"Providing both careful ex   ...ous evaluation, Mark
Sinclair's Bergson will prove invaluable to students and instructors
alike. The book situates Bergson in his historical, philosophical and
political contexts, as well as locating where his positions fall in contemporary discussions. Highly recommended."
                        – John Protevi, Louisiana State University, USA

"Mark Sinclair has written a wonderfully accessible and exhaustive
introduction to Bergson's thought. In the style of engaged history
of philosophy, Bergson is a remarkable contribution to the ongoing
Bergson resurgence and an invaluable resource for readers at all levels."
                        – Donald A. Landes, Université Laval, Canada

Bergson

Henri Bergson (1859–1941) was one of the most celebrated and influential philosophers of the twentieth century. He was awarded the 1927 Nobel Prize in Literature for his philosophical work, and his controversial ideas about time, memory and life shaped generations of thinkers, writers and artists. In this clear and engaging introduction, Mark Sinclair examines the full range of Bergson's work. The book sheds new light on familiar aspects of Bergson's thought, but also examines often ignored aspects of his work, such as his philosophy of art, his philosophy of technology and the relation of his philosophical doctrines to his political commitments. After an illuminating overview of his life and work, chapters are devoted to the following topics:

* the experience of time as duration
* the experience of freedom
* memory
* mind and world
* laughter and humour
* knowledge
* art and creativity
* the *élan vital* as a theory of biological life
* ethics, religion, war and modern technology.

With a final chapter on his legacy, *Bergson* is an outstanding guide to one of the great philosophers. Including chapter summaries, annotated further reading and a glossary, it is essential reading for those interested in metaphysics, time, free will, aesthetics, the philosophy of biology, continental philosophy and the role of European intellectuals in World War I.

Mark Sinclair is Reader in Philosophy at the University of Roehampton, UK, and Associate Editor at the *British Journal for the History of Philosophy*. He is the author of *Being Inclined: Félix Ravaisson's Philosophy of Habit* (2019) and co-editor of the *Oxford Handbook of Modern French Philosophy*.

Routledge Philosophers

Edited by Brian Leiter,

University of Chicago, USA

Routledge Philosophers is a major series of introductions to the great Western philosophers. Each book places a major philosopher or thinker in historical context, explains and assesses their key arguments, and considers their legacy. Additional features include a chronology of major dates and events, chapter summaries, annotated suggestions for further reading and a glossary of technical terms.

An ideal starting point for those new to philosophy, they are also essential reading for those interested in the subject at any level.

Also available:

For more information about this series, please visit: https://www.routledge.com/ The-Routledge-Philosophers/book-series/ROUTPHIL

Mark Sinclair

Bergson

 Routledge
Taylor & Francis Group

LONDON AND NEW YORK

First published 2020
by Routledge
2 Park Square, Milton Park, Abingdon, Oxon OX14 4RN

and by Routledge
52 Vanderbilt Avenue, New York, NY 10017

Routledge is an imprint of the Taylor & Francis Group, an informa business

British Library Cataloguing-in-Publication Data
A catalogue record for this book is available from the British Library

Library of Congress Cataloging-in-Publication Data
Names: Sinclair, Mark, 1973– author.
Title: Bergson / Mark Sinclair.
Description: 1 [edition]. | New York : Routledge, 2019. |
Series: Routledge philosophers | Includes bibliographical references and index.
Identifiers: LCCN 2019018430 | ISBN 9781138219489 (hardback : alk. paper) |
ISBN 9781138219496 (pbk. : alk. paper) | ISBN 9781315414935 (e-book)
Subjects: LCSH: Bergson, Henri, 1859–1941.
Classification: LCC B2430.B43 S495 2019 | DDC 194–dc23
LC record available at https://lccn.loc.gov/2019018430

ISBN: 978-1-138-21948-9 (hbk)
ISBN: 978-1-138-21949-6 (pbk)
ISBN: 978-1-315-41493-5 (ebk)

Typeset in Joanna
by Newgen Publishing UK

To *Alan,* for Paris

Contents

Acknowledgements

This book covers a lot of ground, but thankfully a number of Bergson scholars (and other interested parties) have generously commented on its chapters, significantly improved them and saved me from myself on several occasions. For that, I am indebted to Matt Dougherty, Yaron Wolf, Keith Ansell-Pearson, Tatsuya Muruyama, Matt Barnard, Alexandre Lefebvre, Florian Fischer, Dave Deamer, Sylvain Matton and Adi Efal-Lautenschläger. A "Séminaire de Gorze", one bright winter's afternoon in 2017, on *Essai sur les données immédiates* with Florent Jakob and his students preparing for the *concours* brought clarity to my understanding of Bergson's ideas. Steven Holt did fine work with the copyediting. The book has also benefited from the support of Mike Beaney, Len Lawlor, Draginja Stankovic, Hiroyuki Hara, Stephanie Hankey, Christophe Perrin, Gareth George, Joseph Sinclair and Will Large.

A note on translations and abbreviations

In square brackets within the text, I cite the English translations of Bergson's works according to the list of abbreviations below. I have often modified the translations. After the forward slash in each reference, I refer to the pagination of the original French texts, which is maintained in the new Presses universitaires de France critical editions (under the general editorship of Frédéric Worms) and, with one exception, recorded in the margins of the "Centenary Edition": Henri Bergson, Œuvres, ed. A. Robinet (Paris: Presses universitaires de France, 1959). The exception is DS in M 57-244, which also has the original pagination in its margins.

TFW   *Time and Free Will* (*Essai sur les données immédiates de la conscience*, 1889), trans. F. L. Pogson (London: George Allen & Unwin, 1910)

MM   *Matter and Memory* (*Matière et mémoire*, 1896), trans. N. M. Paul and W. S. Palmer (New York: Zone, 1988)

L   *Laughter: Essay on the Meaning of the Comic* (*Le Rire: Essai sur la signification du comique*, 1900), trans. C. Brereton and F. Rothwell (London: Macmillan, 1911)

CE   *Creative Evolution* (*L'Evolution créatrice*, 1907), trans. A. Mitchell (London: Macmillan, 1922)

ME   *Mind-Energy* (*L'Energie spirituelle*, 1919), trans. H. Wildon Carr (New York: Henry Holt, 1920)

DS   *Duration and Simultaneity* (*Durée et simultanéité* (*A propos de la théorie d'Einstein*), 1922 and 1923), trans. L. Jacobson (Manchester: Clinamen, 1999)

TS   *The Two Sources of Morality and Religion* (*Les Deux sources de la morale et de la religion*, 1932), trans. R. Ashley Audra and C. Brereton (New York: Henry Holt, 1935)

CM   *The Creative Mind* (*La Pensée et le mouvant*, 1934), trans. M. L. Andison (New York: Philosophical Library, 1946)

I refer also to untranslated volumes with the following abbreviations:

C   *Correspondances* ed. A. Robinet (Paris: Presses universitaires de France, 2002)

EPL   *L'évolution du problème de la liberté. Cours au Collège de France 1904–05*, ed. A. François (Paris: Presses universitaires de France, 2017)

HIT   *Histoire de l'idée de temps. Cours au Collège de France 1902–03*, ed. C. Riquier (Paris: Press universitaires de France, 2016)

HTM   *Histoire des théories de la mémoire. Cours au Collège de France 1903–04*, ed. A. François (Paris: Presses universitaires de France, 2018)

M   *Mélanges*, ed. A. Robinet (Paris: Presses universitaires de France, 1972)

Chronology

1859 Born in Paris, October 18, to Jewish parents of Polish and British origin.

1863 The Bergson family moves to Switzerland.

1868 The Bergson family moves back to Paris.

1869 Remains in Paris alone as a boarder at the Springer institute in Paris, and receives a grant to study at the Lycée Fontanes (now Lycée Condorcet), when his parents and siblings settle in London.

1876 Finishes his secondary education with the diploma of *bachelier ès lettres*.

1877 Takes French nationality at the age of 18. Obtains the title of *bachelier ès sciences* in order to prepare for the entrance examination to the Ecole Normale Supérieure-Sciences, and wins a national mathematics competition, the Concours général de mathématiques.

1878 Third place in the entrance examination at the Ecole Normale Supérieure-Lettres after having decided not to pursue a career in mathematics.

1881 Second place in the *agrégation de philosophie*, the examination for positions in the national education system. Appointed to a post in philosophy at the Lycée d'Angers.

1882 Appointed Professeur de Littérature at the Ecole supérieure de jeunes filles, Sèvres.

1883 Appointed at the Lycée de Clermont-Ferrand. Publishes a French translation, without putting his name to it, of

Illusions: A Psychological Study (1881) by the English psychologist James Sully. Publishes an edition of Lucretius.

1884   Takes on additional lecturing duties at the University of
Clermont-Ferrand.

1886   First academic publication in *Revue Philosophique*: "On unconscious simulation in states of hypnotism".

1889   Publishes *Time and Free Will*, his primary doctoral thesis submitted the previous year. Appointed Professeur at the Collège
Rollin, Paris.

1890   Appointed at the Lycée Henri-IV, Paris.

1892   Marries Louise Neuberger, whose mother is the first cousin
of Jeanne Weil, the mother of Marcel Proust, best-man at the
marriage ceremony.

1896   Publication of *Matter and Memory*, and the birth of his daughter,
Jeanne.

1897   Appointed as temporary replacement for Charles Levêque in
the Chair of Ancient Philosophy at the Collège de France.

1900   Elected to the chair of Ancient Philosophy at the Collège de
France. Publishes *Laughter: Essay on the Meaning of the Comic*.

1901   Elected to the Académie des sciences morales et politiques,
the philosophical branch of the Institut de France.

1904   Transferred to the Chair of Modern Philosophy at the
Collège de France.

1907   Publication of *Creative Evolution*. Bergson's lectures enjoy an
immense success at the Collège de France.

1908   First meeting with William James in London.

1910   *Time and Free Will* published in English translation.

1911   Beginning of the pre-war "Bergson boom" with a lecture
tour in Great Britain.

1913   First visit to the US is a spectacular success.

1914   Gifford Lectures at the University of Edinburgh. Elected
to the Académie française. His major works are placed on
the Catholic Index of Prohibited Books. Responds to the
German invasion of Belgium with discourses mobilising
his own philosophical doctrines in support of the French
national cause.

1916 Lectures in Madrid as part of an Institut de France delegation organised by the French government hoping to influence Spain's possible entry into the war.

1917 Sent by the French government to Washington and New York in order to convince US President Woodrow Wilson to increase support for the French war effort.

1918 Second wartime mission on behalf of the French government to the US, but his attempts to raise the issue of a reopening of a second front fall on deaf ears in Washington.

1919 Resigns definitively from his Chair at the Collège de France. Publishes Mind-Energy, a collection of his essays on psychology and metaphysics.

1920 Opens an international meeting of philosophers at the University of Oxford.

1922 Debates with Einstein at the French Society of Philosophy and then publishes Duration and Simultaneity, an interpretation of Einstein's theory. Appointed President of the International Commission for Intellectual Co-operation.

1925 Resigns from the Presidency of the ICIC.

1928 Awarded (for 1927) the Nobel Prize in Literature for his contributions to philosophy.

1932 Publishes The Two Sources of Morality and Religion.

1934 Publishes his second volume of essays, The Creative Mind, which contains his essays on philosophical method and a long philosophical autobiography.

1940 Refuses the Vichy government's offer of exceptions from anti-Semitic regulations.

1941 Dies on January 4 from a respiratory infection.

Introduction

It is difficult to think of another philosopher who was as widely celebrated and as influential in his own time as Henri Bergson. From the early years of the twentieth century until the outbreak of World War I, his lectures at the Collège de France were crammed not just with students, many of whom went on to become renowned writers and thinkers in their own right, but also with Parisian high-society, which would send its butlers, much to the displeasure of the students, hours in advance in order to reserve seats. Bergson was an intellectual celebrity, a "star" in the French media of the time. But what came to be called the "Bergson boom" extended beyond France, and crossed the Atlantic as well as the English Channel. Bergson's ideas attracted the favourable attention even of statesmen such as Theodore Roosevelt and Arthur Balfour, and as legend has it the enthusiasm generated by his lecture (in French)on "Spirituality and Freedom" at Columbia University in 1913 caused the first ever traffic jam on Broadway. Philosopher of time as duration, of memory, of life as the "vital impulse", Bergson had become, in a rapidly globalising world, the first philosopher of global renown in his own lifetime. Not only did he greatly influence some of the greatest writers of the century—Marcel Proust's In Search of Lost Time, to take the most immediate example, is in many ways a Bergsonian novel—but he was also a reference point for a range of avant-garde artistic and political movements. As if this extensive philosophical and cultural influence were not remarkable enough, Bergson also had a diplomatic role of world-historical importance, for in 1917 he was sent as an emissary to the White House in order to persuade Woodrow Wilson to increase support for the French war effort.

It is also difficult to grasp now the extent of Bergson's philosophical, cultural and political significance, given the relative obscurity into which he fell later in the century. When he was awarded, in 1928, the Nobel prize for literature for his philosophical achievements, his star was already on the wane. Perceived erroneously by some to have lost his argument with Einstein concerning the nature of time, criticized crudely by others as an "irrationalist", and denounced bitterly by anti-nationalist and Marxist thinkers for having mobilised his philosophy for the French cause in bellicose wartime writings, Bergson came increasingly to be seen as belonging to the old-guard of French academic philosophy. By then, a new generation of philosophers in France was finding inspiration in Germany for a "concrete philosophy", a "philosophy of existence", in the early-nineteenth-century work of G. W. F. Hegel and in the contemporary phenomenological philosophies of Edmund Husserl and Martin Heidegger. At the same time, in the Anglophone world, the rise of what would come to be labelled "analytic" philosophy had much to do with the decline of the "Bergson boom".[1] Bergson was never forgotten, but he became an increasingly marginal figure during much of the twentieth century. In the last few decades, however, there has been a remarkable resurgence of interest in Bergson's ideas, which has given rise to a 20-volume critical edition of his work, the publication of his Collège de France lecture courses, which illuminate anew his major philosophical preoccupations, and a wealth of new scholarship. With a century's distance, Bergson's work has entered the history of modern philosophy as one of its pivotal moments, and it is increasingly recognised as an important resource for contemporary thought.

In the light of this renewed scholarly attention, this book offers a guide to and an extended study of the major themes of Bergson's philosophy as a whole. The particular chapters of the book treat different themes in his philosophy in the order in which they arrive as explicit topics in his path of thinking. Sometimes this order is not the order in which themes appear in the chapters of Bergson's major works, since in his first two published works he adds "first" chapters after having written at least some of the others. Moreover, this order is vague and undecidable at one point: Chapter 8 on Art could easily have preceded Chapter 7 on Knowledge. In attempting to discern, as much as possible, the true order of Bergson's thought, the book attempts to grasp his thinking in its development, to catch his train of thought, as a philosophy that is not only concerned with process and movement but that is a process and movement, right until the end. Although Bergson sometimes stressed that each of his works takes up a new problematic without any concern for a philosophical "system", and although the development of his work is not linear in any simple sense, we can, in principle, think about this development in two ways. His project develops according to what we ordinarily take to be the different "dimensions" of time: *Time and Free Will* concerns, in principle, the present, while *Matter and Memory* addresses the past, and *Creative Evolution* focuses on the future. As one commentator has recently argued, this development is completed with a concern for eternity in *The Two Sources of Morality and Religion*.[2] The development of the idea of duration can be understood in another sense, however, in that Bergson extends duration beyond the psychological realm as it is narrowly defined in *Time and Free Will* in opposition to the spatial world of things, and this to the point where in *Creative Evolution* it characterises not just the human psyche, but the intrinsic nature of all things, even of apparently inert matter.

The present book guides the reader through Bergson's major works, but in so doing it aims to shed new light on his ideas against the background of the history of modern philosophy in general and nineteenth-century French philosophy in particular. In the Anglophone world, Bergson has too often been taken to be a kind of "genius",[3] a solitary thinker whose ideas arrive without precedent in the tradition. A commentator has recently wondered whether Bergson "can be seen as belonging to a philosophical tradition at all".[4] On this point, we need to return to Susan Stebbing's 1914 observation: Bergson's work represents "the continuation of the current of French thought that proceeds from Maine de Biran through Ravaisson and Boutroux. It would perhaps be hardly necessary to point this out—for no philosopher springs from the void—were it not that, to the English-speaking world at least, Bergson's views came with such force of novelty that he seemed to have no roots in the past".[5] A century later, it is still necessary, even more so, to point this out. *Matter and Memory* can appear to fall from the skies, and this is one reason why it is a difficult book, but, in truth, Bergson's ideas respond to his nineteenth-century context, and they develop the French spiritualist tradition. In elucidating Bergson's work against this background, this book aims to shed new light on familiar aspects of his work, and to illuminate aspects that remain under-examined, and sometimes wholly unexamined, in existing English-language studies.[6] The book tries to see, in context, what Bergson was doing, and this with a view to deciding what to do with Bergson.

The book is intended to offer something for a variety of readers. The relative newcomer to philosophy should find an accessible introduction to Bergson's key ideas. A philosopher trained in the "analytic" tradition looking to see what Bergson might have thought about, say, time, perception, freedom, mind or modality, should find clear accounts of his positions in these fields together with attempts to situate his positions in relation to contemporary debates. Those more familiar with post-Kantian European, "continental" philosophy, but less familiar with Bergson, will find a book emphasising his importance in that tradition. For such readers, I hope this book will help to show that essential moments of twentieth-century French and German thinking are post-Bergsonian, just as nineteenth-century German philosophy is post-Kantian. Finally, the Bergson specialist should find a more developed—and often more considered—form of the interpretations and arguments that I have presented in articles published, largely, in history of philosophy journals in the last few years. The book is, indeed, the work of a historian of modern philosophy (but of a historian who considers that the history of philosophy, done philosophically, *is* philosophy), rather than of an avowedly "analytic" or "continental" philosopher. Concerning the latter, although Bergson's influence is clearly visible in the work of a range of twentieth-century continental European thinkers, and although his Anglophilia may only have increased his dismay at Bertrand Russell's critical barbs and the subsequent rise of "analytic" philosophy, he would have made little sense of the idea of a "continental philosophy", given that he was much preoccupied with national traditions in philosophy.

I have profited enormously in writing this book from the superbly erudite critical dossiers in the recent Presses universitaires de France edition of Bergson's work. Far from shrouding Bergson's work in dusty scholarship, these volumes have brought it back to life. An English translation, by Donald Landes, of Arnaud François' edition of *Creative Evolution* is scheduled to appear with Routledge soon, and I hope that the present book combined with that translation will spur resolute and hardy souls into translating, for the benefit of English-language philosophy, other volumes in the critical edition.

Chapter 1 of the book is intended to offer the most extensive intellectual biography of Bergson available in English. Even though this partly serves as a gentle introduction to the key themes of Bergson's thought, the reader impatient to engage directly with his works can turn immediately to Chapter 2, "Time". However, in order to profit fully from the final two chapters of the book, where Bergson's ethical and political commitments as well as his philosophical legacy are discussed, it will be necessary to turn back to this intellectual biography beforehand.

Notes

1 It certainly had something to do with it in the work of Susan Stebbing (cited below), who after publishing her perceptive MA thesis on nineteenth-century French philosophy with the title *Pragmatism and French Voluntarism* (Cambridge: Cambridge University Press, 1914) went on to found the journal *Analysis* and become a prominent figure in the development and the institutions of analytic philosophy. For more on Stebbing, see Chapter 5 of Michael Beaney, *Analytic Philosophy: A Very Short Introduction* (Oxford: Oxford University Press, 2017).

2 See Camille Riquier, *Archéologie de Bergson* (Paris: Presses universitaires de France, 2009).

3 What Edmund Husserl said was also thought by many in the Anglophone world; see Husserl, *Briefwechsel*, vol. VI: *Philosophenbriefe*, ed. K. Schuhmann (Dordrecht: Kluwer, 1994), p. 155.

4 F. C. T. Moore, *Bergson: Thinking Backwards* (Cambridge: Cambridge University Press, 1996), p. xi. Moore acknowledges in a footnote that commonly Bergson is "not entirely inappropriately associated with the French spiritualist philosophers such as Ravaisson" (xi), but this grossly understates the importance of Ravaisson and the spiritualist tradition for him.

5 L. Susan Stebbing, *Pragmatism and French Voluntarism*, pp. 35–6.
6 These aspects include his own account of genius on which much of his later work turns, his doctrine of retroactivity, his philosophy of technology and the relation of his political engagements and nationalist wartime discourses to his official philosophical writings.

One
Intellectual biography

Early years

Henri Bergson was born in Paris in 1859, the second of seven children of Michaël, a distinguished Polish composer and pianist, and Kate (née Levinson), who was from England and, like her husband, Jewish. Four years later, the family moved to Switzerland, where Michaël was appointed as a teacher, and then as director, of the Geneva Music Conservatory. In 1868, when Bergson was nine, his family moved back to Paris. A year after that, when his parents decided to settle in England after his father's musical career had waned, Bergson stayed on in Paris alone in order to attend the Lycée Fontanes (now Lycée Condorcet) with the help of a grant from the French government. He also had the support of the Springer Institute, a Jewish institution where he boarded, but he seems to have lost any attachment to his religious origins in the course of his residence there. In 1870, he had to endure not only separation from his family, but also the siege of Paris and the tumult of the Paris Commune. Still, he excelled in his secondary education as he had at primary school in Switzerland. In his final year, Bergson specialised in mathematics and won the Concours général de mathématiques, a national competition, with a solution to a problem formulated by Pascal in a 1654 letter to Fermat [M 247–56]. In the end, however, he decided to prepare for the entrance examinations to the *lettres* or humanities section of the Ecole Normale Supérieure, and not to pursue a career in mathematics. In 1878, he was received there in third place behind Jean Jaurès, the socialist and anti-militarist who would be assassinated at the outbreak of World War I. The intake that year was illustrious, which made gaining entry to the school all the more difficult. Emile Durkheim, who would become one of the founders of sociology as an intellectual discipline, failed on his second attempt in 1878 and would not be admitted until the following year.

Bergson had not gained French nationality by being born in France. In order to gain state funding to pursue his studies, he took French nationality at the age of 18. His family was now in England, and he was perfectly Anglophone after having spent his school holidays there, but he loved France with something of the passion of the convert.

Intellectual roots

At the end of his time at the Ecole Normale Supérieure, in 1881, Bergson was received in second place (ahead of Jaurès this time) in the *agrégation*, the competitive examination for positions in the national education system. The examination committee was presided over by Félix Ravaisson, and the subject Bergson drew from the hat for his major lecture (it was, indeed, a hat, which was legendary, and must have had a forbidding air[1]) was "What is the value of contemporary psychology?". Bergson's admirable essay on Ravaisson's life and work—published in 1934 as the final essay in his final book, but read in 1904 after he had replaced him in seat no. 2 of the philosophy section at the Academy of Moral and Political Sciences (Académie des sciences morales et politiques)[2]—helps us to divine how he might have answered the question.

In 1867, on the occasion of the Exposition Universelle in Paris, Ravaisson had published an official report on the progress of nineteenth-century French philosophy, the final section of which, as Bergson writes, "twenty generations of students learnt by heart" [CM 284/275] in order to pass the *agrégation* in the following years. These pages had a great influence on "philosophy as studied in our universities", but this was an influence, as Bergson continues with an analogy that contains more than a hint of autobiography, "whose precise limits cannot be determined, nor whose depth be plumbed, nor whose nature be exactly described, any more than one can convey the inexpressible colouring that a great enthusiasm

of early youth sometimes diffuses all over the whole life of a man"
[CM 284/276]. Ravaisson foresaw a "philosophical epoch soon to
come whose general character will be the predominance of what
one can call a spiritualist positivism or realism, having for its generative principle the consciousness that the mind has in itself of an
existence, on which all existence depends, which is nothing other
than its action".[3] Such a prognosis may have seemed unlikely given
that the nineteenth century had seen a rise in the natural, "positive"
sciences and a decline in the standing of philosophy in the guise of
metaphysics. However, Ravaisson's key claim, as Bergson puts it, was
that "the serious study of the phenomena of life would lead positive
science to enlarge its framework and to go beyond the pure mechanism in which it has been enclosed for the last three centuries"
[CM 284/276]. Biology would increasingly rediscover a principle
of life as irreducible to any notion of inert matter, and as continuous with the principle of mind, which Ravaisson understands
in an originally Aristotelian sense, as "action" or "activity". Even
the founder of the positivist school, August Comte, in his *Course of
Positive Philosophy*,[4] came to isolate life from physical and chemical
facts after originally supposing that living beings were of the same
nature as inorganic things. Under the weight of the facts, Ravaisson
argued, biology would increasingly have to renounce the project
of understanding life on the basis of the inorganic, just as science
as a whole and philosophy in general would have to renounce the
project of understanding the "higher" (life and the mind) from the
perspective of the "lower" (matter).

Ravaisson claimed the idea of a "positive philosophy" for a spiritualist doctrine, and his report announced a renewal of the French
spiritualist tradition that had shaped philosophy in the French
universities earlier in the nineteenth century. It concludes with
these words:

> If the genius of France has not changed, there will be nothing
> more natural for her than the triumph of the high doctrine
> which teaches that matter is only the last degree and, so to
> speak, the shadow of existence over systems that reduce every-
> thing to material elements and to a blind mechanism; which
> teaches that real existence, of which everything else is only an

imperfect sketch, is that of spirit; that, in truth, to be is to live, and to live is to think and to will; that nothing occurs without persuasion; that the good and beauty alone explain the universe and its author; that the infinite and the absolute [...] consist in spiritual freedom; that freedom is thus the last word on things.[5]

When Bergson was preparing his *agrégation* lecture in the Sorbonne library before delivering it in the amphitheatre in front of Ravaisson, these prophetic words would have been present to his mind. Bergson, as he said later, went "full bore against not only contemporary psychology but also psychology in general to the great displeasure of one member of the committee who fancied himself as a psychologist, and who had formulated the question". One imagines that he would also have emphasised that the development of empirical psychology in recent years could take little away from the promise of a spiritualist metaphysics. Bergson would become a perceptive psychologist, but whatever exactly he said in the amphitheatre, it was "to the satisfaction of Ravaisson".[6]

Ravaisson was in a position to have his hopes at least partially realised within French philosophy, and a new generation of spiritualist philosophers did indeed emerge. The talk in 1860 had been of a "philosophical crisis" after the teaching of philosophy had been suppressed in 1852 under the French Second Empire of Napoleon III. In the mid-1870s, however, a "new phase of spiritualist philosophy", one that was also influenced by the philosophy of Immanuel Kant, was clearly visible in the new, Third Republic.[7] Ravaisson's report was followed by Jules Lachelier's 1871 *The Grounds of Induction*, and then by Emile Boutroux's 1874 *The Contingency of the Laws of Nature*. Bergson would have read all of these works before he took the *agrégation*, and, later, *Time and Free Will*, his primary doctoral thesis in 1888, was dedicated to Lachelier, just as those of Lachelier and Boutroux were dedicated to Ravaisson.

This new phase of spiritualist philosophy did not entirely vanquish its opponents, and a more materialist and determinist current of thinking was represented by Hyppolite Taine and Ernest Renan, two disciples of Comte for whom the philosophical crisis of the 1860s was the birth of a new post-metaphysical and largely post-religious era. Bergson was influenced by this current of thought also, particularly in that during his years at the Ecole Normale he shared with the likes of Taine a keen interest in the evolutionary philosophy of the Englishman Herbert Spencer. Bergson seems to have appreciated Spencer's concern to ground theory on the wealth of facts that he invokes, and even, for a while, to have wholly accepted his mechanistic account of evolution. In a 1908 letter to the American philosopher William James, Bergson wrote that at the Ecole Normale he was "wholly taken [...] by mechanistic theories to which he had been led by his reading of Herbert Spencer, the philosopher to whom I adhered the most" and that his intention was only to apply these theories more rigorously in the "philosophy of science" [M 765]. If Bergson was Spencerian during these years, however, Spencerianism was not received in France as wholly antithetical to spiritualism (or to the Kantian philosophy that had influenced it). The first part of Spencer's 1862 First Principles was concerned with "The Unknowable", with the reality of fundamental scientific and religious ideas that escape our intellectual grasp, and the first chapter sought to establish the conditions "for a real and permanent peace" between science and religion. Science and religion "express opposite sides of the same fact: the one its near or visible side, and the other its remote or invisible side".[8] Spencer, then, did not promote a reductive materialist doctrine.

In any case, it was in coming to reflect on the inadequacy of the idea of time, one of Spencer's unknowable ideas, in this evolutionary theory that Bergson was led, between 1881 and 1883, to a quite different philosophical perspective:

I noticed, to my great surprise, that scientific time has no *duration* [*ne dure pas*], that nothing would be changed in scientific knowledge of things if the totality of the real was deployed all at once, instantaneously, and that positive science consists essentially in the elimination of duration [*la durée*]. This was the starting point of a series of reflexions that brought me, gradually, to reject almost everything that I had then accepted, and to change perspective entirely. [M 765–6]

According to the older Bergson, as we will see in more detail in Chapter 2, it was in reflecting on the notion of time that he was awakened from his dogmatic, positivist slumber and led back to a more "spiritualist" perspective. Nevertheless, one of the reasons for the success of Bergson's work is that it developed in dialogue with the positive sciences.[9] As he put it in a lecture of 1903, "philosophy has some value only on condition of being always, constantly verified by contact with the positive sciences" [HTM 26].

After the *agrégation*, Bergson was appointed as a teacher of philosophy at the Lycée d'Angers, and then contemporaneously as a teacher of literature at the Ecole supérieure de jeunes filles, Sèvres. In 1883, he was appointed to a position in philosophy at the Lycée de Clermont-Ferrand, and the five years he spent there before returning to Paris were years as a provincial bachelor with little to distract him from his philosophical work. In addition to teaching at the Lycée and occasionally at the University of Clermont-Ferrand, he published a French translation, without putting his name to it, of *Illusions: A Psychological Study* (1881) by the English psychologist James Sully, which was a sign of his growing interest in questions of perception, dreams and memory. The same year, 1883, he published an edition of *On the Nature of Things*[10] by the Roman philosopher-poet Lucretius.[11] 1886 saw his first academic publication in *Revue Philosophique*: "On Unconscious Simulation in States of Hypnotism", based on his interest and his own experiments in hypnotism.[12]

After this, Bergson must have been wholly occupied by his doctoral theses, which he submitted in 1888 when he moved back to Paris to teach at the Lycée Louis-le-Grand and then the Collège Rollin. His primary thesis was *Time and Free Will*, which was published the following year, while his secondary thesis in Latin concerned the idea of space in Aristotle.[13] To his "fury", as Bergson would say later,[14] the examiners, led by Boutroux, said little about his arguments concerning the psychological experience of duration as irreducible to spatialised clock-time. They said just as little about the conception of free will that Bergson introduced on that basis. Instead, they focused on his critique of experimental psychology, and of the psychophysics of Gustav Fechner, within the opening chapter of the thesis, which Bergson had added after having finished a first draft of the chapters on time and freedom in 1886. Were the judges confused by the "absolute philosophical novelty" of the second chapter on time as duration?[15] If absolute novelties are ever possible in philosophy or elsewhere (Chapter 8 returns to this question in relation to Bergson's own notion of novelty), *Time and Free Will* is probably not one of them. Centuries earlier, Descartes had distinguished time from a different principle that he called duration; time is merely a mode of thinking, merely a way of measuring duration with reference to the movement of celestial bodies.[16] In Spinoza, subsequently, time is merely a function of the imagination, whereas duration characterises things and perhaps even divinity and eternity.[17] In the nineteenth century, ideas of duration as characterising not things directly but rather a psychological, "lived" time wholly distinct from space and more primitive than time as counted by clocks were already in the air before Bergson. In 1865, the Belgian Joseph Delboeuf criticised the representation of time according to the image of a line, whereby time "is no longer properly duration", but becomes "so to speak, a *fourth dimension of space*".[18] In France, Albert Lemoine argued in his posthumous 1875 *Habit and Instinct* that there is "an indissoluble solidarity between the different moments of flowing duration [*la durée qui s'écoule*]" and that "the three elements of time are fused together [*solidaires*] with each other ... it is not true to say that the past is no longer, nor even that the future is not yet".[19] In 1881, his student and then editor Victor Egger subsequently distinguished "the non-Self [*non-moi*] and extension", i.e. space from "the Self [*moi*] and duration", which he described as "pure succession".[20] Moreover, in 1884 William James published "On Some Omissions of Introspective Psychology", which contained reflections on "thought's stream" that were comparable to those of *Time and Free Will*.[21] Bergson later denied having any knowledge of James' article when writing his thesis, but admitted that his own path of thinking was part of a "movement of ideas that has been developing everywhere [*un peu partout*] and that has its own more general and profound causes" [M 658]. His February 1888 foreword to his dissertation does not announce any grand philosophical novelties about time, and presents his account of time as merely preparatory for the apparently more fundamental problem of freedom. His account of duration, although it goes further than and is irreducible to those of his predecessors, "was no cataclysmic insight for French philosophy".[22] It was more like a ripe fruit than an absolute novelty.

In 1890 Bergson was appointed at the Lycée Henri-IV, where he taught students in the intensive preparatory classes (the "khâgne") for the entrance examinations to the Ecole Normale Supérieure. Bergson was gaining a reputation in Paris as a brilliant teacher. In 1892 he married Louise Neuberger, whose mother was the first cousin of Jeanne Weil, the mother of Marcel Proust, who was best man at the marriage ceremony. The proximity of the philosophy of Proust's *In Search of Lost Time* (1913–27) to Bergson's accounts of time and memory, a proximity which is no less evident for the fact that Proust occasionally denied it, would therefore be a family affair. Bergson, in any case, published *Matter and Memory* in 1896. That key sections of it were released in advance to the leading philosophical journals earlier in the year indicates the degree to which *Time and Free Will* had been considered as a significant philosophical event. But although *Matter and Memory* was generally received as a work of great originality in the philosophy of perception and memory, it was often seen to be unclassifiable in that it superseded traditional oppositions between idealism and realism, spiritualism and positivism. Moreover, it did nothing to assuage the concerns of those who had rejected Bergson's anti-rationalism and non-Kantian conception of freedom in the earlier book.[23]

The "Bergson boom"

1896 also saw Bergson became a father, to Jeanne. She was born deaf but, through the efforts of her parents, learnt to speak and became an accomplished painter and sculptor. In 1897, Bergson was named as a temporary replacement for Charles Levêque in the Chair of Ancient Philosophy at the Collège de France, but in 1898 he was rejected a second time for a position at the Sorbonne. The preferred candidate was Gabriel Séailles, who had published in 1883 a thesis on genius and artistic creation[24] that would be significant for Bergson in *Creative Evolution* but little that could be compared in its originality to *Matter and Memory*. Although the Dreyfus affair was raging at the time, the decision was not the effect of anti-Semitism. Séailles himself was a Dreyfusard, friend of Emile Zola and socialist. He was also something of a Kantian in his aesthetics and ethics, and it was doubtless this that gave him the advantage over Bergson, who had positioned himself in opposition to Kant. This resistance to Bergson's philosophy at the Sorbonne was reinforced once Durkheim was nominated there in 1902. In the Dreyfus affair, it should be noted, Bergson refused to intervene. He simply regretted that it had become more than a matter of judicial process, and that it had unleashed so much obscene anti-Semitism.

After teaching for some time at the Ecole Normale Supérieure, Bergson was elected to the chair of Ancient Philosophy at the Collège de France in 1900, and then, upon the death of the previous incumbent, Gabriel Tarde, to the chair of Modern Philosophy in 1904. Though certainly prestigious, a Chair at the Collège de France, which is without degree-awarding powers, was then a slightly marginal position in French philosophical life. The position did not allow Bergson to have doctoral students. That said, his lectures would not have been able to attract Le Tout-Paris if he had been teaching his own students at the Sorbonne. Press photographs of the day show groups of his audience, which was often predominantly female,[25] standing at windows and doorways, craning their necks in order to hear something of his lectures.[26] Given the crush, it was proposed that the lectures be held outside of the college, even at the Opéra, but the Collège decided against it. Bergson seems to have coped with all this attention with admirable equanimity, and only occasionally to have complained about the intellectual commitment of his audience.

Bergson's name had become familiar to a broader, popular audience with his 1900 *Laughter: An Essay on the Meaning of the Comic*. Comprising three chapters originally published in 1899 as articles in *Revue de Paris*, a literary periodical, this was one of Bergson's most widely read books. It is easily his most readable. With apparently minimal philosophical presuppositions, Bergson addresses the questions of what makes us laugh and why we laugh, questions that had begun to occupy him already in 1884.[27] The subject was evidently dear to his heart, for the book displays a deep familiarity with comic literature and theatre. The questions belong to the domain of aesthetics as well as that of psychology, and *Laughter* presents some of Bergson's most programmatic statements about art. His celebrity rose to new heights, however, with the publication of *Creative Evolution* in 1907. In sharp contrast to *Matter and Memory*, the success of the book "was almost instantaneous", "went far beyond the narrow circle of philosophers" and attracted "the popular press".[28] Now Bergson was not just the philosopher of mobility and duration, but of the *élan vital*, the vital impulse, as the principle of biological and psychological life. It was described with pyrotechnic metaphors as the burst of a firework, an explosive force, a bomb or rocket. He was now, after the important 1903 essay "Introduction to Metaphysics", also promoting "intuition" as the means through which consciousness gains access to this living principle. To cap it all, he was now a celebrant of novelty and creation. Duration and mobility rather than stasis, intuition rather than intellect, the spontaneity of life rather than the inertia of matter, creativity rather than repetition, the new rather than the old. *Creative Evolution* is a serious philosophical engagement with evolutionary theory and the history of philosophy, but its immediate attractions to an early-twentieth-century audience avid for novelties were such that the book would go through 16 editions in seven years.[29]

In these years, Bergson's philosophy became a cultural phenomenon influencing a remarkable range of contemporary artistic and political movements. Commentators, including Jaurès,[30] had noted the proximity of his views in *Time and Free Will* concerning art as a kind of suggestive, indirect revelation of reality to those of the Symbolists in *fin de siècle* France. The Symbolists had claimed the German philosopher Arthur Schopenhauer as a philosophical source, and Bergson's continuation of Schopenhauerian positions was remarked.[31] In the decade prior to World War I, however, theoreticians of the avantgarde explicitly claimed Bergson's notions of duration, intuition and life as an influence. In their 1912 *Du cubisme*, Albert Gleizes and Jean Metzinger, for example, used Bergsonian phraseology to account for their concern to render successive aspects of an object, and thus the passage of time, in the artwork. Bergson, for his part, regretted that he had not seen any of their work, and stressed that fine art should be a function more of genius and intuition than of the application of a theory.[32] He was even forced to admit in a conservative newspaper that he "disapproved of revolutionary forms of art".[33] This was a peculiar admission from a celebrant of novelty, and it did not stop Fauvism, and F. T. Marinetti's Futurism, also being influenced by him. Marinetti's notion of becoming rather than static being "as the sole religion", and his rejection of the "beautiful but false intellect" were clearly Bergsonian in inspiration. Moreover, he drew on the use the anarcho-syndicalist Georges Sorel had made of *Creative Evolution* to justify class warfare in his 1908 *Reflections on Violence*. Sorel contrasted the violence of intuitive, pre-rational myth, the myth of a general strike, to the violent force of bourgeois order. Bergson read Sorel with interest and corresponded with him [C 202].[34]

On the political right in France, Bergsonism split Charles Maurras' nationalist, anti-republican and anti-Semitic Action Française movement. Bergson was criticised by Maurras and Pierre Lasserre, editor of the *Revue de l'Action française*, as anti-rationalist, romantic and gothic rather than "classical", and, ultimately, as more German than French. After a temporary left–right rapprochement, this led to the departure of an important Sorelian faction in the movement. In more traditional Catholic circles, Bergson also encountered a mixed, even predominantly negative reception. *Creative Evolution* invoked God, but Bergson's work was vocally opposed by the neo-Thomist Jacques Maritain, who had assiduously attended Bergson's lectures before converting to Catholicism.[35] Bergson's work was associated with the Catholic modernism suppressed by the Church authorities, and it was placed on the Index of Prohibited books in 1914.

In 1911, public enthusiasm for Bergson's works spread to Great Britain—the idea of a "Bergson boom" was first used to describe his reception there—where *Time and Free Will* had appeared in translation the previous year. In May, he was awarded an honorary doctorate from the University of Oxford, where he presented "The Perception of Change", and shortly afterwards he gave the Huxley Lecture at the University of Birmingham on "Life and Consciousness". Later that year he returned in order to lecture on "The Nature of the Soul" at University College London. As Bertrand Russell observed, these lectures were "reported in the daily newspapers—all England has gone mad about him for some reason".[36] Bergson made the acquaintance of two prominent Scots in England: Lord Haldane, Minister of War and sometime Hegelian philosopher, and Arthur Balfour, former Conservative Prime Minister, who published a response to Bergson's doctrines that year in the Hibbert Journal. In 1912, Russell published "The Professor's Guide to Laughter" and "The Philosophy of Bergson" which, though occasionally insightful, were as jaundiced as they were jaunty. Bergson, understandably, did not consider it worthwhile to respond to Russell, but he returned to the British Isles in 1914 to deliver the Gifford Lectures on "The Problem of Personality" at the University of Edinburgh. The year before that, however, he had visited the US. William James had done much to create an American audience for Bergson's philosophy, and the former US president Theodore Roosevelt recommended the "lofty" ideas of both to any "true person of science or religion".[37]

World War I

Bergson cultivated friendships with politicians, and he seems to have dreamt of playing an active role in politics, of becoming a philosopher-statesman.[38] When the opportunity arose in 1914, he seized it with both hands. On August 9, shortly after the declaration of war and the invasion of Belgium with which Germany had responded to France's mobilisation, he proclaimed to his colleagues at the Academy of Moral and Political Sciences:

> [t]he struggle initiated against Germany is a struggle of civilisation against barbarism. Everyone feels this, but our Academy has perhaps a particular authority in order to say it. Dedicated, mainly, to the study of psychological, moral and social questions, it carries out its simple scientific duty in pointing out Germany's brutality and cynicism, and in its disdain for all justice and all truth, a regression to a state of savagery.[39]

The physical conflict had already begun, but with this address Bergson fires the first salvo in the intellectual hostilities. As president of the Academy, he characterises the conflict not as a clash of civilisations, but as a struggle between a bastion of civilisation and savage barbarism. This "scientific" observation, relayed in the press, was soon much acclaimed throughout France and became a recurrent motif in French war propaganda. It caused consternation in Germany, and it met a response two months later in the "Manifesto of the Ninety-Three German Intellectuals". To them, it seemed that with such a reductive view of the conflict France's greatest philosopher had succumbed to "chauvinism".[40] To his credit, Bergson

resisted the proposal in August to expel associates of German nationality from the Institut de France (of which the Academy of Moral
and Political Sciences is one wing). Nevertheless, his admission a
few months later that if he had to choose between indignation and
understanding in relation to Germany, he would prefer indignation,
together with his assertion that German philosophy was merely "the
intellectual transposition of its brutality, its appetites and its vices",[41]
seemed only to confirm the views of his adversaries.

In adopting such a stance in August 1914, Bergson was perhaps
partially motivated by a desire to outflank the ambient anti-Semitism
in France and to silence his critics on the right.[42] Earlier in the year,
Action Française had campaigned against his election—he was the
first ever Jewish member—to the Académie Française. Whatever the
case may be in this regard, Bergson followed this August address
with other interventions. His second, "The Force That Wastes and
the Force That Does Not", was written in November for a military
newssheet, the *Bulletin des armées de la République*. At a time when Germany
was beginning to suffer as a result of the British naval blockade,
Bergson contrasts Germany's dwindling material force with France's
moral force, which is inexhaustible in that it is fuelled and guided
by respect for freedom, justice and international law.

It was, however, in another address to the Academy of Moral and
Political Sciences that Bergson offered his most concerted interpretation of the war. This address expands on the idea of "two
Germanies", an idea much discussed in France after its humiliating
defeat by Prussia in 1870. Echoes of these discussions can be heard
in the later critical theories of Germany's *Sonderweg* ("special path")
that tried to account for the disaster of National Socialism in the
1930s and 1940s. For Bergson, a nation of poets and thinkers, of
Kant, Jacobi and Goethe, had been transformed by Bismarck in its
political unification on the occasion of the Franco-Prussian war into
a rapine "nation of prey" guided by Hegel's philosophy (French
Hegelians in the 1930s would not forgive Bergson for this remark)
and the crude doctrine that might is right.[43] Bergson develops the
idea of "two Germanies", however, in analysing Prussian militarism
as conditioned by "machinism", by modern industrial technology.[44]
The "idea peculiar to that century of diverting science to the satisfaction of men's material wants"[45] led in Germany to breakneck

industrial development and a new social form structured as a kind of military–industrial complex.[46] But this ultimately produces "automatically, a very different effect to that which its constructors intended". Like Goethe's sorcerer's apprentice,[47] Germany has set in motion a process that "sooner or later, was to escape all control and become a race to the abyss".[48] Full of frenzied ambition, and having let the technological genie out of the bottle, Germany has become bent on "world-domination" and stops at nothing short of total war in the pursuit of its imperialist expansion: "from the time when Prussian militarism, now turned into German militarism, had become one with industrialism, it was the enemy's industry, his commerce, the sources of his wealth, his wealth itself, as well as his military power, which war must now target", and to this end "it will massacre women, children and the elderly; it will pillage and burn; the ideal will be to destroy towns, villages, the whole population".[49]

This analysis of twentieth-century total war is important, but the ascription of these phenomena solely to Germany is propagandistic. Germany had committed war-crimes in Belgium, but Bergson could have offered a similar sociological analysis with respect to France and Great Britain, nations which, as one commentator has written recently, "extended their industrial and commercial power around the entire globe, and colonised at will African and Asian countries".[50] Georges Friedmann put the point more strongly in 1936: "Bergson never had a single word to say […] about colonial terror, the exploitation of the weak, the violence of imperialist appetites, of which France and the Allies provide the example".[51] This is not strictly true, it is important to note. For within a brief post-war review of Alfred de Tarde's 1915 *Le Maroc, école d'énergie*, which concerns France's "spiritual mission" in Morocco, Bergson recognises "a secret force that since the war of 1870, has led us to colonise: a revolt of the frustrated energies of our race, a need to act and teach action".[52] It is not only Germany, then, that has been possessed by an imperialist drive since 1870.

In any case, in response to German "scientific" or "systematic barbarism",[53] Bergson totally mobilises the basic framework of his own philosophy: France is a dynamic and self-renewing power of creation, in opposition to the German *Reich*, which, as the force of a spiritless and static mechanism, is bound, despite its might, to wear itself out: "[o]n the one hand, mechanism, the manufactured unable to repair itself; on the other, life, power of creation, which makes itself and remakes itself at each instant."[54] France, in other words, is the nation of the *élan vital*, and thus it can revitalise itself from its own inexhaustible resources. This is not to say that "Bergson now insists that vital energy can only be sustained by ideals of freedom and justice higher than the life force itself",[55] for this gets things the wrong way around. Bergson now posits the *élan vital* as a more fundamental source of French strength than its concern for justice and international law. It is evident, as Georges Politzer wrote acerbically in 1928, that Bergson had decided that "sanctifying the war in the name of freedom was already quite good, but sanctifying it in the name of life is better".[56] In advancing according to such a living impetus, the morale of French soldiers, as Bergson will also say in April 1915, is like that of great religious mystics, but instead of directly accessing the divine they commune with "*l'âme de la patrie*" [M 1154–5], the spirit of the nation.

Bergson's analyses of modern techno-scientific barbarism and the necessity of a spiritual response to it anticipate by nearly two decades his reflections on mysticism and the modern technological condition in the final chapter of *The Two Sources of Morality and Religion*, as we will see in Chapter 10. In the course of the war, however, rather than develop his philosophical reflections, Bergson undertook a series of diplomatic missions. The first was to Madrid as part of an Institut de France delegation organised by the French government hoping to influence Spain's possible entry into the war. During this mission, Bergson spoke on "French Philosophy", and claimed that "[t]he role of France in the evolution of philosophy is quite clear: France has been the great initiator and has remained perpetually inventive, sowing new ideas" [M 1157]. It is important to appreciate Bergson's register here: he writes not of philosophers in France, nor of French philosophy, nor of the French "spirit" or "genius", but simply of France and its role in philosophy, which it has initiated in its modern form. Bergson personifies France, and modern philosophy, he seems to say, is essentially French. A "delightful little summary of French philosophy" it may be,[57] but with such a nationalist purpose, the essay clearly belongs to Bergson's war writings.

Bergson's second mission was of another order of significance entirely. In 1917, he was sent in secret to Washington in order to meet with US President Woodrow Wilson, former President of Princeton University. Bergson's philosophical prestige and celebrity in the US, it was thought in Paris, would help to convince Wilson of France's moral and philosophical commitment to his conception of a League of Nations, and thus to persuade him to maintain and even increase US support for the French war effort. Bergson met with Colonel House, and soon after sent a telegraph to Paris indicating that US support could include "an immense reservoir of men" [C 695]. After meeting Wilson at the White House on February 18, Bergson travelled to New York and in March gave rapturously received lectures, at the France–America Society and the American Academy, on France and America as two nations sharing a "deep and indefeasible love of justice and freedom" and on the US as realising fully the European "ideal".[58] Shortly afterwards, on April 2, Wilson declared to Congress the imminent US entry into the war.

The post-war years

With the war, Bergson, the philosopher of national and then international renown, had become a public and political figure, one celebrated even for having "saved France and European freedom".[59] His 1918 inaugural address at the Académie française, which he had delayed since his election as a member in 1914, was a media event reported on by all the national press. The war's end some months later allowed him, at least for a few years, to devote more of his energies to his philosophical work. He retired from teaching in 1919, due to his increasingly severe arthritis, but that year saw the publication of his collection of essays on psychological questions, Mind-Energy. Bergson seems to have decided at this point to group his essays into two volumes: Mind-Energy was followed in 1934 by The Creative Mind, which contains essays principally on methodological issues. Mind-Energy developed the perspectives of both Matter and Memory and Creative Evolution, but it was not a major departure from them. The following year he opened and closed an international meeting at Oxford, a "meeting" that would have been an international congress of philosophy, the first of which had occurred in 1900, had it not been for the practical impossibility of German participation.[60] Bergson's spoke on "Foresight and Novelty", with an early version of the important late essay (to which Chapter 8 returns) "The Possible and the Real" published in *The Creative Mind* in 1934.

Bergson's most high-profile philosophical engagement in these post-war years was his polemic with Albert Einstein. In 1922, he published *Duration and Simultaneity*, a work responding to Einstein's theory of relativity. Bergson had been working on the book for some time, but it appeared just a few weeks after Einstein's official visit to Paris, which included a talk at the Société française de philosophie. Bergson and Einstein had thus the opportunity to exchange views. In his brief talk, which was essentially what would be published as the preface to the book, Bergson was clear that his intention was not to criticise Einstein's theory of relativity, but only to assess its philosophical significance: "[a]ll that I want to establish is simply this: once we admit the Theory of Relativity as a physical theory, all is not finished" [DS 158/M 1345]. His aim was to shed light on the philosophical significance of the theory rather than simply to dismiss it as unreal or purely a function of mathematical convention. Rather than reject the theory—with its multiple times depending on diverse frames of reference and its famous paradoxes—as a fiction, Bergson's project is more difficult and contentious in that he aims to reconcile science and philosophy by distinguishing what is "real" and what is "fictive" within the theory itself. He argued that although "there is nothing to change in the mathematical expression of the theory of relativity [...] physics would be of service to philosophy in abandoning certain ways of speaking that lead the philosopher astray, and which risk misleading the physicist herself about the import of her views" [DS 145/207–8]. Bergson's attempted reconciliation involves, in fact, leading the physicist to see that relativity theory as ordinarily discussed rests on a naïve, crude ontology, and that expunging this naïve ontology will reveal that the theory confirms rather than contradicts "the natural human belief in a unique and universal time" [DS 59–60/86]. The "real time", *le temps réel*, of *Duration and Simultaneity* is not the "real duration", *la durée réelle*, of *Time and Free Will*, but rather something like the origin and the intersection of both pure duration and spatialised time.[61]

The discussion on the day, as is the way of these things, was inconclusive. Einstein rejected the idea that philosophy had any rightful claim to a time that only it could address: "there is no time of the philosophers; there is only a psychological time different from the time of the physicist" [M 1346]. For Einstein, the physicist's time is not radically different from psychological time, and so on his account science can inform us of the nature of time *tout court*. The polemic was continued with critical responses to Bergson's book by French physicists supporting Einstein.[62] It was supposed that Bergson had made a simple error in understanding the theory, and that he had somehow rejected it, but in the appendix to the second edition of *Duration and Simultaneity*, Bergson claimed that he had been misunderstood: "[w]e have already said it, and cannot stop repeating it: in the Theory of Relativity the slowing-down of clocks by their displacement is, rightfully, as *real* as the shrinkage of objects in terms of distance" [DS 127/216] in ordinary perception. Nevertheless, Einstein repeated the accusation in letters which were made public: "Bergson […] made huge mistakes; may God forgive him for them". He claimed that Bergson's response was simply an "error", and that this error "was purely of a physical order, and quite independent of any discussion between philosophical schools".[63] Bergson published a sixth and final edition of *Duration and Simultaneity* in 1931, but after this he seems to have withdrawn from the fray, tired of the misunderstandings to which the book had given rise. He was perceived to have come off worse in the encounter, and this perception was a factor in the decline of Bergson's influence. His reluctance to pursue the debate should not be taken as an admission of defeat, however, and he returned to the issue within a long footnote to *The Creative Mind* in 1934. The argument was certainly not one that Bergson could claim to have won, but it was not one that he lost. Einstein did not emerge from it unscathed, for, as Jimena Canales has noted, Bergson's critique of Einstein's interpretation of the theory of relativity was mentioned in the presentation speech for Einstein's Nobel Prize in 1922, a prize awarded "for his services to theoretical physics, and especially for his discovery of the law of the photoelectric effect" and not directly for the theory of relativity.[64]

Bergson's fractious dispute with Einstein occurred just as they were supposed to be working together at the League of Nations'

International Commission on Intellectual Co-operation, the fore-runner of UNESCO. The first meeting of the Commission took place in 1922, just a few months after Einstein's talk at the Société française de philosophie. Bergson was France's nomination, Einstein was that of the new German Republic, but before the first meeting the French philosopher was appointed President of the Commission. Bergson seems to have accepted this appointment not only as a national honour, but also as a means of making good on the internationalist promises he had made to Wilson in 1917. Einstein, from the begin-ning, was much less convinced of the international mission of the Commission, and he resigned from it upon the French occupation of the Ruhr in 1923. He accused the Commission of being "even worse" than the League of Nations itself, and of "appointing members whom it knew stand for tendencies the very reverse of those they were bound in duty to advance".[65] Einstein was persuaded to return in 1924, but Bergson's acceptance of the French government's offer to provide a home for the Commission in Paris did nothing to ease tensions. Bergson tried to reassure Einstein that the Commission would remain "rigorously and completely international" [C 1161], but the French philosopher resigned in 1925 on grounds of ill health, just after Einstein had vigorously renewed his critique of the organisation. With this decision, Bergson ended his three years as an international administrator, years spent dealing not with grand philosophical principles, but with practical and bureaucratic tasks.

At the same time, Bergson retired from the Conseil Supérieur de l'Instruction Public, a committee advising on national educa-tional policy, where he had also been involved in a fierce polemic concerning the modernisation of the French secondary education system. In 1922, the "right", including the Minister of Education Léon Bérard, a Catholic conservative, aimed to maintain a clas-sical education and delay specialisation, and proposed obligatory Latin and Greek for all pupils during the first four years of sec-ondary education. The "left" saw in this proposal a reactionary, anti-democratic defence of aristocratic privilege. Bergson made his own views known in an address—"Classical Studies and the Reform of Secondary Education (*Les études grécos-latines et la réforme de l'enseignement secondaire*)" [M 1366–1379]—to the Academy of Moral and Political Sciences, which was published in the *Revue de Paris*. According to

Bergson, the only viable way to maintain the roots of French culture in classical culture is to form an intellectual elite that would move from secondary to higher education, an elite that would be educated separately from a technical and practical elite. Bergson, a philosopher for so long accused by Action Française writers of promoting romanticism and irrationalism rather than their preferred variety of classicism and rationalism, was now stressing France's classical Latin and Greek roots. Bergson's position was, in fact, at the far end of the spectrum of conservative views,[66] and was opposed by a large majority of the Conseil, but it informed the law that was passed in 1923. The separation that Bergson proposed would be enacted, but only in the final three years of secondary education, and not from the beginning. In any event, the success of a left coalition in the 1924 national elections meant that the new Minister of Education was able to reinstate a "modern" pathway parallel to the "classical" pathway to the *baccalauréat* qualification and higher education. The winds of change, as François Azouvi has remarked, were no longer blowing favourably for Bergson.[67]

Eclipse

Bergson was engaged in public controversies in these years, but his work was no longer quite the same reference point for, as it had seemed, everything radical and novel in contemporary culture. Gradually he was becoming "a classic", as Raymond Aron later wrote in his homage to the French philosopher, in the sense that a classic "is someone that everybody knows, that some read, but whom virtually no one takes as a contemporary".[68] Bergson's ideas were taught and in some circles met increasingly less resistance; but with no new major work since 1907, *le bergsonisme* began to be examined in the past tense, as belonging to a very different, pre-war world.[69] Bergson's Nobel Prize for Literature in 1928 was a moment in this process. Although he was awarded the prize as a philosopher, his work was discussed in literary, aesthetic terms by the president of the Nobel Committee: "in the account, so far definitive, of his doctrine, *L'Evolution créatrice*, the master has created a poem of striking grandeur, a cosmogony of great scope and unflagging power, without sacrificing a strictly scientific terminology [...]

one always derives from it, without any difficulty, a strong aesthetic impression. […] The poem, if one looks at it this way, presents a sort of drama".[70] This seems not to have perturbed Bergson, and he said that he recognised the "value" of the prize "even more, and I am even more moved by it, when I consider that this distinction given to a French writer, may be regarded as a sign of sympathy given to France".[71]

The Nobel Prize was perhaps the zenith of Bergson's glory, but between 1927 and 1932 three influential texts appeared that denounced both his philosophy and his politics. The first was Julien Benda's *The Treason of the Intellectuals*, in which Bergson was one of the "immense majority" of European intellectuals to have ignored the universal demands of reason and taken part in the early-twentieth century "chorus of racial hatreds, political factions" and "national passions".[72] This argument was an extension of the campaign against Bergson's "irrationalist" philosophy that Benda had led before the war. The second, in 1928, struck a new note. This was *Le bergsonisme: La fin d'une parade philosophique* (a title echoing Ford Madox Ford's 1924–8 *Parade's End* tetralogy), which, though published under the pseudonym of François Arouet, was the work of the philosopher and Marxist theoretician of Hungarian origin Georges Politzer. This pamphlet was of pivotal significance for a new generation of philosophers, and the course of subsequent French philosophy cannot be understood without it.[73] It is perhaps the principal reason for the rapid decline of Bergson's influence in the 1930s. Politzer speaks in the name of a *genuine* philosophy of the "concrete" and attacks Bergson for offering only the semblance of such a philosophy, a semblance which served the interests of an imperialist, capitalist ruling class. Chapter 10 returns to this argument, but, for Politzer, Bergson's nationalist political engagement was far from accidental or incidental, and it was a direct expression of the philosophy of the *élan vital*. *Les chiens de garde* by the communist Paul Nizan was a variation on the same theme: the old-guard of supposedly detached philosophers, including Bergson, were, in truth, "guard dogs" for the bourgeoisie.[74] The fact that in the 1940s Politzer and Nizan both died heroically at the hands of the Nazis only lent more prestige to their denunciations of Bergson and traditional French university philosophy. Moreover, it cannot be denied that in the 1920s and afterwards his philosophical supporters were often Catholic conservatives and predominantly on the political right. Gone were the days of Sorel's Bergsonian anarcho-syndicalism. Jacques Chevalier, one of Bergson's philosophical heirs, went on to serve as Minister of Education in the Vichy government in 1941.

Commentators before the war had already begun to wonder about the ethical implications of Bergson's metaphysics of the vital impulse. *Creative Evolution* brought Bergson national and then international philosophical celebrity, but of the three books that he had published, not one, and not even part of one, had been directly concerned with ethics. What would a Bergsonian moral philosophy look like? To what ethical expression could and should his "vitalist" metaphysics lead? Responding to the pressure to develop a moral philosophy, in 1912 Bergson seemed to worry that he had nothing clear or concrete to say in this regard, nothing that could match the achievements of his previous books. His official commitments as French diplomatic emissary during the war and then as President of the ICIC after the war certainly did not help him to develop his reflections. The whole of the 1920s passed without Bergson, in increasingly frail health due to arthritis, publishing anything on the issue, and commentators even tried to formulate a Bergsonian ethics without him.[75] And then, "one fine day" in 1932, as Jacques Maritain put it, "without any publicity, without any press release, without anyone, even among the author's closest friends, having been informed, the work that had been anticipated for twenty-five years appeared in bookstores."[76]

The book was *The Two Sources of Morality and Religion*. Within it, Bergson invokes two sources or modes of morality that are the prior condition of any rational moral rules, namely closed morality, which is a function of habit, social pressure and a body politic opposed to others, in contrast to open morality, which is an expression of a universal love for humanity in general. In the same sense, Bergson contrasts closed religion with an open religion of creative mystical heroes. On the basis of this distinction between closed and open moral and religious tendencies, in the final part of the book Bergson returns, as we will see in Chapter 10, to the principal themes of his war writings, namely the socio-political problems facing humanity in the industrial age. *The Two Sources of Morality and Religion* did not provoke controversy, however, but rather was warmly received as the crowning moment of Bergson's philosophical work. Two years after this, in 1934, he published his final book, a collection of essays, *The Creative Mind*, which contains his long intellectual autobiography as an introduction, reflections on philosophical method and essays on his key influences, such as Ravaisson and William James.

In 1940, Bergson refused the Vichy government's offer of exceptions from anti-Semitic regulations. The following year, on January 4, he died from a respiratory infection that he contracted, as some have said, while queueing outside in inclement weather in order to register as a Jew. In his will, written in 1937, Bergson asked for a Catholic priest to say prayers at his funeral. "My reflections", he wrote, "have brought me closer and closer to Catholicism in which I see the completion of Judaism. I would have converted had I not seen coming for many years the terrible wave of anti-Semitism about to break upon the world. I have preferred to remain with those who tomorrow will be the persecuted."[77]

Summary

Between 1889 and 1907 Bergson published three major works that secured his philosophical reputation and with which he gained international celebrity: *Time and Free Will*, *Matter and Memory* and *Creative Evolution*. His ideas about time, memory and biological life in these three books develop the spiritualist tradition in nineteenth-century French philosophy that included Pierre Maine de Biran, Félix Ravaisson and Emile Boutroux. He moved beyond an early allegiance to the evolutionary philosophy of Herbert Spencer when he realised that it, and science in general, methodically overlook the pre-mathematical, lived experience of time. Bergson took French nationality at the age of 18, had a passionate attachment to France, and in the first months of World War I mobilised his philosophy in the service of the French cause. After the war, he published an important philosophical critique of Einstein's theory of relativity in 1922 and was the first president of the League of Nations' International Commission on Intellectual Co-operation (the forerunner of UNESCO) during the years 1922–5. He was awarded the Nobel Prize for Literature in 1928 before publishing *The Two Sources of Morality and Religion* in 1932.

Notes

1 Bergson spoke of his intellectual formation prior to *Time and Free Will* to Charles Du Bos, who recorded the account in his diary. This is reproduced in Bergson, *Œuvres*, pp. 1541–3.

2 Bergson's eulogy was first published as a preface to an edition of Ravaisson's *Testament Philosophique* (Paris: Boivin et Cie, 1933).

3 Félix Ravaisson, *Rapport sur la philosophie en France au XIXème siècle* (Paris: Hachette, 1889), p. 275.

4 Auguste Comte, *Cours de philosophie positive* (Paris: Hermann, 2 vols., 1975). The original edition was freely translated and condensed by Harriet Martineau: *The Positive Philosophy of Auguste Comte* (London: J. Chapman, 1853).

5 Ravaisson, *Rapport sur la philosophie en France au XIXème siècle*, p. 320.

6 Bergson, *Œuvres*, pp. 1542–3.

7 Paul Janet, an older spiritualist philosopher, had written of a "philosophical crisis" in 1860, but in 1873 published an article entitled "Une nouvelle phase de la philosophie spiritualiste", *Revue des deux mondes* 108/2 (1873), 365–88. On this point, see François Azouvi, *La gloire de Bergson: Essai sur le magistère philosophique* (Paris: Gallimard, 2007), pp. 23–5.

8 Herbert Spencer, *First Principles* (London: Watts & Co., 1937 [1862]), pp. 16–17. In this connection, see Azouvi, *La gloire de Bergson*, p. 35, and Daniel Becquemont and Laurent Muchielli, *Le Cas Spencer: Religion, science, politique* (Paris: Presses universitaires de France, 1998).

9 See, on this point, Azouvi, *La gloire de Bergson*, p. 26.

10 James Sully, *Les illusions des sens et de l'esprit* (Paris: Baillière, 1883).

11 *Extraits de Lucrèce, avec un commentaire, des notes et une étude sur la Poésie, la Philosophie, la Physique, le texte et la langue de Lucrèce* (Paris: Delagrave, 1883), reprinted in *Mélanges*, pp. 265–310.

12 Bergson, 'De la simulation inconsciente dans l'état d'hypnotisme', *Revue philosophique de la France et de l'étranger*, 22 (1886), 525–531.

13 *Quid Aristoteles de loco senserit*, translated into French by R. Mossé-Bastide in *Mélanges*, pp. 1–56.

14 Bergson, *Œuvres*, p. 1542.

15 Arnaud Bouaniche, "Dossier Critique", in Bergson, *Essai sur les données de la conscience* (Paris: Presses universitaires de France, 2007), p. 280.

16 René Descartes, *The Principles of Philosophy*, §57, in *The Philosophical Writings of Descartes*, ed. John Cottingham, Robert Stoothoff and Dugald Murdoch, vol. 1 (Cambridge: Cambridge University Press, 1985), p. 212. See also Geoffrey Gorham, "Descartes on Time and Duration", *Early Modern Science and Medicine* 12 (2007), 28–54.

17 See Bruce Baugh, "Time, Duration and Eternity in Spinoza", *Comparative and Continental Philosophy*, 2/2 (2010), 211–33.

18 Joseph Delboeuf, *Essai de logique scientifique* (Liège: Desoer, 1865), p. 152.

19 Albert Lemoine, *L'habitude et l'instinct* (Paris: Germer Baillière, 1875), pp. 59 and 26. On this, see my "Habit and Time in Nineteenth-Century French Philosophy: Albert Lemoine between Bergson and Ravaisson", *British Journal for the History of Philosophy* 26/1 (2018), 131–53.

20 Victor Egger, *La parole intérieure* (Paris: Germer Baillière 1881), p. 113, for example.

21 William James, "On Some Omissions of Introspective Psychology", *Mind* 9/33 (1884), 1–26.

22 Ben-Ami Scharfstein, *Roots of Bergson's Philosophy* (New York: Columbia University Press, 1942), p. 43. See the whole of Scharfstein's second chapter, "The Root in Time", for a fuller account of Bergson's predecessors.

23 On the immediate reception of *Time and Free Will* and *Matter and Memory*, see Azouvi, *La gloire de Bergson*, Chapter 2.

24 Gabriel Séailles, *Essai sur le genie dans l'art* (Paris: Germer Baillière, 1883).

25 In this connection, see Emily Herring's "Henri Bergson, Celebrity" (May 2019): https://aeon.co/essays/henri-bergson-the-philosopher-damned-for-his-female-fans.

26 For a reproduction of such press photographs, see Mark Antliff, *Inventing Bergson: Cultural Politics and the Parisian Avant-Garde* (Princeton, NJ: Princeton University Press, 1993), p. 5.

27 See "Le Rire: Conférence de M. Bergson", in *Mélanges* 313–15 and *Cours* Vol. II (Paris: Presses universitaires de France, 1991), pp. 43–4.

28 Albert Thibaudet, *Trente ans de vie française III: Le bergsonisme* (Paris: Gallimard, 1923), pp. 225–6.

29 See Azouvi, *La gloire de Bergson*, p. 136.

30 For Jaurès, Bergson's position in 1889 was "the metaphysics of decadent art"; cited in Azouvi, *La gloire de Bergson*, p. 62.

31 See Azouvi, *La gloire de Bergson*, "Une philosphie décadente, symboliste et impressioniste", pp. 59–76.

32 On all of this, see Antliff, *Inventing Bergson*, Chapter II: "Du cubisme between Bergson and Nietzsche", pp. 39–66.

33 As cited in Azouvi, *La gloire de Bergson*, pp. 226–7.

34 Georges Sorel, *Réflexions sur la violence* (Paris: Marcel Rivière, 1908)/*Reflections on Violence*, trans. T. E. Hulme and J. Roth (New York: Dover, 1950). On all of the material in this paragraph, see Antliff, *Inventing Bergson*, "Introduction", pp. 3–15. On Sorel's appropriation of Bergson's ideas, see Hisashi Fujita, "Anarchy and Analogy: The Violence of Language in Bergson and Sorel", in *Bergson, Politics, and Religion*, ed. A. Lefebvre and M. White (Durham, NC: Duke University Press, 2012), pp. 126–43. See also Ellen Kennedy, "Bergson's Philosophy and French Political Doctrines: Sorel, Maurras, Péguy and de Gaulle", *Government and Opposition* 15/1 (1980), 75–91.

35 See Azouvi, *La gloire de Bergson*, pp. 141–72.

36 Bertrand Russell, *The Collected Works of Bertrand Russell: Logical and Philosophical Papers*, vol. 6: 1909–1913 (Abingdon: Routledge, 1992), p. 318.
37 See Theodore Roosevelt, "The Search for Truth in a Reverend Spirit", *Outlook* 99 (1911), 819–26.
38 On this point, see Soulez and Worms, *Bergson*, p. 101.
39 Bergson, "Discours prononcé à l'Académie des sciences morales et politiques le 8 août 1914", in *Mélanges*, p. 1102.
40 Wilhelm Wundt, "Plagiator Bergson, membre de l'Institut. Zur Antwort auf die Herabsetzung der deutschen Wissenschaft durch Edmond Perrier, président de l'Académie des Sciences par Hermann Bönke", *Literarisches Zentralblatt für Deutschland* 66 (1915), 1131–8, p. 1137.
41 Both quotations: "Discours en séance publique annuelle de l'Académie des sciences morales et politiques—samedi 12 décembre 1914", M 1107–29. This address has been translated as "Life and Matter in Conflict", in Bergson, *The Meaning of the War*, trans. H. Wildon-Carr (London: T. Fisher Unwin, 1915), pp. 15–40. For the two quotations, see *The Meaning of the War* 17/M 1108 and 30/ M 1113, respectively.
42 See Johann Chapoutot, "La trahison d'un clerc? Bergson, la grande guerre et la France", *Francia* 35 (2008), 295–316, p. 297.
43 Bergson's analysis, including his remarks on Hegel, derives from E. Caro's "Les deux allemagnes: Madame de Staël et Henri Heine", *La revue des deux mondes* (November 1871), 5–20.
44 On this point, see Florence Caeymaex, "Les discours de guerre: propagande et philosophie", in *Annales bergsoniennes VII: Bergson, l'Allemagne, la guerre de 1914*, ed. Arnaud François, Nadia Yala Kisukidi, Camille Riquier, Caterina Zanfi and Frédéric Worms (Paris: Presses universitaires de France, 2014), pp. 143–66, p. 156.
45 Bergson, *The Meaning of the War*, p. 23/M 1110.
46 Bergson, *The Meaning of the War*, p. 22/M 1110.
47 Both quotations: Bergson, *The Meaning of the War*, pp. 22–3/M 1110.
48 Bergson, *The Meaning of the War*, p. 25/M 1111.
49 Bergson, *The Meaning of the War*, p. 31/M 1113.
50 See Roger Bruyeron, *1914: L'entrée en guerre de quelques philosophes* (Paris: Hermann, 2014), p. 116.
51 Georges Friedman, "La prudence de M. Bergson, ou Philosophie et caractère", *Commune* 30/3 (1936), 721–36, p. 730.
52 Bergson, "Rapport sur 'Le Maroc, école d'énergie' d'Alfred de Tarde", in *Mélanges*, 1395–6, p. 1396. See Alfred de Tarde, *Le Maroc, école d'énergie* (Rabat: Imprimerie du Bulletin Officiel du Protectorat, 1915); available at http://gallica.bnf.fr/ark:/12148/bpt6k62652277, and particularly p. 7 for the questions that the review addresses: "Qu'est-ce que la France est venue apporter au Maroc de neuf et de fécond? Qu'est-ce que l'âme indigène, qu'est-ce que l'âme française elle-même gagnent à ce contact?"

53 See Philippe Soulez, *Bergson politique* (Paris: Presses universitaires de France, 1989), p. 140.
54 Bergson, *The Meaning of the War*, p. 38/M 1116.
55 Donna V. Jones, "Mysticism and War: Reflections on Bergson and his Reception during World War I", in *Annales bergsoniennes* VII, pp. 167–79, p. 178.
56 Georges Politzer, "La fin d'une parade philosophique: Le bergsonisme", in *Contre Bergson et quelques autres. Ecrits philosophiques 1924–1939*, ed. R. Bruyeron (Paris: Flammarion, 2013), pp. 127–244, p. 230.
57 J. Alexander Gunn, *Bergson and His Philosophy* (London: Methuen, 1920), p. 31.
58 For Bergson's 1917 US speeches, see *Correspondances*, pp. 715–49.
59 Frank Grandjean, *Une revolution dans la philosophie. La doctrine de M. Bergson* (Geneva and Paris: Atar, 1916), p. 211.
60 On the history of these international congresses, see Frédéric Worms and Caterina Zanfi (eds.), *Revue de métaphysique et de morale* 2014/4, special issue *L'Europe philosophique des congrès à la guerre*.
61 On all of this, see the Introduction to Elie During's superb critical dossier in Bergson, *Durée et simultanéité* (Paris: Presses universitaires de France, 2009), pp. 219–44. For a peerless critical evaluation in English of Bergson's response to Einstein, see Milič Čapek, *Bergson and Modern Physics: A Reinterpretation and Re-evaluation*. Boston Studies in the Philosophy of Science, Vol. 7 (Dordrecht: D. Reidel, 1971).
62 For more historical detail concerning Bergson's engagement with Einstein, see Jimena Canales, "Einstein, Bergson, and the Experiment That Failed: Intellectual Cooperation at the League of Nations", *MLN* 120/5 (2005), 1168–91, and *The Physicist and the Philosopher: Einstein, Bergson, and the Debate That Changed Our Understanding of Time* (Princeton, NJ: Princeton University Press, 2015).
63 The three remarks: Letter to Maurice Solovine, Pentecost 1923, in Albert Einstein, *Correspondances françaises*, ed. M. Biezunski (Paris: Editions du Seuil, 1989), p. 287; Isaac Benrubi, *Souvenirs sur Bergson* (Neuchâtel: Delachaux & Niestlé, 1942), p. 108; and *Mélanges*, pp. 1450–1.
64 See Canales, "Einstein, Bergson, and the Experiment That Failed", p. 1177.
65 Cited in Canales, "Einstein, Bergson, and the Experiment That Failed", p. 1174.
66 R.-M. Mossé-Bastide describes his position as "extremist"; R.-M. Mossé-Bastide, *Bergson Educateur* (Paris: Presses universitaires de France, 1955), p. 151.
67 Azouvi, *La gloire de Bergson*, p. 247.
68 Raymond Aron, "Hommage à Bergson" (January 14, 1941), in *Essais sur la condition juive contemporaine*, ed. Perrine Simon-Nahum (Paris: Editions de Fallois, 1989), p. 18.
69 See Thibaudet, *Trente ans de vie française III: Le bergsonisme*.
70 Per Hallström, President of the Nobel Committee of the Swedish Academy, "Presentation Speech" (December 10, 1928), in *Nobel Lectures, Literature 1901–1967*, ed. Horst Frenz (Amsterdam: Elsevier, 1969). In this connection, see the conclusion of Canales, "Bergson, Einstein and the Experiment That Failed".

71 See Bergson, "Banquet Speech", in *Nobel Lectures, Literature 1901–1967*, ed. Horst Frenz, pp. 246–7.

72 Julien Benda, *The Treason of the Intellectuals* (Abingdon: Routledge, 2017), p. 29.

73 For the importance of Politzer's text, see Chapter 8 of Frédéric Worms, *La philosophie en France au XXe siècle* (Paris: Gallimard, 2009), particularly p. 194, and Giuseppe Bianco, *Après Bergson: Portrait de groupe avec philosophe* (Paris: Presses universitaires de France, 2015), who compares its effect to a "fragmentation bomb" (p. 169). Strangely, English-language commentary seems to be largely unaware that Bergson's fall from grace and glory had political causes.

74 Paul Nizan, *Les chiens de garde* (Marseille: Agone, 2012). Alan D. Schrift notes the importance of Nizan, but not of Politzer, in his *Twentieth-Century French Philosophy* (Oxford: Blackwell, 2006), p. 17.

75 Jacques Chevalier and Alfred Thibaudet attempted this, and Bergson underlined that these attempts were theirs not his; see, in this connection, *Correspondances*, pp. 1060 and 1182, respectively, and Camille Riquier, *Archéologie de Bergson*, p. 409.

76 Jacques Maritain, cited in Soulez and Worms, *Bergson*, p. 229.

77 Bergson's will was published in the *Gazette de Lausanne*, September 9, 1941.

Further reading

Mark Antliff, *Inventing Bergson: Cultural Politics and the Parisian Avant-Garde* (Princeton, NJ: Princeton University Press, 1993). The leading study of Bergson's influence on artistic and political movements in the first decades of the twentieth century.

Ben-Ami Scharfstein, *The Roots of Bergson's Philosophy* (New York: Columbia University Press, 1942). This is still the best study in English of Bergson's sources in nineteenth-century philosophy.

Sanford Schwartz, "Bergson and the Politics of Vitalism", in *The Crisis of Modernism: Bergson and the Vitalist Controversy*, ed. Frederick Burwick and Paul Douglass (Cambridge: Cambridge University Press, 1992), pp. 277–305. An excellent study of the complex cultural context of Bergson's work.

Philippe Soulez and Frédéric Worms, *Bergson* (Paris: Presses universitaires de France, 2002). The standard biography of Bergson, but it has not been translated into English.

Two
Time

Where does *Time and Free Will* begin?

The title of Bergson's 1888 doctoral thesis that was published as a book the following year, *Essai sur les données immédiates de la conscience*, is literally translated as *An Essay on the Immediate Data of Consciousness*. "Data", however, works less well than "*données*", for it sounds considerably more technical and abstract (such that the uninitiated might even wonder whether Bergson's thesis had artificial intelligence for a topic); *donner* is the ordinary French for "to give", whereas *data* is Latin (from *dare*, "to give"). It was perhaps for this reason that in F. L. Pogson's 1910 English translation, which Bergson authorised, the English phrase forms merely the subtitle that is preceded by the rather more incisive title: *Time and Free Will*. Whether it was Pogson or Bergson who proposed this new title, adopting it was a fine decision, for it expresses directly not only the central issues of the text, but also the order in which the French philosopher addressed them. *Time and Free Will* is first of all a book about the nature of time, a book that proposes a revolutionary account of temporal experience. Consequently, Bergson is able to challenge the traditional parameters of debates concerning free will, and to offer an original defence of a notion of human freedom, as we will see in the following chapter of this study.

The English title *Time and Free Will* signals, in fact, that the order of its three chapters is not the order in which Bergson proceeds philosophically. For, in the final version, the chapters on time ("Of the Multiplicity of Psychological States: The Idea of Duration") and freedom ("Of the Organisation of Psychological States: Freedom") are preceded by a first chapter ("Of the Intensity of Psychological States") that Bergson added only after having completed between 1884 and 1886 what became the second and the third. This first chapter addresses the issue of whether psychological states (my joy, for example, the pain in my arm or the blue of the sky) have a quantifiable intensity. Bergson thus enters into the controversy concerning the promotion of quantitative methods in psychology under the heading of "psychophysics" and, more specifically, concerning Gustav Fechner's 1860 proposal for a method to measure the intensities of sensations. Bergson denies that psychological states are quantifiable and measurable, and he even denies Aristotle's claim that such states,[1] though qualities rather than quantities, are intrinsically orderable according to a "more or less". Bergson added this first chapter because:

> it seemed to me that a study of the notion of intensity would constitute, between the notions of quantity and quality studied in the rest of the work, a bridge [un trait d'union] capable of making my views clearer and more accessible; besides, [...] Fechner and psychophysics were popular at the time, and on the terrain of an examination of Fechner's theory, I had the chance of being understood and followed.[2]

If Bergson's intention was to make his views about time and freedom more accessible, it was hardly successful at his thesis defence: his examiners, headed by Emile Boutroux, spent most of the allotted time discussing his arguments about intensity without paying much heed to his argument about time.[3]

Time and Free Will, then, does not really begin where it seems to begin. As Bergson underlined subsequently in a letter, the real starting point of the book lies in its reflection on time, and, more specifically, in its critique of the quantification of time in the sciences:

> the starting point of my Essai sur les données immédiates is to be found in the pages 88–91 [TFW 116–20] and 147–9 [TFW 196–9] relating to homogeneous time, and I can say that it is the consideration of time that detached me from mechanistic philosophy

and led me to a "psychologism" to which I became more and more attached, first in the "immediate data", and then in *Matter and Memory*. [C 145–6]

The pages of the second and third chapters to which Bergson refers here argue that the "sciences operate on time [...] only in immediately eliminating its essential and qualitative aspect" [TFW 115/86]. These pages record, in fact, his conversion in the early 1880s from a concern to complete and extend Herbert Spencer's mechanistic philosophy to a quite different, anti-mechanistic concern for the psychological experience of time. Spencer, as we noted in Chapter 1, had declared that time, as one of the "ultimate scientific ideas", was "wholly incomprehensible",[4] but it dawned on Bergson that it was not possible to fill in this fundamental lacuna in Spencer's philosophy while maintaining the principles of his system as a whole.

Bergson saw first of all that Spencer was led to his sceptical view because mathematical physics methodically abstracts from the real experience of time. A simple calculation of, say, the speed of a uniformly moving body is achieved by dividing the distance by time: d/t. The time is measured by a unit whose length is drawn from a repeatable movement that we take as a standard; a minute, for example, is $1/1440$ of a day, of a full rotation of the earth (ignoring, for the sake of simplicity, its more precise measure, given the variations in the earth's rotation, in terms of the cycles of a caesium atomic clock). On the face of a functioning clock, one revolution of the minute-hand is simultaneous with that portion of the daily movement of the earth. Therefore, when we measure the time elapsed in, say, someone running 1500 metres with and by means of the clock, we compare two simultaneous movements: we compare the locomotion of the runner to that of the earth around the sun.

In all of this, when we quantify time, "there is", as Bergson saw, "no question of duration, but only of space and simultaneities" [TFW 116/86]. In order to measure the period of time elapsed, we mark the beginning and end of each of the movements, but we thereby focus on the beginning and the end of the period of time elapsed rather than the elapsed time; "it is always on the extremity, however small it considers it to be, that mathematics installs itself. As for the interval itself, as for duration and movement itself, they are necessarily left out of the equation" [TFW 119/89]. The intervals separating the extremities cannot be constituted by any series of such extremities, since from the perspective of mathematics, space and time are infinitely divisible. No spatial point can be contiguous with another, just as no temporal instant can immediately succeed another, for between any two points or two instants, no matter how close together, there is always an infinitely divisible interval between them. At the hands of mathematics, the interval separating the extremities disappears "in a dust of moments not one of which has duration, each one being instantaneous" [CM 219/208]. Grasping time mathematically, no matter how concrete the grasp might super-ficially appear, is necessarily to have time slip between one's fingers.

"These unities of time that constitute *la durée vecue*, lived duration", in contrast, "are precisely what interests the psychologist, for psych-ology", at least the one that Bergson proposes, "bears on the intervals themselves, and no longer on their extremities" [TFW 196/147]. As he will write later in *Creative Evolution*:

> If I want to mix sugar in a glass of water, I must, willy-nilly, wait until the sugar melts. This little fact is big with consequences. For here the time I have to wait is not that mathematical time which would apply equally well to the entire history of the material world, even if that history were spread out instantan-eously in space. It coincides with my impatience, that is to say, with a certain stretch of my own duration, which I cannot pro-tract or contract at will. It is no longer something *thought*, it is something *lived*. [CE 10/9-10]

The experienced interval of time, the time I have to wait for the sugar to melt, is not a homogeneous time without quality that, independ-ently of its contents, is identical to any other stretch of time marked out by the mathematician's instants. My impatience, the experienced quality of the passage of time being a burden, is constitutive of that interval of time itself. This is what the passage of time, as we might say, "feels like" for me—and what, at bottom, it "feels like" for me, according to Bergson, is what it is.

In the third chapter of *Time and Free Will*, Bergson draws out the difference between lived and mathematised time with a thought experiment: were the world to be sped up by an evil demon, one "even more powerful than Descartes' evil demon", so that everything within the world happened twice as fast, nothing would change in the "equations allowing us to predict", say, astronomical phenomena.

> [F]or in these equations, the symbol t does not designate a duration, but a relation between two durations, a certain number of unities of time, or, in the end, in the final analysis, a certain number of simultaneities; only the intervals separating them would have diminished, but these intervals count for nothing in the calculations. [TFW 194/145]

Time passing twice as fast would change nothing in the calculations, for the scientist would count the same number of unities of time in the movement whose temporal span is being measured. But everything would change for the person experiencing the accelerated events. Although it could not be measured, since the mathematical measurement of time remains unaffected, there would have to be a qualitative transformation in the experience, "in the ordinary enrichment of the being", i.e. of the person, and "a modification in the progress that it customarily realizes between dawn and dusk" [TFW 194/145]. Descartes' hypothesis in his *Meditations* of an evil demon that would make us take for true what is in fact false led to the one principle that he famously supposed cannot be doubted: *cogito ergo sum*, "I think therefore I am".[5] Bergson's evil demon leads us back to the temporal experience that, although mathematical calculation methodically overlooks it, is also beyond doubt.

Scientific calculations would not be altered if time were sped up, but "when an astronomer foretells, for example, a lunar eclipse, he merely exercises in his own way the power which we have ascribed to our evil demon".

> He decrees that time shall go ten times, a hundred times, a thousand times as fast, and he has a right to do so, since all that he

thus changes is the nature of the conscious intervals, and since these intervals, by hypothesis, do not enter into the calculations. Therefore, into a psychological duration of a few seconds he may put several years, even several centuries of astronomical time; that is his procedure when he traces in advance the path of a heavenly body or represents it by an equation. He does nothing but establish a series of relations of position between this body and other given bodies, a series of simultaneities and co-incidences, a series of numerical relations; as for genuine duration, it remains out of the calculation. [TFW 194/146]

In predicting the movement of the body years or even centuries in advance, the scientist pictures it as already having occurred, just as the equations by which the movement is predicted involve units of time that stand for time that has passed rather than the experience of time that is passing. If the scientist "foresees a future phenomenon, it is only on condition of making it to a certain extent a present phenomenon" [TFW 195/146], in which the completed movement is already there to see, if only in the mind's eye, and thus in which the movement has, in a sense, already occurred. Thus: "all foreseeing is in reality seeing [toute prévision est en réalité une vision]" [TFW 197/148].

Space as quantitative multiplicity

Bergson's train of thought in *Time and Free Will* begins, then, in the passages of its second and third chapters concerning the inability of science, with its mathematical measurement of time, to grasp lived duration. The second chapter starts, however, with an analysis of that by which time is measured, namely number, and this analysis shows exactly why numerical measurement passes over lived duration.

Number is a "synthesis of the one and the many [le multiple]" [TFW 75/56]. A particular number—the number 9, say—is a unity, since it is apprehended as a unity, and bears a single name, but this unity is, at the same time, a sum that allows for division into smaller units and that thus contains a multiplicity of parts that can be considered in isolation. In order to count these units in, say, a flock of sheep, we ignore the individual differences of the sheep and take into account only what is common to them all. The units of a number must in some way be identical, for otherwise there would be nothing that could be added up to make a sum. If we focus on the differences ("Flossy", "Molly", …), we are "enumerating", like the army sergeant calling the roll ("Smith", "Sir!", "Jones", "Sir!", …), rather than counting, for we do not arrive at a sum. To do that, Bergson argues, each must be considered simultaneously, and thus as juxtaposed in a certain space, such as a pen. But if counting the sheep requires that their individual differences are ignored, they must be distinct in the places they occupy in the pen, for otherwise, if they were identical in all other ways, they would all merge into one. Counting physical things, then, requires the simultaneous presence of those things differentiated by their position in space. Similarly, when, during a bout of insomnia, we try to count nine sheep in our minds, we have to imagine them together in an ideal space, an ideal pen, after each has jumped over the fence; otherwise, "it will only ever be a matter of a single sheep" [TFW 76/57] repeatedly jumping.

The same applies, Bergson claims, even in the case of an abstract number. We can conceive the number nine, for example, without the idea of any particular group of nine things. Of course, we can and usually do manipulate numbers without the vision of unities in an ideal space—we are normally perfectly happy to acknowledge that $9 \times 9 = 81$ without doing so—but here "we have ceased to have an image or even idea of it; we have kept only the symbol which is necessary for reckoning and which is the conventional way of expressing number" [TFW 78/58]. "Any clear idea of number", he claims, "implies a vision in space" [TFW 79/59]. It is important to note that Bergson writes "implies" here rather than "requires": if Bergson's position were that there is no clear idea of a large number, say, 50, without envisaging 50 units, it perhaps would be untenable. It is not certain that it is ever possible to envisage, either mentally or in the objective world, such a multiple of units, and to be sure that the multiple units thus envisaged do add up to 50 without introducing intermediary sums. One way to be certain that there are 50 coins on the table, of course, is to arrange five of them in a pile, and then makes ten such piles, but in doing so, the piles of five coins become sums themselves.[6] It would seem, then, that Bergson's position about a "clear idea of number" is not that we have to apprehend the requisite number of single unities, in this case 50, but only that smaller numbers, in order to be apprehended in their truth, can be grounded in an intuition or vision, and that mathematics can develop on that basis.

In the sense that Bergson intends it here, space is a "homogeneous empty milieu", whose parts, without any intrinsic differences, are all of the same nature. "There is", in fact, "scarcely any other possible definition of space: it is what enables us to distinguish a number of identical and simultaneous sensations from one another", and is thus "a principle of differentiation other than that of qualitative differentiation, and, consequently, a reality without quality" [TFW 95/71]. Space is a principle of quantitative difference, of quantitative multiplicity. Although Bergson already points in these pages to a different notion of a qualitative space that would somehow precede homogeneous, geometrical space (a notion that he will develop in *Matter and Memory*),here he accepts, as an essential philosophical breakthrough, Immanuel Kant's interpretation of space in this sense as a condition of possibility of experience, an "*a priori* form of intuition". According to Kant's *Critique of Pure Reason*, space is not a thing like any other, but nor does it derive from things, as an abstraction from them, since a thing cannot be what it is without already being in space.[7] As a "transcendental" condition of the possibility of experience, as a principle that precedes empirical experience such that it makes the latter possible, space is a form that would remain even if there were no things in it, without any matter, a form that belongs to the mind that apprehends the world. But if "it is only from the human standpoint that we can speak of space, of extended things",[8] as Kant put it, space is not just "transcendentally ideal" but also "empirically real" in that it is valid for all possible objects of external experience. In this sense, Bergson can even argue that Kant's view confirms rather than offends common sense [TFW 92/69].

Bergson follows Kant concerning space, but he has also borrowed the argument about quantification from Félix Ravaisson's 1838 doctoral dissertation, *Of Habit*. In a passage concerning consciousness, and its principal faculty, the understanding, Ravaisson writes:

> the understanding grasps quantity only under the particular and determining condition of distinguishing parts—that is, in the

form of the unity of plurality, of discrete quantity, of number. The idea of distinct parts is, in turn, determined within the understanding only under the still more particular condition of distinguishing the intervals separating them; in other words, the understanding represents number only within the plurality of the limits of a continuous quantity. Yet continuity can be grasped by the understanding only on the basis of coexistence. Continuous, coexisting quantity is extension. Thus quantity is the logical, knowable form of extension; and the understanding represents quantity to itself only in the sensible form of extension, in the intuition of space.[9]

Quantity, then, implies number, number implies coexistence, coexistence implies extension, and extension implies space; and if Bergson seems to take this argument in the opening pages of his second chapter as a given, as his arch-enemy Bertrand Russell complained, it is presumably because he expected his examiners to be familiar with it.[10] Moreover, given its Ravaissonian origin, it is clear that *Time and Free Will*'s account of number does not derive, as Russell supposed, from the psychological peculiarity of its author as a "visualiser". This, in any case, is to misconstrue the French philosophers' thesis, which concerns the "intuition of space" rather than simply, in a narrower sense, vision. Space, for Bergson, as a "pure intuition", is homogeneous, completely absent of the qualitative sensory differences that vision apprehends. As Bergson writes, "we know two different orders of reality: one, that of sensory qualities, is heterogeneous, the other, that of space, is homogeneous. The latter, clearly conceived by human intelligence, allows us to produce sharp distinctions, to count, to abstract, and perhaps even to speak" [TFW 97/73]. Space in Bergson's sense is not a space of things with sensory, and thus visual, qualities.

Russell, as Milič Čapek saw, has "confused 'intuition of space' with a *crude visualisation*", although Bergson helps him to do so when he rather loosely states, as we have seen, that any clear idea of number requires a "vision [*vision*] in space" [TFW 79/59].[11] Bergson has not adopted in his philosophy of mathematics the classically empiricist view that all thinking requires mental imagery; and thus he has not simply failed to heed Descartes' lesson concerning the distinction between the imagination and the understanding as faculties of the mind (I can understand the concept of a chiliagon, a thousand-sided figure, without being able to make it present to myself in the form of an image). Instead, Bergson qualifies Descartes position with the Kantian claim that number relates not immediately to the empirical imagination and perception but to an *a priori* form of intuition. To be sure, other views are possible in the philosophy of mathematics, and the reduction of mathematics to logic that Russell espouses retreats from all intuitive elements within it. But Bergson's correlation of number and spatiality, as Čapek has shown, "is not as isolated as Russell wanted to suggest",[12] since a variety of philosophers and mathematicians have expressed similar views.

Bergson departs from Kant and Ravaisson—the latter follows the *Critique of Pure Reason* in this—in rejecting their supposition that number also relates, and perhaps more essentially, to time. In the *Prolegomena to Any Future Metaphysics*, Kant came to hold that "geometry is based on the pure intuition of space", whereas "arithmetic produces its concepts of number through successive addition of units in time". Geometry relates to the pure *a priori* form of space, arithmetic to the pure *a priori* form of time. Kant had already said something similar, though rather more obscure, about number and time in the *Critique of Pure Reason*: although "the pure image of all magnitudes (*quantorum*) for outer sense is space", time is necessary for the application of the concept of magnitude to appearances. The "rule" or "schema" through which this concept is applied is what Kant calls number, which is "a representation which comprises the successive addition of homogeneous units", and "number is therefore simply the unity of the synthesis of the manifold of a homogeneous intuition in general, a unity due to my generating time itself in the apprehension of the intuition".[13]

Kant's claims about number and time seem to have a strong and a weak version, depending on whether the view is that time is what is counted or that it is just necessary for the process of counting. The strong version, seemingly expressed in the *Prolegomena*, Bergson considers to be a confusion deriving from the "habit we have acquired of apparently counting in time rather than space" [TFW 78/58]. We might count to 20 when, say, playing hide and seek, and Bergson can even admit that in so doing it is "incontestable" that we have thus "counted moments of time rather than space". In "counting" in this way, however, we do not arrive at a sum, and we have, in the end, merely enumerated a learnt sequence of numbers in time, numbers whose sense derives from space. To count in a genuine way, we have to "fix in a point of space each of the moments that we count", and "it is on this condition alone that the abstract unities form a sum" [TFW 79/59]. With the strong version of his view, Kant has succumbed to the confusions of habit (as has also Ravaisson, in a treatise on habit!), but the weak version, which may or may not be the one expressed in the *Critique of Pure Reason*, fails to establish anything specific about counting. Time is necessary for counting, certainly, but all psychological acts and processes occur in time, so this fact alone constitutes no reason to think that number has any special relation to it. Calculating fast never changes anything in the result of the calculation—at least when haste does not produce error.[14]

Quantity, then, seems to be intrinsically related to space; quantification is spatialisation. It becomes clear, therefore, why time as conceived by the scientist in mathematical equations passes over duration. Time quantified and mathematised is time spatialised: "it is to be presumed that time understood in the sense of a medium in which one distinguishes and one counts is merely space" [TFW 91/68]. Bergson might exaggerate here, but time in this sense is at the very least time spatialised, time seen through the prism of space, even if it is not exactly identical with space.[15] The homogeneous time thus quantified is a "fourth dimension of space" [TFW 109/81]. From this perspective, the notion of space-time that Hermann Minkowski considered Einstein's special theory of relativity to presuppose, a notion according to which time is no longer separate from space and is treated as another dimension of the latter, only develops and radicalises the spatialisation implied in any mathematical grasp of time. "What has been insufficiently remarked", as Bergson will write in 1922, "is that a fourth dimension of space is suggested by any spatialisation of time; it has always been implied by our science and our language" [DS 103/149].

Here we can also situate Bergson's approach in relation to J. M. E. McTaggart's famous 1908 distinction, one pivotal in much contemporary philosophy of time, of an A-series and a B-series.[16] The

B-series is expressed by words such as "before", "after" and "at the same time as", or "the day before", "that day", and the "day after", and the truth of propositions containing such expressions is unchanging as time passes. Taking the present tense of the verb in a *tenseless* sense, "McTaggart writes his essay after *Time and Free Will* but without referring to it", is true now, and has been true, the typical B-theorist holds, at all times. Often with the aim to accommodate Einstein's theory of relativity, B-theorists of time claim that this unchanging series is the most fundamental aspect of time, and that the experience of temporal passage is secondary or even illusory. Such a view, for Bergson, is no arbitrary hypothesis, but the "metaphysics immanent to the spatial representation of time". Once we conceive time by means of space, it is "inevitable". The spatialisation of time leads us to think that past, present and even the future are already there, lined up, and that the "flow of time is only […] the gradually obtained vision of what was waiting, globally, in eternity" [DS 43/61].

The A-series, in contrast, involves the tensed notions of past, present and future in propositions featuring expressions such as "yesterday", "today" and "tomorrow", propositions whose truth-value can change, since what is present becomes past, and what is future will at some point become present. Tomorrow will be another (to)day, and "Bergson is writing *Creative Evolution*" was true for some time prior to 1907, but false afterwards. Bergson would certainly endorse McTaggart's view that the fact of change cannot be captured adequately by the B-series, but he would have to reject his claim that the A-series is incoherent and inherently contradictory in a way that would lead us to the Scottish philosopher's conclusion that time does not exist. Bergson is certainly closer to an A-theory than to a B-theory of time in *Time and Free Will*, but his originality lies in his account of the experience of succession and passage in time as real duration, an account which A-theory does not provide. Bergson asks whether time in its most profound sense can be conceived as a *series* at all. The notion of a temporal series seems to require discrete moments, but discrete moments, as will become clearer in what follows, require space. From Bergson's perspective, an A-theory of time, if it is not guided by a vigilant critique of our spatialising tendencies, leads us almost inexorably to a B-theory insofar as the A-theory already begins to spatialise time.

Duration as qualitative multiplicity

Bergson's own path of thinking, as we saw in the first section of this chapter, begins with an attempt to elucidate what Spencer claimed to be unintelligible, namely the nature of time. Ravaisson, with his analysis of quantification as spatialisation, as we have just seen, seems to have helped Bergson to discern why science is unable to grasp it. *Time and Free Will* draws out the implications of the analysis of quantification as spatialisation, however, in a manner that goes beyond anything Ravaisson said explicitly.[17] If time is different from space, then time, we might think, at least in its most primitive sense, may well be something other than a quantifiable, homogeneous milieu. "Duration must be something else" [TFW 91/68], as Bergson asserts. In this way, he aims to challenge the parallelism of space and time firmly established by Kant. There are, of course, evident differences between space and time that Kant recognises: space has three dimensions, whereas time has one; and time appears to flow in a particular direction, while space does not. Still, Kant considered both space and time to be quantifiable, homogeneous media, with space characterised as the form of "outer sense", and time as the form of "inner sense".

But if time is something other than a quantifiable, homogeneous milieu, and if the mind is essentially temporal rather than spatial, then mental states in their multiplicity will not be external to each other like things are external to each other in space. "If one accepts this conception of number, it will become clear", claims Bergson, "that not all things are counted in the same way, and that there are two quite different types of multiplicity" [TFW 85/63]. When hearing a peal of church bells, to take his first example, "either I retain each of the successive sensations to organise it with the others and to form a group that recalls a familiar tune or rhythm: in this way, I do not count the sounds, and limit myself to gathering the, so to speak, qualitative impression that their number has on me. Or else I propose explicitly to count them, and thus it is necessary to dissociate them, and that this disassociation is carried out in some homogeneous milieu" [TFW 86/64]. I can retain the past sounds, by means of a certain involuntary, primary memory, which allows the sounds to have something of the unity of a melody, without them being explicitly counted, which is to say explicitly disassociated and juxtaposed in an ideal space.

We are thus led to glimpse at least the possibility that there exist "two types of multiplicity: that of material objects, which immediately form a number, and that of the facts of consciousness, which cannot adopt numerical form without the intervention of some symbolic representation, in which space necessarily intervenes" [TFW 87/65]. The notes of a melody are certainly multiple, and seem to be heard successively, but even so, "can we not say that [...] we still perceive them each in the other, and that their whole is comparable to a living being, whose parts, though distinct, penetrate each other by the very effect of their solidarity?" [TFW 101/75]. Bergson finds evidence for this in the fact that if, playing the piece, we dwell too much on a particular note, it is not so much through the exaggerated length of the particular note as through the "qualitative change brought thus to the whole of the musical phrase" that we become aware of it. Hence, "we can conceive succession without distinction, and as a mutual penetration, a solidarity, an intimate organization of elements, of which each, representative of the whole, distinguishes and isolates itself from it only for thought capable of abstraction" [TFW 101/75].

This succession without distinction that is a mutual penetration is precisely what Bergson attempts to conceive as duration. In order to grasp it, we have to overcome our "obsession" [TFW 224/168] with space. Bergson is concerned with the immediate data of consciousness, concerned to reveal the data of immediate self-awareness—of "immediate apperception" [TFW 90/67; Pogson rendered this as "immediate perception"], to use the term that he takes up from his early nineteenth-century French forebear, Pierre Maine de Biran.[18] This immediacy, however, has to be gained, to be won by combatting the spatialising tendencies of thought that mediate our own self-awareness. As Bergson wrote to Harald Høffding in 1915, "the immediate is far from being what is easiest to apprehend [*appercevoir*]" [M 1148]. One might suppose, in fact, that "there is hardly anything *less immediate* [...] than Bergson's immediate data",[19] but this is true only if we take "immediate" to mean "without" and "prior to" mediation, rather than a negation of mediation, a negation occurring after the fact of mediation. It is in this light that we should understand Bergson's more serene description of his philosophical procedure in *Time and Free Will*: "pure duration is the form that the succession of our states of consciousness adopts when the self lets itself live [*se laisse vivre*], when it stops establishing a separation between its present and former states" [TFW 100/74–5]. If Bergson's philosophical method in 1889—and note that he has not yet arrived at the idea of "intuition" as essential to that method (see Chapter 7 of this study)—involves letting oneself go, a certain relaxation, then it also, paradoxically, involves a "vigorous effort of analysis", by means of which we can "isolate internal psychological facts from their image first of all refracted and then solidified in homogeneous space" [TFW 129/96]. Bergson's method involves analysis in his critique of mathematical time and his account of the relation of number to space, but also in the constant vigilance against the spatialising tendencies of thought. All of this is required in order to apprehend duration in its purity. Bergson therefore does not simply oppose what a contemporary philosopher has called "manifest time" to "scientific time", to the images or notions of time advanced in the contemporary sciences.[20] Duration is not quite a "manifest time".

What makes Bergson's psychological project still more difficult, however, is that the spatialising tendencies of thought are a function of ordinary language. Words—and Bergson is clearly thinking in particular of nouns—signify one set of things rather than another, as distinct from others, and what we all find in things rather than what I individually experience in those things; "the word, with its sharply defined contours, the brutal word, which stores what is stable, common and consequently impersonal in the impressions of humanity, destroys or at least covers over the delicate and fugitive impressions of our individual consciousness" [TFW 132/98]. Language transforms the inter-penetration of our psychological states into "a juxtaposition of inert states", and records the generic unity rather than the individual, particular and therefore unrepeatable qualities apprehended. We speak of love and hate while forgetting

that each of us loves and hates in his or her own way; and we speak
of streets and buildings in the city familiar to us by name as if they
were self-identical, when in truth the experience I have of them is
always qualitatively different, like the clouds in the sky, each time
I walk down or past them [TFW 129/96]. Of course, this function
of language is useful for communication and thus social life, but it
nevertheless veils the primary truth of experience. The philosophical
psychologist—like the bold novelist or poet [TFW 133/99]—has
somehow to use language against its own spatialising, generalising
and separatist tendencies. It was not by accident, then, that *Time and
Free Will* was understood, in relation to late-nineteenth-century artistic movements, as a sort of philosophical impressionism of the
inner life, whose task is to capture the fleeting truths of experience;
or as the philosophical extension of the symbolist movement, for
which truth could only be suggested rather than directly expressed
or depicted.[21]

It is true that Bergson says what duration *is* by first of all saying
what it *is not*. The terms in which he describes duration are largely a
negation, the photographic negative, of the characteristics of homogeneous space: space is opposed to duration as simultaneity to
succession, homogeneity to heterogeneity, and exteriority to mutual
penetration. "At first glance" it might appear that as a function of
this approach, Bergson's idea of qualitative multiplicity, as opposed
to quantitative multiplicity, is "utterly unconvincing", and "an *ad hoc*
notion created out of embarrassment and reluctance to apply the
usual concept of plurality".[22] It becomes more convincing, however, when we understand Bergson's more positive characterisation
of duration as a "mental synthesis", a synthesis "carried out by our
consciousness [*opérée par notre conscience*]" [TFW 124/83] that is of a
quite particular "type", since it is not the quantitative synthesis of
the one and the many constitutive of number.

According to *Time and Free Will*, the synthesis that is duration is a
"qualitative synthesis" that reorganises itself as it proceeds, where
not just the experience as a whole, but also the "parts" within it,
would not be what they are without each other. The present, in other
words, does not just add itself to the past, but melts into it, and
continuously merges with it [TFW 111/75]. As such a qualitative
synthesis, duration is not contrasted with change, in the way that we

might ordinarily think that something enduring resists change, but rather is a continuous process of qualitative change. Even listening to the "same" musical note continuously is a continuous process of psychological, qualitative change, precisely because I apprehend it, and because the I apprehending it now is different from the I that existed three seconds ago, if only because I have existed for three seconds more.

As a qualitative synthesis, duration is also an *immanent* synthesis, since it does not operate on originally separate moments: the present retains the past, as Bergson emphasises, while emerging from it. Synthesis is thus here a form of stretching-out of what has already been, a *self*-stretching out, since there is no external agency acting on what has already been from the outside. Bergson criticises associationist psychology—as had the English philosopher James Ward before him, who seems to have influenced Bergson in this connection[23]—which begins with an isolated, independent item in the present, and supposes that other psychological items are associated with it after the fact. Associationism atomises the life of the mind, and passes over the real flow of lived time. The immanent synthesis that is duration is not a combination of separate moments. If we conceive of it as combinatorial in any sense, Bergson's notion of duration will slip through our fingers.[24] In this connection, it is crucial not to be misled by Bergson's later apparent rejections of an idea of synthesis as an adequate characterisation of duration. When he writes in *Creative Evolution* that "if our existence was composed of separate states whose synthesis had to be carried out by an impassive self, then there would be no duration for us" [CE 4/4], he is criticising a common idea of synthesis as a synthesis of separate states, of synthesis as a combination, but not the idea of synthesis that he presents in 1889.

Noting this allows us to distinguish Bergson's position from "retentionalism" as a position in the contemporary philosophy of temporal experience. Retentionalism is the view that our "direct experiences of change consist of episodes of consciousness that are in fact momentary" and that "these durationless episodes possess contents which appear dynamic and to extend through a brief interval of time, even though in reality they do not".[25] To understand Bergson's description of duration as a "mental synthesis" as the expression of a retentionalist position is to fail to grasp the nature of the immanent, qualitative synthesis he describes. Given that retentionalism is closely related to "presentism", the position in the metaphysics of time according to which only the present moment exists, it is clear at the same time that even in *Time and Free Will*, before he came to write of memory, Bergson is no "presentist": there is no present moment wholly distinct from the past to which we can grant the title of "existence". Bergson is closer to an extensionalist position, as we will see more clearly, according to which "the episodes of experience which house our immediate experiences of change and succession are not momentary, but themselves unfold over periods of (objective) time, in much the way they appear to".[26]

As a qualitative, immanent synthesis, duration is also, and finally, a *passive synthesis*, to borrow an oxymoron from the German philosopher Edmund Husserl, who writes about time, and also the experience of melody, shortly after Bergson. This synthesis may well, as Bergson supposes, be carried out by our consciousness, but it is not and cannot be a voluntary operation, since the fact of duration, as when we are waiting for the sugar to melt, is one to which we have to submit. Duration is a synthesis, and is therefore in some sense an act, but is an act that is as passive as it is active.[27] It happens whether I like it or not. There is nothing outside of consciousness that synthesises duration for it, and so the synthesis occurs "in" consciousness; but this synthesis occurs prior to, and is in the fact the condition of, explicit acts of will and reflective thought.

The idea of a qualitative multiplicity, then, is the idea of a qualitative, immanent and passive synthesis. Thinking in an *ad hoc* fashion, in relation to the particular situation, is sometimes a positive virtue. Bergson's duration is not simply the photographic negative of space. If space is a principle of homogeneity, duration is not quite the "pure heterogeneity" [TFW 104/70] that Bergson posits hypothetically, for as he will write in an 1891 review of Jean-Marie Guyau's posthumous 1890 *La genèse de l'idée de temps* (*The Genesis of the Idea of Time*), although "duration begins only with a certain variety of effects", "absolute heterogeneity, if it was possible, would exclude time, whose principal character is continuity" [M 349]. Duration is not quite "pure difference", as Deleuze supposes it is in 1956. One can admit, with

Deleuze, that "duration is what differs from itself", but it remains the case that, for Bergson, there is no "pure difference", for the very idea of a "self" of duration presupposes a fundamental continuity.[28] Still, the idea of qualitative multiplicity is an attempt to account for the particular experiential fact that there are "two species of multiplicity, two possible senses of the word distinguish, two conceptions, one qualitative and one quantitative, of the difference between the *same* and the *other*" [TFW 121/90]. There are two species of difference, the second of which does not obey the "principle of identity" as a fundamental law of logic. In duration, A = A certainly, but it also equals B and C, since the present merges and melts into what we extract and abstract as the separate past moments of B and C. That duration contravenes logic in this way does not entail that we should consider duration as somehow illusory; instead, we are called to consider that the laws of logic do not hold the keys to temporal experience.

Of these two forms of difference, in any case, duration is primary and the more fundamental. This Bergson establishes in noting that counting numerical unities has a "double aspect". Although, on the one hand, we "suppose that they are identical, which can be conceived only on condition that these unities are aligned in space", on the other hand, "the third unity, for example, in being added to the first two, modifies the nature, the aspect, and something like the rhythm of the whole; and without this mutual penetration and this in some way qualitative progress, no addition would be possible". Qualitative multiplicity is, for Bergson, the condition of possibility of quantitative multiplicity, which itself is never pure. "It is thanks to the quality of quantity", he writes, "that we form the idea of a quantity without quality" [TFW 123/92].

Homogeneous time and movement

Bergson, as we have seen, sometimes identifies mathematicised time, time as represented in equations, with space. But what of the homogeneous time of actually perceived events, the time where things in the world seem to happen before and after each other, which, before we look at a clock, we experience prior to any explicitly mathematical or numerical thought? Bergson argues that this homogeneous time arises "from a type of exchange [...]" between space

and duration "that is near enough to what biologists call a phenomenon of endosmosis" [TFW 109/81], which is the biological
process in which fluid flows through a membrane into a region of
different density. It is important to attend to the detail of Bergson's
argument here in order to see that *Time and Free Will* does not simply
identify homogeneous time, which has characteristics "borrowed"
from pure duration, with space.[29]

Bergson supposes that at the beginning of the endosmosis there
are two principles untouched by each other: in ourselves, in pure
duration, there is "succession without reciprocal exteriority",
whereas "outside of the self" there is "reciprocal exteriority without
succession". At any given moment of its revolution on the clock
face, the second-hand of the clock is where it is, Bergson assumes,
and not anywhere else, and succession, which involves the present
following on from a previous position, is a function of the mind
perceiving it. However, because we can distinguish the positions of
the second-hand in space clearly from each other, as clearly before
and after each other, and because the second-hand is no longer
where it was when it is in a new position, "we contract the habit
of establishing the same distinction between successive moments
of our conscious life". In decomposing our own duration in this
way, we gain the "erroneous idea of an internal homogeneous duration analogous to space". This is illusory, but the very same process of endosmosis—through which duration becomes a form of
homogeneous time *analogous* rather than *identical* to space—has the
more positive and productive effect of allowing the movement of
the second-hand to "benefit in a certain way from the influence" it
has "exerted on our conscious life", and to exist in an external time.

> Owing to the fact that our consciousness has organised them as
> a whole in memory, they are first preserved and then arranged
> in a series: in short, we create for them a fourth dimension
> of space that we call homogeneous time and which allows the
> movement of the pendulum, though occurring on the spot, to
> be continually set in juxtaposition to itself. [TFW 109/81]

Bergson does not emphasise this positive aspect as much as he might
when he tries to determine "what is real and what is imaginary in

this very complex process" of endosmosis, but it would seem that the homogeneous time produced in the process of endosmosis is a reality in the case of extended things—a reality that is a function of our *consciousness* of the world, certainly—but an illusion as an account of pure duration.

More detail is added to this account of the endosmosis of duration and space when Bergson asks whether movement is given in perception. Again, he *begins* by claiming that although ordinarily, pre-philosophically, we might think that we perceive movement in space, on reflection "we see that the successive positions of the mobile indeed occupy space, but that the operation by which it passes from one position to the other, an operation that occupies duration and that is real only for a conscious spectator, escapes space" [TFW 111/82]. The space that a moving body has traversed can be measured and is thus a homogeneous quantity; the time required for the movement, in contrast, is apprehended only by means of time as duration, which is qualitative, and can be divided only by being spatialised in some sense. In the endosmosis of experience, however, not only are we led, illegitimately, to suppose that the time the movement takes, the duration, can be divided as a quantity, like the homogeneous space traversed, but we also project what Bergson terms the "act" or progress of movement into space itself; "we become used to projecting this act itself into space, to applying it to the length of the line that the mobile traverses, in a word, to solidifying it: as if this localisation of a *progress* in space did not amount to affirming that, even outside of consciousness, the past co-exists with the present!" [TFW 112/83–4]. Bergson seems to find this surprising, but he comes to the recognition that the movement from A to B, the transition of the thing *from* somewhere *to* somewhere else, is immediately visible. By the time of *Matter and Memory*, he will state this without any surprise at all: "when I put aside all preconceived ideas, I soon perceive that [...] even my sight takes in the movement from A to B as an indivisible whole, and that if it divides anything, it is the line supposed to have been traversed, and not the movement traversing it" [MM 188/210]. There is an immediate perception of movement in experience, which implies that the presentness of things is not punctual, but a stretch. If the present in things were merely punctual I would see, in truth, not movement but a succession of static points, a succession of immobilities. I do, however, perceive the from–to structure of movement, and thus the present in things is, as William James will famously put it, a "specious present". The process of endosmosis, then, gives rise to a kind of world-duration that is a stretch in which events can occur. This extended presence of the world is no illusion, as Bergson comes to recognise, but rather constitutive of things as they appear to us. In this way, Bergson's position seems to look more like an "extensionalist" position, even though extensionalism as such does not require commitment to his idea of duration in the self.

Not all commentators have seen this clearly, but Čapek was right to note that "already in this first phase of his thought Bergson admitted, reluctantly and without realising the full significance of his concession, the reality of time even in the physical world".[30] This concession makes Bergson's refutation—which he developed in the fourth chapter of *Matter and Memory* and the fourth chapter of *Creative Evolution* after the second chapter of *Time and Free Will*—of Zeno's paradoxes concerning movement more convincing. Zeno of Elea is thought to have devised his paradoxes with the intention of defending Parmenides' claim that, contrary to the evidence of the senses, the belief in change and movement is unreal. Zeno's arrow paradox has it that at any moment of its flight, the arrow is stationary, and that if time is composed of such moments, then there is no time for it to move in. According to the paradox known as "dichotomy", in order to walk a metre, I first have to cross half a metre, and in order to cross half a metre I have to cross a quarter of a metre, and given that space is infinitely divisible, I will have to perform an infinite number of tasks to get anywhere, in this instance a metre, which is impossible. Bergson contends that in these paradoxes analysis has replaced the real movement in process, the qualitative durational act, with the infinitely divisible space that has been traversed. Zeno's arguments "all consist in making time and movement coincide with the line which underlies them, in attributing to them the same subdivisions as the line, in short, in treating them like that line" [MM 191/213]. With this idea of indivisible duration, Bergson thus offers a slightly different refutation of Zeno than Aristotle, who had argued that the moment, the "now", is no real part of time, for it has no temporal span, just as a mathematical point is not a real part of a line, for it has no spatial span. If the point is as little part of the line as the "now" is part of time, it is hardly surprising or paradoxical that movement cannot be constituted on their basis.[31]

Profound and superficial selves

There are, as we have seen, "two forms of multiplicity, two quite different appreciations of duration, two aspects of conscious life" [TFW 127/95]. By the same token, there are two "aspects of the self [du moi]": a superficial and a profound self. Bergson's elaboration of this distinction between aspects of the self allows us, in fact, to comprehend more clearly the nature of the difference at issue between the two forms of multiplicity. It allows us to comprehend the difference between these two forms of difference.

The superficial self is that aspect of the self, of what and who I am, that "touches the world by its surface; our successive sensations, although merging into each other, retain something of the reciprocal exteriority that objectively characterizes things; and this is why our superficial psychological life unfolds in a homogeneous milieu without this mode of representation requiring much effort" [TFW 125/93]. This aspect of the self is the one bound up with external, discontinuous spatial things; it is the one closest to the body that I inhabit in the world. It is a worldly, social self, whose states are more or less clearly distinguished, and which can thus be expressed in language. At this level, my desires, for example, can easily be separated from the rest of who I am and can be described and discussed as independent motives. The profound self, in contrast, is the durational self that is constituted by a mutual penetration of psychological states, wherein everything is a "perpetual becoming", a "fleeting duration" [TFW 130/97].

How exactly to conceive of this self as a perpetual becoming? We can start by underlining what it is not. The durational self is not a self-identical subject or substance that remains the same through temporal change, and that is thus somehow independent of that change. The durational self is not a mental substance in a traditional sense of the term; it is not a Cartesian "thinking thing". Certainly, Bergson will later speak of "our substance", and thus of the substance of the self, but this is not the dogmatic affirmation that the self is *a* substance. In fact, Bergson approaches and, indeed, forces the traditional issue of substance according to what may appear *prima facie* a contradiction in terms: "the permanence of substance" is "a continuity of change" [CM 103/96]. This does not mean that the self is just a loose bundle of changing impressions and ideas in time, as David Hume supposed, impressions and ideas somehow collated to give the illusion of a persistent, substantial self. Nor, to be sure, is Bergson's position, as he emphasises in the Conclusion of *Time and Free Will*, that the profound self stands outside of time in the manner of Kant's transcendental ego that has everything that happens within time, including the empirical ego, as an object. Bergson's contrast of the superficial and the profound self is not Kant's distinction of a transcendental and empirical ego. For Bergson, the consistency of the self, its persistence, and thus what we call "personal identity", is constituted by nothing (by nothing) more than the immanent and passive temporal synthesis that is duration.[32] That synthesis is the "substance", i.e. the persistence or existence, the persistent existence of the self.[33] As he will say in 1911:

> Radical instability and absolute immutability are therefore mere abstract views taken from outside of the idea of the continuity of real change, abstractions which the mind then hypostatizes into multiple states, on the one hand, and *thing* or substance, on the other. The difficulties raised by the ancients around the question of movement and by the moderns around the question of substance disappear, the former because movement and change are substantial, the latter because substance is movement and change. [CM 184/174]

The self is the change that it synthesises in duration. The being, the existence of the self consists in being, as it were, stretched out in the synthesis of the past and future. *Matter and Memory*, as we will see in Chapter 4 below, in discussing more directly the past, will approach this thought under the heading of *character*: one's character is who and what one is, but character is this only as the synthesis or contraction of the past in the present.

Bergson summarises his distinction between the profound and superficial self thus: "our perceptions, sensations, emotions and ideas present themselves in two ways [*sous un double aspect*]: the one sharp, precise, but impersonal; the other confused, infinitely mobile, and inexpressible, because language cannot grasp it without fixing its mobility" [TFW 129/96]. Nevertheless, despite often writing in terms of a duality, Bergson can also write in these pages that there is "a gradual incursion of space in the domain of pure consciousness" [TFW 126/94]. Similarly, later in *Time and Free Will*, as we will see in the following chapter of this study, he describes the freedom of the self as admitting degrees: an act is more free, the more it belongs to the profound self. The difference between the profound and superficial selves, and consequently the distinction between two forms of multiplicity, is therefore a *difference of degree*. Space and duration are certainly different in nature, but in experience they are united by degree. This idea will be crucial in the development of Bergson's philosophical project in *Matter and Memory*.

Summary

Bergson's 1889 *Time and Free Will* is based on the recognition that the sciences overlook *real duration*, which is the real experience of the passage of time. Science, in measuring time, focuses on the beginning and end of a period of time elapsed, rather than on elapsing time. Moreover, as soon as we quantify time, we view it through the prism of space, since, as Bergson shows, any true grasp of the meaning of a number requires the intuition of simultaneously existing units in a real or ideal space. Given that quantity requires space, and that our psychological states are in time but not space, Bergson can conclude, in distinguishing time as it is originally experienced from space, that our temporal, psychological experience is not, at bottom, a quantifiable multiplicity of atomistic states. There are superficial aspects of the mind that present themselves in this manner, but, at its most profound levels, the stream of psychological experience consists rather of what he terms a "qualitative multiplicity", where the present merges into the immediate past and future, and where any one psychological state characterises the whole of the life of the mind.

Notes

1 Aristotle, *Categories*, trans. H. P. Cooke and Hugh Tredinnick (Cambridge, MA: Loeb Classical Library, 1938), 10b26.
2 As cited by Du Bos in Bergson, *Œuvres*, p. 1542.
3 As we noted in the previous chapter of this study.
4 Herbert Spencer, *First Principles*, p. 41.
5 See René Descartes, *Meditations on First Philosophy* (Cambridge: Cambridge University Press, 1996).
6 On this point, see A. R. Lacey, *Bergson* (Abingdon: Routledge, 1999) p. 15.
7 See the "Transcendental Aesthetic", in Immanuel Kant, *Critique of Pure Reason*, ed. P. Guyer and A. Wood (Cambridge: Cambridge University Press, 1999). See also, in the same series as the present book, Paul Guyer, *Kant* (Abingdon: Routledge, 2014), pp. 58–80.
8 Kant, *Critique of Pure Reason*, B43.
9 Félix Ravaisson, *Of Habit*, ed. C. Carlisle and M. Sinclair (London: Continuum, 2008), pp. 39 and 41.
10 Bertrand Russell, "The Philosophy of Bergson", *The Monist* 22 (1912), 321–47, reprinted in H. Wildon Carr (ed.), *The Philosophy of Bergson* (Cambridge: Bowes and Bowes, 1914).
11 Milič Čapek, *Bergson and Modern Physics: A Reinterpretation and Re-evaluation* (Dordrecht: D. Reidel, 1971), p. 181. Čapek perhaps exaggerates when he writes that Bergson "explicitly avoided this confusion" given that he writes that any clear idea of number requires vision in space, but his point still stands.
12 Čapek, *Bergson and Modern Physics*, p. 183.
13 Kant, *Critique of Pure Reason*, A142–3/B182.
14 I borrow this *aperçu* from Camille Riquier, *Archéologie de Bergson*, p. 278.
15 Chapter 11, below, returns to this issue when assessing Heidegger's critique of Bergson.
16 J. M. E. McTaggart, "On the Unreality of Time", *Mind* 17/68 (1908), 457–74. See also Lacey, *Bergson*, p. 41 in this connection.
17 This despite Ravaisson's own interesting remarks about *durée*. In this connection, see Arthur Lovejoy, "Some Antecedents of the Philosophy of Bergson: The Conception of 'Real Duration'", *Mind* XXII(10) (1913), 465–83 and my "Habit and Time in Nineteenth-Century French Philosophy: Albert Lemoine between Bergson and Ravaisson".
18 See Pierre Maine de Biran, *Of Immediate Apperception*, ed. A. Aloisi, M. Piazza and M. Sinclair (London: Bloomsbury, forthcoming).
19 Čapek, *Bergson and Modern Physics*, p. 86.
20 See Craig Callendar, *What Makes Time Special?* (Oxford: Oxford University Press, 2018), pp. 1–18.
21 "Bergsonism is a philosophical 'debussysme'", as René Berthelot put it: see René Berthelot, *Un romantisme utilitaire; étude sur le mouvement pragmatiste* (Paris: Alcan, 1911), p. 23.

22 Čapek, *Bergson and Modern Physics*, p. 97. This, even if, as Deleuze argues, Bergson's concern for two forms of multiplicity derives from the mathematician Riemann; see Deleuze, *Le bergsonisme* (Paris: Presses universitaires de France, 1997), p. 31.

23 See James Ward, "Psychology", in *Encyclopaedia Britannica*, 9th edition, Vol. 20, (Edinburgh: Black, 1886), pp. 37–85. On this point, see also Jean-Louis Veillard-Baron, *Bergson* (Paris: Presses universitaires de France, 1993), p. 41.

24 It is easy to miss the real sense of Bergson's notion of synthesis. See, for example, in an otherwise careful and helpful study, Heath Massey, *The Origin of Time: Heidegger and Bergson* (Albany, NY: State University of New York Press, 2015), p. 21: "While Bergson wants to establish a fundamental difference between time, or duration, and space, he follows Kant in regarding temporal succession as the result of a mental synthesis whereby sensations are retained and combined with others to produce an experience of continuity such as we have when listening to a melody".

25 Barry Dainton, "Bergson on Temporal Experience. Durée Réelle", in *The Routledge Handbook of the Philosophy of Temporal Experience*, ed. Ian Phillips (Abindgon: Routledge, 2017), pp. 93–106, p. 97.

26 Dainton, "Bergson on Temporal Experience. Durée Réelle", p. 97.

27 On Bergson's qualitative synthesis as at once an "immanent synthesis" and a "passive synthesis", see Riquier, *Archéologie de Bergson*, pp. 292–3.

28 Riquier qualifies Deleuze on this point; see Riquier, *Archéologie de Bergson*, p. 293.

29 English-language commentary has said remarkably little about "endosmosis" in TFW, but see John Mullarkey, *Bergson and Philosophy* (Manchester: Manchester University Press, 1999), p. 21, and Massey, *The Origin of Time*, particularly p. 68 for exceptions.

30 Čapek recognises this without tying it to Bergson's notion of endosmosis; see Čapek, *Bergson and Modern Physics*, p. 97.

31 For more on this, see Bradley Dowden, "Zeno's Paradoxes", *Internet Encyclopedia of Philosophy*: www.iep.utm.edu/zeno-par/#potential.

32 On this issue more generally, see, for example, Eric. T. Olson, "Personal Identity", *Stanford Encyclopedia of Philosophy*: https://plato.stanford.edu/entries/identity-personal/.

33 Bergson follows Ravaisson in reflecting on "substance" in this way. On this, see my "Habit and Time in Nineteenth-Century French Philosophy: Albert Lemoine between Bergson and Ravaisson".

Further reading

Henri Bergson, *Histoire de l'idée du temps. Cours au Collège de France 1902–03*, ed. Camille Riquier (Paris: Presses universitaires de France, 2016). This important lecture course, in which Bergson addresses conceptions of time in the history of philosophy, is due to appear in English translation soon.

Milič Čapek, *Bergson and Modern Physics: A Reinterpretation and Re-evaluation* (Dordrecht: D. Reidel, 1971). This is one of the best specialist treatments of Bergson's account of time, particularly in its relation to modern physics.

Ian Phillips (ed.), *The Routledge Handbook of the Philosophy of Temporal Experience* (Abindgon: Routledge, 2017). This is a comprehensive source for contemporary discussions of temporal experience, and see Barry Dainton (pp. 93–106) on Bergson's approach in relation to those discussions.

Three
Freedom

The experience of freedom

Bergson claims that we have an experience of freedom, a direct experience of our freedom to shape our own acts. Freedom, according to *Time and FreeWill*, is in some sense a psychological fact. For this reason, the "respectful homage" to Jules Lachelier with which the book begins is slightly strange. Although Bergson had read Lachelier's 1871 *On the Ground of Induction* with enthusiasm as a young student, he had never been taught by him, and on the basis of the philosophical breakthrough that is his account of "real duration", he approaches the issue of freedom in direct opposition to his dedicatee. Bergson writes in the foreword that he has "chosen among the problems the one that is common to metaphysics and psychology, the problem of freedom" [TFW xxiii/3], but Lachelier concluded his influential 1885 "Psychology and Metaphysics" with the claim that although we must posit freedom as the highest metaphysical truth, this truth is not available in experience as a psychological fact. For Lachelier, freedom—the "idea of ideas",[1] the highest idea—can only ever be a metaphysical rather than psychological issue. Bergson, in contrast, aims to develop a new form of metaphysics in showing that and how freedom belongs to the "immediate data" of consciousness.

What seems to separate Bergson from Lachelier here is the work of Immanuel Kant—which influenced French philosophy in the new, Third French Republic—with its doctrine that freedom is an unknowable *noumenon* (a "thing in itself" or, more literally, a "thing of thought") but never a *phenomenon* (something given in experience).

Of the philosophers constituting the "school of contingency" that runs from Ravaisson through Lachelier and Boutroux to Bergson, the author of *On the Ground of Induction* was the most marked by Kant's philosophy. Bergson, in contrast, as the conclusion of his thesis makes clear, considers Kant's "critical philosophy" as a problem. It is possible that the dedication in *Time and FreeWill* was really a necessarily indirect homage to Boutroux, the president of the jury judging Bergson's thesis, who had been taught by Lachelier. In "Of Man", the final chapter of his own 1874 doctoral dissertation *On the Contingency of the Laws of Nature*, Boutroux argued that mechanical laws, together with the principle of the conservation of energy underlying them, do not apply to the "psychic energy" that is consciousness. From this, as we will see, Bergson draws key elements of his own treatment of the problem of free will, with its claim that time as duration is a form of energy, a force or cause, that does not obey mechanical laws.[2]

In effecting a purification or reduction of the idea of time by relieving it of everything it owes "to the intrusion of the sensory world and, to say it all, to our obsession with space" [TFW 224/ 168], Bergson discovers, as we have seen, real duration as a qualitative multiplicity and, concomitantly, the profound self as distinct from the superficial self. This is the primary breakthrough in *Time and FreeWill*, and if, as Bergson said, all philosophers have only one key thought, the idea of duration is his. The task of his third chapter, however, is to effect on this basis a purification of the idea of "voluntary determination" [TFW 224/168], of the traditional idea of the will as the faculty that executes and produces our actions. In the foreword to the dissertation, Bergson even presents this final purification as the fundamental task of the book, such that his account of duration would be merely preparatory for an elucidation of what he seems to take, after Lachelier and Boutroux, as the highest idea, namely free will. Bergson defends an idea of free will, but he does so only in shifting the terms of traditional debate, in putting an end to "insurmountable difficulties" arising from poorly posed philosophical problems. For he wants to establish that traditional debates "between determinists and their adversaries imply a fundamental confusion of duration with space, and succession with simultaneity" [TFW xxiii/3]. By reflecting on the will *sub specie durationis*, according to the thought of a non-spatialised time, he aims to defeat

determinist positions denying human freedom, while also quali-
fying libertarian positions affirming the absolute spontaneity and
freedom of the will. His arguments in this regard, which the present
chapter examines, have lost nothing of their pertinence and importance, for the perspectives he criticizes still determine much of the
contemporary work in the metaphysics of free will.

Physical and psychological determinism

In determinist doctrines, determination is usually taken as a kind
of conditional necessity: if the determining cause of an event
obtains, and if there are no external factors overriding that cause
and preventing the occurrence of the event typically produced by
that cause, then that event must occur. On Bergson's analysis, however, given that the human being can be considered as both mind
and body, determinist positions can take two distinct but interrelated
forms: physical determinism and psychological determinism. The
physical form can be expressed by a version of the so-called "demon
hypothesis" formulated by Pierre-Simon Laplace in 1814. This
is the hypothesis of a mind knowing exactly and totally the state
of the world at a given point in time as well as the laws of classical mechanics: "the mathematician, knowing the position of the
molecules or atoms of a human organism at a given moment, as well
as the position and the movement of all the atoms in the universe
capable of influencing it, would calculate with an infallible preci-
sion the past, present and future actions of the person to whom this
organism belongs, just as one predicts an astrological phenomenon"
[TFW 144/108]. Of course, Bergson is writing at a time prior to
such anomalies as quantum theory and its uncertainty principle, and
an all-embracing deterministic physical science is no longer either
a credible promise or a real threat. All the same, twentieth-century
challenges to the Laplacian or Newtonian determinist vision of the
physical universe have hardly led to a retreat *en masse* from determinist positions in the metaphysics of free will.

At issue in Bergson's version of the demon hypothesis is not
just a physical event among inert objects, but the actions of a *person*
who has consciousness. The physical determinist therefore has to
account for the determining of consciousness, unless she resorts to

an "identity theory", according to which consciousness or mind just *is* the body and nothing more. Resorting to an identity theory, however, would be to deny freedom by means of a metaphysical position that is inherently unstable (if mind really just is the body in the sense that it is just another name for the body we probably should account for why it took us so long to realise this and why we do not just stop using the term) and looks more like a negation of philosophy than philosophy itself.[3] Identity theory, and the kind of eliminative materialism it leads to, might satisfy some, but we certainly do not need much philosophy to be satisfied by it. So, beyond any identity theory, the physical determinist has to demonstrate that our psychological life is subject to the same determination as physical things. This move will require the thesis of psycho-physical parallelism, according to which there is a one-to-one correspondence between brain-state and mind-state. Here the argument is that mind-states are determined because brain-states are determined, and because there is a one-to-one correspondence between brain-state and mind-state. Now, there may well be a correspondence between brain-state and mind-state in a limited range of phenomena, as Bergson acknowledges, particularly in those phenomena where it is possible to provide some kind of mechanical explanation of the mind-state (the perception of sound, for example). By virtue of recent brain imaging technologies, we may now even know that every time I think, there is some kind of corresponding brain activity. However, "to extend this parallelism to the series themselves in their totality is to decide *a priori* on the problem of freedom" [TFW 146/110]. The theory of psycho-physical parallelism, and Bergson will devote time to this in his lectures at the Collège de France [HTM 310], is not an empirical finding but a philosophical theory that comes to the fore in the seventeenth century, particularly in the work of Spinoza. Of course, the modern determinist may prefer the offshoot of psycho-physical parallelism that is *epiphenomenalism*, according to which there is a correspondence between brain-state and mind-state because the former *produces* the latter. But this replaces philosophical theory with a pseudo-scientific pseudo-explanation, since we have absolutely no idea how the brain-state causes a mind-state (this is an aspect of what contemporary philosophers of mind call the "hard problem of consciousness"), and "it can never be demonstrated that the psychological fact is necessarily determined by the molecular movement" [TFW 147/111]. Moreover, if matter can produce mind, there is no reason *a priori* why mind could not effect change on matter; and if there is not, we have to examine the mind to see whether determined processes occur in it independently of matter.

In order to show that the human person is determined, physical determinism must presuppose that all psychological states are determined, but it cannot justify this claim. A physical determinism that aims to be all-embracing and thus to embrace the human person presupposes a form of psychological determinism, which is the view that psychological states are causally determined by each other independently of any relation they may have to the physical world. The idea is that each mental state is caused and thus necessitated by prior states. Bergson's basic point is that this form of determinism implies an atomistic and "associationist conception of mind" [TFW 155/117] of the sort that came to prominence with the tradition of British empiricism in the eighteenth century. Associationist positions pictures the mind as an "assemblage of mental states of which the strongest exerts a predominant influence and carries the others with it". They suppose that, say, a decision was caused by desire, hatred or fear as distinct things in the mind. This approach pictures the mind as akin to a snooker table with balls of varying degrees of force that produce a certain result in their collision. Language encourages us to accept this picture, because we talk of the fear, the hatred, the desire, as if, to take the last example, the desire was something isolated in the life of the mind and essentially identical in all its instances.

We are but the "dupe" [TFW 165/124] of language when we think in this way, and Bergson makes his general point against associationist conceptions of mind with the compelling example of smelling a rose, where immediately "confused memories of childhood come back to me. In truth, these memories were not evoked by the scent of the rose: I inhale them in the scent itself; it is all that for me. Others will smell it differently" [TFW 161/121]. This example of involuntary memory, of memory inhabiting things, is at the root of one of the monuments of twentieth-century literature, namely Proust's *In Search of Lost Time*. The associationist, of course, considers Bergson's description to be merely a poetic metaphor, and the memory merely to have been evoked by the past; I remember, on this account, smelling the scent in the past when smelling a similar scent in the present, and consequently the memories associated by contiguity to that past event come back to me—in the mind, but not in the sense-experience of the flower. For Bergson, the associationist thus offers a reconstruction of experience rather than accounting for what is actually given in experience: associationism "confuses the explanation of the fact with the fact itself". In explaining the given phenomenon, it *explains it away*; it "makes the mistake of replacing the concrete phenomenon that occurs in the mind with the artificial reconstitution of it provided by philosophy" [TFW 163/123].

In *Matter and Memory*, which Proust claimed not to have read, Bergson will offer the additional argument that appealing to resemblance as a principle cannot provide an explanation of how the association occurs, since everything, at bottom, resembles everything [MM 163/183]. Moreover, as we will see in the following chapter, he will provide his own perfectly philosophical but non-associative account of *how* memories are instantiated in things. Here, however, he limits himself to showing that associationism fails to distinguish the two types of multiplicity, "between a multiplicity of juxtaposition and a multiplicity of fusion or mutual penetration. A particular feeling, a particular idea encloses an indefinite plurality of conscious states; but the plurality will not be observed unless it is, as it were, spread out in this homogeneous medium that some call duration but that is in reality space" [TFW 162–3/122]. It is only at the level of the superficial self that such easily separable psychological atoms can appear, but this, as we saw above in Chapter 2, is preceded and conditioned by the confusion (literally: being fused together) of the durational immanent synthesis that is the fundamental self. Since, at this level, no aspect can be wholly dissociated from the rest of psychological life, it can be said that, if the hate or love is profound, each of us has "our manner of loving and hating, and this love, this hate, reflects one's whole personality" [TFW 163/123].

Mind-energy

The psychological determinist's view that volition is caused by a variety of isolated, psychological motives has "no other value than that of a symbolic representation" that ignores the "internal dynamism" of the mind [TFW 172/129]. The determinist atomises and thus spatialises mental life. Moreover, in claiming that psychological facts obey psychological laws the determinist holds that the same causes produce the same effects, which is to suppose that the "same cause can appear several times on the stage of consciousness" [TFW 199/150]. The same cause cannot repeat itself in psychic life, Bergson argues, because duration is not an indifferent, homogeneous medium in which repeatable psychical events occur. The "same" event occurring a day later would not be the same event precisely because it is a day later and I am a day older since it last occurred. The moment in which it occurs can never be repeated, and is constitutive of the singular quality of the event itself. Given that psychical life is a qualitative multiplicity, quality without quantity, there is no repeatable element within it that could serve as the basis of a causal law describing necessary relations between causes and effects.

To think there is such an element is the second of the "fundamental illusions" underlying the determinist position. Not only does the determinist spatialise mental processes, but in so doing he illegitimately imports quantity into the realm of quality. The determinist considers particular psychological states to have, in principle, a calculable force or intensity; and "sees in intensity a mathematical property of psychological states, and not [...] the special quality, and proper nuance of these diverse states" [TFW 190/142]. In the first chapter of *Time and Free Will*, Bergson attacked the traditional hybrid notion of intensive magnitude and argued that the intensity of psychological states can be accounted for purely in qualitative terms. The significance of that argument for his critique of determinist positions can be seen by returning to the earlier nineteenth-century philosopher William Hamilton, who had quantified a psychological determinist approach: "on the supposition that the sum of influences (motives, dispositions and tendencies) to volition A is equal to 12, and the sum of influences to counter-volition B equal to 8, can we conceive that the determination of volition A should not be necessary?"[4] In reifying the mind, and in quantifying its operation, Hamilton "affirms", according to J. S. Mill's commentary, "as a truth of experience, that volitions do, in point of fact, follow determinate moral antecedents with the same uniformity, and with the same certainty, as physical effects follow their physical causes".[5]

Bergson and the spiritualist tradition he develops offer a remedy for this physicalist and scientistic delirium. In the brief passage that separates the discussion of physical determinism from psychological determinism,[6] he does so not by denying that forces operate in the mind, but only by denying that the principle of the conservation of force or energy is applicable in psychology. According to the principle of the conservation of force, a principle that was often taken in the nineteenth century as the explanatory ground of causality itself, in causal processes there can be no more force or energy in the effect B than in the cause A; the quantity of force must remain the same in a closed physical system. However, Bergson asks, in developing the ideas of Boutroux, his examiner, "whether there is not much to be said for the hypothesis of a conscious force or free will that, subject to the action of time and storing up duration, would escape for that very reason the law of the conservation of energy?" [TFW 154/116]. Boutroux had already criticised the principle and its application in psychology. Psychological life, he argued, is essentially active, constituted as and by activity, which implies progress and genuine novelty; "a psychological consequent", he wrote in On the Contingency of the Laws of Nature, "never finds in its antecedent its complete causes and its sufficient reason".[7] In psychological life, there is always, Boutroux claims, more in what follows than in what preceded it, such that what follows cannot be explained by what preceded it in the way that we ordinarily take a physical cause to explain a physical effect. In this sense, Boutroux argues, there is "creativity" and "novelty" in psychological life. Although Bergson does not adopt these terms in Time and FreeWill, he will do so emphatically in 1907.

According to Boutroux, this "disproportion" between the psychological "cause" and "effect" "is particularly manifest in voluntary acts", for:

> [i]n the resolution that follows the consideration of motives, there is something more than in the motives: the consent of the will to the motive preferred above any other. The motive is not the complete cause of the act. Is it, at least, the sufficient reason?

Certainly, it is always the strongest motive that triumphs, but only insofar as we grant, after the fact, this title to the motive elected by the will.[8]

To consider that my decision, say, either to stay at home to look after my ailing mother or to leave to fight in the Resistance (this will be Jean-Paul Sartre's famous example) is caused by motives that have their own force independently of the weight I *put on them* is to fall victim, as Bergson will say explicitly in his later work, to a retrospective illusion. It fails to understand—and this, admittedly, is a difficult thought, as we will see in Chapter 8—that the past *was* not always what it *is* for us now. It fails to take into account the real dynamism of psychological life; a "more attentive psychology reveals to us", as Bergson writes, "that effects precede their causes" [TFW 156/119] in the mind. Deliberation takes time, and during this period there is not an unchanging self who would assess the force of independent, unchanging feelings; "in truth, the self, merely by virtue of having experienced the first feeling, has already changed when the second feeling arrives: in all the moments of the deliberation, the self changes and consequently also changes the two feelings that act on it" [TFW 171/129].

Bergson develops Boutroux's insights concerning the dynamism of the life of the mind with his conception of duration. As he argues, "the vague and instinctive belief in the conservation of one identical quantity of matter, and of force, depends on the fact that inert matter does not seem to exist in time or at least does not conserve any trace of past time" [TFW 152/115]. The law of the conservation of force may well apply to the spatial things that we are not, but duration escapes it. Consequently, the processes occurring within it are irreducible to any form of determination and causal necessity. The idea of force has come to be associated with necessity only by a bad habit, as Bergson argues towards the end of the third chapter.

The idea of force, which excludes in reality that of necessary determination, has contracted, so to speak, the habit of being merged with necessity, as a result of the use that is made of the principle of causality in nature. [...] we know of force only through the testimony of consciousness, and consciousness does not affirm, and even fails to understand the absolute determination of the acts to come: this is all that experience teaches us, and if we stick with experience, we would say that we feel that we are free, that we perceive force, rightly or wrongly, as a free spontaneity. [TFW 216/163]

The argument here is that we gain the idea of force as a free spontaneity from our experience of effort, as Pierre Maine de Biran had proposed earlier in the nineteenth century (against the eighteenth-century Scottish philosophical sceptic David Hume, who claimed that we have no direct experience of force, not only in things, but even in our actions).[9] We then use this idea of force to account for natural processes in the things beyond us, where the idea of force serves to interpret what we take to be relations of causal necessity (given X and Y, Z will have to happen if there are no external overriding factors). Then, unwittingly, we transfer the idea of force now understood as necessary connection back onto our understanding of psychical processes. In truth, although there is causation, there is no necessitation in duration. It is a shame that anti-necessitarian conceptions of causation in contemporary metaphysics have not paid more attention to Bergson and the tradition of contingency theorists that he develops.[10]

Free will without alternative possibilities

The idea of duration as a qualitative multiplicity helps us to reject the application of the principle of the conservation of energy in psychology. We can thereby defeat the determinist without having to appeal to an extra-temporal principle of freedom that would act as a kind of *deus ex machina*. But what of the traditional "libertarian" position in the metaphysics of free will, which considers that a free act has occurred only if the agent could have done otherwise than she did, only if alternative possibilities of action were open to her? These alternative possibilities, Bergson's libertarian holds, complete the diagram the determinist draws to represent the process of decision and volition. At the point of volition, Bergson names it O, after the antecedent M, the trajectory from O to the act X was just as possible as the trajectory from O to the different act Y [TFW 176/117]:

At the point O there is a volition that is not determined by its antecedents to choose either of the two possibilities. If it is unconditioned by any motive, this volition seems to be, as Bergson will write in *Matter and Memory*, a "an arbitrary *fiat*, a veritable creation *ex nihilo*" [MM 186/207]. Bergson does not rehearse standard objections to this notion of an unmotivated, absolute voluntary spontaneity, as barely intelligible, and as presenting a notion of freedom that resembles chance more than a deliberate action, but he will tip his hat to them in 1896. His primary concern here is to show what the libertarian concedes in accepting the determinist's schema. The libertarian views the volition from the perspective of its having already taken place, from its having taken place in one of two ways, even if these ways are supposed to be merely possibilities rather than actualities, since the trajectories OX and OY are already traced out. In doing so, she is led to do battle on terrain that favours her adversary. For to claim that the self at point O "chooses indifferently between X and Y is to stop halfway along the path of geometrical symbolisation" [TFW 176/117]; it is, in the end, to be inconsistent. If the process is in the past, X or Y will have been realised, and then it is easy to say that, if X was realised, MO led necessarily to X; and it is equally easy to say that if Y was realised, MO led necessarily to Y. In short, the libertarian attempts to add a principle of freedom to a symbolisation of the process of volition as essentially mechanical, but this unwittingly promotes the view of her adversary.

In truth, in time as it unfolds, "there is no line MO, no point O, no path OX, and no direction OY". To think there is amounts to admitting "the possibility of representing time adequately by space, a succession by a simultaneity" [TFW 180/135]. To consider alternative possibilities as a condition of the free act is to spatialise psychical life, to risk ceding victory to the determinist, and to pass over a more primitive sense of freedom present in immediate experience. We must, Bergson argues, "look for freedom in a certain nuance or quality of the action itself and not in a relation of this act to what it is not or what it could have been" [TFW 182/137]. The third chapter of *Time and Free Will* offers several positive characterisations of the free act: it is an act where "the self alone will have been the author of it, since it will express the whole of the self" [TFW 165/124]; "in truth, the profound states of our mind, those that are translated by free acts, express and summarise the whole of our past history" [TFW 185/139]; "it is from the whole soul, indeed, that the free decision emanates; and the act will be freer the more that the dynamic series to which it is bound tends to identify itself with the fundamental self" [TFW 167/125-6]; and "we are free when our acts spring from our whole personality, when they express it, when they have that indefinable resemblance to it which one sometimes finds between the artist and his work" [TFW 172/129].

Wholly free acts, then, are rare, they express one's whole self, which is to say, the entirety of one's past, and freedom is a matter of degree. An act can be more or less free, depending on the degree to which the fundamental self, our character, expresses itself in it. Freedom, on this account, is a function of expression. Bergson's, we might say, is an "expressivist" conception of freedom: the free act expresses its motives and the self that has them. Rather than being determined by its motives, the free act gives form and shape to, and thereby "determines", the motives for the act and the self that has them. Expression here is not mechanical causation, and Bergson's is not simply the soft-determinist, compatibilist position, according to which freedom requires the power or ability to do what the agent wills or desires and an absence of external constraints. For the compatibilist, determination of our acts, if that determination is self-determination, is compatible with freedom; an act needs only to be caused internally, by the self and its desires, in order to be free.

It might be tempting to suppose that Bergson's critique of the principle of alternative possibilities would lead him to support what contemporary philosophy calls, after Harry Frankfurt, "Frankfurt-style examples". To their advocates, these show that moral responsibility, and thus freedom, does not require alternative possibilities. If a lazy, nefarious neuroscientist somehow (we don't have to worry too much about the details of the thought experiment) will intervene to ensure that I do the wrong thing even if I choose to do the right thing, and if, in fact, I choose to do the wrong thing such that the lazy, nefarious neuroscientist does not have to intervene, I am morally responsible while having had no alternative possibilities for action, no realisable ones at least.[11] It is more than a little doubtful, even with all the details, that these supposed counter-examples to the principle of alternative possibilities are effective, but the Frankfurtian compatibilist claims that they show that freedom does not require alternative possibilities, while the "semi-compatibilist" rejects the inference from moral responsibility to freedom, and preserves the thought that freedom, but not moral responsibility, requires alternative possibilities.[12] In any case, Bergson is not, on the question of freedom, in the business of thought experiments. He is trying to lead us to apprehend the particular nuance or quality of the free act itself in the dynamism of our own temporal experience.

In advancing his notion of the free act as an expression of the self, Bergson appeals, as we have just seen, to the procedure of the artist, to the production of fine art. He thus signals his later, more deliberate concern to understand duration according to a notion of art-production, a notion of creation irreducible to creation *ex nihilo*. As he puts it in his 1904–5 lectures:

> freedom is a creation in the sense that one takes this word when one says there is creation in a work of art. [...] We don't mean by this that the work of art is an *ex nihilo* production, that it comes from nothing; we mean rather that given the conditions involved in the production of the work, the work, if it is truly the work of an artist, adds to these conditions something absolutely new, absolutely unforeseeable. [EPL 118]

We will examine Bergson's later account of creation and novelty fully in Chapter 8, but suffice it to note here that the analogy supposes that the work of art, if it is an "expression", is not the realisation or externalisation of a conceptually determined intention. That would be craft rather than fine art. This is why, as Bergson remarks, the relation between artist and work is itself "undefinable", and not the relation between an archetype in the artist's head and a copy. In this sense, fine-art production, though purposive (it does not happen wholly by accident), is not the realisation of an express, conceptual purpose; there is a "purposiveness without purpose" (to borrow a phrase from Kant, developing the sense he gives it only slightly) in the production of the work. It is more like the expression of her whole self, of her most fundamental orientation and attunement to the world. Of course, the artist may have some kind of idea of what she wants to produce, but, as Bergson will later write of the free act in general, there is always, in the event, an element of unscripted novelty in our free actions: "if I deliberate before acting, the moments of the deliberation offer themselves to my consciousness as the successive sketches, each particular in its own way, that a painter would draw of his painting; and the act itself, in being carried out, may well realise something desired and consequently foreseen, but it has nonetheless its own original form" [CM 108/100]. Art production gives us the idea of a form of spontaneity, and thus freedom, that is prior to and more fundamental than rational deliberation concerning alternative courses of action. In the process of the artist's work, just as in the process of our deliberation, "there are not, in truth, two tendencies, or even two directions, but a self that lives and develops by means of its very hesitations, until the free action", or the finished artwork, "drops from it like an over-ripe fruit" [TFW 176/132].

We find this kind of spontaneity, Bergson argues, in the most serious of our free actions; "it is in grave and solemn circumstances, when the opinion that others will have of us and that we will have of ourselves is in question, that we choose without taking into account what is called a motive; and this absence of all tangible reason is all the more striking the deeper our freedom goes" [TFW 170/128]. The more that our fundamental self as duration is involved in the free act, the less can the motives be made out and considered rationally as isolated states. It is for this reason that Bergson can suppose that there is sometimes a certain kind of (what later philosophers will call) inauthenticity or bad-faith in deliberation: "in investigating ourselves scrupulously, we see that sometimes we weigh up motives, that sometimes we deliberate, when our decision has already been taken. An internal, hardly perceptible voice whispers: 'Why this deliberation? You know what it will produce and you know what you are going to do!'" [TFW 158/119]. What happened first was a kind of "willing for the sake of willing that consequently allowed the completed act to be explained by its antecedents of which it is the cause". It is only after the fact that the decision dissociates identifiable motives from the dynamic flux of duration. But this willing for the sake of willing that Bergson posits tentatively is not an absolute spontaneity, the "liberty of indifference" promoted traditionally by the libertarian. Deciding in these grave situations is not like choosing a main course from the menu when one is unmoved by any of the options. The decision rather occupies one's whole being, one's whole self, and the sense of one's past in its entirety. These decisions are not arbitrary, and arguably they can feel more like necessity than a liberty of indifference. It is in this sense that Bergson can argue that the free action carried out by the fundamental self does not:

> express some superficial idea, almost external to ourselves, distinct and easy to account for: it agrees with the whole of our most intimate feelings, thoughts and aspirations, with that particular conception of life which is the equivalent of all our past experience, in a word, with our personal idea of happiness and of honour. Hence it has been a mistake to look for examples in the ordinary and indifferent circumstances of life in order to prove that man is capable of choosing without a motive. [TFW 170/128]

Bergson does not deny that there is a degree of freedom in these instances of an indifferent choice, but he does argue that the more isolated motives are apparent in a decision, the more that decision occurs in a manner that resembles, at least, the determinist's schema.

On this basis, we can understand Bergson's informative remarks in his 1910 brief contribution to the dictionary entry on Liberté in André Lalande's *Vocabulaire technique et critique de la philosophie* (*Technical and Critical Vocabulary of Philosophy*). This dictionary was originally published in installments within the journal of the French Society for Philosophy, but it is still in print in book-form and much used by French philosophers. It is helpful to present these remarks in their entirety, all the more so in that the passage does not seem to have been translated elsewhere:

> The word *freedom* has for me a sense intermediate between those that one usually gives to the two terms freedom [*liberté*] and free will [*libre arbitre*]. On the one hand, I think that freedom consists in being entirely oneself, in acting in conformity with oneself: this would therefore be the "moral freedom" of the philosophers, the independence of the person with regard to all that it is not. But it is not exactly this sort of freedom, since the independence that I describe does not always have a moral character. Moreover, it does not consist in depending on oneself as an effect depends on the cause that determines it *necessarily*. In this way, I would come back to the sense of "free will". And yet I do not accept this sense completely either, since free will, in the usual sense of the term, implies the equal possibility of two contraries, and since it is not possible, I claim, to formulate or even conceive the thesis of the equal possibility of two contraries without serious misunderstandings concerning the nature of time. I could say therefore that the point of my thesis, on this particular issue, was precisely to find an intermediate position between "moral freedom" and free will. *Freedom* as I understand it is situated between these two terms, but not at the same distance from the one as from the other. If it were absolutely necessary to merge it with one of them, I would have to opt for "free will".[13]

Bergson steers between a moral idea of self-determination, which informs the soft-determinist claim that determination as self-determination is compatible with freedom, and a libertarian notion of free will. If there is self-determination this is not as a function of necessitation, and here Bergson may even attempt to tease apart the ideas not just of causation and necessitation, but also of determination and necessitation. Still, if there is freedom, this is not as a function of alternative possibilities. The traditional libertarian and the determinist both fail to apprehend the real temporal nature of psychic life. Although Bergson is closer to the libertarian, it remains the case that freedom, on his account, cannot be defined. Insofar as it requires us to spatialise time, "any definition will support the determinist" [TFW 219/165]. Bergson thus says, in the final passages of his third chapter, what Boutroux said about consciousness as psychic energy: it is an "irreducible datum that explanation obscures and analysis destroys".[14] Duration, as a temporal force of freedom, is primitive in that it cannot be explained by anything else.

Is there not a danger in locating free will in a principle that operates prior to rational thought? Does not such an apparently anti-rationalist position lose a sense of real autonomy and rational self-determination that has traditionally been taken (by Kant, among others) as constitutive of human freedom? In 1890, in one of the first reviews of Time and Free Will, Gustave Belot found "A New Theory of Freedom" within it, but worried that this new theory was as much a negation as a defence of free will precisely in that it seemed to reject any sense of rational autonomy.

> If freedom was in the profound self, it would be better for man perhaps to renounce it and to work to destroy rather than conquer it. For, in order to rediscover it, a veritable step backwards would be necessary: a regression of intelligent thought towards unreflective spontaneity, from humanity towards animality, from social life towards individual isolation.[15]

This new theory of freedom supposedly retreats from the rational and social aspects of human life. Moreover, if, as the philosophical tradition has often held, everything pre-rational and pre-social in the human being belongs to the animal part of the rational animal, then Bergson is simply a celebrant of the animal in man.

In the fourth chapter of Matter and Memory, after restating his own position, Bergson responds to this critique thus:

> freedom is in no way reduced in this way, as has been said, to sensible spontaneity. At the very most, this would be the case in the animal whose psychological life is affective above all. But in the human being, a thinking being, the free act can be called a synthesis of feelings and ideas, and the evolution that leads to it, a reasonable [raisonnable] evolution. The artifice of this

method consists simply, in the end, in distinguishing the point of view of ordinary and useful consciousness and that of true consciousness. Duration *in which we watch ourselves act*, and in which it is useful that we thus watch ourselves, is a duration whose elements become disassociated and are juxtaposed; but the duration *in which we act* is a duration in which our states merge into one another. [MM 186/207].

Bergson does not deny the role of ideas, and thus a form of reasoning, in freedom, just as he does not deny that the fine artist needs to think about what she is doing. His point is rather that it is impossible entirely to separate feelings from reasoning as isolated psychological elements in duration. The free durational act has its own form of "reasonableness", even though it is not the product of pure rationality. The response seems to rely on the idea, developed explicitly in *Matter and Memory*, of degrees in depth of the self: in any particular act, any number of different degrees of the self will be in operation. Hence his point is not that the free act must take place at a level prior to reflective consciousness; it is rather that thoughts and feelings belong in and emerge from the original stream of duration.

Perhaps still unsatisfied with his response, Bergson returns to the issue again in *Creative Evolution*. If there is an expression and thus a "creation" of the self in the free act, then this:

> is all the more complete [...] the more that one reasons about what one does. For reason does not proceed here as in geometry, where impersonal premises are given once and for all, and an impersonal conclusion must perforce be drawn. Here, on the contrary, the same reasons can dictate to different people, or even to the same person at different times, profoundly different, though equally reasonable acts. In truth, they are not wholly the same reasons since they are not those of the same person, or of the same moment. This is why we cannot operate on them *in abstracto*, from the outside, as in geometry, nor resolve for someone else the problems that life poses. [CE 7–8/7]

The reasons for which we act are not bloodless abstractions, and moral reasoning does not have the impersonality of geometrical order. The reasons for the act cannot, in truth, be isolated from the broader psychological life, the duration, of the agent. Bergson's conception of freedom, then, is not irrationalist, even though it is anti-rationalist in that it criticises rationalist accounts of autonomy for offering an abstract idea of freedom.

Real freedom

As he later related, Bergson had finished a first version of the second and third chapters of his doctoral dissertation by 1886, but at that point he realised he had not "taken Kant into account", which, given the importance of the philosopher of Königsberg in French academic philosophy at the time, would, he wrote, "have disqualified my thesis in the eyes of the University".[16] Hence he added a brief critical appraisal of Kant's position on time and freedom to his conclusion. In the "Transcendental Aesthetic" of the *Critique of Pure Reason*, Kant distinguishes time as the *a priori* condition of inner sense, of psychological experience, from space as the *a priori* condition of external experience of the things of the world. The things that I am not are in space and time, whereas my private psychological states are in time but not in space. However, insofar as Kant treats time as a homogeneous medium, he has, following Bergson's arguments that we assessed in the last chapter, implicitly conflated time with space. This conflation conditions his view that the same sort of causality and causal law is operative in the psychological realm as in the physical realm. This, in turn, leads him to cast the principle of human freedom, beyond any known phenomena, into the realm of unknowable *noumena* [TFW 233/174].

Kant's account of freedom, however, is not merely one among many, and Bergson's critical appraisal of his position was not merely a function of philosophical fashion, as he explains in the final session of his 1904–5 Collège de France lectures on *The Evolution of the Problem of Freedom*. Kant presents, on the one hand, the "quintessence" of the modern notion of nature as mathematically knowable and as operating mechanically. On the other hand, and consequently, he articulates the quintessence of a modern notion of freedom as an absolute spontaneity that is external to and opposed to this material realm. For this reason, on the problem of freedom, Bergson can even write that "one can discuss Kant's solution, one can refute it or even reject it, but it is impossible not to start with it, and not to take it in some way as a basis of operations" [EPL 329]. It is not necessary to be a Kantian to recognise the importance of Kant.

In the lectures, Bergson discusses several of the problematic aspects of Kant's "solution". First, this non-empirical, "transcendental" principle is not psychological and seems to belong to the form of consciousness in general, in which all minds share, as much as to any personal self. This will produce, it would seem, a peculiar idea of freedom. Moreover, although its effects are manifest in time, this principle does not operate in time (for it stands outside time), and what such a non-temporal agency could be is difficult to conceive. Somehow, an a-temporal, a-historical, transcendental principle of freedom produces "these successive facts", which, "projected into the sphere of knowledge, find a means to lodge themselves in it". But "how will they do so if all the other facts of nature do not leave room for them?" [EPL 324] This, for Bergson, is the most fundamental problem in Kant's account: "it is impossible to conceive how freedom thus understood can come to insert itself into the mechanism of nature without breaking the unity of nature" [EPL 325]. On the one side, we have the iron rule of mechanical law, according to which any event is wholly explained by its empirical precedents; on the other, we have a pure spontaneity that has to break, mysteriously and magically, the chains of nature in order to manifest itself. In contemporary terms, the principle of "causal closure" governing the physical world, according to which all physical events find their sufficient condition in their antecedents, precludes any understanding of mental causation, of how the mind can effect change in the world.[17]

This is the fundamental problem in Kant's account of freedom, but a version of it still remains unresolved, and even unaddressed, in *Time and Free Will*. Bergson asks "consciousness to isolate itself from the external world, and by a vigorous effort of abstraction, to become once again itself" [TFW 90/67]. Something essential, a decisive philosophical advance, is gained in this effort of abstraction, namely a secure grasp of duration. Still, it tells us nothing about how freedom can be instantiated in the world, about how real duration as a principle of freedom can interact with space. Boutroux, in contrast, with broader ambitions, had sought to "shatter the postulate that renders inconceivable the intervention of freedom in the course of phenomena, the maxim according to which nothing is lost and nothing is created",[18] the postulate that, as we have seen, is the principle of the conservation of force. Certainly, Boutroux was concerned to show that the maxim does not apply in the psychological realm; but this was after having argued that this principle is already a convention, that it has more of a use-value than a truth-value, in its application to the physical world. The principle of causation, as presupposing necessitation and the conversation of force, is a form of thought that we apply to nature, but not an *a priori* form of thought that governs nature in general. The higher one climbs in the scale of beings from the inorganic through the varying stages of life, the clearer it becomes, he argues, that mechanistic principles are abstract. Hence, he can claim that human freedom does not have to smash iron chains of necessity in order to realise itself in the world. And he can confirm Ravaisson's 1867 proclamations that "spontaneity, freedom is the truth" of things, that "nature now, is not, as materialism taught, all geometry, and therefore all absolute necessity", and that determination or "fatality in this world […] is just an appearance".[19]

In order to discover a notion of freedom as duration, Bergson urges us to retreat into the self, but for this freedom to have a meaningful bearing on our lives, we need to understand how it can return into the world. At one point, when discussing the law of the conservation of force early in the third chapter of his dissertation, Bergson does acknowledge that "contingency" can be found in life beyond the psyche: "inanimate things conserve no trace of time passed, but it is not the same in the domain of life. Here duration seems to act in the manner of a cause, and the idea of putting everything back in the same place after a period of time implies a type of absurdity, since such a return has never occurred in a living being [*être vivant*]" [TFW 153/116]. Here Bergson announces the project of *Creative Evolution*. But in order to get there, in order to see duration in biological as well as psychological life, he will first have to undo the uneasy assertions in the conclusion to *Time and Free Will* that duration and space are contradictory principles, that it would be by a "veritable contradiction to place succession in the very heart of simultaneity".

We should not consider, he argues here, that "external things endure [*durent*], but rather that there is in them an inexpressible reason by virtue of which we cannot consider them in successive moments of our duration without noticing that they have changed" [TFW 227/171]. In the concluding chapter of his next major work, *Matter and Memory*, when he is considering modern dualism as a problem, Bergson will clearly reject these assertions and, rather than appeal to a miraculous, pre-established harmony between mind and world, will develop the thought that duration also exists in things.

Summary

Bergson defends an idea of human freedom while arguing that traditional disputes between determinists and libertarians imply a fundamental confusion of duration with space. The determinist view that volition is caused by a variety of isolated, psychological motives, each with a greater or lesser degree of force, is a symbolic representation that ignores the internal dynamism of the profound, durational self. Our genuinely free acts express the self and its motives rather than being mechanically determined by them. The more that clearly defined motives are available before any action, the less that the action is free and the more that action resembles the determinist's schema. Freedom, then, is a matter of degree. The libertarian cannot admit this in adding an absolute power to have chosen another possible course of action (Y instead of X) to the determinist's schema. This addition presupposes, at bottom, that the future can already be mapped out and that it has already happened. There is always, Bergson holds, an element of unscripted novelty in our free actions, which is not conceivable, and thus not possible in the mind of the agent, before it occurs. In this regard, Bergson compares the free act to the creation of works of fine art understood as products of genius. In his later work, Bergson will grapple with objections that this notion of freedom is too far from traditional notions of rational autonomy. Moreover, he will also have to overcome the opposition between duration and space that structures *Time and Free Will* in order to elucidate how freedom can be realised in the physical world.

Notes

1 Jules Lachelier, "Psychologie et métaphysique", *Revue philosophique de la France et de l'étranger* 19 (1885), 481–516, p. 511.
2 See Laurent Fedi, "Bergson et Boutroux. La Critique du modèle physicaliste et des lois de conservation en psychologie", *Revue de métaphysique et de morale* 2001/2 (2001), 97–118. See also Suzanne Guerlac, *Thinking in Time: An Introduction to Henri Bergson* (Ithaca, NY: Cornell University Press, 2006), pp. 78–9.
3 See John Mullarkey, *Bergson and Philosophy* (Manchester: Manchester University Press, 1999), pp. 40–1 for a good treatment of Bergson and identity theory as a position in the contemporary philosophy of mind.
4 William Hamilton cited in J. S. Mill, *An Examination of Sir William Hamilton's Philosophy* (London: Longmans, 1865), p. 498. See Fedi, "Bergson et Boutroux", p. 113.
5 Mill, *An Examination of Sir William Hamilton's Philosophy*, p. 500.
6 The English translation attaches it to the end of the discussion of physical determinism, but in the French text there is a section break here.
7 Emile Boutroux, *On the Contingency of the Laws of Nature*, trans. F. Rothwell (Chicago, IL: Open Court, 1920), p. 141.
8 Boutroux, *On the Contingency of the Laws of Nature*, p. 141.
9 For more on this, see Chapter 6 of my *Being Inclined: Félix Ravaisson's Philosophy of Habit* (Oxford: Oxford University Press, 2019).
10 See Steven Mumford and Rani Lil Anjum, *What Tends to Be: An Essay on the Dispositional Modality* (Abingdon: Routledge, 2018), which has a section on the history of non-necessitarian conceptions of causation, but which does not discuss the French contingency theorists.
11 See Robert Kane (ed.), *The Oxford Handbook of Free Will* (Oxford: Oxford University Press, 2002), particularly Part V: "Moral Responsibility, Alternative Possibilities and Frankfurt-Style Examples".
12 See John Fisher, "Frankfurt-Style Examples and Semi-compatibilism: New Work", in *The Oxford Handbook of Free Will*, ed. Kane, pp. 243–65.
13 See Bergson, *Mélanges*, pp. 833–4 and the entry "Liberté" in André Lalande's *Vocabulaire technique et critique de la philosophie* (Paris: Presses universitaires de France, 1997 [1926]).
14 Boutroux, *On the Contingency of the Laws of Nature*, p. 115.
15 Gustave Belot, "Une théorie nouvelle de la liberté", *Revue philosophique de la France et de l'étranger*, XXX (1890), 361–92.
16 Bergson, *Œuvres*, p. 1542.
17 See Robert C. Bishop "The Causal Closure of Physics and Free Will", in *The Oxford Handbook of Free Will*, ed. Kane, pp. 101–14.
18 Boutroux, *On the Contingency of the Laws of Nature*, p. 171.
19 Ravaisson, *La philosophie en France au XIXème siècle*, p. 269.

Further reading

Henri Bergson, *L'évolution du problème de la liberté. Cours au collège de France* 1904–05, ed. Arnaud François (Paris: Presses universitaires de France, 2017). This important lecture course on the history of the problem of freedom is scheduled to appear in English translation soon.

Vladimir Jankélévitch, *Henri Bergson*, ed. Nils F. Schott and Alexandre Lefebvre (Durham, NC: Duke University Press, 2015). See the first chapter on freedom in this monument of Bergson scholarship.

Robert Kane (ed.), *The Oxford Handbook of Free Will*, ed. Robert Kane (Oxford: Oxford University Press, 2011). A good sourcebook for contemporary formulations of the positions that Bergson criticises.

Mark Ian Thomas Robson, "Is Ultimate Moral Responsibility Metaphysically Impossible? A Bergsonian Critique of Galen Strawson's Argument", *Philosophy* 92/4 (2017), 519–38. A useful attempt to bring Bergson to bear on contemporary arguments in the "analytic" tradition concerning freedom.

Four
Memory

From Time and Free Will to Matter and Memory

Seven years after *Time and Free Will*, Bergson published his second major work: *Matter and Memory*. According to the preface written for the 1911 English translation, the "guiding idea" and "starting point" of the book is that there are "diverse *tones* of mental life", that "life may be lived at different heights, now nearer to action, now further removed from it" [MM 14/7]. Bergson was led to this thought in his doctoral thesis, since freedom, and thus the distinction between the profound self and the superficial self, was there a matter of degree rather than a binary opposition. The diverse tones of mental life in the earlier text were diverse degrees of freedom. *Matter and Memory* departs from this insight, however, and develops the project of the earlier book in two ways.[1]

First, Bergson reworks the opposition between the freedom of mind and the material, external world that, as we saw in concluding the preceding chapter, structured *Time and Free Will*. Hence if Bergson now "affirms the reality of spirit and the reality of matter and tries to determine the relation of the one to the other", he aims to do so "in such a way as [...] to lessen greatly, if not to overcome, the theoretical difficulties which have always beset dualism" [MM 9/1]. As he put it in a letter of 1905, in *Time and Free Will* "he was led to a conception of the self and of freedom that left without a response the question of how [...] the free person can use, in order to act, a material body [...] in space. This led to a series of inquiries that led to *Matter and Memory*" [C 114]. Bergson now considers dualism as a problem and it is in this sense that the subtitle of the 1896 text is *An Essay on the Relation of Mind and Body* [*Essai sur la relation du corps à l'esprit*].

Second, *Time and Free Will* argued, as we also saw in the preceding chapter, that the free act, at the greatest height (or to put the same point in another way, at the greatest depth) of mental life, is one in which the agent contracts and expresses her whole self, her temporal duration and thus her past as a whole. Bergson's reflection on freedom thus implies a notion of the past that his reflection on time could not fully elucidate, since, with its aim to distinguish time from space, it focused primarily on the flow of lived time in the present. It is under the heading of memory that Bergson now addresses the issue of the nature of the past in duration, and he thereby comes to discover that "the very ground of our conscious existence is memory" [CE 17/16]. It is for this reason that Bergson's reflection on memory and its relation to matter can become a general reflection on the relation of mind and matter.

Given, however, that *Matter and Memory* starts from the guiding idea of diverse tones or levels of mental life, the ordering of its chapters does not—and in this it is like *Time and Free Will*—follow the direction of Bergson's train of thought. For it is only in the second chapter, an early version of which he had published as journal articles earlier in the year, that Bergson addresses memory and the degrees of what he now calls "attention to life" [MM 14/7].[2] The third chapter presents the idea of pure memory, which he had not yet discovered in the earlier journal articles. The fourth chapter, a first version of which was also published earlier in the year,[3] addresses dualism as a problem, and attempts to locate duration in things, rather than just in an isolated self, in order to respond to that problem. Before all of this, however, the first chapter provides a novel account of perception, and of the role of the body in perceptual experience, which challenges traditional realist and idealist positions in the philosophy of perception. This first chapter was written after at least two of the others, and is the result of Bergson's reflection on memory.

The published book, then, begins with what was written as a relatively late addition. The decision to structure the work in such a fashion has its advantages: it allows the analysis to move in a linear way from perception of the external world to memory as the essence of mind, and then to illuminate the unity of the whole series in order to respond to the problem of dualism. This structure does not, however, make its first chapter easier to read. Far from it. Bergson's account of the body and perception, which involves a succession of speculative theses and deductions, is difficult (it "was judged obscure by all who had some habit of philosophical speculation" [CM 91/ 83]). It is, however, easier to grasp against the background of the philosophical project laid out in the later chapters. Bergson, in fact, came to recommend that one should begin *Matter and Memory*, after reading the 1911 preface, with the second chapter of the book, and that is exactly how we shall proceed.[4] Here we examine Bergson's arguments concerning memory, and in Chapter 5 we examine his position concerning perception and mind–body dualism.

Two forms of memory

The second chapter opens with Bergson's distinction of two forms of memory. *"The past"*, he writes, *"survives under two distinct forms: first, in motor mechanisms; secondly, in independent recollections"* [MM 78/82]. This is a distinction between remembering how to do something and remembering that something has happened, a distinction that contemporary psychology discusses under the headings of "procedural memory" and "declarative memory". Bergson's formulation of the distinction, according to which its two terms are different in nature rather than just in degree [MM 80/85], has been celebrated even by his most trenchant critic, Bertrand Russell, who considers it "one of the best things in Bergson".[5] The distinction is significant, but the issue of genuine philosophical import is how the terms of the distinction are to be understood. Although Bergson's interpretation of memory proper is original and important, his account of procedural memory or habit here is neither of those two things. It accepts the mechanistic interpretations of the operation of an acquired motor habit that were prevalent in the "scientific" or "empirical" psychology of his time without so much as a backward glance (at least not before, as we will see, the final paragraph of the text!) to the rich tradition of non-mechanistic, vitalist and animist conceptions of motor habit in the foreground of earlier nineteenth-century French philosophy. This, of course, is a reason why Russell would have appreciated it. Understanding just as little of the nineteenth-century philosophical background, commentators more sympathetic to Bergson have even considered his supposed theory of "habit-memory" here to represent a breakthrough crucial for later developments in French thought.[6] In truth, it is far from certain that what Bergson writes here is in his own name or that it can survive his attempt to attenuate the difficulties of mind–body dualism in concluding the book.

Bergson's example, standard at the time, is that of learning a passage of text by heart. His argument is that once we have "committed" the text "to memory", as we might say, through repetition, we have really acquired a habit. I can remember, in principle, each of the occasions that I have read the text. These readings are dated episodes, in that each one happened at a certain point in time, and thus can be recalled through "episodic memory" (which is typically contrasted with "semantic memory", the memory of concepts and present facts, as another species of declarative memory). The result of the repeated readings, however, is not the recollection of an episode at all. It has rather "all the marks of a habit", which I carry out rather than represent to myself in a memory-image: "[l]ike a habit it is acquired by the repetition of the same effort. Like a habit, it demands first a decomposition and then a re-composition of the whole action. Lastly, like every habitual bodily exercise, it is stored up in a mechanism" [MM 80/84]. Bergson recognises that the example is slightly "artificial" [MM 84/89], since this sort of language-use is perhaps not the clearest example of a habit. Repeating a passage of text learnt by heart perhaps requires the operation of thought, whereas less intellectual motor habits can take place without conscious thought, and without conscious thought even having initiated them. In this sense, we might consider learning by heart to be a hybrid phenomenon, straddling both habit and a more intellectual form of memory. Bergson, however, is trying to overturn what he describes in his lectures as a psychological orthodoxy of his time, one that takes this hybrid phenomenon to constitute the model of memory as such, without the difference in nature between habit and memory as recollection being grasped. "If you open any psychology manual […] you'll find in general the view that all memories are acquired in the same way, and are acquired—this proposition is almost a banality— by the repetition of a movement or perception" [HTM 125]. The view he attacks is still orthodox. Contemporary psychology seems to consider more or less unanimously that a phase of "consolidation" is essential to the "encoding" of potentially merely short-term memories as long-term memories. For Bergson, episodic memory not only has no need for consolidation, but it cannot be consolidated; when a memory is consolidated it has become a habit.

On Bergson's account, the acquisition of a motor habit in general consists in the development of motor mechanisms: "[t]hese movements, as they recur, contrive a mechanism for themselves, grow into a habit, and determine in us attitudes which automatically follow our perception of things" [MM 84/89]. Although habits require mental analysis for their acquisition, once acquired they can simply be explained in third-person, neurological terms. An acquired motor habit is, thus, as he will put it in 1904, the "fossilised residue of a spiritual activity" [CM 275/267]. This memorable phrase was supposed to characterise Félix Ravaisson's ideas— according to which, on the contrary, habit does not "become the mechanical effect of an external impulse, but rather the effect of an inclination that follows from the will"[7]—but it was evidently more faithful to Bergson's "own" conception of habit. He did not, in fact, always hold quite such a dualist and mechanistic conception of motor habit, for the record of his teaching before *Matter and Memory* shows him moving away from a position influenced by Ravaisson, to one that incorporates the more materialist and mechanist views of psychologists later in the century.[8]

Is motor habit thus conceived really a form of memory? Although Bergson's original intention was to distinguish, following ordinary talk of habit as a form of memory, two forms of memory, he arrives at the claim that the lesson learnt through repetition is "*habit interpreted by memory* rather than memory itself" [MM 84/89]. If I did not remember the episodes of acquiring the ability to recite the passage, then I would not know that I had once acquired it; I would consider my ability to recite the passage to be innate, and to belong to my "primary" rather than "second" nature. We can talk, it would seem, about habit as memory only in a figurative sense. Unfortunately, Bergson is not consistent on this point, since he continues to talk about habit as a form of memory. What, then, is the genus "memory" such that motor habit and episodic memory are two species of it?

Do the supposed species belong to the genus because they are both modes of the "survival of the past"? If Bergson's view concerning motor habit as merely *interpreted* by memory is his real position, the point should be extended to the notion of two modes of the "survival" of the past in the present. For this is also merely figurative or metaphorical in the case of acquired motor habits understood as a function of material and mechanical changes. Were it not, we might just as well say that the past survives in the letter that I have folded and put in the envelope, because the same sort of physiological change effected by voluntary activity is at issue. This would, I think, be an odd use of English. Intuitively we recognise that there is a difference between saying that the past survives in the present and that the past has causally shaped the present. Hence only in the case of episodic memory—if at all—can the past be said in any literal sense to survive in the present. This would mean that Bergson has distinguished motor habit from memory, but not two forms of memory.

Bergson's basic intention, in claiming that there is a difference in nature between habit and episodic memory, is to grant to the developing neurosciences of his time that acquired habits are, in principle, materially localisable in the body, in bodily mechanisms, while denying that this is the case for episodic memories. On the latter point, he attacks "the strange hypothesis of memories stored in the brain that would become conscious by a veritable miracle, and would bring us back to the past by a mysterious process" [MM 89/95]. Such a hypothesis supposes something inexplicable, and therefore miraculous, namely the passage from a physical fact, some kind of trace in the brain, to a psychological image. This miracle is an expression of the traditional mind–body problem. The process is also mysterious in that physical memory traces are *present*, and this in no way helps us to understand how episodic memories are of the *past*.

Such is Bergson's primary intention, but it has the consequence of opposing mind and body in a dualistic fashion. How mind is supposed to effect change on body in the acquisition of a motor habit he does not say, and he omits to mention in this case the miraculous nature of such mind–body transfers. Moreover, his opposition of mind to mechanical body seems to commit him not just to a mechanical conception of acquired habit, but also, and consequently, to an overly intellectualist account of the acquisition of habit. He supposes that habit acquisition always begins intentionally, in consciousness, by means of mental analysis of a situation, but the acquisition of bad habits (slouching, or filling one's speech with the word "like") immediately gives the lie to that idea. Later French philosophers such as Maurice Merleau-Ponty (and Deleuze, implicitly) will criticise Bergson for this intellectualism, for not adequately observing how it is the body that learns in, say, learning a musical instrument. For Merleau-Ponty, "it is the body", the pre-objective lived-body (*le corps propre*) that is something other than a nexus of mechanisms, "which 'catches' and 'comprehends' movement: the acquisition of a habit is indeed the grasping of a significance, but it is the motor grasping of a motor significance".[9] To be sure, Bergson can *write* similar things: "a movement is learned when the body has been made to understand it" [MM 112/122]. But it would seem that he cannot genuinely *think* the same thought, since if the body is just a machine, the word "understand" here can be taken only figuratively.

If Bergson holds to a mechanistic conception of an acquired habit, then he has not really distinguished two forms of memory. However, earlier in the finished text, in Chapter 1, he presents a different and a genuine distinction between two forms of memory that implies *a real notion of habit-memory*. About the role of memory in perceptual experience Bergson writes this: "[i]n short, memory in these two forms, covering as it does with a cloak of recollections a core of immediate perception, and also contracting a number of external moments into a single internal moment, constitutes the principal share of individual consciousness in perception, the subjective side of the knowledge of things" [MM 34/31]. Memory, in one sense, is the representation, the *re-presentation of the past in the present*, and this, for Bergson, is memory proper and includes episodic memory. But memory, in another sense here, is also a *non-imagistic contraction of the past in the present*. This contraction, which is a function of duration as it was discussed in *Time and Free Will*, occurs according to different depths: it is, first, the contraction or "retention" of the immediate past in the present, in the living-present, in such a way that we can, for example, hear a piece of music as a continuous piece of music, and not as a succession of isolated moments that need to be associated together after the fact. The "concrete and truly lived present [...] consists largely in the immediate past" [MM 150/166]. As Bergson also puts it in extending the idea to the immediate future: "the psychological state that I call 'my present' is both a perception of the immediate past and a determination"—a "protention", as one might say—"of the immediate future" [MM 138/153]. The present of lived-time, then, is not punctual, but something like a stretch; the present is stretched out into the immediate past and the immediate future. Second, and more profoundly, as Bergson will note in the third chapter, the contraction of the past in the present is a contraction not just of the immediate past but of the whole of our past experience: "[i]f we look at the matter closely, we shall see that our memories form a chain of the same kind, and that our character, always present in all our decisions, is indeed the actual synthesis of all our past states" [MM 146/162]. The result of this synthesis, this contraction, of our past as whole is not an image, but our *character*, the ground on which and the way in which we exist in the present. "Our psychological life as a whole reveals itself in our character although none of its past states manifests itself explicitly in character" [MM 148/164].

What, then, is the relation between these two different distinctions between two forms of memory? The Deleuze of 1966 exaggerates in claiming that there is "a completely different principle of distinction"[10] in each. There is, in fact, an implicit relation between the contraction that is duration, on the one hand, and what the second chapter confusedly presents as habit-memory, on the other, taking both as distinct from episodic memory, which is the same across the two distinctions. That there may be a relation between habit and contraction-memory is suggested by Bergson's choice of terms, since in French one speaks of *contracting* a habit, just as in English one speaks of contracting an illness. The contraction that is time as duration, we might suppose, is the condition of the contraction of any particular habits. To understand how this is indeed the case, consider learning a motor action, say, learning to play a piece of music on the piano: from the many different instances of playing—repetition is never wholly repetition of the same, and always involves difference to some degree—we can gain a skill, an unreflective facility (we don't need to think through each time exactly what we're doing, and doing so would only impair the performance, which requires its own kind of concentration). In order to attain this result, however, a power isolating and synthesising the same in the different instances of learning to play the piece is required (for otherwise we would forget everything each time). Crucially, this synthesis is not a function of reflective thought or intellectual analysis, since we are not conscious of carrying it out. Although some degree of reflection and analysis may be required in the acquisition of some habits, habit acquisition in general requires a power or principle that operates prior to the intervention of thought in the guise of memory-images or concepts or judgment. As Ravaisson had argued in *Of Habit*, "it is not action", and by action he means the mental activity that is conscious, reflective thought, "that gives birth to or strengthens the continuity or repetition of locomotion; it is a more obscure and unreflective tendency".[11] This synthesis or tendency is a "passive synthesis", i.e. neither wholly passive nor wholly active, and it is itself the most basic form of habit. Victor Egger develops Ravaisson's point in an 1880 article on "The Birth of Habits": we cannot say simply that repetition gives birth to habit, in the way that repeatedly reading a poem allows us to learn it by heart, for "repetition, from the beginning, needs habit for its explanation".[12] In this sense, habit is the condition of the acquisition of particular habits, and as a synthetic power it develops itself as a capacity for producing acts of the same sort in the future. The power of habit, that is, in synthesising identity in difference, draws out of repetition something new, namely a difference in itself.[13]

Although Bergson does not make it clear, there is a link between duration as a contractive power and acquired motor habits. The former is the ground, the condition of the possibility of the latter. If our character is the dispositions and habits by means of which we tend to do the things that we do, the condition of character in this sense is the contraction that is time as duration, which is but the most primitive form of habit. It remains the case, however, that this account of habit as a contractive power does not accord with a mechanistic and materialist account of an acquired habit. In the first case, a genuine survival of the past is at issue; in the second case, insofar as it involves merely a mechanical and material change, there is, in truth, no such survival. If Bergson really does want to discover a survival of the past in an acquired habit, he will have to see in habit a power, a disposition, a tendency that is irreducible to material, mechanical changes and that belongs to duration itself. But, in *Matter and Memory* at least, he does not do this explicitly, even though he sometimes gestures towards such a thought, and even though his idea of memory-contraction leads him to it.

Recognition

What Bergson discusses as mechanical memory stands at one end of a scale, since memory, on his account, is not just one thing but a spectrum, a continuum of capacities that shade into each other. Recognition, to which the rest of the second chapter of *Matter and Memory* is devoted, is a name for a range of capacities that occupy diverse positions on this scale. Recognition in general is an awareness that we have of knowing something that we encounter in perception, the awareness of having seen something or someone before: I see, and know through seeing, that the person before me is my old friend Marcus, or that the thing on the bench before me is a hammer that I can use for hammering. It would be difficult to explain these forms of recognition by means of the association of ideas as a psychological process, since experience shows us often enough that we can recognise things without having to call previous ideas or images of those things to mind, and without having to compare those images with what is before our eyes. Of course, we can compare the present with an image of the past, but this is, as Bergson put it in his 1903–4 lecture course on memory, a "reflective form" [HTM 60] that presupposes more original forms of recognition. Moreover, clinical psychology has recorded pathological cases where visual memory is intact but the power of recognition is impaired [MM 92/100], which shows that there is a difference between them.

Bergson argues that there is "in the first instance, if we carry the thought to the extreme, an *instantaneous* recognition, of which the body is capable by itself, without the help of any explicit memory image" [MM 92–3/100]. I know what to do with a hammer and immediately recognise it as such; I do not need to see it first as an indeterminate something, and then call to mind memory-images of a hammer. This know-how is a function of "what the Germans call *Bewegungsantriebe*", motor tendencies or drives; "the habit of using the object has […] resulted in organizing together movements and perceptions; the consciousness of these nascent movements, which follow perception after the manner of a reflex, must be here also at the bottom of recognition" [MM 94/101]. About this form of recognition, we have to make a point analogous to the one we made concerning supposedly mechanical habit-memory: if motor recognition is merely a matter of reflex responses to stimuli, motor recognition is not recognition, for it involves no cognition, no understanding or knowledge. We may just as well say (of course, we do say this kind of thing, but only improperly) that the vending machine knows that I have just inserted coins into it when it produces a cup of coffee. Whatever exactly "the Germans" meant by motor drives, Bergson's interpretation of acquired habits as mechanical seems to lead him to interpret these motor drives or tendencies as, at bottom, empty of dynamism and intelligence. We can thus understand why Bergson introduces recognition as a "feeling" [MM 90/96], rather than as anything cognitive. This is merely a feeling of ease, as he acknowledges in 1903–4, a feeling that my motor drives meet no resistance [HTM 113].

Mechanical recognition is, however, merely a limit case at the bottom end of a spectrum. Based on and contrasted with motor recognition is attentive recognition, which requires the "regular intervention of memory images" [MM 98/107]. Bergson's essential point here is that memory-images are constitutive of perceptual experience and not just a result of the latter: "any memory image that is capable of interpreting our actual perception inserts itself so thoroughly into it that we are no longer able to discern what is perception and what is memory" [MM 103/113]. As his lectures show, Bergson is much impressed in this connection with the work of the Danish philosopher and psychologist Harald Høffding, who claimed that in perceptual recognition there is a *fusion* of ideas in experience rather than an *association* of perception to an idea [HTM 71]. Bergson develops this insight: instead of seeing only ready-made ideas, psychological atoms in the mind, we have to apprehend these ideas as the result of a psychological process, one that involves the fusion of memory (pure memory, in fact, but we'll return to this point in the next section) in perception. The fusion of memory in perception produces "*attentive* perception", which "truly involves a reflection, in the etymological sense of the word, that is to say the projection, outside ourselves, of an actively created image, identical with, or similar to, the object on which it comes to mould itself" [MM 102/112]. Instead of thinking of the constitution of experience as linear and unidirectional—in the sense that an external object would produce sense-data in the mind from which memory-images are formed—we should, he urges, consider it as circular, as "a *circuit*, in which all the elements, including the perceived object itself, hold each other in a state of mutual tension as in an electric circuit" [MM 104/114], with memory "fortifying and enriching perception, which, in turn, becomes more and more developed, attracting a growing number of complementary memories" [MM 101/112].

In this way, Bergson accounts for what contemporary philosophers discuss under the heading of "seeing as": we see things *as* things. Bergson refers to experimental studies showing that in the act of reading we do not read words letter by letter. Instead, the mind picks out certain traits and fills in the gaps with memory images, which, "projected on the paper, take the place of the real printed characters and may be mistaken from them" [MM 103/113]. Bergson would have to wait a few years for the full development of Gestalt psychology, but the classic Gestalt images of the duck/rabbit and the candlestick/faces are instructive in this regard. In looking at such images, we *see* one or the other of the duck or rabbit, or faces or candlestick, but never both at the same time; and it takes a peculiar frame of mind, if it is at all possible, to see neither. In this sense, Bergson argues that recognition in perception comes first, that it is "something simple, and indivisible, and yet it contains, virtually, two things; there is perception plus the corresponding memory" [HTM 71–2].

This fusion or projection of memory images into perception within attentive recognition is, however, made possible by what Bergson calls motor schemas, which are, although he does not seem to say this explicitly, a higher—i.e. more reflective, more mental and less mechanical (but whether or not something can be more or less mechanical is an issue to which we return in concluding Chapter 5)—form of habit. Normal auditory language comprehension would be inexplicable if there were no intermediary between purely passive sensory impressions—the impression of a more or less continuous stream of sounds that we experience when, say, listening to a wholly foreign language—and auditory memory "images". Ordinarily "there occurs in our consciousness, in the form of nascent muscular sensations, what we will call the motor schema of the spoken language" [MM 111/121].This motor schema "divides up the speech we hear, indicates […] its salient outlines" and "is to speech itself what the rough sketch is to the finished picture" [MM 112/122].The hypothesis is confirmed, Bergson argues, by cases of echolalia, where the patient repeats spontaneously words and phrases heard. The tendency to repeat in the pathological case bears witness to "a tendency of auditory verbal impressions to prolong themselves in articulatory movements", a tendency which is "more than absolutely mechanical actions, but less than an appeal to voluntary memory" [MM 114/125]. This is not the last time that, following Ravaisson, Bergson will appeal to an idea of tendency or inclination as a bridge between the realms of matter and mind, of mechanism and the will, but this motor schema stands higher up in the continuum of memory than the limit case of purely mechanical, purely automatic responses to stimuli.

Kant, famously, had described the schematism by which concepts are applied to sensory intuitions as "a hidden art in the depths of the human soul".[14] Bergson argues that such schematism is a "motor" phenomenon, that it is a function of tendencies and nascent movement. It is the physiological basis of these motor-schemas and of wholly automatic recognition that can be damaged by lesions in the brain. What we cannot conclude from the clinical studies of aphasia (a label for a variety of problems in understanding and formulating language) caused by brain lesions is that supposed memory-traces corresponding to memory-images in the mind have been destroyed. After Paul Broca had found in the 1860s that cases of aphasia resulted from damage to the left-side of the frontal-lobe ("Broca's area"), subsequent research had attempted to locate specific linguistic functions and auditory or visual linguistic memory images in that region of the brain. But in cases of word-deafness, an inability to recognise words aurally, the loss of word recognition follows certain patterns according to the law of regression formulated by Théodule-Armand Ribot: proper names disappear first, followed by nouns and then verbs. To suppose that the affected region of the frontal lobe is a storehouse of memories is thus to suppose that the physiological damage miraculously eliminates the same category of words in the same order each time, which is absurd. Moreover, as we have already noted, recognition can fail with the patient still able to avail herself of memory-images.

The philosophically informed English neurologist Hughlings Jackson, in a series of articles, had, in fact, already rejected the attempt to localise language centres and memory-images in the brain as unwarranted by the clinical facts: "we must not say that the 'memory of words' is a *function* of any part of the nervous system", as he wrote in 1878, "because function is a physiological term. Memory or any other psychical state emerges *during* not *from*—if 'from' implies continuity of a psychical state with a physical state— functioning of nervous arrangements".[15] Jackson's work was largely ignored until in 1915 it was rediscovered and republished in *Brain* once the theory of localised memory-traces was no longer quite such a neurological orthodoxy. Bergson was familiar with Jackson's work and refers to it in the article on which the second chapter of *Matter and Memory* is based. His arguments are therefore not wholly original, although his omission of the reference to Jackson in *Matter and Memory* has certainly encouraged the view that they are.[16] In any case, the Jackson–Bergson rejection of materialist accounts of memory is as convincing now as it was in the late nineteenth century, for as Rupert Sheldrake has shown recently, "more than a century of intensive, well-funded research has failed to pin down memory traces in brains".[17] In supposing there to be a one-to-one correspondence between the memory in the mind and a physiological trace, modern neuroscience, as Bergson shows, is guided not by empirical findings, but, at bottom, by the *a priori* philosophical thesis of psycho-physical parallelism, since epiphenomenalism presupposes it.

Pure memory

In perception, as we have seen, it is not possible to determine where perception ends and the memory-image begins, which is to say that they are continuous with each other. Any memory can be realised according to an infinite number of degrees of proximity to the action that Bergson takes as constitutive of the present. In his famous image of the cone, the base of the cone represents memories in their pure state, prior to their instantiation, whereas the summit, the point, represents their insertion into the present moment of action. Towards the base of the cone we find personal, episodic memories which allow what Bergson terms in 1903–4 a third "form" of recognition continuous with the two others he treats in *Matter and Memory*, namely personal recognition, which is not the general recognition whereby I recognise, say, a table *as* a table, but one whereby "the recognized object is recognized by me as being part of my own personal experience" [HTM 116], as being this table at which I ate when I lived in the house, for example. Even further towards the base of the cone are dreams, where my past comes back to me, without my expressly willing it, in something like a semi-conscious state. The person of sound common sense exists somewhere in the middle of this spectrum, between the careless impulsivity of purely living and acting in the present and the daydreamer who, submerged by the past, thinks without her thought facilitating action. Between the base and the summit, memory manifests itself according to an infinite number of "degrees of contraction", and, in this sense, it can be "repeated an indefinite number of times in these myriad possible reductions of our past life" [MM 169/188]. This movement, this condensation, is what associationist psychology ignores in seeing in the mind only isolated, atomistic ideas and their interrelation.

Memory-images, in all their different degrees of contraction, presuppose, however, as Bergson came to recognise in 1896, a *pure memory* from which they derive their quality as being of or belonging to the past. In the text, each of the terms *mémoire* and *souvenir* can name both the thing remembered and the act of remembering. The notion of pure memory, however, is the strange notion of a pure past, which although it is the condition of remembering in the present, exceeds anything the mind can do or apprehend. We have to posit this pure past because the quality of pastness in a recollection cannot be accounted for by means of anything that is simply present. Nothing in the present can provide what the contemporary philosophy of memory terms a criterion of "mnemicity" distinguishing imagination from memory.

A classically "empiricist" distinction of memory and imagination according to the different degrees of vivacity of their images in the mind fails, at any rate, to account for it. Whether or not we agree with Hume[18], that memory images are more vivid, this approach will not be able to explain why some memories are perfectly vivid and why some less vivid images do not present themselves as memories. "The truth is that we will only ever reach the past if we place ourselves within it from the outset. Essentially virtual, the past can be grasped as past only if we follow and adopt the movement by which it emerges into a present image, emerging from the shadows into the light of day" [MM 149/173]. The past is *sui generis*, inexplicable by anything other than itself. As Jankélévitch puts it with his usual brilliance, "between the most immaterial *pianissimo* and a melody remembered there is an absolute difference, an abyss that no decrescendo will ever traverse".[19] Although, for Bergson, pure memory is instantiated by degrees in experience, there is a difference in nature between pure memory and imagination; and this instantiation by degrees of something, pure memory, in something else that is essentially different, namely imagination, is captured by the hyphen in the phrase memory-image [*souvenir-image*]. We can accept Bergson's point here but still be wary of his claim that "imagining is not remembering [*imaginer n'est pas se souvenir*]" [MM 136/150]. This seems to presuppose that imagination is a wholly productive rather than reproductive faculty, i.e. that the imagination can produce images that are not based on prior sense experience. Bergson will, in fact, implicitly deny this in his later critique of the modal category of possibility, as we will see in Chapter 7 of this study.

When I try to remember something from, say, my childhood, I do not have to go back, from my position in the present, through all the events that separate my childhood from the present. As Bergson describes it, I "leap" into the "past in general and then into a region of the past" [MM 134/148]. Finding the specific memory that I am searching for is "a matter of trial and error [*travail de tâtonnement*], analogous to bringing a camera into focus". At this point, "the memory remains still in a virtual state; we simply ready ourselves to receive it in adopting the appropriate attitude". Then "gradually it appears as a nebulosity that condenses; from a virtual state it passes to an actual one; and to the degree that its contours are drawn and its surface is coloured, it tends to imitate perception". In this way, pure memory can be instantiated in experience, but on Bergson's account, there can be no *pure act of remembering*: pure memory can never be purely remembered. Memory retrieval is always productive or creative precisely insofar as it can actualise virtual memories only with the means available in the present, a present oriented to action now and in the future. There is something essentially tragic about remembering, for it is doomed to failure, destined never to reach exactly what it seeks. Episodic memory, taken as an attempt to retrieve the past as it was, is a Sisyphean, infinite task. The condition of possibility of remembering, pure memory, is at one and the same time the condition of its impossibility. In the contemporary philosophy of memory, "preservationists" and "generationists" argue about the nature of this relation of remembering to the past; Bergson, for his part, is a virtual preservationist and an actual generationist.[20]

But what is this pure memory that is instantiated in, but irreducible to present memory-images? Like the memory-images to which it gives rise, it has no location in space. To ask where the past is stored is to ask the wrong question, for it supposes an answer that locates pure memory in space. Pure memory does not exist anywhere, but this is not to say that it does not exist at all. To think that because the past is no longer actual or present it no longer exists is to "define arbitrarily the present as *what is*, whereas the present is simply what *is being done* [*ce qui se fait*]" [MM 149–50/166]. This is perhaps a more natural thought in French than English, since in French the "actual" (a word deriving from the Latin *actus*, which relates to the verb *agere*, to act) is more obviously another name for the "present"; *actuellement* in French means "now", "right now", in contrast to the cognate English "actually" meaning "in fact".

With such a thought, Bergson criticises what the contemporary philosophy of time terms "presentism", which, as we saw in Chapter 2, is the view that only the present exists and that the past and future do not exist at all. His position resembles that of the "growing universe theorist", who argues that only the present and the past, which grows as time advances, have a claim to reality.[21] He sometimes writes, indeed, as if an expanded frame of reference would show that past and present have the same ontological status, as in the later essay "The Perception of Change":

> An attention which could be expanded indefinitely would hold under its gaze all the prior sentences with the last sentence of the lesson, and the events that have preceded the lesson, and a portion, as large as we choose, of what we call our past. The distinction which we make between our present and our past is, therefore, if not arbitrary, at least relative to the expanse of the field that our attention to life can embrace. [CM 179/169]

We are, however, not Gods. We are finite beings, with a limited range of attention, and we are thus stuck with the distinction between the past and the present. Hence *Matter and Memory* emphasises, in a different sense, that the past has a different ontological status to the present. It exists *virtually* rather than *actually*. In this sense, Bergson is concerned not simply with extending the list of things, beyond those in the present, that can enjoy the privilege of existence. He is concerned rather with the *mode* of existence of the past, as distinct from the mode of existence of the present, the actual. Bergson's reflection on time thus involves, however inchoately, a reflection on different *senses of being*, on being as virtual and being as actual.

Still, what exactly can be said of pure memory as virtual existence? Descartes resorted to the idea that memory is stored in physiological traces in the brain because he was unwilling to accept the survival of memories in the mind when they were not actively being recollected. Mind, for Descartes, is wholly transparent to itself, and so he had to reject any notion of unconscious memories, and, indeed, the notion of anything unconscious in the mind at all.[22] Bergson, in contrast, aims to challenge our unwillingness to accept "unconscious psychological states" [MM 141/156]. But what exactly can be said of these states if they are not available to consciousness? The problem is that the notion of planes of consciousness tells us nothing directly about the unconsciousness that is supposed to stand at one end of the spectrum as, precisely, a limit idea "never attained" [MM 168/187] in any experience, not even in dreams, for these involve a certain degree of consciousness. The difficulty here is more acute than it was in *Time and Free Will* where the task was to grasp the nature of time as duration without the refraction of spatialising forms of thought. At least there what the philosopher had to grasp was not in principle beyond consciousness. We should not be surprised that Bergson claims in 1908 that the "virtual existence" of the past can be described only "in a vague way, in metaphorical terms" [ME 165/136].

There are two fundamental issues here. First, it is not clear what is recorded from the past, and how it is recorded. Bergson writes that pure memory is "co-extensive with consciousness" and "retains and ranges alongside of each other all our states in the order in which they occur, leaving to each fact its place and consequently marking its date" [MM 151/168]. But what exactly could virtual "states" and "facts" be? Although Bergson does write once at the beginning of Chapter 2 of pure memory as the "image itself, envisaged in itself", his real thought, in the end, is that "everything must happen *as if* an independent memory gathered images as they successively occur along the course of time" [MM 77/81]. Bergson may have begun by understanding this "gathering" literally rather than metaphorically, but his discovery of pure memory is a discovery that the past cannot be gathered in the form of an image, since images are of space and belong to the present, whereas pure memory is not spatial and belongs to the past. It is precisely because pure memory is imageless that Bergson invokes it in his lectures to explain forms of remembering that occur without images [HTM 50]. Hence when in 1908 he writes that memory is a "mirror image [*une image en miroir*]" [ME 165/136] of perception, in underlining that memory is contemporaneous with perception and not subsequent to it (which, he argues, explains the experience of *déjà vu*), this has to be taken as a metaphor or analogy.

By what right, then, can we speak of "states" or "facts" here at all? Bergson recognises that "it is difficult to say" [HTM 132] exactly what pure memory contains. He is sometimes agnostic about whether memory contains all or just some of our past. Moreover, although he can talk, as above, of separable states and facts in memory, he also speaks of memory as an "indivisible whole", an "integral memory" [HTM 136]. In this latter sense, pure memory might constitute a whole from which individual memories derive by a kind of process of dissociation. This is how Bergson often describes the relation of the virtual to the actual elsewhere. To be sure, if memory does record states and facts, it risks traducing experience rather than merely recording it, given that temporal experience on Bergson's account is essentially continuous, and is precisely not composed of separable instants like the film reel is composed of stills. To add to this confusion concerning the nature of the pure past, Bergson sometimes writes of the base of his cone as constituted by dreams, but elsewhere recognises that it cannot be, for dreams are at least partially conscious; "I am not saying that in dreaming we are really placed at this extreme level; but it is quite probable that we approach it" [HTM 138].

A second problem concerns how memory returns in the present. *Matter and Memory* is unsure whether the virtual has any real power (and one meaning of the Latin *virtus* came to be "power"). The second chapter asked whether "perception mechanically determines the appearance of memories" or, on the contrary, "memories spontaneously carry themselves to the forefront of perception" [MM 99/108]. In the third chapter, he writes, on the one hand, that "the past is impotent" [MM 137/152], in contrast to the present, which is all consumed by action. This position would account for voluntary memory, where we search in the past by an intellectual effort. On the other hand, Bergson holds that "memory exerts forward pressure [*exerce une poussée en avant*] in order to insert into present action as much of itself as possible" [MM 168/187]. From this second perspective, the past cannot be described as "what by essence acts no longer", and the body's role in relation to it consists in acting as a kind of gatekeeper, letting some memories in and keeping most memories out. Pure memories are (and note that Bergson finds no particular difficulty in speaking of pure memories in the plural) "phantoms desiring materialization" [HTM 127], as Bergson puts it in his 1903–4 lectures, like Leibniz's "possibles" which strive for existence in the best of all possible worlds that is actually created by God. This dynamic notion of the virtual, according to which it tends towards its own realisation, allows us to understand involuntary memory as a function of memories that come back to us without our having sought them. This, of course, is what Proust's narrator in *In Search of Lost Time* experiences when his childhood comes flooding back to him on the occasion of eating a *madeleine*.

Summary

The guiding insight informing the development of Bergson's 1896 *Matter and Memory* is that there are degrees of consciousness, degrees of "attention to life". This insight was a result of *Time and Free Will*'s reflection on freedom and the self. Much of the difficulty of *Matter and Memory*, however, derives from the fact that here Bergson wants also to maintain the dualist idea that there is a difference in nature between mind and body, a difference in nature that he first justifies in distinguishing motor habit, which neuroscience supposes to be inscribed in physiological mechanisms, and episodic memory, which, he argues, does not have the same physiological basis. Although different in nature, motor habit stands at one end of a spectrum of different forms of memory, whereas pure memory, which stands at the other end of the spectrum, is by degrees involved in the intermediate forms of memory that Bergson discusses as different modes of recognition. Bergson rejects the theory of physiological memory traces as an explanation of episodic memory, and posits a "pure memory", which is constitutive of the essence of mind, in order to explain the quality of "pastness" in what we recollect. However, accounting for the nature of this spiritual past-in-itself and for how it returns into the present is a challenge, since in principle it precedes and escapes conscious reflection.

Notes

1 For something like this reconstruction of Bergson's development, see Camille Riquier, *Archéologie de Bergson*, pp. 311–15.
2 Henri Bergson, "Mémoire et reconnaissance", *Revue philosophique de la France et de l'étranger* 16 (1896), 225–48 and 16 (1896), 380–99.
3 Bergson, "Perception et matière", *Revue de métaphysique et de morale* 4 (1896), 257–79.
4 J. Chevalier, *Entretiens avec Bergson* (Paris: Plon, 1959), p. 35. On this point, see, as well as his monograph, Camille Riquier's introduction to his excellent "Dossier Critique" in the critical edition of *Matière et Mémoire* (Paris: Presses universitaires de France, 2012), p. 296.
5 Bertrand Russell, *The Philosophy of Bergson* 22/3 (1912), 321–47, p. 328.
6 See, for example, Ed Casey, "Habitual Body and Memory in Merleau-Ponty", *Man and World* 17 (1984), 279–97.

7 Félix Ravaisson, *Of Habit*, p. 55.

8 See my "Is Habit the Fossilised Residue of a Spiritual Activity?: Ravaisson, Bergson, Merleau-Ponty", *Journal of the British Society for Phenomenology* 42/1 (2011), 33–52.

9 See Maurice Merleau-Ponty, *The Phenomenology of Perception* (Abingdon: Routledge, 1962), p. 143, and Gilles Deleuze, *Difference and Repetition*, trans. P. Patton (London: Athlone, 1994), p. 73, where Deleuze criticises the "illusions of psychology": "[i]t asks how we acquire habits in acting, but the entire theory of learning risks being misdirected so long as the prior question is not posed—namely, whether it is through acting that we acquire habits".

10 Deleuze, *Bergsonism* (New York: Zone, 1991), p. 125, n.1. Deleuze, of course, is otherwise well aware of the connection between memory-contraction and a notion of habit.

11 Ravaisson, *Of Habit*, p. 53.

12 Victor Egger, "La Naissance des habitudes", *Annales de la facultéde lettres de Bordeaux* 1 (1880), 1–15, p. 1.

13 See Deleuze, *Difference and Repetition*, pp. 72–5, for an account of this passive synthesis, an account which does not acknowledge how much nineteenth-century French philosophy before Bergson knew of it.

14 Immanuel Kant, *Critique of Pure Reason*, pp. A141/B180–1.

15 Hughlings Jackson, "On Affections of Speech from Disease of the Brain", *Brain* 1/3 (1878), 304–30, p. 313; republished in *Brain* 38/1–2 (July 1915), 107–29, p. 114.

16 As André Robinet puts it, "[i]n removing this reference, Bergson covered his tracks [*brouillait les pistes*]. But, because he knew well this [Jackson's] work, his book was able to take on the aspect of a work of avant-garde science, and this made its fortune"; see André Robinet, "Le passage à la conception biologique de la perception de l'image et du souvenir chez Bergson", *Les Etudes philosophiques* 15(3) (1966), 375–88, p. 386.

17 Rupert Sheldrake, *The Science Delusion* (London: Coronet, 2012), p. 194.

18 See David Hume, *Treatise of Human Nature*, vol. 1: *The Text*, ed. David Fate Norton and Mary J. Norton (Oxford: Clarendon Press, 2007), Section 1.1.3.1.

19 Jankélévitch, *Henri Bergson*, p. 79/97.

20 See, for example, Kourken Michaelian and John Sutton's Stanford Encyclopedia entry on memory: https://plato.stanford.edu/entries/memory/.

21 See, for example, Ned Markosian's Stanford Encyclopedia entry on time: https://plato.stanford.edu/entries/time/.

22 For an account of Descartes on memory, see Richard Joyce, "Cartesian Memory", *Journal of the History of Philosophy* 35/3 (1997), 375–93.

Further reading

Henri Bergson, *Histoire des théories de la mémoire. Cours au Collège de France 1903–04* (Paris: Presses universitaires de France, 2018). An English translation of this lecture course is forthcoming.

Sven Bernecker and Kourken Michaelian (eds.), *The Routledge Handbook of Philosophy of Memory* (Abingdon: Routledge, 2017). An important sourcebook for the contemporary philosophy of memory, and a good place to start is the reliable entry on Bergson by Trevor Perri, pp. 510–18.

Félix Ravaisson, *Of Habit*, ed. C. Carlisle and M. Sinclair (London: Bloomsbury, 2008). This is Ravaisson's work on habit that was pivotal in nineteenth-century French philosophy.

Rupert Sheldrake, *The Science Delusion* (London: Coronet, 2012). See Chapter 7, "Are Memories Stored as Material Traces?", for a contemporary restatement of Bergson's critique of neuroscientific accounts of memory.

Five
Mind and world

From memory to perception

At the beginning of the preceding chapter, we noted that Bergson's train of thought in 1896 does not really begin with his account of pure perception in the first chapter of *Matter and Memory*. Although it may seem to fall from the skies, and to have no obvious foundations, that account is based on the notion of "image" developed within the analysis of memory in the second and third chapters of the text. It is on the basis of thinking about memory-images—and we should note the centrality of the term image in all the chapter headings of the book: "Of the Selection of Images"; "Of the Recognition of Images"; "Of the Survival of Images"; "The Delimiting and Fixing of Images"—that Bergson addresses the nature of "perceptual images", and thus comes to offer an account of perception and the perceived world.

By "perceptual image", Bergson means nothing more mysterious (although this is not to deny that there is something essentially mysterious about perception) than the things that I see in everyday experience, such as the coffee cup on the table right now before my eyes. The cup, in Bergson's terms, is a perceptual image. That he describes it as an image does not mean that he thinks it is somehow in my head, as the psychological reproduction of an extra-psychological reality. On the contrary, his denial that memory-images have a parallel in physical memory-traces stored in the brain leads him to deny that perceptual images are the psychological translation of more primitive or parallel neurological states. Perceptual images, such as the coffee cup on the table, he argues, are not in the brain, but out there in the world, exactly where they look like they are, and exactly where common sense thinks that they are. With this claim, Bergson is led into a critical engagement with idealist and realist positions in the traditional philosophy of perception. Such is the movement of Bergson's thought, a movement that seems to have taken him by surprise: "we little thought, at the beginning of our inquiries, that there could be any kind of connection between the analysis of memory and the question, which is debated between realists and idealists [...] with regard to the existence of matter" [MM 15–16/8]. The question of the existence of matter is the question of the possible existence of a material world existing independently or our representations of it. The first task in the present chapter is to assess the response Bergson provides to this question with his account of "pure perception". This account has often been found to be obscure, but it appears less so once we recognise that the fourth chapter of *Matter and Memory* not only lays some of its foundations, but also significantly develops his earlier position. After showing this, it will be possible to turn to his attempts in the final sections of the book, passages which are no less challenging than his arguments in the first chapter, to attenuate the problems of mind–body dualism.

Perception and the body

Bergson criticises "realist" positions in the philosophy of perception, but "realism" here denominates what contemporary philosophy terms, more specifically, *indirect* realism. According to indirect realism, there exist "things that produce representations in us but that would be of a different nature from these representations" [MM 9/1]. On this account, we perceive representations or sense-data in the mind, representations which are caused by things existing independently of us. These independently existing things are spatially extended whereas the mental representations are not; like the images we see at the cinema projected onto a screen, or the image of ourselves that we see in a mirror, mental representations as such only appear to be three-dimensional. The perception of depth, and the apparent perception we have of seeing things at a distance, is not the truth of experience, but, rather, a kind of psychological fiction, a trick of the mind. These mental representations possess what in the seventeenth century John Locke termed "secondary qualities" (e.g. colour and taste) whereas the former have just the "primary qualities" (e.g. shape, motion) that can be quantified and apprehended by, not just one, but a variety of senses.[1] In opposition to indirect realism, idealism, in essence, begins from mental representations and tries to account for the unity and structure of experience without positing independent things as their causes.

The notion of a perceptual image is, as Bergson puts it, one of "an existence placed half-way between the thing and the representation" [MM 9/1]. As an image, the coffee cup before me is not a thing, for it is not something behind, as it were, my representations and that causes them. Nor is it a representation, for it is not the representation of such an independently existing thing. In this way, Bergson wants to challenge both realism and idealism by accommodating two conflicting intuitions of common sense. On the one hand, before we engage with natural science or philosophy, it seldom occurs to us to doubt that we see things as they really are, and to suppose that we see merely secondary representations of them. On the other hand, ordinarily we tend not to think that the existence of things depends on us, such that they would no longer exist when I am not perceiving them. For common sense, "the object exists in itself and yet the object is, in itself, pictorial, just as we perceive it; it is an image, but an image that exists in itself" [MM 10/2].

Here in the Introduction, Bergson claims that "this is precisely the sense in which we take the word image in the first chapter" [MM 10/2]. The idea of an "image in itself" may risk a contradiction in terms, but in order to avoid the most extreme consequences of an idealist position, and thus in order to accommodate the common-sense postulate that things do not rely on us for their existence, Bergson wants to assert the independence of his images from any actual perception. An image "may be without being perceived" [MM 35/32], as he writes in rejecting the dictum of the eighteenth-century idealist philosopher George Berkeley, according to which esse est percipii, to be is to be perceived.[2] That said, the unperceived image has only a relative independence from the perceiver, particularly in that when we think of the matter of the universe we still think in terms of an

image: "reduce matter to atoms in motion: these atoms, though
denuded of physical qualities, are determined only in relation to
an eventual vision and an eventual contact, the one without light
and the other without materiality […] they are still images" [MM
35/31]. In this respect, Bergson is closer to Berkeley. He accepts, in
effect, Berkeley's objection to Locke that it is not possible even to
imagine something without secondary qualities such as colour.[3] He
thereby accepts the claim that secondary qualities are as primitive
as primary qualities and thus equally intrinsic to the nature of what
there is.

We will see below that this notion of images in themselves is not
Bergson's considered and final position concerning the existence of
matter. Bergson's primary objective in the first chapter, however, is to
advance a kind of *direct realism* that accommodates the common-sense
view that we perceive "things" as they are in the world beyond us. The
indirect realist claim that we first perceive a two-dimensional image
that is projected as the appearance of three-dimensional perception
cannot explain how the projection occurs, and, Bergson argues, it
presupposes what it attempts to explain, namely a notion of exteriority, for the mind must already have an understanding of this in
order to project the representations onto it [MM 23/18]. Moreover,
Bergson attacks the role that indirect realist theories ascribe to the
brain. Claims that the brain gives rise to representations of the world
harbour a contradiction, at least if they begin from idealist prem-
ises: if we accept that everything in the world as it is present to me
is in some sense an image or representation, the brain being one
of those images (if my skull is opened up, at least), and if we also
accept that the brain produces the representations we have of the
world, such that the images of the wider world are within it, then
we are saying that one image *in* the world, the brain, has at the same
time all the images in the world *within* it [MM 23/18]. The whole
would thus be in the part, as well as the part in the whole, which
is absurd. Bergson finds the most acute expression of this contradictory position in the first pages of Schopenhauer's *The World as Will
and Representation* [HTM 330]. Of course, without an idealist notion
of "representations", or Bergson's notion of images, the problem
is simply that the indirect realist dogmatically affirms, without
any genuine epistemological warrant, a mind-independent world

containing causally connected extended brains and bodies while denying at the same time that we experience that world directly and thus that we can know anything directly of it.

However, if the body with the brain is not something capable of producing representations of the world, what exactly is it? What is the body's role in perception if it is true that I see things where they are, beyond me? Like any direct realist, Bergson has to qualify, if not wholly reject, a now orthodox intromission theory of perception, according to which perception consists in something, namely light, coming from an external object or a point of it (let's call that point P) into the eyes in such a way as to produce a mental representation. For Bergson, "the truth is that the point P, the rays which it emits, the retina and the nervous elements affected, form a single whole; that the luminous point P is a part of this whole; and it is really in P, and not elsewhere, that the image of P is formed and perceived" [MM 43/41]. Perception is more like a circuit than a linear process, and in this circuit, my body does not serve to represent P but to perceive it where it is, outside of and beyond my body itself. The retinal image—which even the indirect realist has to admit we do not perceive directly (since there are two of them, whereas ordinarily we do not have "double vision", and since signals have to pass subsequently through the optic nerve and brain)—is just one moment in the circuit. The body has afferent, "centripetal" nerves, and these seem to transmit movement from the external world into the brain, but it also has efferent, "centrifugal" nerves that transmit movement from the brain to the extremities of the body. These efferent nerves, Bergson reasons, are what complete the circuit of perception: there must be a kind of movement in perception that brings the circuit back out to point P, and the efferent nerves are the means by which this movement is transmitted. Of course, the efferent nerves stretch only as far as the skin, but Bergson reasons that they are what send back the movement transmitted to the thing beyond us, such that we can see it exactly where it is.

On this account, the operation of the efferent nerves, and thus motor activity, is essential to the act of perception; "my nervous system, interposed between the objects that affect my body and those which I can influence, is a mere conductor, transmitting, sending back or inhibiting movement" [MM 45/42]. The brain is more like an old-fashioned telephone switchboard transmitting signals, as Bergson famously puts it, rather than something that can give birth to a representation. In order to entertain this theory, we have to stop thinking of vision as operating like the sense of touch. We cannot feel things at a distance, of course, but we can, Bergson contends, see them at a distance, exactly where they are, out there in the world. To be sure, he does not say exactly how movement in the circuit of perception is transmitted back from the periphery of the body to the externally perceived thing, and in this sense his theory can appear sketchy. But if Bergson's theory is sketchy, all forms of direct realism suffer from the same defect, since experience does not show us *how* it is that I see things beyond me. Experience just shows, putting intromission theories of vision to one side for a moment, *that* I see things beyond me. Even if one might prefer their less physiological approach to the nature of perceptual experience, philosophers in the twentieth-century phenomenological tradition advancing notions of "intentionality" or "transcendence" are not really in a stronger position in this regard, since they suppose a kind of intellectual action at a distance as a primitive, inexplicable given.

Bergson's approach is, indeed, physiological, the expression of a peculiar form of biological metaphysics. He presents the operation of the body in perception as, in principle, wholly independent of memory, mind and any spiritual principle. Although, in actual fact, perceptual experience is always overladen with memory-images, there exists a "pure perception" on the basis of which memory comes into operation. Memory provides the subjective aspects of perception, whereas the operation of the biological, "living body [*le corps vivant*]" [MM 44/43] provides their objective base. Conscious life and conscious perception arrive with the increasing complication of motor mechanisms established in the body, which allow for a wider variety of responses to situations, for more physiological indetermination, and for memory and thus mind to intervene. The "increasing complexity" of the nervous system, as Bergson will put it much later in the text:

> seems to leave an increasingly large latitude to the activity of the living being, the capacity to wait before reacting, and to relate the stimulus received to a richer and richer variety of motor

mechanisms. But this is only the outside, and the more complex organization of the nervous system, which seems to assure
greater independence to the living being with regards to matter,
is only a material symbol of this very independence, and that is
to say, the inner force that allows being to escape the flowing
rhythm of things, to retain better and better the past to influence
more and more profoundly the future. [MM 222/249]

Bergson does not quite say that increasingly mechanical complication in an organism *produces* or *causes* the power of hesitation and
choice which seems to shape—more and more as one "ascends"
the scale of the variety of its forms—animal life. Increasing
mechanical complication is merely the material symbol of the
spiritual force, grounded in memory, that is the real, spiritual
principle of the increasing independence of the animal from the
material world.

From this account of the body in perception, Bergson draws two
further inferences. First, he advances a kind of pragmatist theory
of perception. From his supposition that perception is a function
of the efferent nerves and thus motor activity, he infers that what
the living body perceives is a function of its practical orientation
and purposes: "*the objects which surround my body reflect its possible action
upon them*" [MM 21/16]. Bergson thus moves from the claim that
bodily activity is involved in perception to the claim that perception itself is always a function of practical, biological need. The first
claim does not obviously entail the second, and Bergson does little
to show that it does. We can accept that sense perception is not the
entirely passive reception of an external object, particularly after
having read Bergson's account of the role of memory in perception,
while denying that we always see things as a function of *biologically*
driven purposes. The thesis is not entailed by Bergson's preceding
claims, and what it itself entails may even seem to contradict them.
For the thesis entails that the images encountered in pure perception do not present the truth of what there is. The thesis entails that
there is a more fundamental aspect of reality prior to its perceptual
apprehension.

Indeed, Bergson goes on to account for the relation between
the image pragmatically perceived, and the material world before

I perceived it. He reasons, and this is his second inference, that if there were *more* in the perception than in the image prior to its being perceived, "the passage from matter to perception would remain wrapped in an impenetrable mystery" [MM 36/32]. Consequently, he supposes that there is *less* in the "represented image" than in the "present image" (the image as it is prior to my perception of it). Perception, as a function of biologically driven concerns, apprehends only what interests it in the world, and thus subtracts from the positivity of that pre-given world: "if living beings are […] just 'centres of indetermination', and if the degree of this determination is measured by the number and rank of their functions, we can conceive that their mere presence is equivalent to the suppression of all those parts of objects in which their functions find no interest". Bergson describes, in fact, a world of a kind of universal interaction which obliges an individual image "to act through every one of its points upon all the points of all other images, to transmit the whole of what it receives, to oppose to every action an equal and contrary reaction, to be, in short, merely a road by which pass, in every direction, the modifications propagated throughout the immensity of the universe" [MM 36/33]. Prior to my perception of it, the world is constituted by a kind of universal interaction. When perception occurs on this basis, it reflects back to an object some of its aspects, and thus isolates some of the aspects in it.

Matter as motion

We might fear that in these passages of the first chapter, which are among the most speculative to which Bergson put his name, "we find only an ingenious construction",[4] as one commentator put it in 1902, rather than a convincing interpretation of experience. Ingenuity is not always the greatest virtue in a philosopher. It is necessary, however, to turn to the fourth chapter of *Matter and Memory* in order to grasp the foundations of Bergson's constructions in the first and in order also to recognise that what he wrote there concerning "images in themselves", in taking up the view of common sense, is not his final position.

In the fourth chapter, he explains his notion of universal interaction in the material world by noting that what "science has placed beyond dispute" is the "reciprocal action of all parts of matter upon each other" by means of an idea of force: "between the supposed molecules of bodies, the forces of attraction and repulsion are at work. The influence of gravitation extends throughout interplanetary space" [MM 200/225]. Science had discovered forces like gravity acting at a distance throughout nature, but Bergson goes on to argue that the notion of that on which these forces supposedly act, namely atoms, has more of a use-value than a positive truth-value, and is just an expression of our pragmatically oriented grasp of the world.

> The preservation of life no doubt requires that we should distinguish, in our daily experience, between passive *things* and *actions* effected by those things in space. As it is useful to us to fix the seat of the *thing* at the precise point where we might touch it, its palpable outlines become for us its real limit, and we then see in its *action* a something, I know not what, which, being altogether different, can part company with it. [MM 200/224]

The distinction of atoms and forces is thus a version of our tendency to isolate, as we saw in Chapter 2 above, an unchanging thing from its multiple momentary states when analysing the durational movement of the self. Common sense supposes, a supposition to which David Hume gave clear voice, that "the idea of motion necessarily supposes that of a body moving".[5] Bergson, in contrast, considers that this presupposition, together with the doctrine of atomism to which it gives rise, has a pragmatic, practical origin.

Moreover, he sensed that the development of the sciences was bringing it increasingly into question.

> We see force and matter drawing nearer together the more deeply the physicist has penetrated into their effects. We see force more and more materialized, the atom more and more idealized, the two terms converging toward a common limit and the universe thus recovering its continuity. We may still speak of atoms; the atom may even retain its individuality for our mind which isolates it, but the solidity and the inertia of the atom dissolve either into movements or into lines of force

whose reciprocal solidarity brings universal continuity back to us. [MM 200/224–5]

An ontology of unchanging, discontinuous and essentially inert things changing position according to relations of force which act upon them from the outside is dissolving in the development of the sciences, Bergson suggests, into an ontology of vibratory movements and lines of force showing up against a background of universal continuity. Bergson now claims, as Čapek puts it well, that the "concept of immutable, material substance is just as illegitimate as that of immutable, mental subject. The immutable particles in physics are just as fictitious as the mental atoms of Hume [...] in psychology".[6] Bergson, as we saw in Chapters 2 and 3 above, had criticised associationism as a doctrine of mental atomism in *Time and Free Will*, but now he criticises physical atomism also. If it is true that Hume's associationist "science of man" was modelled on Newton's physics,[7] Bergson now attacks the physical model after having attacked its psychological offshoot. We should conceive, he argues, matter as motion, rather than as occasionally in motion.

Remarkably, Bergson advanced these ideas decades before wave mechanics, for example, and the discovery of the materialisation and dematerialisation of "particles" in quantum physics. As he stated later, "[w]hen I began to write" *Matter and Memory* "physics had not yet made the decisive advances which were to bring a change in its ideas on the structure of matter. But convinced, even then, that immobility and invariability were only views taken of moving and changing reality, I could not believe that matter, whose solid image had been obtained through the immobilization of changes [...] was composed of solid elements" [CM 84/76]. The passages of the fourth chapter concerning matter, as Čapek has it, initially "appeared, in contrast to the prevailing classical picture of the physical world, so grotesquely improbable, that they were largely ignored."[8] They were confirmed, however, by developments in physics, and already by 1911 Bergson could assert confidently:

the more it [modern science] progresses, the more it resolves matter into actions moving through space, into movements dashing back and forth in a constant vibration so that mobility becomes reality itself. No doubt science begins by assigning a support to this mobility. But as it advances, the support recedes; masses are pulverised into molecules, molecules into atoms, atoms into electrons or corpuscles; finally the support assigned to movement appears merely as a convenient schema—*a simple concession of the scientist to the habits of our visual imagination.* [CM 175/165]

Atomism is merely a concession to our habitual modes of thought, an expression of our natural tendency to think by means of pictures and images. In contrast, Bergson's own "theory of matter is an attempt to find the reality hidden beneath these customary images which are entirely relative to our needs, from these images it must first of all set itself free" [MM 200/224].

This rejection of customary images and the habits of our visual imagination can be taken in two ways. First, we might take Bergson to demand a *better* image of the natural world, but this interpretation is hardly licensed by the fact that the term "image" is employed almost exclusively pejoratively in the fourth chapter. Instead, it seems that Bergson's true thought is one that dismisses the suggestions of the first chapter concerning "images in themselves": the image is the meeting point of consciousness and the world, certainly, but matter in itself is pre-imagistic.[9] Recall that when, in the first chapter of *Matter and Memory*, Bergson claimed that if we think of the material world existing independently of us we have to think of it in terms of an image, he conceived of matter as atomistic; "reduce matter to atoms in motion: these atoms, though denuded of physical qualities, are determined only in relation to an eventual vision and an eventual contact, the one without light and the other without materiality [...] they are still images" [MM 35/31]. This atomistic conception of matter is, as we have just seen, precisely what he rejects in the fourth chapter. Hence it seems that just as he had come to recognise that pure memory is not imagistic, so too he arrives at the— comparable, if not exactly parallel—thought that pure perception operates on a non-imagistic basis. Thus understood, Bergson urges us to recognise that the "book of nature", to use the age-old metaphor, is not at bottom a picture-book, and that it cannot be grasped adequately by the faculty of the mind that is the imagination. This position, perhaps, does not sit easily with Bergson's claim that there is only a difference in degree between matter and images perceived, a claim that he repeats in the fourth chapter; "we seize in the act of perception, something which outruns perception itself, although the material universe is not essentially different or distinct from the representation we have of it" [MM 208/343]. But perhaps we can conceive of matter as pre-imagistic by degree; and even if we cannot, it is not obvious that we would thus introduce, despite Bergson's worries, intractable mysteries. Perceived images would just be what occur when the animal body encounters the pre-existing and pre-imagistic material world.

The idea of "images in themselves", then, was an idea that Bergson borrows from common sense and then *destroys* in the course of his analysis. Still, we might consider, following Merleau-Ponty in 1947–8, that with this talk of a pre-existing material world, Bergson has not avoided falling back into a crude, dogmatic realist position.[10] This would be a legitimate response if Bergson said nothing more on the issue, but the fourth chapter of *Matter and Memory* will show, as we will see in the following section, that this pre-existing material world already belongs to spirit, even though it is prior to any representative perception.

Rhythms of duration

As we have seen, the first chapter of *Matter and Memory* is concerned with pure perception, while the second and third chapters lead to the discovery of pure memory. Pure perception and pure memory are different in nature, different in principle, even though they work together, and even though each is never found without the other, in experience. In the fourth chapter, however, Bergson addresses the problem of the "union of mind and body", and thus the union of memory and perception, by claiming that the earlier chapters allow us to grasp "if not a means for resolving the problem, at least a side from which to approach it" [MM 180/200]. This, if one had not read the preface to the book, would come as a surprise. It is not obvious how separating mind and body as different in nature can provide grounds for a response to the problem of mind–body dualism. Hence even Jankélévitch, one of Bergson's most eloquent and resourceful advocates, admits that the pages in the fourth chapter where this is attempted "are among the most obscure and the most embarrassing of his entire *œuvre*".[11]

The "obscurity" and intractability of the mind–body problem, Bergson writes, "derives from the fact that the dualist hypothesis considers matter as essentially divisible and every state of mind as rigorously without extension, in such a way that one begins by cutting the communication between the two terms" [MM 220/ 248]. Once we separate, in a Cartesian fashion, the mind understood as *res cogitans*, thinking substance, from spatial things as *res extensa*, we have "inextension and quality on one side, and quantity and extension on the other" [MM 220/248]. According to an opposition that still structured *Time and Free Will*, everything "in" the mind (nothing really is in the mind, because it is not spatial) is quality without quantity (for quantification is spatialisation, as we saw in Chapter 2), whereas everything in space is quantifiable and without the qualities that are irreducible to quantities. This produces an apparently insoluble problem, insofar as we have supposed that there are "no degrees, no possible transition" between them. But Bergson's account of the actualisation of memories in perception has shown that there is, indeed, a "gradual passage from the idea to the image and from the image to sensation" and that "the more that it evolves towards actuality, towards action, the more the state of mind approaches extension" [MM 220/248]. Pure memory can be actualised all the way down in the extended perceptual image itself, according to a spectrum where memory shades into perception, a spectrum on which we cannot say where perception begins and memory ends. It is the discovery of this continuum of planes of consciousness, then, of degrees of attention to life, that leads Bergson to think that he has a response to the mind–body problem.

For this response to be successful, Bergson has to show that there is a possible transition between, first, the dichotomy of extension and inextension. The task, in fact, is to show that the spatiality of the perceived world "once reached, remains undivided and is thus not out of harmony with the unity of the soul" [MM 220/248], that the space in which things appear is not antithetical to the mind. Bergson argues that because memory images are always actualised in perceptual experience, because subjective qualities constitute the reality of the perceived world, "material extension [*étendue*] is not and can no longer be" a mathematical space; it is no longer "that composite extensity [*extensité multiple*] of which the geometer speaks" [MM 182/ 202]. Kant supposed that infinitely divisible, geometrical space, which is homogeneous in that any of its sections is like any other, is an *a priori*, necessary condition of the possibility of any experience whatsoever. Bergson argues, and he had already suggested this in *Time and Free Will*, that homogeneous geometrical space is a conceptual abstraction from a more primitive, immediately experienced spatiality. Homogeneous space arises as the work of "solidification and division that we effect on the moving continuity of the real in order to obtain within it starting points for our operation, in short, to introduce into it real changes"; it is merely a "schema of our *action* on matter" [MM 211/237]. The idea of homogeneous space is simply an expression and development of our ordinary biologically driven, pragmatic concerns. As the ground of modern mathematical physics, it certainly helps us to become, as Descartes put it, "masters and possessors of nature", but it is not a primary truth. The primary truth is that duration resides in things (as Bergson had already recognised, perhaps reluctantly, in *Time and Free Will*) and that this makes possible their movement in a pre-mathematical, *indivisible* space. As soon as we have analysed the space the mobile traverses as constituted by discrete, homogeneous points, just as soon as we have analysed the time it takes to move as consisting of distinct temporal moments, we are no longer dealing with a movement but rather with its symbolic representation as a succession of static points. "*All movement, as a passage from one point of rest to another, is absolutely indivisible*" [MM 188/209], indivisible in space, as well as in time, as Bergson now claims. Since it is indivisible, Bergson argues, this space is no longer quite as antithetical to the temporal mind as is homogeneous space.

In itself, this notion of a lived spatiality and of duration forming the horizon of worldly events is not a significant departure from *Time and Free Will*. However, Bergson's response to the second dichotomy, that between quality and quantity, does represent a significant departure from his earlier work. He aims to reduce "the difference between the heterogeneous qualities that succeed each other in our concrete perception and the homogeneous changes that science puts behind these perceptions in space" [MM 182/ 203]. Science explains the heterogeneous qualities of the perceived world by invoking homogeneous changes supposedly occurring in a world independent of our perception of it; the colour blue, from this perspective, is a certain frequency of a light-wave emitted from an external source (which has in itself no colour), which is received by the eye and transmitted to the brain by the optic nerve. Bergson now wants to lessen this difference between the perceived quality and the scientifically determined quantity, between what Wilfred Sellars called the "manifest image" (things as they appear) and the "scientific image" (the matter in motion that science describes) of the world.[12]

In one sense, Bergson does not have to do this. Like much of the later phenomenological tradition, he could argue that the scientific explanation of colour perception in terms of a quantifiable frequency of light-waves is a theory rather than a fact; a theory that can never, however useful it may otherwise be, explain the abyss, the absolute difference separating the experience of "qualia"— the quality of, say, this blue—from the movement of colourless light-waves. In fact, the first chapter of *Tine and FreeWill* was concerned to protect the psychological domain from any intrusion of quantification. There, as we saw in Chapter 2, he criticised the traditional hybrid notion of "intensive magnitudes" (according to which psychological qualities are intrinsically orderable, such that it is meaningful to say that I am happier now that I was last year, even though they are qualities not quantities), and this to the point where it sometimes seemed like he was rejecting the very idea that psychological states have an intrinsic intensity.[13] Bergson, however, now considers it necessary to reconcile quality and quantity on the grounds that if the quantitative "elements are external to the qualities of which they are meant to explain the regular order, they can no longer render the service demanded of them, because then the qualities must be supposed to come to overlie them by a kind of miracle" [MM 205/230]. In order for science not to be vitiated by reliance on something inexplicable, namely the passage from quantity to quality, we have "to put these movements in these qualities, as a form of internal vibration, to consider these vibrations as less homogeneous and these qualities as less heterogeneous than they appear to be superficially" [MM 205/230]. This is a clear and pivotal instance of the later Bergson's concern to reconcile science and philosophy. He argues that there is no difference in nature between the experienced colour and the movements because light works like sound. Just as we can hear and see the chord in a piano vibrate while we hear its sound, we could see the vibrations of light were we able to contract all of them together in a single duration. Each one of the millions of vibrations requires a before and after, and thus duration, in order to be a movement; but in our less condensed and less tense experience of duration we are unable to grasp it. "If we could stretch out this duration, that is to say, live it at a slower rhythm, should we not, as the rhythm slowed down, see these colours pale and lengthen into successive impression, still coloured no doubt, but nearer and nearer to coincidence with pure vibrations?" [MM 203/228] The scientist may find curious Bergson's affirmation that the light-wave is coloured, but this is an interesting hypothesis, and could well help, if it is in any way convincing, to reconcile the manifest and the scientific image of the world.

With this attempt to reconcile quantity and quality, Bergson is led to the thought, a thought whose difficulty he recognises, that existence is constituted by a plurality of rhythms, or as he otherwise puts it, a plurality of tensions of duration.

> In reality, there is not one unique rhythm of duration; one can imagine many different rhythms, which, slower or faster, would measure the degree of tension or relaxation of consciousness, and would thereby fix their respective places in the series of beings. This representation of durations of unequal elasticity is perhaps painful for our minds to entertain, because our minds have contracted the useful habit of substituting a homogeneous and independent time for the real duration experienced by consciousness. [MM 207/232]

The point is no longer simply that movements in the material world occur within the horizon of my own duration insofar as I perceive them. The point is rather that all movement requires some degree of contraction of the present in the past, and that the undulating movement of light occurs at a rate that I can never perceive or contract myself. According to the low tension of my duration, in a genuinely free action I can contract the whole of my past life, whereas the undulation of the light-wave occurs in tiny, for me unnotice-able, fractions of a second. The light-wave undulates according to a different rhythm or tension of duration than mine, and thus we cannot account for it solely in terms of my own experience of dur-ation. Bergson admits that we will struggle to conceive this because we are used to thinking of time as a homogeneous medium, as an invisible framework indifferent to the processes that occur within it, but we are called to recognise that duration has different rhythms, different degrees of contraction of the past, degrees that are nested within each other.[14] Does this mean that there are many different durations in the world rather than one? Although Bergson does occasionally speak in that way, his genuine thought seems to be that there is one duration that is itself the potential multiplicity of an infinity of different levels of contraction and tension, and that these levels are but the different planes of consciousness exposed earlier in *Matter and Memory*.[15]

This reconciliation of science and metaphysics implies a form of panpsychism that may not be music to the scientist's ears: if things have their own tension of duration, and the different tensions of duration are a function of the different planes of consciousness, then things have their own form, however minimal it may be, of con-sciousness. On this hypothesis, the matter that "in the act of per-ception [...] surpasses perception itself" [MM 208/233] is still a function of mind and consciousness, even if it is not a reflective, self-aware consciousness. It is for this reason that Bergson's claim that perception arises as a subtraction from a pre-given world does not amount to a dogmatic materialist realism. If it is a realism, his position is a panpsychic, spiritualist realism: the world that pre-exists my perception of it is a tensed, minimally conscious world of duration.

Mind and body united?

In this light, we can approach Bergson's claim that "*questions relative to the subject and to the object, to their distinction and to their union, should be put in terms of time rather than space*" [MM 71/74]. There is a continuum of intensities of duration that, he argues, underlies the distinction of pure memory (the subject) and pure perception (the object).

Matter and Memory does not go as far in this direction as it might—not as far as *Creative Evolution*, at any rate. Rather than attempting to account for or explain degrees of spatial extension by the *ex-tension* or relaxation of duration, as he will in 1907, here Bergson remains with a certain parallel between them: "by the idea of *tension* we have striven to overcome the opposition between quality and quantity, just as, by the idea of *extension*, that between the inextended and the extended. Extension and tension admit of degrees, multiple but always determined" [MM 247/278]. Let us note in advance that in order to interpret extension in terms of the tension and ex-tension of duration, Bergson will have to invert—in a manner that threatens the coherence of his philosophy in its development—the position of *Matter and Memory* according to which our memories "adopt a more banal form when memory is the more contracted, more personal when it is dilated" [MM 167/188]. Here contraction seems to be on the side of matter, while dilation is on the side of memory (although Bergson might not be wholly consistent on this issue), but *Creative Evolution*, as Chapter 9 shows, will claim that the opposite is the case. Consequently, Bergson's interpretation of dreams will be transformed: rather than approaching the excellence of pure mind, the dilation of dreams amounts to a descent into material dispersion.

But how do the claims of *Matter and Memory* concerning tension and extension help us with the mind–body problem? Bergson's position is far from unambiguous. In one sense, he wants only to show "that spirit can rest upon matter and, consequently, unite with it in the act of pure perception, yet nevertheless be radically distinct from it" [MM 220/248]. Union here is not the mind–body union that Descartes, in his non-dualist moments, opposed to both mind and body as a third, *sui generis*, ontological category that cannot be explained by either of the other two. Bergson "leaves to one side the theories that are content to state the 'union of soul and body' as an irreducible and inexplicable fact" [MM 11/4]. Union with the body, for Bergson, means rather working with and "resting upon" matter. In this sense, Bergson does not have to choose between mind–body union or mind–body dualism; all he wants to do is to make more intelligible how mind can interact with body, and he claims to have done so in showing that one cannot say where one begins and the other ends. Thus, "on the first hypothesis, the one that conceives of the difference between body and mind in spatial terms, body and soul are like two railway lines that cut across one another at right angles; in the second, the rails line up with one another on a curve, so that one can pass from one track to the other imperceptibly" [MM 222/250].

In another sense, however, Bergson wants to do more and *has to* do more than this. He is aware that in order to respond adequately to the problem of dualism, the most fundamental conceptual opposition he has to deconstruct is that of freedom and necessity, as we saw in concluding Chapter 3. We have no real hope of adopting a meaningfully non-dualist position if we remain with an opposition of the freedom of spirit and the necessity of matter. The very last passages of the "Summary and Conclusion" that follow the fourth chapter, and that thus form the final passages of the book as a whole, are devoted to this question, and here Bergson shows that he still belongs in 1896, though not as its most faithful student, to the French "school of contingency".

Boutroux's 1874 *On the Contingency of the Laws of Nature* had concluded with the claim that the necessity in natural processes is merely apparent and no real necessity at all.[16] In prolonging his Boutrouxian critique in 1889 of the principle of the conservation of energy, Bergson now asks whether in a physical process "each moment can be mathematically deduced from the preceding moment", and thus whether everything happens because it has to, just as the pistons rise in a car engine because they are made to rise without fail by the ignition of petrol. He answers thus:

> [w]e have throughout this work, and for the convenience of the study, supposed that it was really so; and such is, in fact the distance between the rhythm of our duration and that of the flow of things, that the contingency of the course of nature, so profoundly studied in recent philosophy, must, for us, be practically equivalent to necessity. So let us keep to our hypothesis, though it might have to be attenuated. [MM 248/279]

Bergson is clearly referring to Boutroux here, and his position is close to that of *On the Contingency of the Laws of Nature*. For Bergson, nature operates according to a principle that is *practically equivalent* to necessity, but which is not *theoretically*, i.e. in truth, necessity itself; the idea of a necessity in things was adopted merely for the *convenience of the study*. The notion that the physical world operates mechanically is merely a working hypothesis that, as Bergson states in concluding his lectures on memory in 1903–4, and in announcing his course on human freedom for the following academic year, is an *a priori*, metaphysical theory rather than any kind of empirical fact [HTM 337]. The "natural atmosphere of the intelligence is necessity" [EPL 99], as Bergson will say in those lectures on freedom; the human mind is somehow naturally inclined to think about things mechanistically. This does not, however, imply that mechanism is a primitive truth of the material world.

Now, given that the form of necessity operative in nature in the classical scientific paradigm is a mechanical necessity, Bergson is admitting here, to return to an issue that we raised in Chapter 4 above, that his mechanical conception of habit and the body earlier in *Matter and Memory* was a *mere hypothesis*, and *not even his own*. But that hypothesis does not and cannot conform to his Boutrouxian insight that there are degrees of elasticity in things, which he interprets as degrees of tension in the rhythms of duration in which all things partake. The absolute inflexibility that we ordinarily understand by the terms "mechanical necessity" is, of course, as little a degree of elasticity as death is a degree of life. Necessity, and it is important to recognise this, admits no degrees; something is either necessary or it is not. This entails that if Bergson genuinely intends to provide a compelling response to the problem of mind–body dualism by overcoming the opposition of freedom and necessity, he will have to reject the mechanical account of habit presented earlier in the book. By the same token, he will have to reject the account of pure perception presented in its first chapter, if that account is supposed to reveal the thoughtless and mechanical base or bedrock of all perceptual experience. "Pure perception", that is, has to be something other than a mechanistic realm on which the infinite degrees of duration as memory are posed if Bergson is to provide an adequate response to the problem of dualism.

However, if pure perception is no longer a dead mechanism (it was, after all, supposed to be the realm of the "living body"), and involves a degree of consciousness, then it is not pure. If we think in this direction, we have to reject the idea of pure perception *tout court*. Bergson's claim that pure perception exists "rather in theory [*en droit*] than in fact" [MM 218–19/246], it is important to note, can be taken in two ways. It can mean either that pure perception forms, as we have just said, the ever-present basis of perceptual experience, a basis that is always accompanied by memory. Or it could mean that pure perception does not exist at all, that it is a mere *ens rationis*, a mere hypothesis, an extrapolation from the fact that degrees of memory are instantiated in actual perceptual experience all the way down into matter. Bergson might seem to begin from the first interpretation and then move towards the second. We might wonder, consequently, whether in the course of *Matter and Memory* Bergson has destroyed the idea of pure perception, just as he destroyed the idea of "images in themselves". In this second sense, once Bergson has discovered that duration inhabits the material world, we might suppose, following Čapek, that he has to "show to what extent the structure of the physical world *approaches* the world of classical physics", with its "strict determinism", "without, however, coinciding with it".[17]

The ambiguity in Bergson's position, however, remains in the crucial, final paragraph of *Matter and Memory*. Bergson is non-commital: he wants to defend and maintain the necessitarian hypothesis, on the one hand, while recognising that it is merely a hypothesis, and also while somehow attenuating it, on the other. The contradictory nature of this gesture becomes obvious when he states his intention to maintain the mechanical hypothesis while admitting that the physical world "might be regarded as a latent consciousness" [MM 248/279]. It is far from obvious how a supposedly wholly dead, mechanical thing such as the car engine can be conceived as a latent consciousness. In *Matter and Memory*, one might say, Bergson wants to have his cake and eat it; in one sense, he supports a mechanistic philosophy, and, in another sense, he does not. In the light of this contradiction, claims that he has somehow solved, resolved or dissolved the mind–body problem in *Matter and Memory* appear over-enthusiastic, and not to have seen the real extent of the problem. Four years later, however, in reflecting on the nature of laughter and the comic, Bergson will begin to attenuate further this contradiction by adopting more clearly—but how much he does so is debatable—the vitalist and anti-mechanistic ideas about nature advanced by Boutroux and Ravaisson before him.

Summary

With his account of images and pure perception in the first chapter of *Matter and Memory*, Bergson offers a direct realist position that accommodates the common-sense belief that we see things as they are in the world beyond us. However, Bergson also advances an idea of the perceiving, living body as dissociating its "images" of the world from a pre-given reality; there is less not more in our "images" of the world than in the world itself. According to the fourth chapter of *Matter and Memory*, this pre-given reality is not an "image in itself", as the first chapter had supposed; pure perception is pre-imagistic, just as pure memory is pre-imagistic. This pre-imagistic truth is matter not just *in* motion but *as* motion, which is a function of duration. With his notion of rhythms of duration, Bergson argues that matter in this sense is a degree of mind and consciousness. This approach could certainly help to think beyond modern mind–body dualism, but Bergson does not apply it consistently, since in the final passage of the book he seems reluctant to renounce the mechanistic conception of the material world that had informed his account of motor habit in the first chapter.

Notes

1 On this issue, the uninitiated can refer to William Uzgalis' Stanford Encyclopedia entry on Locke: https://plato.stanford.edu/entries/locke/.

2 For more detail, see Lisa Downing's Stanford Encylopedia entry on Berkeley: https://plato.stanford.edu/entries/berkeley/.

3 George Berkeley, *A Treatise Concerning the Principles of Human Knowledge* (Oxford: Oxford University Press, 1998), §10.

4 P.-L. Couchoud, "La métaphysique nouvelle, 'Matière et Mémoire' de Bergson", *Revue de métaphysique et de morale* X (1902), 225–43, p. 229. Bergson seems to respond directly to Couchoud's claim that *Matter and Memory* is based on "hypo-thetical constructions" [CM 105/ 97] in concluding the Introduction to *The Creative Mind*, but not in a way that is particularly enlightening for us.

5 David Hume, *Treatise on Human Nature* IV, 4. See, in this connection, Čapek, *Bergson and Modern Physics*, p. 273.

6 Milič Čapek, *Bergson and Modern Physics*, p. 274. See also, in this connection, Joel Dolbeault, "From Mind to Matter: How Bergson Anticipated Quantum Ideas", *Mind and Matter* 10/1 (2012), 25–45.

7 See Eric Schliesser's Stanford Encyclopedia entry on "Hume's Newtonianism and Anti-Newtonianism": https://plato.stanford.edu/entries/hume-newton/.

8 Čapek, *Bergson and Modern Physics*, p. ix.

9 For this reading, see also Riquier, *Archéologie de Bergson*, pp. 336–41.

10 Merleau-Ponty, *The Incarnate Subject: Malebranche, Biran and Bergson on the Union of Mind and Body*, ed. A. G. Bjelland Jr. and P. Burke, trans. P. Milan (New York: Humanity Books, 2001), p. 89.

11 Jankélévitch, *Henri Bergson*, p. 95/p. 116.

12 See Willem de Vries' Stanford Encyclopedia entry on Sellars: https://plato.stanford.edu/entries/sellars/.

13 In this connection, see Lacey, *Bergson*, Chapter 1, and Deleuze's remarks in *Bergsonism*, pp. 91–2.

14 On this point, see John Mullarkey, *Bergson and Philosophy*, p. 54.

15 On this point, see Deleuze, *Bergsonism*, Chapter IV.

16 See Boutroux, *The Contingency of the Laws of Nature*, conclusion.

17 Čapek, *Bergson and Modern Physics*, pp. 192–3.

Further reading

Milič Čapek, *Bergson and Modern Physics: A Reinterpretation and Re-evaluation*. Boston Studies in the Philosophy of Science, Vol. 7 (Dordrecht: D. Reidel, 1971). See the third and final section for Čapek's account of Bergson's philosophy in relation to modern physics.

Gilles Deleuze, *Bergsonism*, trans. H. Tomlinson (New York: Zone, 1988). See Chapter IV, "One or Many Durations?", for an excellent treatment of the issue of the unity or plurality of duration.

Vladimir Jankélévitch, *Henri Bergson*, ed. Nils F. Schott and Alexandre Lefebvre (Durham, NC: Duke University Press, 2015). See Chapter 3 on *Matter and Memory* and the mind–body problem.

Six
Laughter

No laughing matter

With his 1900 *Laughter: An Essay on the Meaning of the Comic*, Bergson belongs to the small number of major philosophers to have addressed in depth the topic of laughter and the comic as its source. Aristotle's book on comedy, the second volume of his *Poetics*, was lost, and subsequently in the philosophical tradition the questions of what makes us laugh and why we laugh were often addressed only in passing.[1] This may have been because laughter was considered ignoble, because philosophers feared treating something unserious seriously, or because they found it, following Cicero, a subject too difficult and diverse to encapsulate in a single theory.[2] Bergson, at any rate, considers philosophers to have failed to provide an adequate account of comic laughter, despite renewed attention to the question in modern philosophy.[3] The definitions provided (in terms, say, of incongruity or absurdity) are all too broad—as he claims in the preface and appendix added to the 23rd edition of his text in 1924, which do not appear in the 1911 English translation—and describe many things which are simply not funny. At best, they capture only the necessary rather than the sufficient conditions of the comic, and thus they fail to provide any "rules for producing [*procédés de fabrication*]" comic effect [L /vi]. After an early 1884 intervention on the topic, of which only a review in a local Puy-de-Dôme newspaper remains [M 313–15], *Laughter* presents Bergson's considered attempt to solve this "little problem, which has a knack of baffling every effort, of slipping away and escaping only to pop up again", a problem that, rather like a jack-in-the-box, has continually reappeared as "an impertinent challenge thrown down to philosophical speculation" [L 1/1].

Even though it had occupied him since the 1880s, *Laughter* may appear, after the rigours of *Matter and Memory*, to address this "little problem" merely as a matter of light relief. It is the shortest of his monographs, and, written for a popular audience, it contains little explicit discussion of his major metaphysical concerns. The impression is reinforced when Bergson explains in the preface that the book does not offer, beyond occasional remarks in the text, an in-depth critical assessment of existing views on laughter and the comic, since that would entail a volume whose size would be out of "proportion to the importance of the subject" [L /v]. The topic, Bergson appears to claim, is hardly of fundamental significance, and his approach to it would consequently have little import for his philosophy as a whole. Yet *Laughter* is not just a book by Bergson, a punctual and more or less incidental intervention on unresolved questions relating to aesthetics and psychology, but a Bergsonian book, one that has its place in the train of his philosophical thought. It takes up the perspectives offered by his previous work, for Bergson applies, as we will see, the ontology of *Matter and Memory* in addressing the problem of the nature of comic laughter. *Laughter*, however, develops as much as it applies the text of 1896, and this in a way that points towards his later work.[4] His famous thesis that the comic derives from "something mechanical plastered on the living [*du mécanique plaqué sur du vivant*]" [L 37/29] points the way to his theory of the *élan vital* as the ground of non-mechanical psychological and biological life in *Creative Evolution*, just as his argument concerning the social function of laughter points towards his engagement with questions of society and with the new science of sociology in *The Two Sources of Morality and Religion*. *Laughter*, then, is not just an incidental contribution to a particular topic dear to its author, but a transitional, pivotal moment in Bergson's philosophy as a whole.[5]

Situating *Laughter*

Theories of humour in the philosophical tradition can be grouped under three headings.[6] According to superiority theories, formulated notably by Plato and Aristotle, but also by Hobbes in the early modern period, we laugh from feelings of superiority. As Hobbes puts it in *Human Nature*: "the passion of laughter is nothing else but sudden glory arising from sudden conception of some eminency in ourselves, by comparison with the infirmity of others, or with our own formerly."[7] We laugh, that is, when we suddenly grasp the inferiority of others or of our former selves, and thus there is something essentially vainglorious, arrogant and mean-spirited about it. The superiority theory of humour, which holds laughter in low esteem, was predominant in the history of philosophy until the eighteenth century.

Hobbes points to another theory of humour when he mentions that we laugh at "*absurdities* and infirmities abstracted from persons",[8] and this idea was developed first in Scotland by Francis Hutcheson and James Beattie, and then in Germany by Kant and Schopenhauer. On these accounts, laughter arises from a felt incongruity between what is the case or what we expect to be the case, and what actually happens in the situation, depicted or real, at which we laugh. We laugh at what is absurd in this sense, and as Kant puts it in *The Critique of Judgment*, "laughter is an affection arising from the sudden transformation of a strained expectation into nothing".[9] Explanations of the nature of the incongruity differ according to particular incongruity theorists, but if superiority theories appear to be less about jokes or the comic and more about mere scornful laughter, Kant's incongruity theory preserves Hobbes' emphasis on *suddenness*. Timing, of course, is essential to comic effect. According to more recent relief theories, however, Kant's "strained expectation" is to be taken in a physiological sense as pent-up nervous energy, and laughter is understood as its release, which is intrinsically pleasurable. This more or less hydraulic approach was sketched in the eighteenth century in Shaftesbury's "An Essay on the Freedom of Wit and Humour", developed in Herbert Spencer's "On the Physiology of Laughter", and then articulated most famously later by Freud in his *Jokes and Their Relation to the Unconscious*.[10]

The status of Bergson's own theory of the object of laughter is a matter of some difficulty, as it is not offered as a simple "definition" [I. 1/1] of the comic. We will return to this issue at the end of the chapter, but his approach involves a kind of incongruity theory and a kind of superiority theory. It is introduced by three general observations bearing "less on the comic itself than on the field within which it must be sought" [L 2/2]. These observations respond implicitly to fundamental questions concerning the nature of comic laughter: what do we laugh at? How or when do we laugh? Who laughs?[11] First, Bergson's provisional answer to the question of what we laugh is: the human being. The human being is not only the laughing animal, but also the "animal which is laughed at [*qui fait rire*]" [L 3–4/3]. Bergson considers it strange that so important a fact has escaped the notice of philosophers, but is it true that we laugh at an animal only because we have "detected in it some human attitude or expression" [L 3/3]? Do not donkeys provoke mirth because of the incongruity of their small frame with their powerful voice and staunch determination?[12] We might also laugh because their ears just seem too big for their heads and bodies, and this not just in comparison with human beings but also with other species. It is not obvious how Bergson can deal with these instances of laughter. Nor is it immediately obvious that he had to make such a sweeping initial claim, since his basic theory about the mechanisation of life does not have to be restricted to human life.

Second, in response to the question of how or when we laugh, Bergson's view is that laughter is "usually" occasioned in an "absence of feeling [*insensibilité*]" [L 4/3]. The experience of abruptly stopping laughing when we realise that the thing we thought funny is, in fact, grave and serious is common enough, and it teaches us that emotions such as pity, worry and fear are forces opposed to laughter. Bergson, however, seems to exaggerate his case in broadening the claim to emotions in general, and in claiming that laughter requires a "soul that is calm and unruffled" [L 4/3]. Laughter can be bitter and sardonic,[13] and is compatible with affects such as pride on which superiority theories focused. Even so, his positive claim that the comic is addressed primarily to the intellect rather than to the emotions still stands, and this is hardly surprising given that the "laughing animal" is also, as the philosophical tradition has it, the "rational animal".

Third, in response to the question of who laughs, Bergson argues that laughter is an essentially social phenomenon. It is possible to laugh alone, but even in these cases laughter involves an implicit appeal to others, and one tends to laugh more when others join in. "Laughter is always the laughter of a group", of, that is, a finite social grouping, a "closed circle" [L 6/5]. Laughing at someone is always laughing with, implicitly or explicitly, others. But this answer to the third question gives rise to a fourth: why do we laugh in a social grouping? In offering a preliminary response to this question, Bergson offers a hint of the "guiding idea" [L 8/6] of the whole book: laughter has a particular social function and signification. This function, as Bergson will clarify, is corrective: its purpose is to chastise and reform human behaviour. This is, in fact, the reason why Bergson restricted the object of laughter to humanity in his first observation, since laughing at other species evidently has no effect on their behaviour. His response to the question of why we laugh guides and shapes, as he admits, his response to the question of what we laugh at.

Ridiculous rigidity

We laugh at human beings, but at what exactly in the human being? *Laughter* turns first to the most primitive modes of the comic in nature, in what naturally and spontaneously produces laughter, rather than to comic art. In everyday life, there is a kind of spontaneous sense of the comic, a natural comic imagination, and this is developed in the artifices of comedy; "the stage is a magnified and simplified view of life" [L 67/51]. The example of a person who, paying insufficient attention, trips in the street is not unfamiliar to philosophers, since Thales, the early Greek thinker, is supposed, as Plato reports, to have fallen into a well when observing the night skies, which amused a passing Thracian maid.[14] What we find in this distraction is "a certain *mechanical rigidity* exactly where one would hope to find the attentive suppleness and the living flexibility of a person" [L 10/8]. When an able-bodied person slips, trips or falls harmlessly, the loss of dignity, the absent-mindedness and the irruption of physicality can make us laugh. It is such irruption of spiritless physicality, of a kind of mechanical rigidity that Bergson sees as the root of all comic laughter; the comic is a function of rigidity rather than ugliness, of *raideur* rather than *laideur*, which Brereton and Rothwell translated with verve as "the unsprightly rather than the unsightly" [L 26/22].

Bergson thus criticises Aristotle's version of the superiority theory according to which we laugh at what is ugly.[15]

The whole of Laughter, in subtle and persuasive ways, attempts to trace the expression of this principle, according to which we laugh when we detect rigidity in human life, throughout the manifold forms of the comic, in the comic of forms, gestures and movements (Chapter 1), of situations and words (Chapter 2) and then of character (Chapter 3).

The "*attitudes, gestures and movements of the human body*", as the first chapter shows, "*are laughable to the exact degree that this body makes us think of a machine*" [L 29/23]. Hence the repeated gestures of the hands and arms of a lecturer can make us laugh. "Our states of mind change from moment to moment, and if our gestures faithfully followed our internal movements, if they lived as we live, they would not repeat themselves", which is to say that "fully vital life" "should not repeat itself" [L 31–2/24]. In this regard Bergson takes up the idea of duration in Time and Free Will and advances towards Creative Evolution, since what he had said in 1889 about psychological experience now seems to characterise life in general. From this observation, Bergson traces three diverging lines of comic fantasy. The first concerns disguise. In everyday experience, we do not separate someone's clothing from their person, and their clothes seem to belong to them. But add an element of surprise and novelty, as when we see a photograph of Bergson in his belle époque attire replete with top hat, "our attention is attracted to the clothing, we distinguish it absolutely from the person [...] and the risible side of fashion passes from shadow to light" [L 39/30]. The person might seem to be wearing a kind of disguise, a merely external, lifeless addition to his or her person, and we find it, however mildly, amusing. Something of the comic virtue of disguise explains why, says Bergson, in a manner that is as naïve as it is offensive, "why one laughs [*pourquoi on rit*]" at "a negro". He clearly considers it unnecessary to address morally and politically the fact that at the turn of the twentieth century white Europeans often laughed at black people in their vicinity. According to his explanation, the cab driver (surprise!) he heard hurling "comic" abuse at a black person by describing him as "unwashed" (*mal lavé*) is not really doing so from scorn and from an uneasy European assertion of superiority, but from an uneasy feeling that the person is in disguise, is "blacked up", when she is not. Here "disguise has passed something of its comic virtue to cases where the person is not even disguised" [L 40/31]. People of colour, as Bergson will allow, may well have laughed at white people in similar ways, at least when subjugation and the horrors of slavery did not preclude the requisite "calm and unruffled state". His treatment of the example is naïve both politically and philosophically, however, for although he may well offer a partial explanation of laughter at people of different races, it is clear that only a broader superiority theory of laughter can account for the negative connotations of being unwashed and thus for the obvious scorn in the example. Bergson's naïvety concerning the racism he encountered actually brings into focus the limitations of his own theory. It demonstrates its inability to deal adequately with racist jokes.

According to the second line of development, "*any incident which draws our attention to a person's bodily existence when something mental is at issue is funny*" [L 51/39], as when we laugh at the orator with an itchy nose or ear during a solemn address. According to the third line, "*we laugh when a person gives us the impression of being a thing*" [L 58/44], just like the child laughs at a Punch and Judy show, when puppets in human form are repeatedly bashed on the head.

In the comedy of situations, Bergson finds that "*any arrangement of acts and events that gives, in a single combination, the illusion of life and the distinct sensation of mechanical arrangement [agencement] is comic*" [L 69/53]. Bergson draws out this mechanisation at the level of comic plot by analogy with the toys and play of children. On the stage—and, we might add now, particularly in children's animated cartoons—effects resembling a jack-in-the-box, a puppet on strings or a snowball rolling out of control all draw a laugh. At a higher level, Bergson isolates three comic effects that subvert, he argues, three characteristics of temporal life. Life involves a continual change of aspect, the irreversibility of phenomena, and each living being is a closed system of phenomena in the unity of a single organism. The theatrical subversion of these characteristics amounts to "*repetition, inversion, and the interference of series*" [L 89/68]. Repetition suggests an inanimate process, and Bergson analyses the comic effect of the repetition of the same events in different circumstances within Molière's plays. Inversion, analogous to repetition, involves the "inversion of *roles*, and a situation which recoils on the head of its author", as when the persecutor becomes the victim of his persecution, the conman the victim of his own con [L 95/72]. By the "interference of series" Bergson is thinking of situations, such as those of mistaken identity, which *"belong at the same time to two absolutely independent series of events, and that can be interpreted at the same time in two wholly different senses"* [L 96/73]. Mistaken identity, a device familiar from Shakespeare's comedies, introduces an air of mechanism into a story, as if the characters were marionettes, and it is this, at bottom, that makes us laugh.

Under the heading of the comic of words, of verbal humour, Bergson examines cases of the comic where language does not just express something funny but is what is essentially funny. On the way to this distinction, however, *Laughter* distinguishes *le spirituel* and *le comique*, wit and the comic. The nature of wit, he argues, in all its varieties, will appear too diffuse and intractable for the theorist if we do not recognise that its forms are grounded in the comic. The essence of wit, in fact, consists in seeing things theatrically, *"sub specie theatri"* [L 107/81]. When, to take Bergson's example, Madame de Sevigné writes to her daughter "your chest hurts me [*j'ai mal à votre poitrine*]", in expressing how her daughter's illness causes her emotional pain, she plays on the image of them being attached as if by invisible strings like a puppet. This effect, as Bergson remarks, is worked out in a scene by Molière, where a doctor diagnoses a daughter's illness by taking her father's pulse. Thus "between wit and the comic there is the same relation as that between a completed scene and the fugitive indication of a scene still to be created" [L 108/84]. This continuity between wit and the comic facilitates Bergson's further claim that in purely verbal humour, where language creates the comic rather than just expresses it, the same three comic functions of repetition, inversion and interference are to be found. Manifest absurdities in a ready-made phrase ("I don't like working between meals"), taking a figurative expression literally ("The stock market is a dangerous game. You win one day, you lost the next—Well, I'll play on alternate days"), and transposing the natural expression of an idea in another tone all make us laugh. Under this latter heading, Bergson discusses parody, satire, irony and exaggeration. But these forms of incongruity, he argues, are funny because they rely on a certain rigidification in and of language itself. This rigidification is particularly manifest in professional jargon, an easy target for the parodist and satirist.

Jargon, as a certain rigidification of the character of a profession, leads from the comic in words to the comic in character, with which, Bergson argues, it is essentially continuous. In this, we laugh at a "rigidification against social life" [L 134/102]. Given that Bergson takes laughter to have the social function of chastising such anti-social behaviour, he considers the comic in character to be the comic in its purest form. The anti-social behaviour it chastises, however, is not immoral behaviour but a rigid lack of sociability. In this sense, even a moral virtue such as honesty, when practised dogmatically without regard to circumstances, can be risible, as is Alceste in Molière's *Misanthrope*. When such rigidity of character is manifestly conditioned by automatism and distraction, as in *Don Quichotte*, we have, for Bergson, "the comic itself, drawn from as near as possible to its source" [L 146/112]. But all character contains the seeds of the comic, insofar as it consists of habits and typified ways of being.

In all of these diverse but continuous levels of the comic, Bergson finds the same motif at their source: mechanism plastered on the living. As I suggested, this theory is, in the end, a particular form—a possibly all too narrow form, but we will return to this issue—of incongruity theory in that it supposes that it is the incongruous contrast between life and apparent mechanism in the human being that makes us laugh.[16] Bergson seems to be aware that we need to apprehend this contrast, even and precisely when he tries to distinguish his theory from incongruity theories, for he asserts that "many things are comic *de jure* without being comic *de facto*, the continuity of custom having deadened within them the comic quality" [L 39/30]. In order to laugh, we need to be surprised by the comic and thus to notice the contrast it contains. As a particular form of incongruity theory, Bergson's position is close to that of Alexander Bain in his treatment of the ludicrous in the 1853 *The Emotions and the Will*. Bain criticised general incongruity theories for being too broad, and attempted to provide a more fitting definition with the claim that "the occasion of the ludicrous is the degradation of a person or interest, possessing dignity, in circumstances that excite no other strong emotion".[17] Bergson, it might be thought, is also pointing to phenomena of spiritual degradation. However, he considers his own theory of "the mechanical plastered on the living" to be both more flexible and broader, in that it accounts for the fact that "if the transposition of the solemn into the trivial, the worse into the better, is comic, the inverse transposition can be all the more so" [L 124/95].[18] Does this mean that Bergson, beyond transposition in words, would be able to account for comic situations where we might laugh at a person in whom the higher cannot adapt itself to the lower when it needs to, at the person who acts elastically and spontaneously where and when a form of automatism is required? It is easy to imagine a comic situation involving a person unable to adapt to the rigours and discipline of work. Perhaps Bergson could account for such cases as instances of inflexibility on a kind of meta-level (for the inflexibility consists in sometimes not being able to be inflexible!), but in this way his own position would still more obviously belong under the more general heading of an incongruity theory, for it would rely still more broadly on an idea of contrast.[19]

It is also significant in this connection that Bergson presents at least the echo of a release theory, which, as we saw above in relation to Kant, can complement, rather than contradict, an incongruity theory. Socially and inconveniently inelastic behaviour makes one "uneasy" [L 20/15]. We only have to look at the rictus grin of a clown mask, a staple in horror films, to feel the proximity of the comic to what is uncanny and discomforting. Laughter could then be understood as the release from this tension and discomfort. To be sure, Bergson does not say this, not even when addressing the idea that in laughter "there is a movement of release [détente] which has often been noticed" [L 195/149]. On the contrary, he claims here that release and relaxation, with the sympathy that it [L 199/151] involves, is but a prelude to laughter rather than laughter itself. But although he could have said much more about relief theories, his own gesture towards one in the first section of the book perhaps does not flatly contradict his concluding remarks about relaxation. For it is possible that this relaxation can be accompanied by or at least produce unease, just as enjoying oneself can be accompanied by a bad conscience (when, say, a pile of exam scripts is still to be marked). This would explain why we laugh rather than just acquiesce in the relatively deviant behavior.

Hilarious habit

Bergson's theory of "mechanism plastered on the living" clearly relies on the account of degrees of consciousness first presented in *Matter and Memory*. The 1896 text focused on the degrees of "attention to life", but it is *inattention to life* that Bergson now finds to be the source of the comic. However, *Laughter* develops and even challenges the ontological framework of *Matter and Memory*, as much as it applies it. In the earlier work, Bergson accounted for motor habit in mechanistic terms, even if mechanism is a mere "hypothesis" as he admitted in the final pages of the text. In 1896, automatism served the necessity of action that was life, but now he explicitly contrasts "life" with the mechanical, for the experience of this contrast is, precisely, the source of the comic. Life is now understood as a synthesis of a physical and a spiritual principle, a synthesis that is both "*tension* and *elasticity*" [L 18/14]. Elastic, flexible life, that is, consists in the tension that unifies matter and mind, and the release of that tension constitutes the distraction and rigidity proper to the comic. From the perspective of *Laughter*, therefore, the habituated "living body" in the account of pure perception in *Matter and Memory* is the inflexible, mechanical body that is worthy of ridicule and closer to death than life.

The notion of flexibility derives from Boutroux, who had sought to reveal an "elasticity",[20] a certain contingency or non-necessity, in existence—in life certainly, but more generally in all the domains of existence, and thus even in the inorganic realm. What we take to be the "laws" of nature, he argued, do not have an "absolute existence" for "they are the image, artificially obtained and determined [*fixé*], of an original that, in essence, is living and movable [*mobile*]". Laws of nature are really habits, and maintain something of the vital flexibility of habit. It is habit that "gives the lower beings the appearance of a fabric of lifeless laws", but habit, as Boutroux argues after Ravaisson, is "not the substitution of a substantial fatality for spontaneity", not a mechanical necessity, but a "state of spontaneity itself".[21] What *Laughter* does after Boutroux's argument concerning elastic contingency, then, is to construe the more or less mechanical image or representation of flexible, elastic life in the human being as constituting the essence of the comic.

Does this mean that Bergson considers all habit to be intrinsically ridiculous? It often seems so. "Deep rooted in the comic", he writes, "there is always the tendency to take the path of least resistance, generally that of habit" [L 196/149], and "what is essentially laughable is what is done automatically" [L 146/111]. Bergson would thus merely elaborate Kant's view in his *Anthropology from a Pragmatic Point of View* that because habit "leads to thoughtless repetition of the very same act", it "becomes ridiculous".[22] The qualification "generally" in the first sentence above is, however, not accidental, and Bergson seems to acknowledge earlier in the text that a graceful movement, grace being opposed to inelasticity as beauty is to ugliness, has its own form of "contracted habit [*pli contracté*]" [L 24/18]. Boutroux's position was that habit, which is "grace when active and regarded as a stage enabling one to rise still higher, becomes a cause of weakness, of dissipation of energy, and of decay, when regarded as an ultimate term, when it is passive",[23] and Bergson seems implicitly to accept this contrast. Although he often speaks of habit negatively, in *Laughter* he seems able to recognise that habit and grace are not antithetical, for the absence of effort and laboured movement is a necessary condition of the one as much of the other. It is only when habitual movements lose the flexibility and mobility of grace, when they become one-tracked and inelastic, that they become ridiculous. Repetition is not intrinsically comic, and repeated movements in a ballet do not make us laugh. It is repetition that gives the impression of mindlessness and mechanism that makes us laugh. In this sense, if we laugh at Charlie Chaplin in *Modern Times* when he manically continues, outside the factory, his production-line manoeuvre of tightening bolts, we are not laughing so much at habit as we are at its degeneration into an apparently wholly mindless mechanism, at an absurd, theatrical exaggeration of a natural tendency to repeat, with less and less awareness and effort, actions already performed.

Mechanical or quasi-mechanical representations or performances of human action are intrinsically ridiculous. We find the same representations, albeit in theory rather than on screen or stage, in supposedly serious behaviourist philosophy, and thus *Laughter* allows us to see clearly how behaviourism is a ludicrous, risible theory. The joke about the two behaviourist lovers in a moment of post-coital inquiry ("How was it for me?") relies on this. But this implicit lesson of Bergson's account of humour can perhaps also be applied to the author's own philosophy in *Matter and Memory*. There Bergson had described the idea of the mechanical living body operating in pure perception as a limit idea that is unrealisable in experience. But is this limit idea not just, as he now writes in describing puppetry, "a very artificial exaggeration of a certain natural rigidity in things" [L 102–3/78]? *Laughter* perhaps does not decisively move beyond the ambiguities of the concluding paragraphs of *Matter and Memory* since it never really clarifies whether it is mechanism in the human being or merely an apparent mechanism in the human being that makes us laugh. Still, the last quotation concerning puppetry shows that he can lean towards the latter view, and thus it may appear that by 1900 Bergson has brought the dualistic metaphysics of *Matter and Memory* more profoundly into question. In any case, *Laughter* might lead us to see, beyond Bergson's own intentions, the dualism in *Matter and Memory* as a bit of a joke, even if it is not nearly as ridiculous as behaviourism.

The social function of laughter

We have already noted that Bergson's response to the question of what we laugh at is bound to his account of why we laugh. Laughter, he argues, serves the needs of social life. What both "life and society require from each of us is a constantly alert attention that discerns the outlines of the present situation, together with a certain elasticity of mind and body to enable us to adapt ourselves to it". Social life requires flexibility and "a constant effort of reciprocal adaptation", but it is all too easy for us lazily to "let ourselves go in the easy automatism of acquired habits", and thus to lose the elastic alertness that makes such adaptation possible. Although it makes us laugh only when it has no serious consequences, "society" is generally "suspicious of any inelasticity of character, of mind, and even of body, because it is the possible sign of a slumbering activity, as well of an activity with separatist tendencies [qui s'isole], that inclines away from [qui tend à s'écarter de] the common centre around which society gravitates" [L 18–19/15]. Thus when we laugh at something, Bergson concludes, we laugh in order to repress and correct the socially deviant and inconvenient inelasticity: "the comic is rigidity, and laughter is its punishment" [L 21/16].

Bergson adds this social concern for repression and correction to traditional superiority theories, to which his own account of the function of laughter belongs. Laughter, he claims, is always mockery, and there is a scorn for imperfection, condescension and even malice that is essential to the comic.[24]

> Laughter is above all a corrective. Being intended to humiliate, it must make a painful impression on the person against whom it is directed. By laughter, society avenges itself for the liberties taken with it. It would fail in its object if it bore the stamp of sympathy or kindness. [L 197/150]

One might suppose that beneath the corrective cruelty of humour, there lies a certain kindness, but Bergson still considers that it relies on a "spark of spitefulness, or, at least, of mischief", and that dwelling on the question would not produce "anything very flattering to ourselves" [L 198/151]. In line with traditional superiority theories, and despite his sociological development of them, he seems to hold laughter in relatively low esteem.

The laughter of a child may appear to stand as an obvious counter-example to this sociological superiority theory. The child may well be laughing at mechanism plastered on the living, but the supposition of any intention of social correction in that laughter is implausible, in the case of a young child at least. This, however, is precisely why Bergson invokes the intentions of "society", and thus a kind of collective consciousness that precedes and conditions the thoughts and behaviour of any individual. This sociological approach is new in Bergson's philosophy, and he will develop it more fully over three decades later in *The Two Sources of Morality and Religion*. That text will be much more Durkheimian than *Laughter*, however, in that there Bergson will radically revise his views about habit and society. *Laughter* opposes the good functioning of society to habit, whereas later, following Durkheim, Bergson holds that the good functioning of society *is* habitual. According to *Laughter*, it is, in effect, only when social convention and custom becomes habitual in the sense of unthinking and inelastic that it becomes comic. *The Two Sources of Morality and Religion* makes no such distinction between custom and habit, and treats deviation from ethical and social norms as a product of the intellect, as we will see, rather than of habit. It is not easy to say which view is the more convincing, and perhaps both are true, and both exaggerations, in their own ways.

In *Laughter*, Bergson also diverges from Durkheim's sociology in reducing the social to the natural. Given that the tendency to laugh does not depend on education or vary to any great extent from society to society (which is not to deny that certain societies have tried to suppress it), Bergson finds reason to suppose that the corrective social function of laughter is somehow natural. "Nature has utilized evil" in the humiliation of the ridiculous "with a view to good", and "[l]aughter is simply the result of a mechanism set up in us by nature or what is almost the same thing, by a well-established habit [*par une très longue habitude*] in social life" [L 198–9/151]. It is not surprising that Bergson does not dwell on this issue, however, for it is replete with problems. He seems to sense that there is no viable explanation for how nature produced this social function. In the terms of evolutionary theory, a Larmarckian explanation might seem to be the most viable approach, as Bergson seems to suggest, according to which laughter as a now natural chastisement of automatism derives from the inheritance of acquired characteristics, by the inheritance of a habit, but by the time of *Creative Evolution* Bergson will clearly reject, following biological orthodoxy, the theory of the inheritance of acquired characteristics. A Darwinian explanation, according to an idea of chance mutations and natural selection, may appear unlikely, since the laugher gains no evolutionary advantage in laughing at others, but recent approaches have supposed that it is particular social groupings that enjoyed better communication and thus an evolutionary advantage through laughter.[25] Still, in either approach, if the social function of laughter were acquired in an evolutionary process, the physiological fact of laughing would have had to have been produced first without its social function, without the intention to humiliate, since that intention presupposes that individuals know—that "society knows"—that being laughed at is a humiliation, rather than, say, a sign of respect. Laughter may well have arisen because the laugher held someone in contempt, as a spontaneous physiological reaction to the object of derision, but it cannot have arisen in order to deride someone. This means that the social function of laughter is parasitic on laughter as a spontaneous physiological response to the comic, and thus that we laughed at least once for reasons other than an intention to humiliate. But if we laughed once in this way, it seems that it is possible for us to laugh now in the same way, and thus there seems no need to deny our ordinary intuitions that we can laugh in any number of situations without the intention of humiliating someone. Bergson has focused too narrowly on one particular form of laughter, mocking laughter, but the existence of that form presupposes that there are others.[26]

It is due, in any case, to the purposeful social function of laughter that Bergson considers the comic not to belong to the domain of aesthetics, of fine art. Although they are supposed to occasion a non-sensory pleasure, the comic arts are not ethically disinterested in that they are still motivated by a concern for the social good. This social function may become increasingly refined, but it is still present, Bergson argues, even in the highest expressions of the comic. That said, there is something "aesthetic about the comic, since it emerges precisely when society and the individual, freed from the concern of their preservation, begin to treat each like works of art". The comic arises when people respect each other as having a value and dignity beyond utility, as requiring persuasion rather than direct physical repression. In this sense, the comic hovers "between life and art" [L 21–2/17]. There is, however, another sense in which the comic remains at the level of the artisan rather than the fine artist: comedy is addressed to the intellect, and concerns types which we have met before and will meet again. It is for this reason, Bergson observes, that comedies more naturally carry general types as their titles than tragedies. It is hard to imagine *Othello* under the name of *The Jealous Man* or *Macbeth* as *The Ambitious Man*, but Molière's comedies carry titles like *The Misanthrope*, *The Bourgeois Gentleman* and *The Imaginary Invalid*. Even *Tartuffe* was originally *Le Tartuffe ou L'Hypocrite* and later *Le Tartuffe ou L'Imposteur*, but, of course, Cervantes' *Don Quichotte* is an obvious counter-example.[27]

In contrast to the comic concern for generality, fine art, to which tragedy belongs, on Bergson's account of art that we will study in Chapter 8 below, is concerned for things in their particularity; "what the artist fixes on his canvas is something he has seen at a certain spot and on a certain day at a certain hour, with a colouring that will never be seen again" [L 161/124]. Bergson has a point here, but we should be wary of exaggerating it. Surely, comedy requires at least some particularity in order to be effective, and one wonders what he would make of the idea of "comic genius", given that genius— and he will accept this traditional understanding of the term in his later reflections on art, as we will see in Chapter 7—transcends clear conceptuality and thus the generality of the intellect. Moreover, surely tragedy conserves some generality. Aristotle emphasised this in the *Poetics*, arguing that tragedy has much of its effect because the tragic hero could be anyone, including you.[28]

The expansive source of the comic

Bergson argues that existing incongruity theories are too broad, and fail to determine the sufficient conditions of the comic, but his own approach to the object of laughter, as a type of incongruity theory, may easily appear, as he recognises in his appendix, too narrow, and to offer sufficient conditions of the comic at the cost of these no longer being necessary. Commentators have often taken his theory in this way, and even as an example of risible pedantry, as mechanical thinking insensitive to the open and multi-faceted texture of comic reality.[29] An aspect of life being presented as mechanical and inert may well be intrinsically humorous, but is it not obviously the case, particularly when we move beyond gestures and movements, that the comic has other sources, that other things can make us laugh? Take novelty, for example. Novel works of art, novel scientific theories, novel dietary regimes can all, quite easily, appear risible. We might describe such novelties, which are incongruous with our expectations, as surprising, bizarre, eccentric and, precisely, as ridiculous. It is plausible that we laugh at such novelties with the aim, implicit or explicit, of suppressing social eccentricities, but it is less obvious that such novelties are funny because they suggest a kind of automatism. Novelties in fashion may have this suggestive power, but it is hard to see how this can be transferred to novelties in general. Novelty and surprise may well be not just a condition of the comic, but also a source of the comic itself, and if this is the case there exist instances of the comic to which Bergson's social correction theory of laughter might apply, but to which his automatism theory does not.[30]

Bergson qualifies his theory in two important ways, however. First, he seems to accept that it does not apply to all instances of the comic, including the comic unintentionally produced, when, in the (untranslated) preface to the text that he wrote in response to his critics, he states that his aim is to produce "rules for the production of the comic [*procédés de fabrication*]" [L–/vi]. *Laughter*, that is, is concerned with comic craft, the conditions of making something funny, and not with the comic in general, regardless of where it is to be found. This even though the main motif for comic craft, namely "mechanism plastered on the living", can be found in things not intentionally produced to be funny or intentionally produced at all (such as tripping up, as we saw). In this way, Bergson's attempt to narrow down traditional incongruity theories would have only a limited sphere of application; and those theories would still be valid in relation to aspects of the comic not intentionally produced.

F. C. T. Moore has emphasised, *pace* Lacey, that no such rules can provide the sufficient conditions for the production of the comic, since, as Bergson seems to recognise, comic effect requires additional ingredients such as a degree of novelty and a sense of timing, just as the successful realisation of a culinary recipe might require a good oven.[31] This may well explain why Bergson does not quite or does not directly describe his own procedure as that of providing sufficient conditions for the production of something funny, even when, as in the appendix to *Laughter*, he seems to criticise traditional theories for not providing sufficient conditions for the comic in general. But only in a very particular sense, as Lacey sees, can Bergson be taken to account even for the necessary conditions of comic production. The first page of *Laughter* clearly states, in fact, that the aim is not to offer a definition of the comic:

> [o]ur excuse for attacking the problem in our turn is that we do not intend to enclose comic fantasy in a definition. We see in it, above all, something living. We will treat it, as minor as it may be, with the respect due to life. We will limit ourselves to watching it grow and develop. From form to form, by insensible gradations, it will undergo before our eyes quite singular metamorphoses. [...] Perhaps we will gain from this close contact something more than a theoretical definition—a practical and intimate knowledge, like that born from a long friendship. [L 2/1]

A definition stating the necessary conditions of the comic, which together would constitute its sufficient conditions, it would seem, is not *Laughter*'s aim. The comic belongs to psychical life, and life, as Bergson will argue later in *Creative Evolution*, cannot be captured in this way. "A perfect definition", he writes there, "applies only to ready-made reality; but vital properties are never entirely realized, but always on the way to their realization; they are less *states* than they are *tendencies*" [CE 13/13]. Life is a process, which involves evolution and change. Hence a philosophy of the comic, as an aspect of life, should seek only "supple" concepts and definitions able to follow the changing contours of comic reality.[32]

This is the second way in which Bergson qualifies his aims and the range of his formula "mechanism plastered on the living". Later in the first chapter, he develops the point:

> we must not accept this formula as a definition of the comic. It is suitable for cases that are elementary, theoretical and perfect, in which the comic is free from all adulteration [*de toute mélange*]. Nor do we offer it, either, as an explanation. We prefer to make it, if you will, the *leitmotiv* which is to accompany all our explanations. [L 21/16]

The formula neither explains nor defines the comic, but it can identify the comic in the simplest, purest cases, as in the absent-minded person tripping up. Rigidity where elastic life is expected is the "source" of the comic—and Bergson uses the term "source" in *Laughter* as he will later in *The Two Sources of Morality and Religion*—in the way that pure perception and pure memory are sources of factual, perceptual experience in the text of 1896. The crucial point is that this source of the comic is not a genus to which things either belong or not; it is not the "external conformity to a genus", as Bergson put it in a letter of 1900 [M 437]. The source of the comic is "more or less" present in particular comic instances, and this according to infinite gradations and degradations, which a generic unity cannot have. A horse, for example, cannot be more or less of an animal. If it is a horse it is an animal; and if it is not an animal, it is not a horse. The source of the comic, in contrast, unifies all comic instances, but its most far-flung expressions have only the most distant relation to it, even if they can never be entirely cut off from it. There is a "force of expansion" in the comic—a "comic *élan*" as the Bergson of 1907 might have said—that ties its more distant expressions by association and analogy [M 437] to its primitive forms. It is in this sense that his formula for the comic is more like a *leitmotiv*, a dominant recurring theme that changes in its different forms and actualisations in the development of a piece of music. This *leitmotiv* underlies the gradual, continuous gradations that distinguish one expression of the comic from another at more of a remove from the source; but it is not the genus to which all instances of the *leitmotiv* belong.

Perhaps Bergson's thought can be translated, without regard to *Matter and Memory*, into an Aristotelian concern for "focal meaning", as Lacey suggests: health is a physical condition of the body, but we say that particular foodstuffs are healthy insofar as they can produce health, that a walk is healthy because exercise can lead to good health, and that someone has a healthy complexion because this complexion is a sign of good physical health. All of these three senses relate to health as a bodily condition, but the bodily condition is not the genus of which the other senses are species.[33] But this is how Bergson expresses his thesis in a letter of 1904 published in the *Journal des débats*:

> My thesis consists in supposing that there exist a certain number of risible or dominating effects, reducible to a relatively simple formula, but that what is comic in these effects immediately rebounds on other effects that resemble them in some way, and those on others that resemble them *without necessarily resembling the first*, and so on, infinitely. A particular phrase, a particular situation is comic only because it evokes in our minds an image (that is fleeting, hardly graspable) which invokes another, which invokes a third etc. [M 632–3]

This is not so much a question of focal meaning as a chain of associations and analogies, through which comic effects have an increasingly distant relation and "family resemblance" to their source.

It is not clear that *Matter and Memory*'s ontology of gradations and degradations can work in the case of the comic, where there seems to be no other positive principle of a different nature opposed to it. For if there is less and less of the source of the comic in its increasingly sophisticated and far-flung expressions, of what is there more and more? The unfunny? Or another source of the comic? If it is the unfunny, then Bergson's source of the comic risks becoming a generic unity, because what is funny in things is funny to the same degree in all of its expressions; it just gets more and more mixed up with what is unfunny. If it is another source or other sources of the comic, then Bergson should not speak of the source of the comic. Whatever the case may be, it is because of his notion of the expansive source of the comic that Bergson cannot, in any straightforward sense, be held to provide the necessary conditions for the production of the comic: the condition of automatism and rigidity is not always or necessarily present in the same way, to the same degree, in order for something to qualify as funny. Of course, as Lacey notes, this approach "tends to disarm criticism"[34] automatically, since Bergson can always respond to critics of the apparent narrowness of his theory by claiming that although the "cause that he indicates is not manifest in the immediate impression" [M 436], comic instances have a mediated, more distant and covert relation to the source of the comic that is mechanism plastered on the living.

Summary

Bergson argues that we laugh at rigidified and ossified manifestations of human life, at "mechanism plastered on the living". This explicit contract of mechanism and life points beyond the horizon of *Matter and Memory* (which had considered the "living body" to operate mechanically) and towards *Creative Evolution*. Bergson's theory can be classed, in traditional terms, as a hybrid of an incongruity theory and a superiority theory, the latter of which is present in his view that we laugh in order to chastise and correct inflexible behaviour in society. Thus understood, the comic forms a bridge between the domain of morality and the domain of aesthetics, even though it belongs to neither. Bergson's account of what we laugh at has often been taken to be impossibly narrow, and to exclude other sources of the comic, but he defuses this criticism by emphasising that he does not propose a "definition" of the comic, and is rather interested only in bringing to light a guiding thread or *leitmotiv* that can be more or less present in particular instances of the comic.

Notes

1 See Walter Watson, *The Lost Second Book of Aristotle's Poetics* (Chicago, IL: Chicago University Press, 2012).

2 See David Heyd, "The Place of Laughter in Hobbes' Theory of the Emotions", *Journal of the History of Ideas* 43/2 (1982), 285–95, p. 285.

3 See Bergson, *Cours* vol. II: *Leçons d'esthétique. Leçons de morale, psychologie et métaphysique* (1887–1888) (Paris: Presses universitaires de France, 1992), p. 43.

4 Stephen Crocker is right to note that *Laughter* "offers some of Bergson's most interesting insights on the tension between mechanism and vitalism that informs all of his work"; see Stephen Crocker, "Man Falls Down: Art, Life and Finitude in Bergson's Essay on Laughter", in *Bergson and Phenomenology*, ed. M. Kelly (Basingstoke: Palgrave, 2010), pp. 78–97, p. 78.

5 On the pivotal nature of Bergson's reflection in *Laugher*, see also Frédéric Worms' introduction to the critical edition of the text by Guillaume Sibertin-Blanc: Bergson, *Le Rire: Essai sur la signification du comique* (Paris: Presses universitaires de France, 2012), pp. 5–13.

6 On all this see John Morreall (ed.), *The Philosophy of Laughter and Humor* (Albany, NY: State University of New York Press, 1987), and his "The Philosophy of Humor", Stanford Encyclopedia of Philosophy: https://plato.stanford.edu/entries/humor/.

7 See also Thomas Hobbes, *Leviathan*, ed. N. Malcolm(Oxford: Oxford University Press, 2012), I, iv: "[s]udden Glory, is the passion which maketh those Grimaces called LAUGHTER; and is caused either by some sudden act of their own, that pleaseth them; or by the apprehension of some deformed thing in another, by comparison whereof they suddenly applaud themselves".

8 Hobbes, *Human Nature*,in *Human Nature and De Corpore Politico*, ed. J. C. A. Gaskin (Oxford: Oxford University Press, 2008), p. 54.

9 Immanuel Kant, *Critique of Judgment*, trans. N. Walker (Oxford: Oxford University Press, 2007), p. 161.

10 See, in particular, the section of Morreall's "The Philosophy of Humor" entry on "The Relief Theory".

11 On this point, my reading is indebted to Guillaume Sibertin-Blanc's lucid analytical synopsis of Bergson's text in *Le Rire: Essai sur la signification du comique*, pp. 263–77.

12 For this observation, see Louise Mathewson, "Bergson's Theory of the Comic in the Light of English Comedy", *University of Nebraska Studies in Language, Literature and Criticism* 5 (1920), 1–27.

13 As Lacey notes: *Bergson*, p. 138.

14 Plato, *Theaetetus* 174a; Plato, *Theaetetus, Sophist*, trans. H. N. Fowler (Cambridge, MA: Loeb Classical Library, 1921).

15 See Aristotle, *Poetics* V 1449a; *Poetics*, ed. D. W. Lucas (Oxford: Oxford University Press, 1968).

16 On this point, see D. Parodi, "Le Rire. Essai sur la signification du comique par H. Bergson", *Revue de métaphysique et de morale* 9/2 (1901), 224–36, pp. 229–30.

17 Alexander Bain, *The Emotions and the Will* (London: Longmans, 1865), §37, p. 248.

18 Bergson's further critique of Bain that "degradation" is "just one form of transposition, which is itself just one of the means of obtaining laughter" [L 124/446] is perhaps not convincing. This is a key moment in *Laughter* where a more concerted response to the ideas of his forebears would have been helpful.

19 See Parodi, "Le Rire", p. 230.

20 Boutroux, *On the Contingency of the Laws of Nature*, p. 70.

21 Boutroux, *On the Contingency of the Laws of Nature*, p. 195.

22 Kant, *Anthropology from a Pragmatic Point of View*, ed. and trans. Robert B. Louden. The Cambridge Edition of the Works of Immanuel Kant: Anthropology, History and Education (Cambridge: Cambridge University Press, 2011), §12, p. 261.

23 Boutroux, *On the Contingency of the Laws of Nature*, p. 195.

24 For this claim, see Morreall (ed.), *The Philosophy of Laughter and Humor*, p. 15.

25 See, for example, M. Gervais and D. S. Wilson, "The Evolution and Functions of Laugher and Humour: A Synthetic Approach", *The Quarterly Review of Biology* 80/4 (2005), 395–430.

26 For this argument, see Parodi, "Le rire", pp. 233–4.

27 See Mathewson, "Bergson's Theory of the Comic in the Light of English Comedy", pp. 8–9 for the argument that Bergson's approach in general has been overly influenced by Molière's comedies, whose comic target, addressed with the sort of absence of feeling that Bergson promotes, is wayward individuals who stray from custom and common sense in behaving inflexibly.

28 Aristotle, *Poetics*, 55b2–12.

29 See, in particular, Bertrand Russell, "The Professor's Guide to Laughter", *The Cambridge Review* 33 (1912), 193–4.

30 For this argument also, see Parodi, "Le Rire", p. 234.

31 F. C. T. Moore, *Bergson: Thinking Backwards*, pp. 68–9.

32 On this point, see Guillaume Sibertin-Blanc's helpful initial note to Chapter 1 of *Laughter*: Bergson, *Le Rire*, pp. 172–3.

33 On focal meaning in Aristotle, see Michael T. Ferejohn, "Aristotle on Focal Meaning and the Unity of Science", *Phronesis* 25/2 (1980), 117–28.

34 See Lacey, *Bergson*, p. 141.

Further reading

Alexander Bain, "Of the Ludicrous", in *The Emotions and the Will* (London: Longman, 1865), pp. 247–51. This is Bain's "degradation" theory of the comic, to which Bergson's own account is close.

Simon Critchley, *On Humour* (Abingdon: Routledge, 2002). An engaging and informative treatment of humour with a chapter devoted to Bergson's views.

John Morreall (ed.), *The Philosophy of Laughter and Humor* (Albany, NY: State University of New York Press, 1987). A comprehensive source book for approaches to humour and laughter in the philosophical tradition.

Seven
Knowledge

Method and metaphysics

Bergson sought to reclaim the lived experience of time as duration for many years before offering a concerted reflection on the
methods available in order to do so. As if finding his way in the dark,
relying on touch rather than sight, in attempting to bring duration
into the light he philosophised before reflecting on what it is to
philosophise. This was apparent in *Time and Free Will*. His description
of the apprehension of duration as requiring the thinker to "let herself live", was vague and open to misinterpretation. Moreover, it was
necessary to clarify the sense in which duration could be one of the
"immediate data of consciousness", when the mediation of a critical
philosophical stance seemed necessary in order to turn to it. Bergson
had made significant discoveries in his earlier work, but in order to
defend and develop them it was necessary to determine how it is
possible to arrive at them.

Such methodological issues must have increasingly nagged
at Bergson. Finally, in 1903, he published "An Introduction to
Metaphysics", which concerns the method of his metaphysics, and
at the same time the basic elements of his epistemology, his account
of what we can know and how we can know it. Here Bergson
distinguished two ways of knowing, namely "analysis", which is
proper to scientific enquiry, and "intuition", which is essential to
philosophical method. The first depends "on the viewpoint chosen
and the symbols employed, while the second does not depend on
a point of view and rests on no symbol" [CM 187/178]. Intuition,

and thus philosophy, is a kind of immediate knowledge that is independent of the generalising tendencies of language and conceptual
thought. "We name intuition here", Bergson writes, "the *sympathy*
by which one is transported into the inside of an object in order to
coincide with what is unique and consequently inexpressible within
it" [CM 190/181]. Philosophical intuition thus attains truths that
analysis cannot reach, and it does so by means of a certain sympathetic identification with the individuality of its object.

"Introduction to Metaphysics" was a catalyst in Bergson's
increasing intellectual celebrity in Paris. Symbolist poets, encouraged
by his remarks on art in *Laughter*, adopted the notion of intuition as
an account of their own poetic practice.[1] Although the term was not
yet in use, Bergson, by circumstance much more than by design,
was becoming a philosopher of the *avant-garde*, and was drawing an
increasingly broad public to his lectures. At the same time, the essay's
contrast of philosophical intuition with scientific method, and its
epistemological critique of the claims of all conceptual thought, left
him even more open than before to charges of "irrationalism". It was
argued that in declaring intuition to be a form of "co-incidence",
Bergson was offering a mystical and mythical notion of philosophical method as a kind of return to a pre-lapsarian, instinctive contact
with reality. According to Bertrand Russell's famous jibe, "intuition
is at its best in bats, bees and Bergson".[2]

The present chapter examines Bergson's account of intuition—
about which, as he complained, "so much nonsense" [C 889]
had been written—as it is developed not just in "Introduction to
Metaphysics", but also in his later work. Subsequently, the chapter
turns to his related views, which are fully developed in the second
chapter of *Creative Evolution*, concerning, first, the "intelligence", as
the operation of conceptual thought and as the organ of scientific
inquiry, and, second, instinct, a form of unreflective and innate
knowledge shared by both humans and other animals.

Intuition and the absolute

What, then, does Bergson mean by "intuition"? Recall that in *Time
and Free Will* intuition was essentially related to space: any clear idea
of number, as Bergson argues at the beginning of his second chapter,

requires the "intuition" of a homogeneous multiplicity in a physical or mental space. "Intuition" here was no crude visualisation,
but it was related to space rather than time.[3] In 1903, however,
Bergson has decided—and he seems to have been encouraged to do
so by his disciples, by Edouard Le Roy in particular[4]—to take "intuition" in a rather different sense as describing the mind's apprehension of duration, of non-quantified and thus non-spatialised
time. This new sense of intuition he promotes as the very method of
metaphysics, which has for its object, according to the first sentence
of "Introduction to Metaphysics", the "absolute".

The text of the essay in *The Creative Mind* is a slightly altered version
of a 1903 journal article of the same name, but this article was, in
turn, based on the introduction to his 1902–3 lecture course at the
Collège de France concerning the history of the idea of time. The
problem of time is "the central problem of metaphysics in general",
and in the first lecture, Bergson attempts to gain some initial clarity
on "obscure notions" that have shaped accounts of it in the history of philosophy. The notions of "absolute, relative, infinite, perfect", he notes, are "badly defined" and "equivocal" [HIT 17]. When
Bergson begins his essay published a year later with the assertion that
metaphysics has for its object the "absolute", he is, therefore, self-
consciously attempting to redefine and clarify a traditional, problematic term in metaphysics. Here he is not creating new problems,
but approaching traditional problems in a new light.

The absolute/relative conceptual doublet is, for Bergson, an epistemological as well as metaphysical distinction: one and the same
thing can be known relatively, as relative, or absolutely, as absolute.
His first example is movement, which can be understood relatively
for two reasons. First, "I perceive it differently according to the point
of view from which I look at it" [CM 187/178]; if I am going at the
same speed in the same direction as the mobile, it will have the same
position in relation to me, and thus will appear, purely in terms of
that relation, immobile, whereas if I move in the opposite direction,
it will appear to move more quickly away from me than if I were
stationary. Second, "I express it differently […] as I relate it to the
system of axes or reference points […], according to the symbols
by which I translate it". The reader unfamiliar with Bergson's earlier
work might think that knowing movement geometrically in this

way is to know it objectively, and thus properly or adequately, even "absolutely", but *Time and Free Will* showed that movement cannot be constituted by points in space, which are immobile. To know movement in this way is to know it by means of that which it itself is not, namely axes and points, and for this reason such knowledge is relative. Relative knowledge has subjective and objective modes, but "in either case, I place myself outside the object itself". In contrast, I can understand the movement absolutely, from the inside, which means that really (when I am in actual fact the mobile), or merely by an "effort of imagination", I place myself in the position of the mobile.

Bergson has in mind here Thomas More's response to Descartes' account of the relativity of movement.

> When Descartes spoke of the reciprocity of movement, it is not without reason that Thomas More answered: "If I am sitting quietly, and someone else, taking a thousand steps away from me, is red in the face from fatigue, it is definitely he who moves and I who rest". Everything that science can tell us about the relativity of movement perceived by our senses, measured by our rulers and clocks, will leave intact the profound feeling that we have of carrying out movements and making efforts that we dispense. [DS 21/37–8]

Descartes, looking at movement from the outside, "went very far on the path" [HIT 20] of an idea of the relativity of movement, for he conceived all movement as reciprocal: if A moves away from B, it is exactly the same thing, he argues, as B moving away from A, and there is no geometrical means of determining which is the case. Thomas More, in response, imaginatively putting himself in the shoes of the person who is clearly making the effort to move, treats it as an absolute. Descartes analyses, whereas More intuits; and intuition involves sympathy. In the original, 1903 version of "Introduction to Metaphysics", it should be noted, Bergson described this sympathy as an "intellectual sympathy", but the word *intellectuelle* disappeared in the final 1934 version of the text, since, as we will see in the following section of this chapter, the term "intellect" has taken on a quite particular sense for him.[5]

Intuition in this sense delivers over an "absolute", "while all the rest has to do with *analysis*" [CM 190/181]. The absolute is "synonymous with perfection", since it is perfectly, entirely what it is, but it is not synonymous with the "infinite". For an infinite, countless number of mathematical points can be found in the trajectory traced out by the mobile, but this endless infinity—this "bad" infinity, as Hegel would have said—is only one side, the external product of the absolute movement, which in itself is indivisible [CM 190/181]. In contrasting relative and absolute knowledge thus, Bergson is taking sides with French philosophers such as Ravaisson (who had already spoken of "intuition" as the "method of metaphysics"[6]), and distancing himself from Herbert Spencer, who expounded and promoted the influential doctrine of the Scottish philosopher William Hamilton, according to which all knowledge is relative.[7] Bergson also reads Kant's work as an expression of a relativist position, since according to his critical philosophy all knowledge is relative to the mental forms by which it is known. That said, after the post-Kantian philosophers in Germany such as J. G. Fichte and F. W. J. Schelling, Bergson finds in Kant's own ideas the antidote to this relativism: "one of the most important and the most profound ideas of the *Critique of Pure Reason* is that if metaphysics is possible, it is so by means of vision, and not by a dialectic", i.e., by means of reason. In other words, Kant "has definitively established that, if metaphysics is possible, it is this only by an effort of intuition" [CM 164/154–5]. While Kant denied that any kind of non-sensory or intellectual intuition was possible, and thus denied that metaphysics was possible, Bergson affirms that it is possible and thus that there can be knowledge of the absolute. Certainly, Bergson initially speaks in a hypothetical mode [CM 190/181], which is understandable given that his first example in "Introduction to Metaphysics" concerns the intuitive, sympathetic identification with someone else's experience, and even with the movement of a non-thinking thing, rather than the immediate apprehension of the truth of one's own experience.

Bergson's doctrine of intuition is different from those available in post-Kantian Germany philosophy in that it is, at bottom, intuition of duration. For this reason, he hesitated to use the term, and was concerned that its long philosophical history would distort the sense he wanted to lend to it:

numerous are the philosophers who have felt how powerless conceptual thought is to reach the core of the mind. Numerous, consequently, are those who have spoken of a super-intellectual faculty of intuition. But as they believed that the intelligence worked within time, they concluded that to go beyond the intelligence consisted in getting outside of time. [CM 30–1/25]

The task of philosophy is not to escape time in this sense, for in beginning from the perspective of reflective thought we have already escaped it. In returning to time in its primitive sense, we come to know time absolutely, as duration, and not relatively, as a spatialised time; but if it is to be known absolutely, it is by intuition that we know it. Difficult as it may be to achieve, there is nothing particularly mysterious in this: given that the self, as we saw in Chapter 3, is its own duration, intuition is the means by which the mind apprehends itself. But perhaps knowing oneself is the most difficult thing of all.

Bergson considers that the term "intuition" lends itself to confusion, and he even wrote later that he could have passed over the term and not used it at all [M 1520], but he may well add to the confusion in using it in both a broad and a narrow sense. In the broad sense promoted in "Introduction to Metaphysics", intuition is identified with philosophical method as a whole. This raises a problem, for it is hard to see how any kind of direct apprehension can be methodical and thus procedural. How can intuition, as a non-symbolic, non-conceptual form of knowing, be the path (the Greek *hodos* in the word "method" means path) to the destination rather than the destination itself? As Aristotle argued, vision is not a process; it is the same thing to see and to have seen, since vision is completed as soon as it occurs.[8] If intuition is an immediate apprehension of something, like vision, and if method involves some kind of mediation, a path towards a goal, then their identification seems impossible. Later, however, Bergson will write of intuition in a narrower sense as the result of preparatory philosophical and critical work, as a part of philosophical method and not the whole of it:

[p]hilosophical method, as I represent it, includes two successive mental procedures. The second of these moments, the final procedure, is what I call *intuition*—a difficult and troublesome

method by which we break with preconceived ideas and ready-made intellectual habits, in order to place oneself by sympathy into the interior of reality. [M 1197]

In this 1916 lecture in Madrid, intuition takes over from an initial methodological procedure.

Hence, even while agreeing with Deleuze's rejection of anti-methodological, "intuitionist" interpretations of Bergson, we should be wary of his identification of Bergsonian philosophical method with intuition.[9] Certainly, we can go some way towards accommodating Bergson's divergent accounts of it by noticing his view that the "intuitional effort" can be "accomplished at different levels at different points" [CM 33/29]. Intuition can be carried out at different degrees of intensity, degrees which are but the degrees of attention to life, and perhaps it is for this reason that Bergson admits that he understands intuition "in senses that cannot be mathematically deduced from each other" [CM 34/30]. It remains the case that when Bergson speaks of intuition in art, he sometimes holds that intuition is independent of method and can occur without it. "Painters or sculptors, musicians or poets", if they are artists of genius, are capable of a "more direct vision of reality"; and this talent is bequeathed to them by "nature" rather than being a capacity that is learnt. The task of philosophy, therefore, is to gain by more methodical procedures the same sort of truths: "what nature does from time to time, by distraction, for certain privileged individuals, could not philosophy, in such a matter, attempt, in another sense and another way, to do for everyone?" [CM 163/153]. Philosophical method can stand in for the intuitions of genius, which move not just the fine artist, but also the great, revolutionary scientists, and even the mystic, as Bergson writes in his Madrid conference text of 1916 on the "human soul".

> The mystic, you will say, is a privileged person. Certainly, the great mystics are geniuses; what we call method is precisely the way of partially replacing genius, and an appropriate method will be precisely what will allow us, allow us all, to contemplate without veils, in a direct vision, the things of interior life. [M 1201]

Philosophical method thus enables "mere mortals" to attain the truths intuited by genius, and, in this sense, method is necessary when intuition is lacking. We should note parenthetically that Bergson did not think, as he admitted in a letter, he had any special gift for intuition: "Alas! far from feeling that I have the slightest genius, I know only too well how many impasses I have got myself into, how many insurmountable obstacles I have come up against in my research" [M 1574].

If intuition can occur without method, it seems that it should be considered as a *source* of philosophical method—in the sense that Bergson will speak of *The Two Sources of Morality and Religion*—rather than as identical with method.[10] We might be tempted to understand intuition as a source in this sense as a *means*. Intuition would be a means for the philosopher like the submarine is for the marine biologist examining deep-water species. Philosophy begins with the critical, rational discourse of the philosopher, who then sounds the depths of pre-reflective, pre-conceptual temporal experience. Her vessel, however, has to return to the surface, since the philosopher has to communicate her thoughts by means of language to others. Philosophy has thus the peculiar task of making silence speak. From this perspective, we can understand that although intuition somehow "surpasses intelligence", Bergson can still write that it is "from intelligence that it received the impulse" to do so [CE 187/193].

In another sense, however, Bergson underlines that intuition is *not simply* a tool in the service of reflective, conceptual thought. For intuition can lead to analysis, as much as analysis can lead to intuition. In appearing to recount his own discovery of duration, his own recognition of the limitations of spatialised conceptions of time, Bergson suggests that our apprehension of the inadequacy of analysis is itself the result of intuition:

> Faced with currently-accepted ideas, theses which seemed evident, affirmations which had up to that time passed as scientific, it whispers into the philosopher's ear the word: *Impossible!* Impossible even though the facts and the reasons appeared to invite you to think it possible and real and certain. … What a strange force this intuitive power of negation is. [CM 129/120]

Intuition here is a kind of confused resistance to reason and accepted truths, an involuntary "hunch" that all is not what it seems. If this particular "power of negation" is not, for Bergson, pure intuition, intuition at its most profound, it is at least a product and offshoot of the latter. That intuition can be involuntary in such a way seems to be one reason why Bergson writes that we cannot arrive at it by means of analysis; "from intuition one can pass onto analysis but not from analysis to intuition" [CM 213/202]. Intuition begins from nothing but itself; it is, in traditional philosophical terms, *sui generis*. This may appear to contradict Bergson's claim that, as we have seen, intuition is the second stage of a philosophical method, but it is perhaps reconcilable with it. Analysis can clear the ground for intuition, but it cannot wholly command it, and it must, if it is to guide intuition for reflective philosophical goals, *have already been guided by it*. Philosophical method, in other words, consists of the mutual support of intuition and reasoned, conceptual discourse, and both, in actual fact, are always intrinsically related to each other. It is in this sense that we can understand Bergson's dictum that "our intuition is reflection" [CM 103/95].

Intuition is intrinsic to reflection and the intellect, but what, at bottom, Bergson intends by the term "intuition" relates quite closely, as he admits, to an ordinary sense in which "some [*certains*] take the term today" [M 1577], namely as a kind of uncertain view, an awareness of something whose evidence may or may not convince. Intuition is not the apprehension of an absolute certainty, the mental apprehension of clear and distinct ideas, as Descartes supposed, but rather the awareness of duration that, itself, is neither distinct nor clear. Rather than absolute certainties and a total co-incidence, intuition, as Bergson emphasises in *Creative Evolution*, provides "vague suggestions" [CE 187/178], "indistinct and indeterminate" intimations at the outer limits of conceptual thought, intimations that are often momentary and "will disappear into the night" [CE 294/278]. In the human being, "intuition is almost entirely sacrificed to intelligence" [CE 282/268], and thus the task of philosophy is to attempt a kind of gradual expansion or "dilation of consciousness" [CE 282/268], by means of both intuition and conceptual thought. This task, in all its detail and difficulty, as Bergson emphasises, cannot be realised all at once in a particular individual and is thus necessarily a collective task. Bergson rejects the "exaggerated confidence of philosophy in the powers of the individual mind" [CE 201/192]. For these reasons, when he describes the task of philosophy as one of "going beyond the human condition" [CM 57/51], this cannot be taken as an affirmation of the possibility of simply turning away from conceptual thought in order to bask in the supposed certainties of intuition.[11]

Practical intelligence

In *Creative Evolution*, Bergson develops his account of what, in "Introduction to Metaphysics", he opposed to intuition, namely analysis. Now his claim is that analysis is the product of a particular faculty of the mind: the intellect. This account of the intellect is an extension of *Matter and Memory*'s pragmatist account of perception, according to which (see Chapter 5) we perceive not simply what there is but what meets our biologically driven needs; "*the objects which surround my body reflect its possible action upon them*" [MM 21/16]. *Creative Evolution* expands the claim to the intellect (what Kant called the "understanding") as the faculty of concepts: "our intelligence, in a narrow sense of the term, is destined to assure the perfect insertion of our body in its milieu, to represent the relations of external things to each other, and, at bottom, to conceive matter" [CE ix/v]. Our intelligence is "an annexe of the faculty of action": not only do we *see* what we want and need, but also we *conceive* according to our wants and needs.

We might naïvely consider that theory is independent of practice, but Bergson argues that our theorising, from the ground up, is intrinsically practical and purposeful. If the "intellect" is the faculty of concepts, the basic *schema* of our conceptual thought are intrinsically a form of *scheming* that allows us to manipulate and profit from things. We pride ourselves in our knowledge, and name ourselves *homo sapiens*, "the knowing human", but we also recognise ourselves as *homo faber*, "the human maker". For Bergson, our knowing has always been in the service of our making: "*intelligence, envisaged in what seems to be its original procedure, is the faculty of producing artificial objects, tools to make tools in particular, and to vary infinitely their fabrication*" [CE 146/140]. The intelligence is naturally disposed towards "un-organised solids" [CE 162/154], the dead stuff that it can easily manipulate. It can grasp things only in supposing that their edges are the product of an arbitrary division; "it makes us consider every actual form of things, even the form of natural things, as artificial and provisional; it makes our thought efface from the object perceived, even though organised and living, the lines that outwardly mark its inward structure" [CE 164/156]. The natural forms of living beings, as Bergson now writes, are effaced by the intellectual function of regarding all matter as arbitrarily divisible. Seeing only continua of an infinite number of points and instants, the intellect betrays the life and movement in things [CE 164/156]. With its natural inclination towards inert things and mechanistic thinking, it cannot grasp life in its spontaneity: "[i]ntelligence, by means of the science which is its own product, will deliver up to us more and more completely the secret of physical operations; of life it brings us only, and claims moreover to bring us only, a translation in terms of inertia" [CE 186/177]. Life is not death, just as movement is not immobility; and the mechanistic schema of the intellect will always strangle the life out of movement in attempting to grasp it.

This critical delimitation of the intellect is a product of Bergson's evolutionary epistemology, of what we might understand as a quite particular form of "evolutionary psychology" (one quite different from what is advanced under that heading today). "A theory of knowledge", he argues, "that does not put the intellect back into the general evolution of life will teach us neither how the forms of knowledge have been constituted, nor how we can expand or surpass them" [CE xiii/ix]. He approaches all the faculties of the mind as products of biologically determined needs:

In the labyrinth of acts, states and faculties of mind, the thread which one must never lose is the one furnished by biology. *Primum vivere*. Memory, imagination, conception and perception, generalisation in short, are not there "for nothing, for pleasure". It really seems, to listen to certain theorists, that the mind fell from heaven with a subdivision into psychological functions whose existence simply needs to be recognised: because these functions are such, they will no doubt be used in such a manner. I believe on the contrary that it is because they are useful, because they are necessary to life, that they are what they are; one must refer to the fundamental exigencies of life to explain their presence and to justify it if need be. [CM 61/54]

The "understanding" or "intellect" has to be explained; and explanation here amounts to a biological account of its genesis and purpose. This may appear to be a shockingly reductive approach for a supposedly "spiritualist" philosopher, but it is not as materialist as it seems, given that Bergson argues, as we will see in Chapter 9, that the principle of biological life, the *élan vital*, is already, by degrees, conscious and spiritual. From Bergson's perspective, "nature", as Ravaisson hypothesised before him, is the "history of the soul, a history continued and realised by humanity and its art".[12]

In the middle of the nineteenth century, evolutionary biology had led, quite naturally, to the idea that human cognitive functions could be explained in evolutionary terms; this, as Čapek noted, was part of the "intellectual atmosphere"[13] of the period. In 1855, prior not just to Darwin's own limited forays into the domain,[14] but even to the publication of his On the Origin of Species, Herbert Spencer offered a statement of an evolutionary psychology in his Principles of Psychology. Bergson's evolutionary psychology, however, involves a rejection of Spencer's approach. He arrived at the discovery of duration, as we saw in Chapter 2, by reflecting on the nature of time as one of Spencer's "first principles", and this led to the claim that mechanical principles do not apply to the domain of the mind. In 1907, Bergson extends this claim to life as such, to biological as well as psychological life, and attaches it to a critique of the intellect: the intellect, with its mechanical principles, is "created by life, in definite circumstances, to act on definite things", but it cannot "embrace life" as a whole, precisely because it is "only an emanation or an aspect" of it [CE x/vi]. Hence at the same time as rejecting Spencer's mechanistic account of biological evolution, Bergson rejects his Victorian assurance that the mechanical principles of modern science represent the culminating stage of epistemological development.

Mechanism as a "methodological rule" is certainly an "effective research instrument" but we err in "converting this methodological rule into a fundamental law of things" [CE 374/348] in general. Although it is true that in Creative Evolution "it is not the mechanistic viewpoint but its extension beyond matter to life"[15] that Bergson *explicitly* criticises, his position on mechanism is *still* (see the conclusion to Chapter 5) ambiguous. On the one hand, he affirms that although the intellect, with its mechanistic tendencies, is intrinsically pragmatic in orientation, we can assume, at least until we know otherwise, that science gets to the heart of matter, or that it is, at least, on the way to doing so:

> If the intellect is made for using matter, it is on the structure of matter, perhaps, that the structure of intelligence has modelled itself. Such is at least the simplest and the most probable hypothesis. We'll have to accept it for as long as it has not been demonstrated that intelligence deforms, transforms, constructs its object, or touches only its surface or grasps only its appearance. [CM 38–9/35]

This may seem to retreat from Bergson's notion of matter as durational in the final pages of *Matter and Memory*, but it is only when the mechanistic intellect encroaches on the terrain of philosophy and its concern for life—when science becomes "scientism" [CM 78/71]—that it is to be combatted. On the other hand, Bergson affirms that "mechanical systems" [CE 10/10] are abstracted and isolated from a prior, more organic totality, from a "universe" that "endures" [CE 11/11], and this idea could swiftly lead back to the idea that mechanistic schema indeed deform a more primitive truth, one continuous with consciousness, in things as a whole.

The ambiguity in Bergson's position is contained in the idea that "matter has a tendency to constitute isolated systems that can be treated geometrically" [CE 10/10]. The third chapter of *Creative Evolution* accounts for this tendency by developing the conclusions of *Matter and Memory* concerning a form of extension prior to geometrical space. Both intelligence and the inert matter with which it is made to function, Bergson argues, presuppose geometrical extension, but he now considers (as we will see in more detail in Chapter 9) extension as *ex-tension*, i.e. the relaxation of duration. As such a relaxation, geometrical extension is a natural tendency of both mind and matter, one that arrives, by degree, on the basis of a common origin. It is not the case, as Kant thought, that there are only "three options in the theory of knowledge: either the mind models itself on the structure of things, things are modelled on mind, or we have to suppose between things and the mind a mysterious harmony". For there is a fourth option, according to which both have a common origin in the movement, the tension and ex-tension, of durational life: "the more consciousness is intellectualized, the more matter is spatialized" [CE 199/190], and "gradually intelligence and matter have adapted themselves to each other to then finally come to rest at a common form" [CE 217/207].[16] On this basis, Bergson can argue that classical modern physics does not have merely relative knowledge of its object—even though this knowledge is sometimes "approximative" [CE 199/190]—while still maintaining the idea that it is the gradual result of a more fundamental development.

From the perspective of Kant's critical philosophy, attempting to account for the genesis of the categories of the understanding in this way would be impossible and absurd, the product of a "category mistake", since the attempt would presuppose, like all knowledge, the categories it was trying to explain. Kant's position is that the fundamental forms or categories of the "understanding", categories which are involved in all our thinking, are *a priori*, timeless and inexplicable. Bergson claims, in contrast, that they have a genesis and origin, but he accepts that another faculty of the mind is necessary in order to grasp this, namely intuition. His argument does not necessarily imply that we have to renounce the idea of *a priori* forms of knowledge, as long as we are able to recognise, according to Bergson's lecture at the 1900 International Congress of Philosophy in Paris, that "*a posteriori* and *a priori* designate differences of nature or value, but not a chronological anteriority or posteriority" [M 419]. The idea that forms of knowledge are *a priori* does not preclude, at least if we are prepared to stretch ordinary understandings of the Latin phrase, that they have arisen in time.

Although he is critical of the over-extension of modern mechanism, Bergson's "biological" approach to the practical intellect— and it is important to note this in relation to his reflection on the perils of modern techno-science in *The Two Sources*, which Chapter 10 addresses—does not allow him much scope for critique of the particular forms that the intellect has adopted within history. In relation specifically to modern science, he claims that "the mathematical form which physics has taken is, at one and the same time, what best corresponds to reality and what is most satisfying to our understanding" [CM 52/45]. We might wonder, however, whether the advent of mathematical physics—as, in the words of one of its founders, an attempt to gain "mastery and possession" (Descartes) of nature— is not rather a contingent, historical event, a cultural and historical paradigm shift producing a new interpretation of things, one which is neither simply a more accurate representation of reality nor simply an expression of biological need. Bergson was rebuked on this score by thinkers as diverse as the Marxist Georg Lukács and the Thomist Jacques Maritain. Bergson, they argued, makes something natural of the modern mathematisation of reason, normalises the pernicious forces of modernity and leaves us with only a dubious, "irrationalist" doctrine of intuition as a response.[17] It is not necessary to accept their interpretations of Bergson's doctrine of intuition to see that they make an important point concerning his notion of the intellect.

Vital instinct

Creative Evolution distinguishes the intellect from instinct. Instincts, in the plural, we can define as the more or less fixed patterns of behaviour in animals, whereas instinct, in the singular, is, the force or capacity that produces these behaviours. Bergson admits that "the most essential of primary instincts", as in the chick's breaking the shell of its egg with its beak, do not in any immediate or obvious sense appear to involve forms of knowledge or consciousness [CE 176/ 167]. Higher, more complex forms of instinct, however, appear increasingly mysterious, and seem to require a cognitive principle for their explanation. Just as birds seems to know when and where to migrate, the wasp, to follow Bergson's example, somehow knows how and where to sting the caterpillar in order to paralyse it; "it knows that the cricket has three nerve centres … or at least it acts as if it knew this" [CE 182/173]. This knowledge or quasi-knowledge is instinct, "a *sympathy* (in the etymological sense of the word)", as Bergson writes, evidently enjoying the irony. It is a "fellow-feeling" or "feeling-with", "which teaches it from within, so to speak, concerning the vulnerability of the caterpillar" [CE 183/ 173]. "Instinct is sympathy" [CE 196/186], but not the *intellectual* sympathy that, for the Bergson of 1903, was intuition. Instinct tends to be "assured of immediate success" in realising what appear to be its ends, its purposes, "but limited in its effects", since those ends are specialised and relatively invariable. Intelligence, in contrast, is "hazardous", and will meet less frequently with success, but its "conquests, if it should reach independence, might be extended indefinitely" [CE 147/141] in an infinity of circumstances. Instinct has a "blind lucidity"[18] that assures the living being of success; its range is narrow, but it is profound and prompt. It knows in its own way what it has to do better than intelligence ever could. Intelligence is shallow and hesitant, but by means of calculation and reasoning is able to turn its hand to a horizon of possibilities. And in contrast to intelligence, which is geared to inert matter and the manufacture of tools, instinct uses the living organs of the body, instruments that "produce and repair themselves" [CE 147/141], to realise its ends.

To say that the bird and wasp know what to do is not, for Bergson, anthropomorphic, an illegitimate application of a concept deriving from human capacities to other animals. For "if instinct and intelligence both involve knowledge, knowledge is much rather *played* and unconscious in the case of instinct, and rather *thought* and conscious in the case of knowledge". This, however, "is a difference of degree rather than nature" [CE 152/146]. Different instincts differ in the degree of self-aware knowledge that they possess, and thus in their degree of consciousness. One cannot say where conscious knowledge begins and where unconscious knowledge ends, since both are continuous with each other, differing only by potentially ever-decreasing degrees. Bergson justifies this claim by analogy with our own experience of habit. We directly experience degrees of the spectrum of consciousness in our own actions as they become habitual [CE 151/145]. Here, by degrees, the "representation of the act is held in abeyance by the execution of the act itself", and thematic, reflective consciousness arises only if the "carrying out of the act is stopped or hindered" [CE 151/145]. Consciousness rises and declines by degrees, and it arrives when our actions are unable to be executed as if all by themselves, without any explicit guidance of the will and reflective thought.

The degrees of what *Matter and Memory* termed "attention to life", Bergson now finds, therefore, not just in human life, but across the whole range of animal life, and even in plant life. However, although in actual fact intelligence and instinct differ by degrees, they are no less different in principle; there are "profound differences of internal structure" between them. Both instinct and intelligence are products of evolution, but they are "divergent, equally elegant solutions to one and the same problem" [CE 150/144], namely the problem of survival and of the furtherance of life. Instincts are not, as the neo-Darwinist of Bergson's time held them to be, namely a "mosaic of reflexes juxtaposed by genetic variation and natural selection". Nor are they an originally "intelligent discovery on the part of a few individuals of the species" that has been "degraded by habit and transmitted by heredity" as the neo-Lamarckian would have it.[19] Instinct and intelligence are coeval principles, and life has two means to achieve its goals. Intelligence is not higher than instinct, and for this reason instinct can derive from it just as little as it can be reduced, following contemporary evolutionary psychology, to a development of instinct. Consequently, Bergson rejects the humanist position that the human being is higher than other animals because of its alleged exclusive possession of intelligence, and holds that humanity differs in nature from other animals only because intelligence predominates in it [CE 193/183]. Like memory and perception in sense experience, instinct and intelligence are different in principle, while always accompanying each other in fact in living beings. However, instinct and intelligence have a common origin, which is the principle of life itself: "they are divergent tendencies emerging from a common source, tendencies that are never completely isolated from each other" [CE 150/144]. In some species instinct comes to the fore, while in the human being intelligence is pre-eminent, but the two, Bergson argues, are never wholly without at least a glimmer of the other.

With these notions of life as divergence and tendency, we arrive at Bergson's conception of the *élan vital*. Before addressing it directly in Chapter 9, the following chapter addresses the reflection on art and the account of artistic creation that guides it. To conclude this chapter, it is important to note how Bergson relates intuition to instinct as well as to intellect. *Creative Evolution* presents intuition as a kind of synthesis of both instinct and intellect: "by intuition, I mean an instinct that has become disinterested, self-conscious, capable of reflecting upon its object and of expanding it indefinitely" [CE 186/178]. Or as he writes elsewhere, "human intuition prolongs, develops and transposes into reflection what remains of instinct in man" [M 1150]. Intuition, then, is not a faculty in its own right, but a synthesis of instinct and intelligence. This, of course, left Bergson open to Russell's jibe about the birds and the bees, but it saved him from having to address potentially difficult questions about the evolutionary origin and purpose of intuition.

Summary

In his 1903 "Introduction to Metaphysics", Bergson accounts for his own philosophical method by taking up the notion of intuition widely discussed in nineteenth-century post-Kantian German philosophy. Intuition, on Bergson's account, is distinguished from analysis, and is the means by which we apprehend duration. Bergson seems to employ the term in both a narrower and a broader sense: intuition can denominate philosophical method in general, including its analytical aspects, but it can also denominate the non-analytical and immediate apprehension of the primary truths of experience. In contrast, as *Creative Evolution* argues, analysis is the product of the intellect as a mental faculty that is intrinsically oriented towards manipulating inert matter. The intellect and the geometrical space it is apt for understanding have a common origin, as the third chapter of the 1907 text argues, in a more fundamental principle accessible to intuition. In the second chapter of the text, Bergson distinguishes the intellect from instinct as two equally elegant solutions, which can both be found to varying degrees in humans and other animals, to the problems encountered by life in its evolution. Intellect is just as little a higher form of instinct as instinct is a degraded form of intellect.

Notes

1   On this, see Azouvi, *La gloire de Bergson*, Chapter 5.
2   Bertrand Russell, "The Professor's Guide to Laugher", *The Cambridge Review* 33 (January 18, 1912), 193–4.

3 On this point, see Léon Husson, *L'Intellectualisme de Bergson. Genèse et développement de la notion bergsonienne d'intuition* (Paris: Presses universitaires de France, 1947), p. 6.

4 See Husson, *L'Intellectualisme de Bergson*, pp. 54–62.

5 See Bergson, "Introduction à la métaphysique", *Revue de métaphysique et de morale* 11/1 (1903), 1–36, p. 3. On this point, see also Riquier, *Archéologie de Bergson*, p. 134.

6 See Ravaisson, *Of Habit*, p. 55: "The obscure intelligence that through habit comes to replace reflection, this immediate intelligence where subject and object are confounded, is a real intuition, in which the real and the ideal, being and thought are fused together". Also p. 59: "habit can be considered as a method—as the only real method—for the estimation, by a *convergent infinite* series, of the relation, real in itself but incommensurable in the understanding, of Nature and Will."

7 On this context, see Laurent Jaffro, "Infinity, Intuition, and the Relativity of Knowledge: Bergson, Carrau, and the Hamiltonians", *British Journal for the History of Philosophy* 18/1 (2010), 91–112.

8 Aristotle, *Metaphysics IX*.

9 Riquier takes Deleuze to task on this point; see *Archéologie de Bergson*, pp. 133–4.

10 If this is the case, in *identifying* intuition with philosophical method, rather than showing how intuition is one of the *sources* of philosophical method, Deleuze would fail to follow the second of his four "rules" of intuition as a method: "struggle against illusion, rediscover the true differences in kind or articulations of the real"; *Bergsonism*, p. 21.

11 See, in this connection, Keith Ansell-Pearson, *Bergson: Thinking Beyond the Human Condition* (London: Bloomsbury, 2018).

12 Ravaisson, "Philosophical Testament", in *Selected Essays*, p. 305.

13 Milič Čapek, *Bergson and Modern Physics*, p. 3.

14 Concerning Darwin's perspective on the mind, see Chapter 5 of Tim Lewens, *Darwin* (Abingdon: Routledge, 2007) in this book series.

15 Michael Vaughan, "Introduction: Henri Bergson's *Creative Evolution*", *SubStance* 36/3 (2007), 7–24, p. 15.

16 See, in this connection, Gilles Deleuze, "Lecture Course on Chapter Three of Bergson's *Creative Evolution*", trans. Bryan Loban, *SubStance* 36/3 (2007), 72–90.

17 On this point, see Sanford Schwartz, "Bergson and the Politics of Vitalism", p. 290.

18 According to Jankélévitch's paradoxical formulation: *Henri Bergson*, p. 158.

19 Both quotations: Raymond Ruyer, "Bergson et le Sphex ammophile", *Revue de métaphysique et de morale* 64/2 (1959), 165–79, reprinted in Bergson, *L'Evolution créatrice*, ed. A. François, pp. 635–50, p. 637.

Further reading

Henri Bergson, *Histoire de l'idée de temps. Cours au Collège de France 1902–03*, ed. C. Riquier (Paris: Presses universitaires de France, 2016). The first chapter, an early version of the essay "Introduction to Metaphysics", contains an important reflection on fundamental metaphysical ideas from the philosophical tradition.

Milič Čapek, *Bergson and Modern Physics: A Reinterpretation and Re-evaluation*. Boston Studies in the Philosophy of Science, Vol. 7 (Dordrecht: D. Reidel, 1971). See the first part of this book for an extended examination and contextualisation of "Bergson's Biological Theory of Knowledge".

Gilles Deleuze, "Lecture Course on Chapter Three of Bergson's *Creative Evolution*", trans. Bryan Loban, in *SubStance* 36/3 (2007), 72–90. Deleuze's notes helpfully situate in the context of post-Kantian German philosophy *Creative Evolution's* attempt to discover a common origin of the intellect and homogeneous space.

Eight
Art

Fragmentary aesthetics

In the preceding chapters of this study, we have seen that Bergson appeals to experience of the arts, to what is traditionally called "fine art", in order to support his metaphysical and epistemological claims. Chapter 2 showed that *Time and Free Will* compares the unity of temporal experience to that of a "phrase in a melody". Chapter 3 showed that Bergson thinks about freedom by analogy with artistic creation: our acts are free when they "spring from our own personality, when they express it, when they have that indefinable resemblance to it that one sometimes finds between the artist and his work" [TFW 172/129]. Moreover, Chapter 7 indicated that Bergson reflects on intuition as a philosophical method against the background of a certain idea of artistic intuition and of truth in art. Some of the motivation and justification for Bergson's claim that intuition can deliver truths to us—that conceptual thought, if left to its own devices, can never attain—derived from ideas about the operation of intuition and genius in fine art.

Bergson did not develop these appeals to art with a book devoted solely to aesthetics or the philosophy of art. The nearest we have to such a work is the section on the purpose or "object" of art in the third chapter of *Laughter*. Although later in the 1920s he seems to have considered writing an aesthetics, the pull of a work on ethics and religion was stronger.[1] When asked in 1934 whether he had the intention to work on "aesthetic problems", he replied negatively and cited his advancing years.[2] Bergson left his published works, as

Frédéric Worms has written, "scattered with the radiant fragments [*les éclats*] of an at once present and absent aesthetics".[3] Consequently, the idea that Bergson offers a "philosophy of art" has to be taken not just as an objective genitive (*genitivus objectivus*, as the grammarians say), whereby philosophy takes art for its object and clarifies it by its own lights, but also as a subjective genitive (*genitivus subjectivus*), according to which the philosophy, as an "artistic philosophy", belongs to the art and is an expression of it. Art, for Bergson, is as much an answer as a question, as much a solution as a problem in its own right.[4]

To understand what Bergson says about art, therefore, is to understand not just a particular aspect of his thinking but his philosophy as a whole. With that aim in mind, this chapter examines first his account of the "object" or purpose of art in both *Time and Free Will* and *Laughter*, while the second section turns to the ideas of creation and genius in the 1907 *Creative Evolution*. On this basis, the chapter turns to two other aspects of Bergson's mature metaphysics that derive from his reflection on artistic creation: the critique of the modal category of possibility and his associated account of retroactivity, the *prima facie* strange idea of a certain kind of backwards causation in history.

Suggestion and revelation

Bergson briefly reflects on the nature of art and aesthetic experience in the first chapter of *Time and Free Will*, in a passage which presents the outline of what we might term an aesthetics of *suggestion*. "The object of art", he writes, "is to lull to sleep the active or rather resistant powers of our personality, and to bring us thus to a state of perfect responsiveness in which we realise the idea suggested to us and sympathise with the sentiment expressed" [TFW 14/11]. Poetry, for example, relies on "the regular movements of rhythm, through which our soul is lulled into self-forgetfulness, and, as in a dream, thinks and sees with the poet". There is necessarily a power akin to "hypnosis" in art, and in this sense "art aims to impress feelings on us rather than express them; it suggests them to us and does without imitation when it finds more efficacious means" [TFW 15/12]. With their emphasis on the dreamlike and the hypnotic, and on indirect suggestion in contrast to direct imitation or expression,

Bergson's remarks on art in 1889 seem to resonate with the work of the "decadent", "symbolist" poets and painters of fin de siècle France.[5]

Laughter presents a more developed account of the "object of art", one that understands "object [objet]" both in the general sense of the purpose of art and also in the more specific sense of its subject-matter. "If reality came to strike our senses and consciousness directly", Bergson begins, "if we could enter into immediate communication with things and with ourselves, I think that art would be pointless [inutile], or rather that we would all be artists, for our soul would vibrate forever in unison with nature" [L 150/115–16]. This is a hypothesis to which Bergson contrasts his view that art has, indeed, a purpose, and this because the practical necessities in perception and their associated linguistic conventions veil the truth of the perceived world. We perceive not the world in its pure state, as we have seen Bergson argue in Chapters 5 and 7 of this study, but rather as carved up by our pragmatic concerns and general, conventional concepts. Fine art, however, can break this pragmatic spell and gain access to a reality that is veiled in and by everyday experience. Artists are able to "bring us face to face with reality itself", the reality of our own feelings as well as that of the perceived world, and, in the case of poetry or creative language, make language express "what it was not made to express", namely individuality and singularity. Nature inspires "souls more detached from life", souls in which "nature forgets to attach perception to need", and who possess "a virginal manner, in some sense, of seeing, of hearing or of thinking". The fine artist perceives for the sake of perceiving— in privileging different senses according to the different forms and media of art—and thus achieves a "more direct vision of reality". Artistic detachment from practical life produces proximity to reality, and art's "highest ambition is to reveal nature to us" [L 153/119].

It would be easy to criticise these claims for ignoring that the arts are mediated by their own particular forms of technique, and thus are pragmatic each in their own way. Following Raymond Bayer, we could emphasise that the painter sees more for the sake of painting than for the sake of seeing, according to the capacities and possibilities of painting. In this sense, the fine artist is *homo faber* as well as a visionary, and the arts are in large part analytic rather than simply intuitive.[6] But such a critique remains external to Bergson's approach, because he is accounting for what distinguishes fine art from art, i.e. craft in general. In modern philosophy, what distinguishes fine art from craft, since Kant at least, is *genius* understood as a kind of natural, inborn talent contrasted with technique, culture and skill. Hence Bergson does not have to marginalise or minimise the mediating role of technique in art. His position is simply that (1) fine art is the result of something more than technique; and (2) this additional element consists in a better, a truer apprehension of reality than the one that conventional conceptual experience can grasp. With this second point, Bergson is closer to the post-Kantian German Romantic philosophers than he is to Kant himself.

Is it not the case, however, that Bergson's account of art as revelatory of nature remains naïve in that it seems to suppose a faithful reproduction—a "more direct vision"—of a pre-existing reality? Bergson does not, to be sure, promote a narrow form of "realism" or "naturalism" in art (according to which the task of the artist would be to reproduce faithfully what is supposedly "given" in sense-experience), since he admits that some form of "idealism" is an integral element of breaking with pragmatic convention and turning to the truth of and in experience: "it is by means of ideality alone that we can resume contact with reality" [L 157/121]. The artist somehow has to turn away from the world before turning to it in more depth; and what we might describe as more abstract, less naturalistic forms of art may gain access to reality in Bergson's sense. That said, when reflecting again on the purpose of art in the 1911 Oxford lectures "The Perception of Change", Bergson compares the poet to the liquid developing agent in a photographic dark room, which seems to presuppose a quasi-mechanical view of art as a passive registration of the real:

> the poet and the novelist who express a mood certainly do not create it out of nothing; they would not be understood by us if we did not observe within ourselves, up to a certain point, what they say about others. As they speak, shades of emotion and thought appear to us which might long since have been brought out in us but which remained invisible; just like the photographic image which has not yet been plunged into the

bath where it will be revealed. The poet is this revealing agent.
[CM 159/149–50]

This position seems to exclude points of view and interpretation in art. Bergson seems to tie the object of art to an idea of reproduction or imitation in this sense when he writes that "nowhere is the function of the artist shown as clearly as in that art which gives the most important place to imitation, I mean painting". The original painter, and Bergson writes here of the nineteenth-century proto-impressionism of J. M. W. Turner and Jean-Baptiste-Camille Corot, shows us what we have not noticed, what we "have perceived without seeing [perçu sans apercevoir]". Painting focuses on what Leibniz calls our petites perceptions, our small, unnoticed perceptions, and in so doing it makes them grand and remarkable:"the great painters are those to whom belongs a certain vision of things that has or will become the vision of all men". It is on this condition, Bergson supposes, that art can be more than mere arbitrary fantasy and that we can speak of paintings as "true". This is not to deny, as he states, that the painter has "created" a painting, and that it is a product of her "imagination" [CM 159/150], but if it did not show us something of our own experience, there would be no truth in painting.

There is an evident tension in these remarks concerning the purpose of art in that Bergson wants to reconcile a notion of revelation, and thus truth in art, with a notion of artistic creation. On the one hand, he wants to preserve the idea that art has a certain kind of truth function, that it shows us something about the perceived world; on the other hand, he recognises the "creativity" and imaginative powers of the artist, which add something that was not already present. In this latter sense, within "Introduction to Metaphysics", Bergson can write of an artist sketching Notre-Dame cathedral in Paris who "substitutes for the real and internal organization of the thing an external and schematic reconstitution, in such a way that his drawing responds, in sum, to a certain point of view on the object and to the choice of a certain mode of representation" [CM 201/191] of it. The drawing, according to the way in which it represents its object, expresses a point of view, and reconstitutes the perceived world schematically. It is hard to reconcile this position with his earlier, apparently positivistic idea of art as the revelation of a pre-given reality.

In order to attempt to resolve or dissolve this tension in Bergson's position, we have to ask what this "real and internal organization of the thing" before it is represented in art could be. *Matter and Memory* taught, as we have seen, that the idea of pure perception is a theoretical abstraction, since in reality the difference between perception and memory is always a difference of degree. The perceived reality that art can reveal is therefore a reality inhabited and constituted by memory. Memory forms a horizon constitutive of the singularity of things, and thereby our reality is inhabited by our personal histories. Memory in this sense constitutes what Marcel Proust will describe as a "*milieu* that we do not see, but by the changing and translucent means of which we see […], that is to say the beliefs that we do not see but which are no more reducible to pure emptiness than is the air that surrounds us".[7] Hence, if the purpose of art is to reveal reality, it is the horizon of memory constitutive of the things of actual experience that it can reveal. Given, however, that this horizon of meaning is not one of the things constituted within it, revealing it in art can hardly be understood on the model of the imitation of things. Painting, to take Bergson's leading example, could have for its task an illumination and excavation of the layers of memorial meaning, sense and organisation that are constitutive of the things of the perceived world. Bergson does not say this explicitly, but his notion of art bringing us "face to face with reality" can easily accommodate it. Although he sometimes advances an apparently naïve notion of artistic revelation as a more "direct" apprehension of reality, the movement of his own thought allows for a richer understanding of art as revelatory rather than merely imitative of sense-experience. In this way, his approach would be close to later philosophies of art—such as that of Maurice Merleau-Ponty[8]—which emphasise the interpretative nature both of sense experience and of the art that serves to reveal it.

Bergson's notion of artistic revelation is vague and requires elaboration, but it allows him to claim that art and philosophy derive from the same source. What Bergson writes in 1904 of Ravaisson is also a profession of his own doctrine: "Ravaisson's whole philosophy derives from the idea that art is a figurative metaphysics, that metaphysics is a reflexion on art, and that it is the same intuition, diversely employed, that produces the profound philosopher and the great artist" [CM 274/266]. Artistic vision, for Bergson also, is of the same origin as what we have seen he takes to belong to, if not wholly to constitute, the method of metaphysics: intuition. This is not to say that philosophical intuition is wholly identical to artistic intuition, but only that they emerge from the same source: "philosophical intuition, after having engaged itself in the same direction as artistic intuition, goes much further: it takes life before its dispersion in images, while art bears on the images" [M 1148]. Art, in focusing on things in their particularity, as they are before they are carved up by pragmatic vision and conventional concepts, "dilates our perception, but on the surface", while by means of philosophy "all things acquire depth" [CM 186/175], a depth that, as we have seen in previous chapters, is pre-imagistic.

Genius and creativity

In Time and Free Will Bergson elucidated a sense of human freedom prior to the availability of alternative possibilities by appealing to the production of art. This appeal, as we will see in Chapter 9, becomes the basis of a philosophy of life as a whole in Creative Evolution. In the Middle Ages and still in the early Renaissance, it is important to note, the Latin words creatio and creare applied to divine rather than human acts.[9] Only after the struggles of Renaissance humanism was it possible to speak of the essential "creative" dignity of man, of the "fine artist" (the category of "fine art" will not be clearly defined before the eighteenth century) as "creative". In 1907, Bergson extends creative power to living nature as a whole—nature is not just God's creation, but itself creative—but he acknowledges his debt to Gabriel Séailles' 1883 Essai sur le génie dans l'art in this connection. According to Séailles, a "creative power [puissance créatrice]" unites and underlies thought and biological life, such that thought "can be defined, as much as the life of the body, as 'a creation'".[10] Séailles, however, sought to demystify the modern notion of genius as the principle of artistic creation: rather than a quasi-divine capacity to create something from nothing, genius is a talent for the selection and discovery of material in nature and history. Séailles even admitted that genius, as a principle continuous with life, is not, *stricto sensu*, "creative"; genius "does not create, in the strict sense of the word; it does not produce new forms from scratch [*de toutes pièces*]".[11] There is a "creative" principle underlying all the manifestations of life, but this principle cannot be taken in any strict sense as the production of an absolute novelty, a novelty emerging *ex nihilo*.

In perhaps the most important footnote to *Creative Evolution*, since it clarifies one of the terms in the title of the book, Bergson responds to the demystified and deflated sense of production that Séailles attaches to "creation" thus:

> do we have to understand by "creation", as [Séailles] does, a synthesis of elements? Wherever there are pre-existing elements, the synthesis that will be made of them is given virtually [*virtuellement*], being only one of the possible arrangements: and this arrangement, amongst all the other possibilities that surrounded it, could have been apprehended in advance by a superhuman intelligence. We hold, on the contrary, that in the domain of life, the elements do not have a real and separate existence. These are but successive views of the mind on an indivisible process. And this is why there is radical contingency in progress, an incommensurability between what proceeds and what follows—that is, duration. [CE 30/29–30]

That creation is not *ex nihilo* or wholly *de novo* does not entail that it is synthetic in the sense of combinatorial. If the new thing were only an arrangement of already separate elements then that thing was, in principle, even if only in the divine mind, foreseeable, and thus "possible" or "virtual"; but life in its progress cannot be foreseen, Bergson affirms, because it involves contingency and incommensurability between past and future, and thus a form of novelty. Still, unforeseeability, incommensurability and indeterminism do not imply discontinuity and an idea of creation from nothing.

Bergson evidently worries that Séailles has gone too far in demystifying genius, and that he has reduced art-production to craft-production, but while remaining broadly sympathetic to his rejection of the idea of creation *ex nihilo*. Bergson's assertions concerning a "radical" and "absolute" novelty have to be treated with caution.

They are intended primarily in an epistemological sense: something is radically or absolutely new, on Bergson's account, when it cannot be foreseen; and "to foresee consists of projecting into the future what has been perceived in the past" [CE 9/9]. From this perspective, Bergson can understand "maturation" and "creation" as synonyms: after stating that "the more we dwell on the nature of time, the more we will understand that duration signifies invention, creation of forms, continuous elaboration of the absolutely new", he describes time as the "internal work of maturation or creation" [CE 11–12/11]. If creation did involve an idea of absolute and discontinuous novelty the very idea of a creative *evolution* would become a contradiction in terms. That said, it cannot be denied that another, more radical intention emerges elsewhere in Bergson's work. In 1932, Bergson writes of "the unforeseeability of forms that life creates from scratch [*de toutes pieces*], by discontinuous leaps, all along its evolution" [TS 95/119]. Séailles had denied that creation operates "from scratch", but Bergson now affirms it and therefore seems to entertain the potentially contradictory idea of a discontinuous evolution.

Does this entail that "Bergson's philosophy really contains two accounts of creation", as Newton Stallknecht wrote in 1934?[12] It is tempting to think so, and many commentators have made the point in one way or another.[13] There is a way, however, to attenuate the contradiction. This requires us to recognise that discontinuity cannot be an authentic Bergsonian category. For the idea of discontinuity seems to presuppose the image of a line that at a given point is cut, and it thereby seems to presuppose time spatialised. It is hard to see what non-spatial sense discontinuity could have. If so, the idea of discontinuity would be unable to account for duration and evolution in their primitive senses. By appealing to the idea, Bergson would only be trying to emphasise the novelty in the development of life. Bergson would thus not have two distinct and incompatible senses of creation, but rather a single notion of creation that he describes in different and approximate ways. We will return to this issue, but "from scratch" and "discontinuous" would not mean *ex nihilo* or *de novo*, from nothing other than the act of creation itself, and would serve only to emphasise that novelty is unforeseeable and that creation does not occur as a synthesis of pre-existing independent elements.

Nothingness, possibility and novelty

Bergson has to reject the idea of creation *ex nihilo* given that he argues that there is no such "thing" as nothingness. The idea of nothingness, he holds, is not even a figment of the imagination. Nothingness cannot be perceived or imagined, because to perceive or imagine is always to imagine *something*; if you try to imagine nothing, something will always pop up in your imagination while you are trying to imagine it. Nor can it be thought in a non-imagistic sense of thinking. The *idea* of nothingness, Bergson argues, derives from the negation of things expressed in language and thought ("my bicycle is not there!"), but negation, he holds, is merely a covert affirmation, a substitution of one thing for another. When I say that my bicycle has gone, I am really affirming that something else is in its place (air, unfortunately) while expressing my regret that this is the case. Bergson's argument will be famously contested by Jean-Paul Sartre in *Being and Nothingness*,[14] but on this basis he concludes that the idea of nothingness is meaningless and contradictory, like that of a square circle. On Bergson's account, when philosophers have asked "Why is there something rather than nothing?", they have, embarrassingly, been led to a state of apparently profound wonder only on the basis of an "absurdity" [CM 115/107].

Bergson's argument against nothingness is supposed to be therapeutic: nothingness belongs to the set of "grand metaphysical problems" that are "generally badly posed and that can be solved" or, better, dissolved "when the statement of the problem is rectified" [CM 112/104]. As he argues in "The Possible and the Real"—an essay first published in French in 1934, but which was based on the lecture with which Bergson opened the international meeting of philosophy at the University of Oxford in 1920—the idea of possibility also belongs to this set of problems. Much philosophical reflection on the relation of what the tradition calls the "modal" categories of possibility and actuality (which are both contrasted with necessity) presupposes that the possible precedes the real, and is somehow less than it, in that reality is supposed to require possibility plus a power to actualise it. For Bergson, in contrast, the possible is *more* and not *less* than the actual: ideas of what is possible arrive only after the fact of experience: "the possible is merely the real with, in addition, an act of mind that projects its image into the past once it has happened" [CM 118/110]. The traditional notion that the possibility of things precedes their existence is an illusion, a retrospective illusion that occludes "the continual creation of unforeseeable novelty" [CM 124/115] in duration.

The footnote of *Creative Evolution* responding to Séailles features an early expression of Bergson's critique of possibility, but this critique is most fully developed in "The Possible and the Real", where he appeals to examples of "fine art" and literature. *Hamlet* was conceivable, he argues, and thus possible, only after it was written by a person of "talent and genius" [CM 118/110]; "it is clear that the person in whom Shakespeare's *Hamlet* came forth in the form of the possible would have created in this way its reality; this would have been, by definition, Shakespeare himself" [CM 121/113]. If the artwork of the future were already possible, if I could conceive it, "I would" immediately "make it [*je la ferais*]" [CM 118/110]. In fact, I would already have made it, for "as soon as the musician has the precise and complete idea of the symphony he will create, his symphony has been created" [CM 22/13]. This is not to admit an idealist conception of creation according to which the artist first has an idea of the finished product that she then realises in the work material, for "a free action or a work of art [...] can be expressed in terms of ideas only after the fact and in an approximate manner" [CE 236/224]. Original works of art, in their irreducible singularity and particularity, and thus in their novelty, are not possible before they are realised. To think they are possible before their realisation is to import ideas "from the domain of fabrication"—where, after an initial act of creative invention, concepts, plans and schema can be realised identically many times over—into "that of creation" [CM 116/107]. It is to import a notion of craft production into fine-art production.

Kant had already recognised this within his famous analysis of genius as the principle of fine-art production in his 1790 *Critique of Judgment*. Within art in general (i.e. within craft) what is to be produced must first be "represented as possible [*als möglich*]"[15] in the producer's mind, after which the physical process of production makes this representation actual. The design and build of the product occurs according to a process of rational, conceptual deliberation, according to "rules" which can be learnt and applied in different cases. Fine art, in contrast, "does not permit of the judgment of the beauty of its product being derived from any rule that has a *concept* for its determining ground, and that depends, consequently, on a concept of the way in which the product is possible [*wie es möglich sei*]".[16] Fine-art production, as opposed to craft production, does not consist in the actualisation of a pre-given conceptual possibility. It consists in the irruption of a pre-conceptual talent and impetus that produces original works. Later, in *The Two Sources of Morality and Religion*, Bergson will provide a positive account of what in the artwork transcends the cold clarity of conceptual meaning, a positive account that echoes Kant's doctrine of aesthetic ideas, which are ideas associated with a given concept but irreducible to the latter. The creative work, Bergson will argue, necessarily expresses emotion, which is "pregnant with representations, of which none is fully [*proprement*] formed". In this sense "creation means, above all, emotion" [TS 32–3/40]. The fundamental task of art, then, is to convey and evoke a certain kind of emotion that is not wholly distinct from the concepts by which we think. In 1907, however, Bergson's "artistic philosophy" wins out over his philosophy of art, for rather than offer a theory relating only to a particular mode of experience, he extends, as we will see in the next chapter of this study, his account of artistic creation to psychological experience in general and then to the biological domain. Life is lived as a continual work of genius, as the continual irruption of "*génialité*" [CE 173/ 165], "geniality", insofar as there is something qualitatively unique and original in every state of mind, in every moment of phenomenal experience, in every action. Arthur Mitchell's translation of Bergson's neologism as "fervour" served to veil the fact, but an idea of genius is one of the guiding threads according to which he conceives the force of life as an *élan vital*.

Bergson's position on possibility, then, is this: on the basis of an implicit premise familiar from what we now call the empiricist tradition that all ideas or concepts derive from sense-experience, and an explicit premise equating possibility with conceivability, in a traditional manner that can also can be traced back to Hume's philosophy,[17] he concludes that things are not possible before they occur. He could certainly say more about the nature of conceivability and its relation to possibility. He could also say more about the historical doctrines that he is attacking, even if the primary focus of his critique is clear enough: this is the paradigm of modality as alternative simultaneous possibilities that emerged in the twelfth century as a result of difficulties in reconciling Aristotle's "statistical" or "temporal" paradigm of modality (according to which the possible exists at some point in time, in contrast to the necessary, which exists at all times) with the Christian conception of God the creator, a conception which admits some possibilities never being realised.[18] Such a sense of possibility is the basis of, indeed, Leibniz's idea of the possible worlds arrayed before the infinite understanding of God, who, by virtue of his goodness, actualises the best among them; and Bergson later stated in conversation that the target of his essay was, above all, Leibniz's doctrine.[19] On this account, the possible is that which is conceivable without contradiction; a possible world is a maximal collection of compossible things (a set of things that can exist together); and the worlds thus possible already exist in the divine intelligence.[20] For Leibniz's God, the future is wholly foreseeable, and in a sense, it has already "happened" (for everything that I might do tomorrow, there is a different version of me already present in the divine intelligence), even if His possible worlds are not, as they are for David Lewis' twentieth-century modal realism, real spatio-temporal worlds existing somewhere other than this one.[21] In the terms of the contemporary metaphysics of modality, it should be noted, Bergson's is a combinatorial conception of possibility (according to which ideas of the possible are combined from ideas about what is actual) with a radical solution to the problem of "alien qualities", i.e. of novelty, that combinatorial conceptions have faced: a genuinely novel or "alien" event, he argues, is simply not possible before it occurs.[22] This, he argues, should be a cause for celebration rather than consternation.

Bergson does not substantially qualify his thesis when he notes that to claim that the artwork of the future was not already enclosed "in some kind of cupboard reserved for possibles" [CM 118/110] is not necessarily to claim that it was impossible. It certainly was not logically impossible, as is the contradictory idea of a square circle, and there was no "insurmountable obstacle" [CM 120/112] preventing its realisation. "This non-impossibility of the thing" can be thought as "the condition of its realisation", Bergson admits. If we use the word possible to name such non-impossibility, we should recognise that "the possible thus understood has no virtuality or ideal pre-existence [n'est pas du virtuel, de l'idéalment pré-existant]". In this sense of possibility, for Bergson, it is a truism to claim that possibility is the condition of actuality, whereas in the other, stronger sense it is a pure illusion, for it would be tantamount to claiming that Shakespeare pre-existed Shakespeare himself [CM 121/112]. A sense of possibility, then, as a *not being impossible* may precede actuality as its condition, but this pre-existing non-impossibility is nothing like an idea or model of that which is to be actualised.

It is necessary, however, to qualify Bergson's position since his critique of a notion of possibility as foreseeability leaves us with the question of how to understand positively the relation of the past to the present in modal terms. Bergson's analysis was supposed to dispel and dissolve philosophical problems, but it has, in fact, only brought into the open the issue of the relation of the present and future to the past in duration. Bergson's own notion of creation as dissociation from a primal unity, which is precisely not a notion of creation *ex nihilo* as we have seen, requires a more positive modal notion accounting for how the work, in the event, emerges from the past, and how the past stands in relation to the future.[23] We can admit with Bergson that *conceptions* of what something can possibly be arrive after the fact, in the event, but this epistemological delay does not preclude a different sense of pre-existing possibility. Aristotle, for one, was able to recognise that our *preconceptions* are inadequate to the novelty of events, that our *notions* of possibility arrive only after the fact, without having to give up on the idea of a pre-existing possibility. The particular form of a novel work of art in a block of marble, for example, may well be unforeseeable, but it remains the case, he held, that the stone was potentially the statue, that the powers of the stone, along with the capacities of the artist, are what made the statue possible.[24]

Jankélévitch understood this when he argued that there is an unspoken idea of "organic possibility (*possibilité organique*)" in Bergson's work, an idea that characterises all those "nascent states that Bergson excels in describing". Organic possibility is that from which the present event emerges, and it is to be distinguished from mere logical possibility and conceivability as a "promise" is distinguished from "permission". As a promise, it is "an *élan* or drive towards the concrete", and yet it is a "mystical indetermination, rich, profound and sonorous like the silence of the night". It is not a set of distinct "possibles", ghostly proto-things striving to be actualised, but a primal state of interpenetration from which beings emerge in the forward thrust of life. Organic possibility, on this account, is in one sense nothing; it is "nothing at present, but it will be". In another sense, however, it is not a pure nothing; "it is something, but it represents in a compressed state an existence that in its adulthood will blossom freely".[25] Deleuze, however, took a different terminological approach. The two terms "possible" and "virtual", which are traditionally synonymous or at least closely related, are now to be radically distinguished. The realisation of possibility, Deleuze claims, involves reproduction of possibles that are somehow pre-existent, and thus marginalisation of unrealised possibles; the virtual, in contrast, must create its own lines of actualisation in positive and novel acts. Although the essence of the argument is Bergsonian, the terminology is not, for Bergson, as we have seen in this chapter, more often than not (and particularly in "The Possible and the Real") uses *virtuel* as a synonym for *possible*. Deleuze's terminological decision was not groundless, since in *Matter and Memory* Bergson had advanced a more positive idea of the "virtual", but it served to obscure the text of "The Possible and the Real" and its relation to traditional modal doctrines.[26]

Retroactivity

Deleuze's interpretation also occludes the fact that Bergson grapples with a rather more positive conception of possibility when reflecting on the role of history in art-production. Bergson argues that although an original work was not possible before it happened, it *will have been possible* once it has happened. The original work in the present, that is, changes the past in that it allows us to see past works as constituting the possibility of the present. "Let a man of talent or genius come forth", writes Bergson, "let him create a work: it will then be real, and by that very fact it becomes retrospectively or retroactively possible. It would not be possible, it would not have been so, if this man had not come upon the scene. [...] it will have been possible today, but [...] it is not yet so". Although one can cannot "insert the real into the past and thus operate backwards in time [...] there is no doubt that the possible can be lodged in it, or rather that the possible comes to lodge itself in it" [CM 118/111]. It is natural to think that a present that becomes past becomes a necessity, because now we can do nothing about it, but Bergson claims that the past is the realm of possibility insofar as the present places it there.

From a common-sense perspective, these are extraordinary claims. What exactly does Bergson mean by "possibility" in this context and how can it retroactively be lodged in the past by the original work of art in the present? Bergson develops the thought in the introduction to the 1934 volume of essays *The Creative Mind* with an example drawn from Emile Deschanel's 1882 work of literary criticism, *Le romantisme des Classiques*. We may well talk now, after the advent of the Romantic movement in the late eighteenth century, of the already present romanticism of Racine in the seventeenth century, but:

> the romantic aspect of classicism became clear [*ne s'est dégagé*] only due to the retroactive effect of romanticism [...]. If there had been no Rousseau, no Chateaubriand, no Vigny or Hugo, not only would we never have noticed, but there would never really have been any romanticism in the Classics of old, for this romanticism of the Classics is realised only by the lifting-out [*découpage*], in their work, of a certain aspect [*aspect*], and this aspect [*la découpure*], with its particular form, existed no more in classical literature before the appearance of romanticism, than exists, in a passing cloud, the amusing sketch that an artist perceives in it by organising the amorphous mass according to his imagination. Romanticism operated retroactively on classicism, like the artist's sketch on this cloud. Retroactively it created its own prefiguration in the past, and an explanation of itself by its antecedents. [CM 23–4/16]

The Romantic aspects "lifted out" of Classicism entail that we can now talk of Classicism making Romanticism possible, but possibility in this sense is no longer foreseeability or conceivability without contradiction. It is rather a real quality, an "aspect" of past works. It is because it is such a real quality of past works of art that Bergson can now talk just of retroactivity rather than specifically of the retro-activity *of the possible*. Retroactivity is just as much a retroactivity of the actual as of the possible.

It is hard to imagine that this doctrine of retroactivity does not reflect a reading of §34 of Nietzsche's *The Gay Science*, even though there seems to be no particular evidence indicating that Bergson had read it:

> *Historia abscondita*—Every great human being exerts a retroactive force: for his sake all of history is placed in the balance again, and a thousand secrets of the past crawl out of their hiding places—into *his* sunshine. There is no way of telling what may yet become part of history. Perhaps the past is still essentially undiscovered! So many retroactive forces are still needed![27]

Bergson's position on the nature of such retroactivity is, how-ever, delicately poised. On the one hand, he rejects the idea that the romantic aspect of classicism was already present all along, but unnoticed, as a retrospective illusion—an illusion ignorant of the way that the present shapes retroactively the past. The illusion is a function of what Bergson terms the "retrograde movement of truth", and though a natural tendency of the human mind, it is an error, the "mirage of the present in the past" [CM 9/1]. Original artists are often subject to this illusion when critics, once the shock of the new has receded, claim that the work was prefigured in the past. It is "the eternal illusion of criticism, art criticism and literary criticism, to think that because a work can be explained, perhaps, by its antecedents once it has been produced, that these antecedents produced it and were sufficient to produce it" [EPL 119]. The truth is, however, that "the present introduces something into the past, that action goes back in the course of time and comes to impress its stamp on it retroactively". The "new qualities" stamped on the past did not pre-exist the present; they are rather "created from scratch [*de toutes pieces*] and absolutely unforeseeable". Consequently "an aspect [*côté*] of the present exists as an 'aspect' only when our attention has isolated it" [CM 23/15]. In this sense, all creative work, although it is not actual plagiarism, is, in Pierre Bayard's words, *le plagiat par antici-pation*, anticipatory or retroactive plagiarism.[28]

On the other hand, if Bergson's position really is that the new aspect that appears in classicism with the advent of romanticism did not previously exist at all, one wonders why he uses the verbs *isoler* (to isolate), *se dégager* (a reflexive verb with a passive sense and a priv-ative prefix), and the noun *découpure* (also with a privative prefix) to describe the action of the present on the past: the *découpure* or "cutting" *s'est dégagé*, was revealed in, or "lifted out of", as Andison translates it faithfully, classicism by romanticism. These terms suggest that the aspect is *revealed* rather than *created*.[29] This manner of expressing his ideas could be taken as a residual expression of the very retrospective illusion that Bergson criticises, and thus to show that he has not learnt fully his own lessons. In truth, it is more likely an expression of the difficulties of his "creationist" position. He explicitly considers two options: either the aspect was already and actually there in the work of the past, or it is "created" in it by the work of the present. When Bergson extends his conception of retroactivity in the his-tory of art into a broader conception of social and political history, he may seem to push in the direction of a "creationist" position. We may claim, he writes, to discover "premonitory signs" of the modern advent of democracy in the periods preceding it, but these are "signs only because we know the course, because the course has been completed. Neither the course, nor its direction, nor, conse-quently, its end were given when these facts came into being: hence they were not yet signs" [CM 23/15]. Bergson thus seems to pre-sent a picture of history without tendencies, movements or forces— without, at least, tendencies, movements or forces whose future direction can be divined in the present. That said, Bergson admits in a parenthesis that "not just any [*non quelconque*]" [CM 23/15] novel reality is able to emerge from a specific historical conjuncture, and so his position is not as "creationist" as it may otherwise seem.

Bergson, then, seems both to affirm and to deny that the possi-bility of the original work in the present pre-existed that present in the past. We can go some way towards resolving this contradiction by observing that "creation" still means here what it meant in *Creative Evolution*: dissociation from a primal unity that, prior to the creative act, does not yet possess real and separate elements. Bergson would only be forcing, perhaps unhelpfully so, his emphasis on novelty by affirming that creation occurs "from scratch", and his real position would be that the present work of genius dissociates, and thus reveals, aspects or elements in the works of the past. With this position, Bergson seems—from the vantage point of other nineteenth- and twentieth-century conceptions of time and history—to reach out towards the idea of a repetition of the past that would be different from the boring, deadly and habitual repetition that he typically describes.[30] This would be a repetition not of the *same*, but of and with a *difference*. Kant seems to have preceded him in this also, for in discussing canonical succession in the history of art, and, that is to say, how great artists inherit from the past, the *Critique of Judgment* contrasts mere copying of past works of genius with a more original succession, whereby originality is a function of inheritance and *vice versa*—but "how the latter is possible", Kant admits, "is difficult to explain".[31] Somehow, canonical succession, development in art-history, is constituted by a reciprocal play between present-day genius and the exemplarity of past works. The original work in the present does not emerge *ex nihilo*, from nothing, but *ex historia*, from history, and yet this is not to say that the possibility of the original work was ready-made and pre-existed the present in the great work of the past. Bergson, after Kant, seems to point to the idea that the original work in the present reveals what the past made possible— *and* that this possibility is nothing without the original work in the present. On this basis, artistic creation would be intrinsically a form of revelation, and revelation would be intrinsically a form of creation. It would consequently be pointless to wonder whether the historical possibility of the original work chronologically precedes its actuality or *vice versa*, for both arrive together and co-constitute the "shock of the new".

Given that this is not Bergson's explicit position, we have to ask why he did not fully adopt it, and why he affirmed that genius in the present is untouched by the past (that it operates "from scratch") at the very moment that he sees that genius touches the past retroactively. A first answer to this question lies, perhaps, in the ethical motivations that Bergson adduces for his doctrine of "absolute novelty". Novelty, he claims, produces "joy", since it breaks the spell of the dull, monotonous repetition of the same, and allows those who do not have easy access to original art to share in the joy of those who do; "the reality invented before our eyes will give each one of us, unceasingly, certain of the satisfactions that art at rare intervals procures for the privileged; it will reveal to us, beyond the fixity and monotony which our senses, hypnotized by our constant needs, at first perceived in it, ever-recurring novelty, the moving originality of things" [CM 124/116]. If novelty is a source of joy, then one can understand why Bergson might seek its purest form and affirm a present absolutely and radically new, and why one might consequently deny the intrinsic historicality of art-production, the shaping of the present by the past. The idea, however, that novelty is desirable *per se* is scarcely defensible, and one does not have to be a political reactionary to see that novel things can be bad and that constant novelty leads to distraction. Bergson seems to be aware of this, for he admits in a lecture course that novelty is not always good [HTM 175], but he could have done more in his published texts to ensure that he was not mistaken for a celebrant of novelty for its own sake.

But this is not, perhaps, his most fundamental motivation in affirming "absolute novelty" and creation "from scratch". In addition to bringing us joy, as he argues in concluding "The Possible and the Real", appreciating the novelty in our actions and experience will "above all" make us "stronger [plus fort]", "for we shall feel we are participating, creators of ourselves, in the great work of creation which is the origin of all things and which goes on before our eyes". Strength can be gained in recognising that our creative power is one with a more general creative power that underlies life and the movement of time as such. Hence: "humbled heretofore in an attitude of obedience, slaves of certain vaguely-felt natural necessities, we shall once more stand erect, masters associated with a great Master" [CM 124–5/116]. We will return to Bergson's notion of the divine, but here it is evident that the goal of philosophical reflection and life itself is strength and mastery, even if we can never gain a monopoly on this power. At bottom, the idea of creation that guides Bergson is one of the heroic self-creating creator whose autonomy would only be weakened by inherence in history.

Life and art as will

In order to confirm this interpretation of Bergson's position, it is necessary to dig deeper. It is necessary to ask what it is, for Bergson, that enables us to create and thus create ourselves. What allows us to lift ourselves up, to elevate ourselves above natural necessity? To lift oneself up requires effort, of course, and where there is effort, there is will. Creation, then, is a function of the will, and, if Bergson does not state this explicitly in "The Possible and the Real", he nevertheless affirms, not inadvertently, that we are artistic and creative when "we want to be [*quand nous le voulons*]" [CM 110/102]. Such a voluntarist position may appear strange, particularly in the light of ordinary intuitions about "creativity" containing an essential element of "inspiration" irreducible to "perspiration". One wonders how such a voluntarist position could make sense of, say, "writer's block" or the "difficult second album". "Where an author owes a product to his genius," as Kant recognised, "he does not himself know how the *ideas* for it have entered into his head, nor has he it in his power to invent the like at pleasure."[32] Maine de Biran, Bergson's early-nineteenth-century forbear in the French spiritualist tradition, put the same point particularly well. Genius, "this ineffable form of *inspiration*, source of the most amazing *powers* of man, is not itself in his power. What is more, it ceases to exist and loses its ability to influence and move us, as soon as the will tends to give it laws, or aims to reproduce and to imitate its supreme charm".[33]

Bergson's remark about voluntary creation in "The Possible and the Real" is not inadvertent since, in *Creative Evolution*, he had already claimed that "the principle of all life", and thus all duration, is "a pure willing [*un pur vouloir*]". There he wrote: "[w]hen we put our being back into our will, and our will itself back into the impulsion that it extends, we come to understand, we feel that reality is a continual growth, creation that develops without end" [CE 252/240]. Our will is united with the principle of all growth: duration itself. Bergson's philosophy of the will gains only fleeting expression in *Creative Evolution*, and for this reason it has "little drawn the attention of commentators", as Arnaud François has remarked.[34] Yet it shapes not only Bergson's philosophy of life in general but also his philosophy of art. Certainly, if as Bergson writes in "Dreams", initially delivered as a paper in 1901, "waking and willing [*veiller et vouloir*] are one and the same" [ME 127/104], then he might have considered creation, like dreaming, to be a form of relaxation or even negation of the will. If he had done, Bergson would have remained close to Schopenhauer's accounts of both the will and art.[35] Yet he does not, and the reason why not is, in the end, clear enough: if life is creation, and if life is will, then creation itself cannot be anything but voluntary. Bergson evidently wants to hold on to the thought that life is a creative principle, and to develop the idea that life is a function of the will; but given that his idea of creation is developed according to the guiding thread of reflection on art production, he is led to a voluntarist conception of the latter, and of what, for him, is its principle, namely genius. Later, in *The Two Sources of Morality and Religion* Bergson explicitly speaks of genius as a function of the will. There exist "genial volitions [*volontés géniales*]", genial acts of will, unforeseeable volitions that are acts of genius; "the will has its genius", he states, "as does thought, and genius defies all prevision" [TS 44/55]. What exactly this might mean is open to question, but we have reason to wonder whether it is not this emergent voluntarism that limits Bergson's thinking and prevents the authentic development of his notion of retroactivity.

Summary

In his early reflection on art, Bergson claims that the "highest ambition" of fine art "is to reveal nature to us". This claim contrasts with his later emphasis on genius, creativity and novelty in fine art. Bergson writes of "radical" and "absolute novelty" in the creative process—which, in *Creative Evolution*, he discovers throughout nature as a whole and not just in the fine artist—but he does not hold to a traditional theological notion of creation *ex nihilo*. He cannot do so since he argues that *nothingness* does not in any sense exist, not even as a consistent object of thought. For this reason, he can write of creation as a process of "maturation". Still, Bergson distinguishes creation as maturation from ordinary craft-production understood as a synthesis or combination of pre-existing elements: the fine artist, as Bergson says of life in general in 1907, proceeds by dissociation rather than association. Moreover, creation does not proceed, as Kant had already shown in his account of genius, by realising pre-determined conceptual possibilities; that also is craft-production rather than creation. Bergson extends this critique of the modal category of possibility in fine art to existence in general: things, in the creative novelty of duration, are not possible before they occur. Bergson provides the lineaments of a more positive conception of possibility in reflecting on canonical succession in the history of art: great art in the present reveals the past as having made it possible, even though it was not possible before it occurred. This account of retroactivity points to a hermeneutic account of history and temporality that would move beyond Bergson's previous reflections on time. The reason why he does not develop this thought lies, at bottom, in his voluntarist affirmations that creation is a product of the will.

Notes

1 In this connection, see Brigitte Sitbon-Peillon "*Les Deux Sources de la Morale et de la Religion* suite de *L'Evolution créatrice?* Genèse d'un choix philosophique entre morale et esthétique", in *Annales bergsoniennes* IV, ed. Anne Fagot-Largeault and Frédéric Worms (Paris: Presses universitaires de France, 2008), pp. 325–38.

2 Isaac Benrubi, "Entretien avec Bergson", in *Henri Bergson: Essais et témoignages recueillis*, ed. Albert Béguin and Pierre Thévenaz (Neuchâtel: Editions de la Baconnière, 1943), pp. 365–71, p. 368: "these problems are of the greatest interest, but I am too old to gather material on them, as I did when I was composing my other works, in order to treat them in depth".

3 Frédéric Worms, "Présentation", in Henri Bergson, *La Pensée et le mouvant*, ed. A. Bouaniche *et al.* (Paris: Presses universitaires de France, 2009), pp. 1–13, p. 9.

4 On this point, see Charles Laro, "Promesses et carences de l'esthétique bergsonienne", *Revue de métaphysique et de morale* 48/4 (1941),301–13, and Ruth Lorand, "Bergson's Concept of Art", *British Journal of Aesthetics* 39/4 (1999), 400–15.

5 See Azouvi, *La gloire de Bergson*, "Une philosophie decadente, symboliste et impressionist", pp. 59–76.

6 See Raymond Bayer, "L'Esthétique de Henri Bergson", *Revue philosophique de la France et de l'étranger* 131 (1941), 244–318, pp. 254–66.

7 Marcel Proust, *A la recherche du temps perdu* (Paris: Gallimard, Bibliothèque de la Pléiade, 1988), vol. III, p. 655.

8 See Galen A. Johnson (ed.) *The Merleau-Ponty Aesthetics Reader* (Evanston, IL: Northwestern University Press, 1994).

9 In this connection, see M. Nahm, "The Theological Background to the Theory of the Artist as Creator", *Journal of the History of Ideas* 8/3 (1947), 362–72.

10 Gabriel Séailles, *Essai sur le génie dans l'art* (Paris: Librairie Germer Baillière, 1883), p. ix.

11 Séailles, *Essai sur le génie dans l'art*, p. 154.

12 Newton Stallknecht, *Studies in the Philosophy of Creation with Especial Reference to Bergson and Whitehead* (Princeton, NJ: Princeton University Press, 1934), p. 53.

13 For more on this, see Leszek Kołakowski, *Bergson* (Oxford: Oxford University Press, 1985), pp. 103–4.

14 Chapter 11 returns to Sartre's critique.

15 Immanuel Kant, *Kritik der Urteilskraft*, in *Gesammelte Schriften*, ed. Preußische Akademie der Wissenschaften/Deutsche Akademie der Wissenschaften zu Berlin/Akademie der Wissenschaften zu Göttingen (Berlin: De Gruyter, 1963), vol. 5, p. 307/*Critique of Judgment*, trans. N. Walker (Oxford: Oxford University Press, 2007), p. 136.

16 Kant, *Kritik der Urteilskraft*, p. 308/*Critique of Judgment*, p. 137.

17 See D. Tycerium-Lightner, "Hume on Conceivability and Inconceivability", *Hume Studies* 23/1 (1997), 113–32.

18 See Simo Knuuttila, "Modal Logic", in *The Cambridge History of Later Medieval Philosophy*, ed. N. Kretzmann, A. Kenny and J. Pinbourg (Cambridge: Cambridge University Press, 1982), pp. 342–57.

19 See Isaac Benrubi, "Un entretien avec Bergson (Fragment de journal)", in *Henri Bergson: Essais et témoignages recueillis*, ed. A. Béguin and P. Thévenaz (Neuchâtel: Editions de la Baconnière, 1942), pp. 365–71, p. 366: "J'ai voulu, dit-il, réagir surtout contre Leibniz qui voyait dans le réel la réalisation du possible".

20 Note, however, that Leibniz's conception of possibility as conceivability without contradiction has an actualist basis, for the simple natures that constitute a consistent, non-contradictory concept derive from divine attributes. On this point, see Ohad Nachtomy, "Modal Adventures between Leibniz and Kant: Existence and (Temporal, Logical, Real) Possibilities", in *The Actual and the Possible: Modality and Metaphysics in Modern Philosophy*, ed. M. Sinclair (Oxford: Oxford University Press, 2017), pp. 64–93.

21 See David Lewis, *On the Plurality of Worlds* (Oxford: Blackwell, 1986).

22 On this issue, see D. M. Armstrong, *A Combinatorial Conception of Possibility* (Cambridge: Cambridge University Press, 1989).

23 In this sense, Pete Gunter was right to note that the critique of the modal category of possibility in "The Possible and the Real" should not be "taken at face value"; see Pete Gunter, "Bergson's Creation of the Possible", *SubStance* 36 (2007), 33–41, p. 34.

24 See Aristotle, *Metaphysics* IX, 1049b13, where Aristotle states that *energeia* is prior to *dunamis* "according to its concept".

25 Jankélévitch, *Henri Bergson*, pp. 180–1; pp. 217–18.

26 English-language commentary has often failed to see this. A. W. Moore's account of Bergson in his The Evolution of Modern Metaphysics. Making Sense of Things (Cambridge: Cambridge University Press, 2012), pp. 411–18 is a recent example of this Deleuzian construal of Bergson as a philosopher of the "virtual".

27 Friedrich Nietzsche, Kritische Studienausgabe vol. III (1988), p. 404/The Gay Science,§34, trans. W. Kaufmann (New York: Vintage, 1974), p. 104.

28 Pierre Bayard, Le plagiat par anticipation (Paris: Editions de Minuit, 2009).

29 In the new critical edition of La Pensée et le mouvant, Arnaud François emphasises that these "découpures" are in fact created (p. 314), but without seeing the tensions in Bergson's position.

30 Although Jankélévitch underlines the importance of Bergson's notion of retrospective illusion and claimed, in fact, that Bergson had developed it in response to the first edition of his Bergson published in 1930, he does not draw out the positive significance of the doctrine of retroactivity that I highlight here.

31 Kant, Kritik der Urteilskraft, p. 310/Critique of Judgment, p. 139.

32 Kant, Kritik der Urteilskraft, p. 308/Critique of Judgment, p. 137.

33 Pierre Maine de Biran, De l'aperception immédiate (Paris: Livre de Poche, 2005), p. 253. An English translation of this 1807 text will appear soon with Bloomsbury: Maine de Biran, Of Immediate Apperception, ed. A. Aloisi, M. Piazza and M. Sinclair.

34 Arnaud François, Bergson, Schopenhauer, Nietzsche: Volonté et réalité (Paris: Presses universitaires de France, 2008), p. 48.

35 When Bergson was accused by German philosophers not just of chauvinism, but also of plagiarising Schopenhauer's philosophy, they failed to see his distance from the German thinker on the question of art. See Arnaud François, "Bergson plagiaire de Schopenhauer? Analyse d'une polémique", Etudes germaniques 60/3 (2005), 469–91 for a study of this polemic, and, for orientation, Sandra Shapshay's Stanford Encyclopedia entry on Schopenhauer's aesthetics: https://plato.stanford.edu/entries/schopenhauer-aesthetics/.

Further reading

Mark Antliff, Inventing Bergson: Cultural Politics and the Parisian Avant-Garde (Princeton, NJ: Princeton University Press, 1992).

Ruth Lorand, "Bergson's Concept of Art", British Journal of Aesthetics 39/4 (1999), 400–15.

Nine
Life

Spiritualist positivism

"One is never compelled to write a book" [CM 106/98], as Bergson remarks in concluding his intellectual autobiography in 1934. Still, one might have the feeling, even when aware of the illusions of retrospection, that he had to write *Creative Evolution*. In one sense, the book was a surprise in 1907, for in the preceding years there were few external signs to suggest that he was examining contemporary research in a variety of biological fields. Bergson did not use his teaching at the Collège de France in the years prior to 1907 to present his new work on biology, but rather to rehearse and develop issues addressed in his first two books; he led courses on memory, time and freedom in these years but no course on biological life.[1] In another sense, the book was no surprise at all. *Time and Free Will* had already signalled the importance of a reflection on living beings: "inanimate things conserve no trace of time passed, but it is not the same in the domain of life. Here duration seems to act in the manner of a cause" [TFW 153/116]. Bergson's forebears in the spiritualist tradition had pointed him in this direction: Ravaisson, as we saw in Chapter 1, had proclaimed in 1867 that the fate of a "spiritualist positivism" or "spiritualist realism" would turn on a non-mechanistic and spiritualist interpretation of biological life. Subsequently, in a chapter entitled "Living Beings" (the chapter preceding "Of Man" that was crucial for Bergson's account of freedom) of his *On the Contingency of the Laws of Nature*, Boutroux had sought to highlight a form of contingency and indetermination in the domain of biological life. The project of a "spiritualist positivism" involved a non-mechanistic biology, and thus Bergson's development of the spiritualist tradition with his account of duration called for its application to biological life.

Ever since the discovery of duration had led Bergson to break in the mid-1880s with Herbert Spencer's mechanistic evolutionary philosophy, and to accommodate a more spiritualist position, he must have been actively reflecting on the possibility of a non-mechanistic but also non-teleological account of biological evolution.[2] The sketch of a spiritualist and theistic evolutionary doctrine that Ravaisson left in his 1900 *Philosophical Testament* was evidently an inspiration for him. This was written during a period later described as the "eclipse of Darwinism" by Julian Huxley,[3] when Darwin's theory was contested by a range of alternative evolutionary doctrines. On Ravaisson's account, a divine principle expands and descends into the world in a primary act of creation which, by installing a "tendency to perfection" in the lowest levels of existence, allows for a "creative ascent" in the scale of beings, all the way back up to the purity of the divine source.[4] Even though, as we will see, he resists the teleological aspects of Ravaisson's doctrine, Bergson is closer to him than ever in *Creative Evolution*. The invocation of God as "incessant life, action, freedom" [CE 262/249] (rather than as a kind of static super-thing) may not be essential to Bergson's project in 1907, but later he will frame that project within an explicitly theistic approach. In a 1912 letter to Father Joseph de Tonquédec, Bergson describes the path of his thinking up to 1907 and considers that it has served to "reveal a free and creative God, generative of both matter and life, and whose creative effort is continued in life by the evolution of species and by the constitution of human personalities" [M 964].

Within Bergson's own path of thinking *Creative Evolution* may appear as a quasi-necessary development in that it serves to complete his earlier work in two ways. Its reflection on biological life in terms of time as duration expands duration into the world in a way that Bergson had been searching for since recognising dualism as a problem after *Time and Free Will*. In this sense, *Creative Evolution* takes up the still hesitant conclusions of *Matter and Memory* concerning rhythms or tensions of duration in the world. In Jean Gayon's words, biological evolution provided "the empirical material capable of offering the largest extension of his [Bergson's] indeterminist theses and his vision of mind".[5] Moreover, Bergson now emphasises the *futurity* of duration in a manner that completes the emphasis on the flowing *present* in *Time and Free Will* and on the *past* in *Matter and Memory*. That said, Bergson's new emphasis on the future bypasses rather than simply adds to the "polarizing"[6] distinction, as Jankélévitch saw clearly, of the past and the present-future in *Matter and Memory*. Now the mind does not belong essentially to memory in opposition to the present and future, but to the present and future first of all. It is no longer a question of finding the "excellence of the mind in the idleness of dreaming", for Bergson's position now is that dreaming amounts to our descent into space, into extension now understood as ex-tension, i.e. relaxation, as we will see. *Creative Evolution* thus inverts the fundamental orientation of *Matter and Memory*, and it returns to *Time and Free Will* in order to "expand its ideas on a cosmic scale",[7] with an idea of creation that was already implicit within the doctoral dissertation, given its analogy of the free act and the work of fine art.

Chapter 7 made an initial approach to *Creative Evolution* by examining Bergson's epistemological triumvirate of intuition, intellect and instinct. Bergson's epistemology, as we saw, involved a form of evolutionary psychology, albeit a spiritualist evolutionary psychology, and one of his basic claims is that "the *theory of knowledge* and the *theory of life* seem to us inseparable" [CE xiii/ix]. The present chapter focuses directly on the details of Bergson's theory of life, a task which has been further facilitated by Chapter 8, insofar as it illuminated the idea of creation and genius that are pivotal, as will become clear, in Bergson's reflections on the *élan vital*. This chapter shows how Bergson applies his account of genial creation to biological life after having examined his arguments against biological mechanism and finalism, and then his arguments against the expression of both in evolutionary theories. After all of that, the chapter will address Bergson's account of the relation of matter and life in the third chapter of *Creative Evolution*, and how this develops the project of *Matter and Memory*.

Mechanism and finalism

"Transformism" or "transmutationism", as it was called before the term "evolution" took hold in the 1860s, is the basic idea that biological life develops by the gradual and continuous transformation of one species into another. To Bergson, the idea suggested that temporal development is intrinsic and essential to biological life, just as *Time and Free Will* had shown that temporal development, i.e. duration, constitutes psychological life: "the more we fix our attention on this continuity of life, the more one sees organic evolution approximate to that of consciousness, in which the past presses against the present and makes a new form emerge from it that is incommensurable with its antecedents" [CE 29/27]. Consequently, the first chapter of *Creative Evolution* criticises mechanism and finalism as accounts of life, just as *Time and Free Will* had argued against determinist and libertarian positions concerning freedom in the human individual.

"The essence of mechanical explanation", he writes, "is to regard the future and the past as calculable functions of the present, and thus to claim that all is given" [CE 39–40/38]. The ideal of mechanistic explanation (as we saw in Chapter 3) is Laplace's demon hypothesis according to which the future is wholly calculable from the present state of affairs in the world. To foresee the future in this way is to make of time something "useless and even unreal" [CE 40/38]. Foreseeing involves *seeing* and thus, at bottom, the transformation of time into space. But the passage of time in actual experience is real and inevitable, and Bergson's position is that it is as real for biological life as it is for us in the psychological experience of duration. Time does not "bite" on inorganic matter in that at any given instant the supposed elementary particles of matter could be re-arranged and returned to the situation in which they were at any given point of time in the past, like chess pieces on a board. In the domain of life, in contrast, "the idea of putting things back in their place at the end of a certain time involves a kind of absurdity" [TFW 153/116]. The very idea of a living being involves something more than an assemblage of inert, self-identical particles capable of being re-arranged. Anti-mechanist doctrines have always, in some way, seen in the living being a whole that is greater than, and inexplicable by, the sum of its parts, but Bergson's originality lies in conceiving this whole in temporal, evolutionary terms according to the idea of duration; "the evolution of the living being, like that of the embryo, implies a continual recording of duration, a persistence of the past in the present, and so an appearance, at least, of organic memory" [CE 20/20]. In ontogeny as well as phylogeny time is of the essence of life: "the more duration marks the living being with its imprint, the more the organism differs from a mere mechanism, over which duration glides without penetrating. And the demonstration has the most force when it applies to the evolution of life as a whole [...] inasmuch as this evolution constitutes, through the unity and continuity of the animated matter which supports it, a single indivisible history" [CE 24/24]. Particular living beings have an apparent individuality, but on closer inspection this always dissolves. Internally, it dissolves into the perhaps infinite number of organic beings of which it is composed (into the infinite number of machines nested within machines, as Leibniz said), such as limbs, organs and cells. Externally, it dissolves into the harmony of the living being with others and into its continuity with its progenitors and offspring. For Bergson, "*life appears as a current that goes from germ to germ through the medium of a developed organism*" [CE 28/27]. Life is a whole, a temporal, durational whole that constitutes all living beings—or it is nothing at all.

Mechanism knows nothing of organic memory (hence Bergson's hesitations, as we saw in Chapter 4, concerning a mechanical conception of habit as a form of memory in 1896). Laplace's demon is concerned only with the present state of things and the laws or forces by which they interact. Mechanism knows just as little of the creative advance of organic memory into the future. It cannot, in principle, entertain any genuine sense of creativity, for it can see in new biological forms only a re-arrangement, a re-assembly of pre-existing elements. We might consider such a mechanistic approach to be a clear-sighted and hard-nosed rejection of any "wooly", anthropomorphic thinking, but Bergson exposes the naïvety of this view: "mechanism [...] holds that nature has worked like a human being by bringing parts together, while a mere glance at the development of an embryo shows that life goes to work in a very different way" [CE 94/90]. Mechanism in biology supposes that nature proceeds like the craftsman who makes a table by associating the wood from which the legs are made with that of the table top, and thus by adding pre-existing entities to each other. But this anthropomorphic approach is wrong-headed, Bergson argues, in that life, as even the basic fact of cell division shows, *"does not advance by the association and addition of elements but by dissociation and division"* [CE 94/90].

From this perspective, Bergson accommodates Darwin's idea of the tree of life—of branching after branching on the basis of a single trunk—albeit with an armory of rather more pyrotechnic metaphors: life advances like an explosion, firework or bomb, in the form of a sheath or bouquet. But Bergson takes dissociation and division to resist and confound mechanistic explanation. Such explanation in biology, just as in psychology, falls victim to a retrospective illusion when it considers that events could have been predicted on the basis of already-isolated and distinct causes in the past. For it is the advance of life that isolates and disassociates these causes, just as a free decision isolates and accords weight to the motives that I may later consider to have determined it [CE 28/28]. It is only retrospectively that life may appear open to mechanical explanation. This is not to deny that there are aspects of life that can be understood chemically and physically, and thus mechanistically, or that science will be able to explain more and more about life in this way [CE 32/31]. Physical and chemical explanations of living phenomena may well be relatively successful when they focus on what is repetitive in life [CE 37/36], and, as a "positive science", biology has to treat the living being in its repetitive aspects as a machine; "only on this condition" can it fulfil its practical purposes and allow us to manipulate living beings [CE 98/94]. Nevertheless, the profound secret of life resides in its creative development of new forms, in the creative advance of organic memory into the future. Biology, as any number of biologists have held since 1907, is irreducible to physics and chemistry.[8]

In contrast to mechanism, finalism focuses on the apparent purposiveness of living beings, what modern biology—in trying to keep traditional teleological, finalist doctrines at arm's length—calls, after Jacques Monod, the *teleonomy* of living beings, which is the basic fact that "all living beings behave as if they have an agenda".[9] Traditional finalist or teleological doctrines hold that living beings do have an agenda, just as we pursue goals and purposes in our actions. Aristotle's biology is shaped by such an analogy. All things, he is traditionally understood to argue, have four causes: material, formal, efficient and final.[10] The material cause of, say, a chalice is the silver from which it is made; the formal cause is its shape; the efficient cause is the silversmith who made it; and its final cause is the purpose for which it was made. The principal difference between the living being and an artefact such as the chalice is that the former—the acorn, say, becoming an oak—brings itself into form, is self-producing, whereas the former finds its efficient cause in another being, in the silversmith. According to this analogy, natural production in the domain of living beings is guided by purposes to the same extent as human craft. The analogy is only strengthened by the later theological notion, foreign to Aristotle, that nature as a whole is a machine of divine creation that works according to His purposes.

Biological finalism thereby focuses on the "attraction of the future" rather than, following mechanism, the "impulsion of the past" [CE 42/40], but perhaps even more explicitly than mechanism it supposes that everything is already given, and thus that time is not itself a productive cause. It cannot admit genuine, creative novelty in the course of experience insofar as biological development is conceived as merely the instantiation of a blueprint, of a plan already laid down. In this sense, "finalism is an inverted mechanism" [CE 41/39]. But in another sense, mechanism is just a weakened, truncated version of finalism [CE 94/90], given that it derives from an interpretation of purposeful craft production, and rejects only the role of final causes. There is a strange dialectic between these positions: mechanism points back to finalism insofar as the idea of a machine supposes a purpose for which it was made, while finalism can always be abbreviated in the form of mechanism. But both are products of the intellect, which, as we have seen Bergson argue (see Chapter 7), has its own quite practical purposes. Both, in fact, are the expression of a "productivist" metaphysics that views life from the blinkered perspective of the technician who can "represent organization only as a fabrication" [CE 97/93]. Both can represent living complexity, to use the cherished phrase of contemporary Darwinists, only as an 'engineering problem'.

Forms of evolutionism

Mechanism and finalism are the two poles of a spectrum which
form the background to the four competing evolutionary theories
of Bergson's day that he addresses successively in the first chapter of
Creative Evolution: neo-Darwinism, mutationism, orthogenesis and neo-
Lamarckism.[11] With the biological "analogy" of the human eye to
the eyes of a bivalve mollusc, the scallop, Bergson assesses the ability
of the doctrines to explain how life produces the same apparatus
by dissimilar means along divergent lines of evolution [CE 57/55].
The analogy may not be quite as strong as he presented it, since
the eyes of the scallop—of which there are as many as 200 on the
lips of their familiar shells—operate by crystalline mirrors (like a
telescope) rather than by a lens, as in the human eye.[12] Still, in the
two cases we have similar forms with the same function on quite
different lines of evolution, long after any possible common origin
of molluscs and vertebrates.

That random variation, prior to the natural selection of those
variations, should have produced such similar structures across
widely different lines of development seems incredible. Science is
supposed to account for the causes of evolutionary development,
but here we are left with a notion of chance that would hardly be
much of a scientific advance beyond notions of divine creation. If
chance, as Darwin sometimes says, is merely a label for effects whose
efficient causes are not yet known,[13] then we remain, in principle,
with the biological version of Laplace's demon that he presented in
his *Essay* of 1844.[14] Darwin will replace the idea of the divine selector
possessing "forethought over future centuries" with "nature" in the
corresponding passage of *The Origin of Species*,[15] but the process of
evolution, insofar as it is mechanical, is still foreseeable, and thus
possibly foreseen. From Bergson's perspective, Darwin's theory of
chance variations, whether they are determined or undetermined,
operates in the shadows of teleological and divine hypotheses. It
is a shame, however, that Bergson does not discuss Darwin's "principle of divergence" (a controversial principle among contemporary
biologists), which might help to account for the analogy of the eyes,
and that might, in fact, be close to Bergson's own conception of life
as disassociation.[16]

Bergson argues that neo-Darwinian theories of naturally selected chance variations face difficulties. August Weismann maintained Darwin's position that the variations are gradual and slight, such that one trait could develop without upsetting the delicate equilibrium in the organism as a whole, while rejecting his commitment to a notion of the inheritance of acquired characteristics (Weismann's theory of the continuity of the germ-plasm, of germ-cells as wholly distinct from soma-cells, excluded that). Bergson asks how the potentially advantageous trait can be selected and stored while it waits for other traits to catch up, but the neo-Darwinian gradualism of our time responds to this objection by affirming that all naturally selected mutations are by definition actually advantageous, however partially and minimally, for the individual.[17] The worry that Bergson expresses seems to have partially motivated the "saltationist" or "mutationist" views that variation occurs in distinct leaps, views proposed by most notably Hugo de Vries, William Bateson and Thomas Morgan, who allowed only a reduced role for natural selection. But if the variations are large and remarkable, they will upset the equilibrium in the organism, and when one trait develops, others will have to develop at the same time. These miraculously mutually supporting developments seem to suggest, Bergson argues, that evolution has a pre-determined direction and even that there is something like an intelligent principle conducting its orchestra in the organism [CE 62/59].

Theodor Eimer's "orthogenesis"—the idea of co-ordinated adaptations, and thus development in a given direction—sought an evolutionary principle in the relation of the organism to its external environment. That a chrysalis subject to heat or cold gives rise to butterflies of different forms or that significant changes can be established in a crustacean, *Artemia salina*, by varying the salinity of the water highlights the possibility of environmental factors causing speciation. Bergson shows, however, that speaking of causation in this connection does not preclude, and in fact presupposes, that the organism has a certain power or capacity to be affected by and to react to environmental factors, and that this power is a function of its own active bearing on the world. The chrysalis or crustacean may appear to play a passive role in the cases above, but the formation of eyes in the process of evolutionary "adaptation" (a term which, as Bergson emphasises, can be understood in more passive or more

active senses, and thus is ambiguous [CE 62/59]) cannot be understood simply as passive. The idea that eyes, along with the rest of the
physiological apparatus (optic nerve, brain etc.) that they require
in order to function, have been caused by external factors would be
rather like the claim—as Bergson allows us to see in an important
development of his Paris International Congress of Philosophy paper
and Collège de France lectures on causation in 1900–1 [M 419–
41]—that the match caused the building to explode while omitting
to mention the gunpowder that it ignited. Eimer aimed to explain
adaptation in mechanistic terms, according to basic laws of physics
and chemistry, but he could not avoid "implicitly attributing to
organized matter a certain *sui generis* capacity, the mysterious power
to invent very complicated machines to utilize the simple excita-
tion that it receives" [CE 76/73]. This adaptive capacity would be
more honestly accounted for, Bergson contends, by appealing not
to chemical and physical causal processes but to an in some sense
purposive response to environmental conditions. Unfortunately,
although it is the latter perspective, as Bergson remarks, "that is truly
useful to the practice of science, […] it is the former that provides
its philosophy" [CE 62/59], i.e. its official doctrine.

Bergson accepts from Eimer's "orthogenesis" the idea that there
is a drive towards new forms throughout life as a whole, while
rejecting his physico-chemical interpretation of that drive. In a certain proximity to neo-Lamarckism—the only theory "capable of
admitting an internal and psychological principle of development"
[CE 81/78]—he interprets this drive as essentially psychological.
The principle of evolution is not, however, the effort of *individual*
living beings: the drive is trans-individual and can be interpreted
as effort only in "distinctly extending the sense of the word"
[CE 82/79]. Moreover, although Bergson sees that Weismann's rejection of the inheritance of acquired characteristics—of adaptations
acquired through effort—is not wholly justified by his experiments,
his position is that such inheritance could only be the exception
rather than the rule and thus that it cannot explain evolution as a
whole. The adaptations are driven through a trans-individual drive
deriving from a single root, and this allows us to understand how
the same result, such as eyes, can be realised across divergent lines
of evolution.

Why does Bergson spend so much time critically assessing the doctrine of the inheritance of acquired characteristics, a doctrine traditionally understood as Lamarckian, given his sympathy for Lamarckism as a psychological account of evolution? In truth, the doctrine of the inheritance of acquired characteristics is an aspect of what Bergson criticises—when coming to a final reckoning with Spencer's evolutionary theory, which relied on the doctrine—as "false evolutionism" [CE 287/272]. False evolutionism "reconstructs evolution with fragments of the evolved" [CE 385/363] and is an expression of the *associationism* that Bergson criticised in his earlier work. False evolutionism can see in biological development only the *addition* and *association* of new elements to old elements, just as false psychology sees in temporal experience only the accumulation of temporal instants. Bergson rejects, therefore, the theory of the inheritance of acquired characteristics as well as the doctrine of random variations insofar as both presuppose that evolution is simply additive, that it consists in adaptations or variations being added to the course of life from outside of the history of the living being.

This critique of false evolutionism also seems to condition the glaring absence of any discussion in *Creative Evolution* of the new science of genetics. On other issues, Bergson cites its founders, namely Bateson (who named the new science), Morgan and E. B. Wilson, but he makes no mention of the rediscovery of Mendel's laws in 1900. What these laws seemed to suppose, namely that there are specific characters or hereditary unities (*Anlagen* or "rudiments", as Mendel said, but Wilhelm Johannsen's "gene" is the name that stuck) that seemed to remain unmixed and merely juxtaposed or superposed in the organic individual was, in short, anathema to Bergson. Even though Weismann's theory of the germ-plasm, for which Bergson has an evident sympathy when he writes that "*life appears as a current that goes from germ to germ through the medium of a developed organism*" [CE 28/27], had in a sense anticipated it (Mendel's laws confirmed "Weismann's barrier"), this was "precisely the adversary that Bergson had made for himself, for metaphysical reasons, in the whole of *Creative Evolution*".[18] Perhaps, as M. and A. Wolsky have emphasised, "it was not easy to see in genetics as pursued at the time anything more than a very 'down to earth' mechanical explanation" of the inheritance of characteristics, and the "far reaching consequences" of this discovery "could not have been foreseen".[19] Still, from the perspective of the "modern synthesis" of population genetics and Darwinian natural selection that dominated biology from the 1930s, Bergson's approach came to appear obsolete and ill-informed. That said, the limits of gene-centric approaches have increasingly come to light since the underwhelming results of the Human Genome Project,[20] and the modern synthesis has come under significant pressure from evolutionary developmental biology ("evo-devo") in particular. Biologists such as Stephen Rose have sought alternatives to reductive genetic approaches and signalled the importance of Bergson's work in this context.[21]

Élan vital

The psychological force throughout life as a whole is what Bergson terms the *élan vital*, a phrase which he borrowed from an 1899 work on evolution by André Lalande.[22] The global drive is expressed and carried forward in particular species and individuals; "each individual retains from the global impulsion of life only a certain drive, and tends to utilize this energy in its own interest; in this consists *adaptation*" [CE 53/51]. This impulsion or drive cannot be taken in a mechanistic sense: "we have either to take or leave mechanistic philosophy", Bergson writes, and "we would have to leave it if even the smallest grain of dust, in deviating from its trajectory traced out by mechanics, showed even the slightest trace of spontaneity" [CE 42/40]. Mechanism does not admit degrees (as we argued in Chapter 4), and thus accounting for, say, the spontaneity in the adaptation of the eye to its environment requires us to reject mechanistic philosophies of life. Finalism, in contrast, comes in a variety of different shades, depending on how exactly the spontaneity and self-directed nature of life is conceived, and Bergson states that it is necessary to admit something of it in rejecting mechanism. Pure finalism is a function of a retrospective illusion insofar as it presupposes that the end or goal of the process is already known, and thus that in a sense the process has already happened. There is, however, a mode of finality in the *élan vital* that is not the deliberate pursuit of a pre-determined goal. Just as *Time and Free Will* ultimately sided with the libertarians while offering an account of free voluntary agency without alternative conceptual possibilities, as something other than the pursuit of conceptual ends, in evolutionary biology Bergson sides with the finalists while offering a much reduced and transformed account of finality.

Bergson's notion of finality is, in Kantian terms, a "finality without end", a "purposiveness without purpose", i.e. purposiveness without a conceptually determined goal. This notion of purposiveness without purposive, as Jankélévitch and Léon Brunschvicg before him noted, is the very essence of the post-Kantian "romantic voluntarism" of which Bergson's thinking in 1907 is a particular expression.[23] Nature has its *génialité*, as we have seen Bergson claim, just as fine art has its genius; but Kant and the German Romantic philosophers after him had already conceived of genius itself as "nature giving the rule to art", as the spontaneous thrust and irruption of a force of nature in what without that force would merely be the work of a technician. According to the idea of purposiveness without purpose, Bergson's notion of an *élan* is the notion of a force—a force as we have seen, that he conceives as will—throughout life as a whole that is reducible neither to mechanical causation nor to final causation as the pursuit of a clearly determined goal, but which, nevertheless, has the form of purposiveness and is thus intrinsically related to purposes. This apparently paradoxical idea is no doubt difficult to grasp. It resists the conceptual understanding that is at home with the whys and wherefores of our pragmatic concern to draw profit from nature, but which clumsily struggles with a principle that is finer and more graceful than its own deliberate efforts.

It is hardly surprising that Bergson struggles to grasp and formulate this principle—it belongs to intuition rather than the intellect—and that his formulations of it can appear now mechanistic, now overly finalistic. In an anti-finalist mode, Bergson accounts for the divergence of the *élan* in divergent lines of biological development with the claim that within it "harmony is not ahead but behind. The unity comes from a *vis a tergo*: it is given in the beginning as an impulsion [*impulsion*], it is not posed at the end as an attraction" [CE 108/104]. Later, however, Bergson senses that opposing the *élan* as an impulsion to attraction risks a return to a mechanistic position. *The Two Sources* will state that the motto of "pure experience" is that the *élan* is "neither an impulsion nor an attraction" [TS 105/119], and thus it states more clearly that it stands somehow between mechanism and pure finalism.[24] The advance of life does not involve "the representation, conscious or unconscious, of a goal to be attained", but nor is it the blind and mechanically necessary consequence of a prior determining cause, and thus it does not preclude "to a greater or lesser degree, contingency" [CE 102/97]. It is the middle term, as Jankélévitch has it, between the past of impulsion and the future of attraction, just as duration is the middle term between any two instants one may abstract from it.[25] One might say, in English, that the *élan* is more of an impulse than an impulsion, if the former suggests more spontaneity than the latter; or, in French, that it is more of a *pulsion* than an *impulsion*.[26]

The most essential concept that Bergson advances in order to understand something of this impulse that is irreducible to mechanical and pure final causation is *tendency*. "Tendency" here is not to be taken in an empirical sense as denominating a statistical regularity ("I tend to go for a drink on a Friday after work"), but as the force or drive that might produce, in the right circumstances, such statistical regularity. Ravaisson had already presented tendency or inclination as irreducible to mechanical causation, on the one hand, and to the explicit pursuit of a goal in final causation, on the other; tendency, on his account, was continuous with the reflective will and consciousness but irreducible to them.[27] By the time of *Creative Evolution*, "tendency" has become a term of art with a similar sense in Bergson's own philosophy.[28] "Life is tendency", he writes, "and the essence of a tendency consists in developing in the form of a sheath, creating, by the fact of its growth alone, divergent directions between which its *élan* will be distributed" [CE 104/100]. This drive unfolds as arborescent differentiation, as Ravaisson had already seen: "the creative principle, with the lines through which it is embodied spreads out like a spring that pours out into every part of the whole".[29] Certainly, Bergson resists Ravaisson's notion of a "tendency towards the best", and writes instead, after de Vries, of a tendency towards change [CE 90/86]. Still, tendency has to have some directionality, if not a definite direction, and when Bergson writes that the *élan* is neither a function of impulsion nor one of attraction, his position implies that it involves *a form of* impulsion and a form of attraction at one and the same time. The basic idea of duration allows us to understand this: the unity of quasi-impulsion and quasi-attraction that constitutes the *élan vital* is but the unity of retention and protention, of a past and future that inhabit the present, that is duration. Duration is futural as much as it is historical, as much as it bears the past within itself as contracted, organic memory. For this reason, Bergson's affirmations that the *élan vital* comes from behind, that it is a *vis a tergo*, have to be treated with caution. They seem to lead us back to a mechanistic, necessitarian conception of force. Bergson warns us that the notion of an *élan* was only an "image" [CE 271/ 258], and the image of a *vis a tergo*, of a force arising from *behind*, may well presuppose exactly what reflection on duration is supposed to combat, namely space and our obsession with it.

Tendency, understood as the pre-teleological directionality of biological life, belongs to the *élan* as essentially durational. With this conception of duration and tendency in genial biological life, Bergson can reconcile the simplicity of the functioning of an organ, vision by means of the eye, and the infinitesimally complicated means by means of which it functions. This is a relation on which mechanistic doctrines, which claim that we can see because we have eyes, can shed no light: the unity of the function can only be, from this perspective, a mysterious, magical product of the multiple means. Finalist doctrines—according to which we have eyes in order to see—are right to consider the simplicity of the function as the condition of the multiple means, but misconceive, Bergson argues, how the potentially infinite complexity of the means arises. We have no need to resort to the idea of a "divine watchmaker" in order to understand its potential infinity. The infinity is the product of the unity and simplicity that is duration itself. The creation of the eye in the movement of biological duration would have been a simple process, Bergson leads us to see, like the simplest of movements. The creation would have been as simple as the movement of my arm is for me, a movement which certainly can be analysed after the fact as an infinite number of points. The creation of the eye would have required no more effort and intention than the sweeping brushstroke of the "artist of genius" [CE 95/90], which we might also take great pains to deconstruct and reconstruct as a mosaic of tiny pieces. Like a snow-flake, the eye could have been formed almost instantaneously (Bergson thus would be able to accommodate the basic idea of "mutationism" as well as its synthesis with gradualism in contemporary "punctuated equilibrium" theory). Nature is more like the fine artist, the artist of genius, than an artisan methodically, deliberately realising a plan. Like the artist of genius, nature does not know exactly what it is doing, and it neither wants nor needs to know. Life is not an "engineering problem", for it is akin to the impetus in fine art.

Although Bergson writes of durational geniality, of his *élan* as an *élan vital*, his teaching at Clermont-Ferrand in 1887–8 concerning vitalism and animism as traditional philosophies of life shows that he is well aware that strictly speaking his position is *not* vitalist.[30] Vitalism, most notably in the eighteenth-century Montpellier school, was a critical response to the early-modern animist trad-ition, which had held that all biological processes, even such appar-ently involuntary ones as blood circulation, were a function of thought (of "pre-conscious thought" at least).[31] For vitalism strictly speaking, the principle of life is different and irreducible to mech-anical forces, on the one hand, and mind, on the other. Given that duration, for Bergson, is the principle of both consciousness and biological life, his is an animist, spiritualist and panpsychic position based on the idea that there are degrees of consciousness throughout nature as a whole: "though not belonging to intelligence, instinct is not situated beyond the limits of mind [*l'esprit*]" [CE 184/176], and "instinct and intelligence both arise [...] on a unique ground that we can call, for want of a better word, consciousness [*la con-science*]" [CE 196/187]. When he uses the term "vitalism" in *Creative Evolution*, it is in fact to characterise doctrines he rejects, the "neo-vitalism" of Driesch and Reinke. The problem here is not so much that these doctrines posit an unknowable force and thus "respond to the question with the question itself" [CE 44/42], but rather that they posit the vital force as internal to the individual organism (and thus in a sense as part of the organism) while resorting, even if despite themselves, to traditional finalist doctrines. If vitalism was originally intended to oppose animist doctrines, neo-vitalism in the work of Driesch, the biologist turned philosopher, ends up as a teleological form of animism positing a kind of "foreman" in the organism [CE 238/226].

Life and matter

In *Creative Evolution*, Bergson often presents the *élan vital* as opposed to matter, and as a principle that could exist independently of it; "we are not the vital current itself, we are this current already burdened with matter" [CE 252/240]. From this perspective, with the proliferation of its physiological forms the *élan vital* overcomes the resistance of matter and ensures its own development. Its victory in adapting to external circumstances is never permanent or absolute, however, for the very forms that life creates to make its own way can bring about a certain torpor, just as our free acts can degenerate into habitual acts that are no longer motivated to the same degree by mind:

> [e]ven in its most perfect works, when it seems to have triumphed over external resistance and over its own resistance, it is at the mercy of the materiality that it had to give itself. Our freedom, in the very movements by which it is affirmed, creates nascent habits that will smother it if it does not renew itself by a constant effort: automatism menaces it. The liveliest thought becomes frigid in the formula that expresses it. The word turns against the idea. The letter kills the spirit. [CE 134/128]

In this way, by analogy with our own experience of habit, Bergson accounts for apparent dead-ends along the minor branches of evolutionary development; lingulae, for example, which Darwin described as "living fossils", have remained unchanged for hundreds of millions of years [CE 107/103]. "Evolution", thus, "is not only a moving forward; in many cases we observe a marking time, and still more often a deviation or turning back. […] the same causes that divide the evolutionary movement often cause life to be diverted from itself, hypnotised by the form it has just brought forth" [CE 109/105]. The materiality of established forms of life can hypnotise the genius of the *élan vital*, just as our creativity can be deadened by our habits.

Bergson does not always characterise habit so negatively, and he recognises that it is necessary to the instantiation of our freedom; "in man, motor habit can have a second result, incommensurable with the first. It can hold in abeyance other motor habits, and, in this way, in mastering automatism, set consciousness free" [CE 193/ 184–5]. Following the second chapter of *Matter and Memory*, Bergson here again accounts for acquired motor habits as bodily mechanisms. How these bodily mechanisms can be acquired if mechanism admits no degrees [CE 41/40], Bergson does not say, but they do not necessarily suffocate and eliminate consciousness; with effort, the mind can use acquired habits to go on to perform new tasks and acquire more developed skills—to acquire new, higher habits. In this more positive light, Bergson can write more generally that matter is not simply the organ and obstacle of consciousness, but also its stimulant. Matter, as Bergson will state in returning to the issue in his May 1911 talk at the University of Birmingham, "Life and Consciousness", is what "divides and specifies" [ME 28/22] in allowing life to develop the rich plethora of its forms. Matter is thus, all at once, "the obstacle, the instrument and the stimulant" [CM 29/23] of consciousness.

As interesting as it may be, if this were all Bergson had to say in *Creative Evolution* about matter and life, he would have retreated from the fourth chapter of *Matter and Memory*. Recall that there Bergson sought middle-terms underlying expressions of traditional mind–body dualism. He discovered tensions (or "rhythms") of duration between the opposition of quality and quantity, as well as a notion of extension underlying the opposition of the inextended and the spatially extended [MM 247/278]. As we saw in Chapter 7, Bergson develops his account of extension in this sense in 1907 by showing that geometrical extension and the intellect that grasps it have a common origin and a more profound source. The final pages of the third chapter of *Creative Evolution* go further in this direction, however, by *applying* the notion of tensions of duration to the notion of extension. Bergson now understands extension as ex-tension, as a function of the slackening or relaxation of duration; "extension appears merely [...] as an interrupted tension" [CE 258/246]. The more the rhythm or tension of duration is slackened, the more it gives rise to moments standing apart from each other, and thus to space. The degrees of attention to life, the degrees of tensed duration, are degrees of externalisation and thus spatialisation.

In order to advance this idea, Bergson has to invert the perspective of *Matter and Memory*, according to which tension was on the side of space and relaxation on the side of mind. Now Bergson holds that mind is tension, a tension with which it carves open the future:

> [t]he more we succeed in making ourselves conscious of our progress in pure duration, the more we feel different parts of our being enter into each other, and our whole personality concentrates itself in a point, or rather a sharp edge, pressed against the future and cutting into it unceasingly. It is in this that life and action are free. But suppose we let ourselves go and, instead of acting, dream. At once the self is scattered; our past, which till then was gathered together in the indivisible impulsion it communicated to us, is broken up into a thousand recollections *made external to one another*. They give up interpenetrating to the degree that they become fixed. Our personality thus descends in the direction of space. […] No doubt we make only the first steps in the direction of the extended, even when we let ourselves go as much as we can. [CE 212–13/202–3]

Bergson's inversion of the framework of *Matter and Memory* has evidently brought with it a new interpretation of dreams. They are no longer at the base of his image of the cone, at the furthest remove from the spatiality of the present. Dreaming is now understood as a relaxation of the mind that introduces spatialisation; the relaxed indifference to our ordinary concerns in dreams, as Georges Canguilhem put it, brings with it the increasing indifference, i.e. the increasing homogeneity, of space.[32]

Dreaming is relaxation and ex-tension, but matter in general, in its distinction from life and consciousness, can be conceived in the same way: "suppose for a moment", as Bergson adds to the passage above, "that matter consists in this very movement pushed further and that physics is simply psychics inverted" [CE 212–13/202–3]. It is, it would seem, because this idea of matter as distended or ex-tended mind inverts the conclusions of *Matter and Memory* that Bergson begins the final paragraph of his intellectual biography thus: "[t]ension, concentration, such are the words by which we characterize a method that requires from the mind, for each new problem, an entirely new effort. We could never have drawn from *Matter and Memory* that preceded *Creative Evolution* a veritable evolutionary doctrine ..."[CM 105/97]. There is a new conception of tension in *Creative Evolution* that is not simply drawn from *Matter and Memory*. Of course, this new conception leaves us with the difficult question, which Bergson does not help us to answer, of how to understand the old conception, which was supposed to overcome the opposition of quality and quantity by finding increased tension in material quantity, in the vibrations of matter. After *Creative Evolution*, it would seem, that approach is no longer available to us.

The conception of extension as ex-tension in Bergson's later work may well be "the most difficult, most elusive as well as the least known and least understood part of Bergson's thought",[33] as Čapek put it, but it becomes clearer once we recognise that *Creative Evolution* inverts the orientation of *Matter and Memory*. In any case, in his 1904 discourse on Ravaisson, Bergson is happy to give the credit for much of the idea to his predecessor. The final sections of Ravaisson's 1867 report on French philosophy show "in the original production of matter, a movement opposite to the one accomplished when matter organises itself"; we should "imagine at the beginning a *distension* [*distension*] of mind, a diffusion of space and time that constitutes materiality" [CM 284/275]. The idea, as Bergson notes [CE 222/ 211], ultimately goes back to the neo-Platonist philosopher Plotinus, but Ravaisson wrote this:

> from the internal and central perspective of self-reflection, the mind does not see itself only as, at bottom, the infinite from which it emanates; it also sees itself, it recognises itself, as more or less different from itself, by degrees down to the extreme limit where, in the dispersion of matter, all unity seems to fade away and all activity disappears in the chains of phenomena. From this point of view, since we find in the soul all that is developed in nature, we can comprehend Aristotle's notion that the soul is the site of all the forms. Since all objects appear to us thus as representing, by forms in space, the phases that the mind traverses in the succession of its states, we can understand Leibniz's dictum that body is momentary mind.[34]

This was a position that Ravaisson had already formulated in 1838, although there it was, perhaps, unclear whether nature included the inorganic realm as well as living beings:

> between the ultimate depths of nature and the highest point of reflective freedom, there are an infinite number of degrees measuring the development of one and the same power, and as one rises through them, extension—the condition of knowledge—increases with the distinction and the interval of the opposites. This is like a spiral whose principle resides in the depths of nature, and yet which ultimately flourishes in consciousness. Habit comes back down this spiral, teaching us of its origin and genesis.[35]

In Bergson's own words in *Creative Evolution*, "life is a movement, materiality is the inverse movement" [CE 263/250]. Mind and body, life and matter, are not two substances, but two movements or two tendencies across a single infinitely divisible spectrum. This is certainly difficult to conceive; no sooner do we think, then we tend to think of *something*. But life and matter here are not two things. The same spectrum can be viewed in the ascendant or in the descendent. In the ascendant, the spectrum is the energy of matter fuelling life, genial life reaching out to ever higher forms; in the descendent, it is life congealing as matter, life becoming fascinated and hypnotised by habit and its own materiality. From this perspective, if we are to hold to it resolutely, matter and habit can only *appear* to operate mechanically, since, as we have noted, dead mechanism can admit no degrees.

Bergson thus presents, in the final pages of the crucial third chapter of *Creative Evolution*, a monist philosophy characterised by a dualism of tendencies.[36] The tendency towards materiality and rest is not external to life itself; there is—to borrow a phrase from the early-modern astronomer Johannes Kepler—an *inclinatio ad quietem*, an inclination towards rest and inertia in the very principle of life. Life contains the seeds of its own downfall and degradation. Life is like steam, says Bergson, that rises only to condense and fall. But matter also belongs to life and can rise to new heights from the ashes of an almost extinguished flame.

Summary

Creative Evolution discovers duration in biological evolution and thus in life as a whole. Bergson criticises mechanist and finalist accounts of biological life, accounts which reduce organisms to artefacts, just as he had criticised determinism and libertarianism as accounts of human action. In so doing, he criticises the predominant evolutionary theories of the time: neo-Darwinism, mutationism, orthogenesis and neo-Lamarckism. With the idea of the *élan vital* he offers a, broadly speaking, "psychological" account of the motive force of evolution whose impetus transcends individual living beings (the apparent unity of which always dissipates on closer inspection) and advances as arborescent differentiation. Bergson develops the nineteenth-century Romantic idea that instead of pure mechanism or pure finalism there is genius at the heart of the creative advance of nature: the *élan vital* proceeds like the fine artist with a "purposiveness without purpose". The third chapter of *Creative Evolution* accounts for the relation of matter and life by showing that matter and the space in which it appears are the result of the relaxation of duration: extension is the ex-tension of duration. Matter is, thus, a tendency of durational life itself, just as life is a tendency of matter, which is never wholly inert and without duration. In this way, Bergson develops the still hesitant conclusions of *Matter and Memory* by presenting a monistic philosophy that contains two opposing tendencies.

Notes

1 Bergson had given lessons on basic issues concerning vitalism and animism as philosophies of life in his lectures at Clermont-Ferrand in 1887–8; see Bergson, *Cours I*, ed. H. Hude (Paris: Presses universitaires de France, 1990), pp. 337–50.

2 Arnaud François makes the same point: Bergson's departure from Spencer "led him to envisage, *from the beginning*, an alternative to Spencerian evolutionism"; Bergson, *L'Evolution créatrice* (Paris: Presses universitaires de France, 2007), p. 392, n.4 to Chapter I. On Bergson's response to Spencer, see also Keith Ansell-Pearson, Paul-Antoine Miquel and Michael Vaughan, "Responses to Evolution: Spencer's Evolutionism, Bergsonism and Contemporary Biology", in *The History of Continental Philosophy*, Vol 3: *TheNew Century: Bergsonism, Phenomenology and Responses to Modern Science*, ed. Keith Ansell-Pearson and Alan D. Schrift (Abingdon: Routledge, 2013), pp. 347–79.

3 For Bergson's influence on Huxley, see Emily Herring, " 'Great is Darwin and Bergson his poet': Julian Huxley's other evolutionary synthesis", *Annals of Science* 75/1 (2018), 40–54. For more detail on turn-of-the-century evolutionary theory, see P. J. Bowler, *The Eclipse of Darwinism: Anti-Darwinian Evolutionary Theories in the Decades around 1900* (Baltimore, MD: Johns Hopkins University Press, 1983).

4 Ravaisson, "Philosophical Testament", in *Selected Essays*, ed. M. Sinclair (London: Bloomsbury, 2016), p. 307. Against this Ravaissonian background, it is hardly, *pace* Lacey, remarkable that such "a 'spiritual' philosopher" as Bergson "should accept so wholeheartedly" the basic idea of evolutionism; see *Bergson*, p. 123–4.

5 Jean Gayon, "*L'Evolution créatrice* lue par les fondateurs de la théorie synthétique de l'évolution", in *Annales bergsoniennes* IV, ed. Anne Fagot-Largeault and Frédéric Worms (Paris: Presses universitaires de France, 2008), pp. 59–93, pp. 61–2.

6 Jankélévitch, *Henri Bergson*, p. 109/132.

7 Jankélévitch, *Henri Bergson*, p. 109/132.

8 On this issue, and for an account of recent attempts to bridge the gap between chemistry and biology by means of replicative "systems chemistry", see Addy Pross, *What Is Life? How Chemistry Becomes Biology* (Oxford: Oxford University Press, 2012).

9 Pross, *What Is Life?*, p. 9.

10 For an account of how Aristotle's own doctrine differs from this traditional, Latinate conception of it, see Martin Heidegger, "On the Essence and Concept of *Phusis* in Aristotle's *Physics* B, I" in *Pathmarks*, ed. W. McNeill (Cambridge: Cambridge University Press, 1998), pp. 183–230 and Chapter 5 of my *Heidegger, Aristotle and the Work of Art* (Basingstoke: Palgrave, 2006).

11 Bergson later speaks of "three grand forms of contemporary evolutionism" [CE 84/85] but only in treating new-Darwinism and mutationism as one.

12 See Bernard Balan, "L'Œil de la coquille Saint Jacques—Bergson et les faits scientifiques", *Raison présente* 119 (1996), 87–106.

13 For an extended treatment of chance in Darwin, see Curtis Johnson, *Darwin's Dice: the Idea of Chance in the Thought of Charles Darwin* (Oxford: Oxford University Press, 2014).

14 On Darwin's demon, see Paul-Antoine Miquel, "Une harmonie en arrière", in *Annales bergsoniennes* IV, ed. Fagot-Largeault and Worms, pp. 133–45, p. 140. The 1909 Cambridge University Press edition of the *Essay* of 1844 is available at http://darwin-online.org.uk/converted/pdf/1909_Foundations_F1556.pdf. Darwin's demon is on p. 85.

15 On this, see the editorial note on p. 85 of the *Essay* of 1844.

16 Arnaud François points this out; see "Les sources biologiques de l'*Evolution créatrice*", in *Annales bergsoniennes* IV, ed. Fagot-Largeault and Worms, pp. 95–109, p. 100, and his edition of *L'Evolution créatrice*, n.171 to chapter I, p. 426. For Darwin's doctrine of "divergence", see Lewens, *Darwin* (Abingdon: Routledge, 2006), p. 69.

17 See Richard Dawkins, The Blind Watchmaker (London: Penguin, 2016), particularly Chapter 3, "Accumulating Small Change".

18 Arnaud François, "Les sources biologiques de l'Evolution créatrice", p. 101.

19 Maria de Issekutz Wolsky and Alexander A. Wolsky, "Bergson's Vitalism and Modern Biology", in The Crisis in Modernism: Bergson and the Vitalist Controversy, ed. Frederick Burwick and Paul Douglass (Cambridge: Cambridge University Press, 1992), pp. 153–69, p. 153.

20 On this point, see Rupert Sheldrake, The Science Delusion (London: Coronet, 2012), Chapter 6.

21 For a variety of contemporary critical responses to the modern synthesis, see Philippe Huneman and Denis M. Walsh (eds.), Challenging the Modern Synthesis: Adaptation, Development, and Inheritance (Oxford: Oxford University Press, 2017). On Stephen Rose and Bergson in contemporary biology, see Keith Ansell-Pearson, Paul-Antoine Miquel and Michael Vaughan "Responses to Evolution: Spencer's Evolutionism, Bergsonism and Contemporary Biology", pp. 371–9.

22 André Lalande, La dissolution opposée à l'évolution (Paris: Félix Alcan, 1899), p. 399: "The living being is characterized by a course of development absolutely without example in the inorganic realm: embryonic germ, differentiation of tissues, adult state, senility and death. It struggles for life, it deforms itself more or less in this struggle. And the species appears to behave in this like the individuals, having a modest start, then an élan vital that tends to multiply them without limit, and finally a more or less complete triumph followed by regression and decadence". See in this connection Ben-Ami Scharfstein, The Roots of Bergson's Philosophy, p. 81.

23 Jankélévitch, Henri Bergson, p. 113/137.

24 Lacey sees Bergson's ambivalence on this point without quite seeing how the French philosopher is attempting to rethink finality, rather than simply to reject it, according to an idea of purposiveness without purpose; see Lacey, Bergson, p. 132.

25 Jankélévitch, Henri Bergson, p. 111/134.

26 In this connection, see the interesting collection of essays Pulsions, ed. Jean-Christophe Goddard (Paris: Vrin, 2006), particularly Arnaud François, "Y a-t-il une théorie de la pulsion chez Bergson? Pulsion et actualisation", pp. 183–211. See also Rudolf Bernet, "La conscience et la vie comme force et pulsion", in C. Riquier (ed.), Bergson (Paris: Editions du Cerf, 2012), pp. 25–54. A version of the latter is available in English as "Bergson on the Driven Force of Consciousness and Life", trans. T. Perri, in Bergson and Phenomenology, pp. 42–77.

27 See my Being Inclined: Félix Ravaisson's Philosophy of Habit (Oxford: Oxford University Press).

28 In this connection, see Matthias Vollet, "Créativité comme Tendencialité", in Bergson, ed. Riquier, pp. 359–73, who examines the use of the term in Bergson's earlier work.

29 For more on this, see my Being Inclined and the introduction to Félix Ravaisson: Selected Essays.

30 Bergson, *Cours* I, p. 345 in particular. Arnaud François is right to note that this strict sense of vitalism is bequeathed to Bergson by Ravaisson; see "Les sources biologiques de l'*Evolution créatrice*", p. 97.

31 For more on this, see the first chapter of my *Being Inclined*.

32 See Georges Canguilhem's 1943 commentary on the third chapter of Bergson's 1907 text: "Commentaire au troisième chapitre de L'*Evolution créatrice*", in *Œuvres complètes* vol. IV, ed. Camille Limoges (Paris: Vrin, 2015), pp. 111–70, p. 153. As Canguilhem also notes, this interpretation of dreams will persist in Bergson's thinking, since in 1908 he will write: "Stop willing, detach yourself from life, become disinterested; in this way, you pass from the waking self to the self of dreams—less *tense*, but more *extended*" [ME 155/136].

33 Čapek, *Bergson and Modern Physics*, pp. 214–15.

34 Ravaisson, *La philosophie en France au* XIXème *siècle*, p. 271.

35 Ravaisson's, *Of Habit*, p. 77. As Canguilhem notes ("Commentaire au troisième chapitre de L'*Evolution créatrice*", p. 149), Ravaisson writes early in *Of Habit* that "habit is not possible in the empire of immediation and homogeneity that forms the inorganic realm [...] Body exists without becoming anything, it is in some way outside of time" (p. 77), which suggests that it presents a dualist philosophy. In my *Being Inclined*, I argue that this apparent dualism is not Ravaisson's final position in 1838.

36 See Jankélévitch, *Henri Bergson*, p. 144/174.

Further reading

Keith Ansell-Pearson, Paul-Antoine Miquel and Michael Vaughan, "Responses to Evolution: Spencer's Evolutionism, Bergsonism and Contemporary Biology", in *The History of Continental Philosophy* Vol. 3: *The New Century: Bergsonism, Phenomenology and Responses to Modern Science*, ed. Keith Ansell-Pearson and Alan D. Schrift (Abingdon: Routledge, 2013), pp. 347–79. A broad-ranging study of Bergson's evolutionary philosophy that is particularly informative in relation to contemporary biology.

Henri Bergson, *Creative Evolution*, ed. Arnaud François, trans. Donald Landes (forthcoming from Routledge). The critical dossier in this translation of the recent critical edition volume of L'*Evolution créatrice* should have a great impact on English-language Bergson studies.

Georges Canguilhem, "Commentaire au troisième chapitre de L'*Evolution créatrice*" in *Œuvres complètes* vol. IV, ed. Camille Limoges (Paris: Vrin, 2015), 111–70. This is a peerless 1943 commentary on the third chapter of *Creative Evolution*, and serious study of the development of Bergson's philosophy has to go through it.

Maria de Issekutz Wolsky and Alexander A. Wolsky, "Bergson's Vitalism and Modern Biology", *The Crisis in Modernism: Bergson and the Vitalist Controversy*, ed. Frederick

Burwick and Paul Douglass (Cambridge: Cambridge University Press, 1992), pp. 153–69. A helpful treatment in English of Bergson's *élan vital* in relation to later developments in biology.

Vladimir Jankélévitch, *Henri Bergson*, ed. Nils F. Schott and Alexandre Lefebvre (Durham: Duke University Press, 2015). The fourth chapter on "Life" is perhaps the most impressive of them all.

Ten
Ethics, religion and politics

The sources of morality and religion

In 1932 Bergson named the book on ethics that had been expected of him for 25 years *The Two Sources of Morality and Religion*. The fact that the book concerned religion *and* morality was no great surprise: Bergson had been interested in religious mysticism for as long as he had been concerned with the possibility of an ethics, and he had begun to emphasise, as we saw in Chapter 9, the theistic aspects of his evolutionary philosophy a few years after 1907. In what sense are the *sources* of morality and religion at issue in the book? "Source" is not to be taken in the sense of historical origin, for these sources still exist in the present. Nor does "source" mean "type" or "sort", since this would suppose that the sources each have a generic unity allowing them to exist independently in the present. Instead, the sources of morality and religion resemble the two fundamental tendencies of life in *Creative Evolution*, tendencies which are not types or genera. On the one hand, Bergson now understands the power of creative genius, which he had shown to lie at the heart of biological life, as a source of morality and religion, and this in taking seriously Romantic notions that there is something divine or quasi-divine in the products of genius. Genius is a principle of "openness" in both morality and religion. This principle of openness is opposed, on the other hand, to a quite different source of morality and religion, a principle of closure that Bergson conceives according to the guiding thread of a notion of habit. Bergson's reflection on the "open" and the "closed" in morality and religion is grounded on the accounts of genius and habit in duration that he had presented in *Creative Evolution*.

Still, as he insisted, the perspective of 1932 cannot be deduced from that of 1907, and The Two Sources completes his previous discoveries by "transposing them to a higher level".[1] In gaining elevation, the idea of two sources of morality and religion may well move away from the idea of habitual materialisation and genial spiritualisation as tendencies of the vital impulse, and may well return to a more dualist position resembling Matter and Memory's affirmations of purity in perception and memory. The second section of this chapter addresses this issue, after the first has examined Bergson's critique of traditional approaches in ethics. The third section addresses his arguments concerning religion, before the fourth shows how his important remarks concerning the modern technological condition in the final chapter of the book are to be understood in the light of his war discourses, whose central themes are repeated in these remarks.

Anti-intellectualist ethics

Bergson presents his account of habit and society, of social habit, in the opening passages of The Two Sources, but later in the first chapter, "Moral Obligation", he poses the meta-ethical question of the foundation of ethical norms, to which the opening passages constitute a partial, initial response. The question is: how and why am I obliged to do certain things and not do others? This meta-ethical problem of moral motivation is a long-standing philosophical issue, but Bergson claims that traditional philosophies have been unable adequately to respond to it to the degree that they presume that morality is essentially a rational, intellectual affair.

In this, Bergson is close to David Hume's claim that the motivational force in morality cannot belong to reason, which can only ever be, as the Scottish philosopher put it, a "slave to the passions": "[n]ever in our hours of temptation, should we sacrifice to the mere need for logical consistency our interest, our passion, our vanity" [TS 23/17]. To think that reason, which can tell us what it would be contradictory or consistent to do, "should be sufficient to silence selfishness and passion" is to have "never heard the voice of the one or the other very loud within oneself" [TS 87/88]. In moral deliberation, reason can help social obligation to regain the upper hand over more selfish tendencies, but it cannot, Bergson argues, be a real source of obligation. At the same time, Bergson accepts Kant's point that no genuinely moral obligation can arise from subjective dispositions or feelings, such as Hume's sympathy and antipathy, whose goals practical reason subsequently pursues in deliberating on the correct means to attain them. "We may be obliged to adopt certain means in order to attain such and such ends", Bergson writes, "but if we choose to renounce the end, how can the means be forced upon us" [TS 90–1/92]? Such feelings or dispositions can produce, in Kant's terms, only hypothetical rather than categorical imperatives, imperatives based on particular desires ("if you don't want to put on weight, don't eat too much ice cream"). In short, Hume's approach passes over a basic feature of moral experience: the awareness of a seemingly non-relative, unconditional obligation. Obligation, on the empiricist account, amounts to merely an "invitation logically to pursue a certain end" [TS 90–1/92] rather than to any kind of demand. An "intuitionist" position, of the sort advanced by Plato, fares no better on the problem of motivation: we may in some sense directly apprehend or perceive objective ethical values, but what could the intuitionist "reply to the man who declared that he places his own interest before all other considerations?" [TS 88/89]. Intuitionism does not tell us why we should pursue the good that we perceive. Bergson's 1904–5 lectures on freedom at the Collège de France show that he was aware of the development of this claim [EPL 290–3], one discussed in the early-modern period under the heading of "moral necessity", according to which our perception of the good in some sense compels and determines us to pursue it, but he does not discuss this account of moral obligation directly in 1932.

All three meta-ethical positions, Bergson argues, presuppose a social and non-intellectual sense of the good. We name "good" only that which moves us [TS 87–8/89], and what moves us is already socially shaped. As soon as we attempt to define "the good" in order to determine whether a given action conforms to it, we introduce socially determined objectives. To posit "the good" as the ground of morality is to convert the product of morality into its principle; it is to elevate above the human being what has been produced by it. Similarly, any "empiricist" attempt to draw moral maxims from "feelings such as honor or sympathy, or pity" presupposes social obligation: "[e]ach of these tendencies, in a man living in society, is laden with all that social morality has deposited in it" [TS 89/90]. We might even try to posit pure self-interest as the basic principle of morality, but given that self-interest consists of "pride, the craving for praise" it becomes "impossible to define" without reference to social morality, and thus "we shall find no great difficulty in building up a rational morality sufficiently resembling" [TS 90/91] current social norms on its basis.

Bergson attempts to make the same point in relation to ethical rationalism with reference to Kant's example of not returning a deposit of money. Moral obligation in this case, Bergson argues, does not pertain to the bare and empty fact of "contradicting oneself, since the contradiction in this case would simply consist in rejecting, after having accepted it, a moral obligation which for this reason was already there" [TS 87/88]. Kant's argument was that the universalisation of my maxim ("it's acceptable for me not to return a deposit") contradicts the social institution of depositing money (no one would ever deposit money if everyone acted as the maxim proposes that I can). I discover a "contradiction in conception" in universalising the maxim and thereby discover that my maxim is immoral. Bergson does not deny this contradiction, but argues that it presupposes a given social institution, namely private property. If I do not presuppose this, then the word "deposit" merely describes a purely physical process (as in a "mineral deposit") without any moral significance and thus there is no contradiction involved in keeping the money. Bergson does not acknowledge this—neither here nor in his lectures at the Lycée Henri-IV during the years 1891–3 where he made the same point[2]—but his argument (curiously, given his rejection of Hegel's philosophy in 1914) rehearses Hegel's critique in his *Philosophy of Right* of the formalism of Kant's ethics. "If it is already established and presupposed that property and human life should exist and be respected", Hegel writes, "then it is a contradiction to commit theft or murder"; "a contradiction must be a contradiction with something, that is with a content that is already present as an established principle. Only to a principle of this kind does an action stand in a relation of agreement or contradiction".[3]

On the problem of moral motivation, we might wonder whether Bergson offered a mere caricature of Kant's position, since the

German philosopher discusses the rational, non-pathological feeling of respect for the moral law and for other rational agents as a motivating force.[4] But respect, as Bergson argues, is an essentially civic feeling, and the Roman citizen's respect for himself and others of his kind "would have been one of a piece with what we could call today his nationalism" [TS 65/66]. Self-respect, in other words, is a function of one's compliance with the demands of society. Moreover, if in Kant's Enlightenment philosophy, respect is respect for reason as possessing the highest value, then this is only because in history "men have divinized humanity, and [...] impressed a divine character on reason as an essential attribute of humanity" [TS 67/68]. Treating people as ends rather than means because and insofar as they are rational requires the kind of religious transformation that saw temples to reason erected in Revolutionary France. Kant's rationalist ethics, Bergson holds, has both social and religious origins that are non-rational.

That Bergson's meta-ethical position is anti-intellectualist in this way does not mean, to be sure, that he sees no place for reason and intelligence in the moral life. On the contrary, "[i]t is on the plane of intelligence, and on that plane alone, that discussion is possible, and there is no complete morality without reflection, analysis and argument with others as well as with oneself". Rational deliberation and discussion gives "confidence and delicacy to the moral sense" [TS 97/99]. It is often necessary to deliberate in order to work out what we should do in a given situation, what exactly the available options are, and to ensure that one course of action is consistent with others. Rational deliberation, that is, enables us to become fully fledged moral agents and belongs to the fact of morality whose sources Bergson attempts to bring to light. Still, rational moral deliberation, he argues, presupposes that we already feel the push or pull of moral obligation. Deliberation can serve to deliver us from temptation and to return us to obligation, but "from the fact that we get back to obligation by rational ways it does not follow that obligation was of a rational order" in the first place; a "tendency, natural or acquired, is one thing" but "another thing" is "the necessarily rational method which a reasonable being will use to restore its force and to combat what is opposing it" [TS 22/16].[5]

Closed and open morality

Given that she is in the business of thinking, it is natural for the philosopher to suppose that morality is essentially an intellectual affair. But the philosopher thus conflates "the feeling of obligation, a tranquil state close to inclination, with the violent effort that we sometimes exert on ourselves to break down what is opposed to obligation" [TS 11/14]. Bergson's at first glance peculiar position is that doing what one ought to do is normally easy, and to do our duty we have only to let ourselves go. Effort and moral deliberation arise only when our tendency to do what we ought to do is opposed by another, more anti-social and egotistical force; or when we have a conflict of duties. In this sense, morality is originally unthinking and habitual, and "social life appears to us as a more or less deeply rooted system of habits responding to the needs of the community" [TS 2/3]. Moral "obligation"—the word derives from the Latin *ligare*, "to bind"—is a function of the social ties that bind us, and it is by, as Hume put it, the "gentle force"[6] of habit that we feel compelled to obey social rules: "each of these habits of obeying exerts pressure on our will. We can remove ourselves from it, but we are drawn to it, brought back to it, like the pendulum which has swung away from the vertical" [TS 2/2]. Kant's intellectualist and dualist presuppositions had led him to argue that habit "deprives even good actions of their moral worth because it impairs the freedom of the mind", and that "as a rule all habits are reprehensible", but in affirming the moral and social value of habit, Bergson joins Hegel in his concern for *Sittlichkeit*, which is customary, habitual and social ethical life, as prior to the rationalisations of morality (*Moralität*).[7]

What exactly does Bergson mean by the force of habit here? He describes its operation as "pressure", but in the opening paragraph of the book he seems unsure whether it operates mechanically, which is what the word "pressure" suggests, or according to a more intrinsically active and perhaps more organic or even spiritual sense of attraction ("we are drawn to it").[8] We might presume that Bergson is relying on his previous accounts of personal motor habit as resulting in biological mechanisms, but if so, *The Two Sources* is developing that account, for he had not mentioned in *Matter and*

Memory that "with all habit, we feel obliged" [TS 2/2]. When he adds
that the inclination and obligation in social habit is "incomparably
stronger" than in other habits, such that there is not just a difference
in degree but a "difference in nature" between them, because each
social imperative forms a "single mass" [TS 2/2] with others, he
certainly goes beyond anything that he had previously said about
habit. Consequently, we might infer that if social habits really are
different in nature to other habits, then they do not operate in the
same way as mechanical motor habits.

Before making such an inference we have to understand that in
conceiving the force of moral obligation as habit, Bergson sets up
what he presents first as an *analogy* between the social and the natural realm, between our "second nature" and our primary nature,
and thus between moral and physical laws: although a "human
community is a collectivity of free beings", the "obligations which
it lays down, and which enable it to subsist, introduce into it a
regularity which has merely some analogy to the inflexible order
of the phenomena of life" [TS 3/3]. Confusingly for the reader
of *Laughter*, where life was conceived of as elasticity, Bergson now
aligns inflexibility with life, but the point is that if an apparent
inflexibility of the phenomena of life is governed by necessity, by
necessary laws, it can be said that "obligation is to necessity, what
habit is to nature" [TS 6/7]. Even though obligation "obliges rather
than necessitates" [TS 3/4], it has something quasi-inexorable,
quasi-necessary about it.

Bergson is responding to, in addition to Hegel, two French intellectual sources in these opening passages. The first is Ravaisson and
the "school of contingency", of which many echoes can still be
heard throughout *The Two Sources*. Ravaisson had argued that habit
allows freedom to be instantiated and incorporated in "inclinations"
and thus to adopt a form of necessity that is a "necessity of attraction
and desire"[9] rather than any mechanical necessity of pressure. This
supposed necessity of attraction in an acquired habit was, in truth, no
real necessity at all, since it was presented as a matter of degree: habits
become more and more necessary as they are acquired, but necessity cannot be a matter of degree (something is either necessary
or it is not), and so it was easy to surmise that habits are never
necessary at all. Boutroux came to this conclusion in his 1874 *On the*

Contingency of the Laws of Nature, as we have noted: the idea of necessity is but the "most abstract translation" of "moral obligation and aesthetic attraction", which govern human pursuits and even nature as a whole.[10] Boutroux's claim, then, is that obligation and attraction are a function of what he terms "contingency" rather than necessity, however much it looks like the latter, and Bergson might seem to rehearse the claim in the opening pages of *The Two Sources*.

Nevertheless, Bergson seems to reject this inheritance and to decide later in the chapter that moral obligation operates mechanically: "obligation stands for the pressure exerted by the elements of society on one another in order to maintain the shape of the whole, a pressure whose effect is prefigured in each of us by a system of habits which, so to speak, go to meet it; this mechanism, of which each separate part is a habit, but whose whole is comparable to an instinct, has been prepared by nature" [TS 42/53]. Each particular ethical habit is "contingent" rather than necessary, since different societies have different ethical forms, but it is necessary that a society has habits; habit is the "great guide" of human life, as Hume said, but in society, Bergson adds, as well as in the individual. On the basis of this claim that having habits is necessary, Bergson slides towards the claim that habits operate by a form of necessity, and thus that they can be interpreted mechanistically. The word "mechanism" appears another three times in the same paragraph, and thus Bergson seems to return to the kind of dualist and mechanistic interpretation of social and ethical habit that he had presented of motor habit in *Matter and Memory*. This mechanical interpretation of ethical habits may appear much less tenable, and it may lead us to wonder whether "mechanism" here quite means what it says. Is it not absurd to suppose that Berliners customarily wait for the green man, the *Ampelmännchen*, to appear before crossing a road empty of traffic because social pressure has been instantiated in physiological or psychological mechanisms? Contemporary neuroethics tries to persuade us that it is not, but further clarification and justification of Bergson's own claims is required in these passages of *The Two Sources*.

Bergson's account of social habit is unsatisfactory and takes rather a lot for granted, but one reason it does so is that he is drawing on the sociology of Emile Durkheim, his fellow student at the Ecole Normale Supérieure, rather than formulating his own position from scratch. Durkheim is not once mentioned by name in this chapter of the *Two Sources*, but the whole chapter is a "tacit and entirely systematic"[11] response to his sociology, as Alexandre Lefebvre and Melanie White have shown. The idea of the primacy of habit in social life and the notion of obligation as the psychological correlate of social constraint and pressure are Durkheimian themes. Nevertheless, Bergson attacks Durkheim on two closely related points. First, Durkheim went to great pains to isolate the social from the biological, social facts from biological facts, in order to establish his new discipline as a science in its own right, one independent of both biology and psychology. In contrast, in the course of the first chapter Bergson's analogy of the social with the biological becomes explicitly an *identification*. The chapter concludes by affirming that society does not "explain itself" and thus that it is not *sui generis*: "everything becomes clear […] if we go and search, beyond these manifestations" of social life "for life itself. Let us then give to biology the very wide meaning it should have, and will perhaps have one day, and let us say in conclusion that all morality […] is in essence biological" [TS 82/104].

It has been objected to Bergson that he thus broadens the sense of a word in a wholly arbitrary fashion, but this is to forget that *bios* in ancient Greek originally means a human way of life, a manner of living, the subject of a *biography*, and precisely not animal life.[12] Bergson's broadening of the sense of the term could spiritualise nature as much as it naturalises spirit, and it is not necessarily the expression of a reductive "biologism". That said, the worry that Bergson advances a kind of sociobiology (the term will not be coined until the 1940s) attempting to reduce social phenomena to forces governing animal life is not unfounded.[13] He ascribes to a form of instinct, and thus to a form of nature, the principle of what he considers as "closed" social morality: "[o]ur social duties aim at social cohesion; […] they compose for us an attitude which is that of discipline before the enemy […] The social instinct we have detected at the basis of social obligation always has in view— instinct being relatively unchangeable—a closed society, however large it may be" [TS 21/27]. Although particular social habits vary from society to society, social habit in essence and as a whole has the instinctive, life-preserving purpose of consolidating a particular human society pitted against and closed off from another. The biological necessity of social habit is, at bottom, a war instinct.

Bergson also attacks Durkheim for his claim that the exclusive ties of family and nation can be progressively expanded into a concern for humanity in general. According to the "cosmopolitan nationalism" that Durkheim promoted, "the state makes its main goal not to expand, in a material sense, at the expense of its neighbours, nor to become stronger or richer than them; but to realize within itself the general interests of humanity. […] From this point of view, all rivalry between different countries disappears and, consequently, so too does the antinomy between cosmopolitanism and patriotism."[14] As Bergson puts it, "[w]e are fond of saying that we learn about civic virtues within the family, and that in the same way, from holding our country dear, we learn to love mankind. Our sympathies are supposed to broaden out in an unbroken progression, to expand while remaining identical, and end up embracing all humanity […]." This approach is not just naïve and picturesque, Bergson argues, but it is also "*a priori* reasoning born from a purely intellectualist conception of the mind" [TS 21/27].

It is a function of *a priori* reasoning, he argues, because it does not take into account the empirical fact of war. In war, "murder and pillage, as well as perfidy, fraud and lies become not only lawful; they are praiseworthy. Just like the witches of *Macbeth*, the belligerents will say: 'Fair is foul, and foul is fair'" [TS 21/27]. That a society at war can suspend so easily its universal duties to mankind suggests that its morality never stretched beyond itself. War, from Bergson's perspective, "is not a mysterious departure from the morality of society; it is instead the key to bringing that morality clearly into view".[15] Habitual morality is intrinsically closed, intrinsically oriented towards consolidation of a particular society against others. Moreover, Durkheim's position is *intellectualist*, since it is natural for the intellect, at home with quantification, to consider that morality begins with one principle, love for the limited number of people in one's family, and ends with a maximal quantitative expansion of that principle in the guise of love for humanity. This is true, Bergson admits, in the case of the development from family to society, since they were originally closely bound together. But in the case of the difference between a particular society and humanity in general, Bergson objects to Durkheim that these moral commitments have two wholly different but equally non-intellectual sources.

The closed principle of habitual morality is of a radically different nature to an open principle of love for humanity as a whole. The difference can be traversed only in a leap, by means of a conversion. "Exceptional souls […] borne on a great surge of love towards humanity in general" [TS 77–8/97] have made this leap and beckoned us to follow them: "before the Christian saints, humanity had known the Greek sages, the prophets of Israel, the Buddhist Arahants and many others" [TS 23/30]. At its limit, Bergson argues, this love without exclusive attachment does not attach just to humanity, or even just to living things: "charity would remain in the one who possesses it, even if nothing else living existed on earth" and "its form does not depend on its content" [TS 27/34]. This aspect of morality is not pressure but aspiration. It does not repeat and reproduce, like habit, constantly turning around itself in a circle, but rather pushes forward into the open, breaking new moral ground. This moral evolution is a biological evolution in Bergson's broad sense of the term; it is the pinnacle and the cutting edge of the *élan vital*. It does not advance by means of the intellect, but by emotion and generosity, by the sort of boundless love that Christianity discussed under the heading of *agape*.[16]

Only emotion, Bergson contends, has the motivating power to defeat the force of closed social obligation. This is the sort of profound emotion that, as we hinted in Chapter 8, for the Bergson of 1932 characterises original art:

> The work of genius has usually emerged from a singular and unique emotion that would have been thought inexpressible, but which *had* to be expressed. But is it not the same with any work, however imperfect it may be, in which creation has a share? Anyone who has undertaken a literary composition has been able to feel the difference between an intelligence left to itself and one burning with the fire of an original and unique emotion, born of the identification of the author with his subject, and, that is to say, engendered by intuition. [TS 34/43]

Like Kant's aesthetic ideas, this profound emotion gives rise to thoughts and concepts, but can never be reduced to the latter; it is "emotion that drives the intelligence forward despite obstacles; it vivifies or rather vitalises the intellectual elements with which it is destined to unite" [TS 34/43]. Genius, then, does not just exist in literature and art [TS 33/42], and great moral innovators and fine artists alike are moved by the same creative, emotive source. We might find this expansion of the idea of genius strange, and worry that it considerably, even impossibly, dilutes traditional accounts of it. What in ethical practice, we might ask, is the equivalent of the artwork, the work that is irreducible to conceptual interpretation?.

In articulating this distinction between closed and open morality, between the genial and the habitual, Bergson distinguishes two kinds of justice. Relative justice "evoke[s] ideas of equality, of proportion, of compensation" [TS 55/69], asserts that each should receive her due, what is owed to her, and is mercantile in origin. Absolute justice is "the assertion pure and simple of an inviolability of right and of the incommensurability of the person with any values whatsoever" [TS 57/71]. In absolute justice, the absolute justice underlying modern notions of human rights (and international law, which Bergson actively defended in his work for the League of Nations after the war), the person becomes an absolute value in her own right: "it is a far cry from [...] the scales held by the justice of the ancients, to a justice such as ours, that of the 'rights of man,' which no longer evokes ideas of relativity and proportion, but, on the contrary, of the incommensurable and the absolute" [TS 59/73]. But the move to absolute justice, Bergson argues, involves a transfiguration and a leap, rather than a quantitative expansion, and it is only in retrospect, according to a retrospective illusion [TS 58/72], that the leap can appear to have traversed a unitary scale of gradations and degradations.

So, from Bergson's perspective, in failing to grasp the two opposed sources of morality, Durkheim's position is dangerously naïve. It fails to recognise not just the natural darkness at the heart of human society but also the higher source of the moral power able to combat it. But who is right in this covert intellectual exchange?

Before attempting to answer, we should notice the historical context of the dispute. In 1914 Bergson and Durkheim responded differently to what the philosopher claims the sociologist has not adequately considered, namely the eventuality of war. Durkheim, with Jewish origins like Bergson, was the enthusiastic secretary of a committee of French intellectuals, which included the author of *Creative Evolution*, formed to produce documents and studies on the war that were distributed in and outside of France in order to undermine German propaganda.[17] Nevertheless, the works on the war to which Durkheim put his name—*Who Wanted War? The Origin of the War According to Diplomatic Documents* and *Germany Above All: German Mentality and War*[18]—were rather more measured in tone than Bergson's. As politically on the left, Durkheim, though patriotic, was not enthused by the nationalist fervour in France, even less so after his son fell in battle in 1915. He seems to have paid for this with accusations of disloyalty before his death, from sorrow as is said, in 1917.[19] Bergson, in contrast, as we have seen, made himself more or less unassailable in this regard. The philosopher and the sociologist had clearly both felt the pressure of nationalism, the pressure of a society at war, but had responded to it in different ways.

Who, then, is right on the issue of morality and war? Is Durkheim dangerously naïve? Or is Bergson not exaggerating, dangerously dabbling in biologism in 1932 just as he had dangerously dabbled in closed mythological nationalism in 1914? When he speaks of closed human society as like a beehive or anthill, the charge of "*a priori* thinking" can, I think, be levelled at him just as forcefully. Certainly, French society may have felt like a beehive when it closed ranks in 1914 under the banner of *l'union sacrée*, the sacred union of all parties and interests. But is it not evidently the case that this closure—which led to the assassination of Jean Jaurès, Bergson's and Durkheim's former Ecole Normale colleague—was a function of *sui generis* political choice rather than some kind of biological necessity?

Bergson's determination to separate love for family and nation, on the one hand, and love for humanity in general, on the other hand, as wholly different principles is questionable. It appears all the more so when we notice that before the war, in his lectures at the

Lycée Henri-IV, a young Bergson supported the expansionary, monistic view that he now criticises.[20] Now he argues that existing moral doctrines are composed from two sources, but one of these sources, if realised in its purity, would be amoral, even immoral. A purely closed morality would not even pretend to be concerned with others beyond the immediate social group, and would be actively opposed to them. History has given us enough examples of extreme racial and tribal hatred of this nature, but it is hard to see how it could merit the label "morality". Isn't a society that cares only about itself, like a person who only cares about himself, simply immoral? The worry is that only one of Bergson's sources is itself moral. At the same time, we might worry that a purely open morality—although "pure mysticism is a rare essence" [TS 181/225], Bergson speaks of this purity as possible and sometimes actual—would be unrealisable in experience, impossible as a way of life. How can a love that favours nobody in particular be bestowed in concrete worldly circumstances on anyone at all? We could point to the idea and institutions of human rights as an instantiation of Bergson's purely open mystical love, but we might be disappointed by this formalistic and perhaps essentially negative (human rights exist principally to protect from oppression) expression of selfless love.[21]

These worries about the purely closed and the purely open might lead us to question the very notion of *sources* of morality and religion. The ontology of sources here is the expression of an ethical evaluation of the human condition that is arguably at once too cynical and too optimistic. Perhaps it would be more convincing to remain closer to *Creative Evolution* and to speak of *tendencies* rather than sources. Is it not the case that welcoming the stranger is made possible by loving one's own, just as loving one's own is an inherent tendency of the realisation of a less exclusive, mystical love and joy?

Myth and mysticism

Bergson distinguishes static from dynamic religion just as he distinguishes closed from open morality, but his discussion of religion in the second chapter of *The Two Sources* involves more explicit responses to the nascent sciences of sociology and anthropology.

How, Bergson asks in opening the chapter, are we to understand the fact, which is humiliating for the human being's self-understanding as a rational animal, that no society has ever existed without a religion, and that religions through the ages have involved a farrago of irrational beliefs and counselled even the most immoral actions? He rejects the proposal of Lucien Lévy-Bruhl—who was influenced by Durkheim and succeeded Boutroux in the Chair of the History of Modern Philosophy at the Sorbonne—that such irrational beliefs and practices belong to a "primitive mentality" that we no longer possess as a result of evolutionary changes. We are hardly immune to superstition in the present, Bergson retorts, and it is only our increased knowledge that can keep the most acute of our superstitions in check [TS 117–18/148]. Moreover, the idea that different beliefs are the result of evolutionary biological changes seems to presuppose the inheritance of acquired characteristics, which Bergson, as we have seen, is not inclined to accept. Bergson also criticises Durkheim's postulation of a social, collective mentality that could explain religion and demarcate sociology from individual psychology: "individual and society reciprocally imply each other: individuals constitute society by their assembly; society shapes a whole side of the individual by being prefigured in each one of them. Individual and society thus condition each other in a circular fashion" [TS 169/209].

For Bergson, the key to understanding religious beliefs and practices—religious "fabulation"—resides in the recognition that "our psychical structure originates in the necessity of preserving and developing" both "social and individual life" [TS 88/111]. Religious beliefs, which have structured human experience through the ages, have to be understood from the perspective of their function for both society and the individual. Rather than arbitrary, unmotivated inventions, they are products of a vital need. Our intelligence, as *Creative Evolution* argued, is a product of the *élan vital*, but the disassociation of intellect from instinct brings dangers, Bergson now contends, from which religion serves to protect it. Religious belief is a "virtual instinct" [TS 90/114], a natural tendency to fabulation that guards against three principal dangers. First, in the guise of egoism and self-interest, intelligence threatens social breakdown, but religion can act, with its threats of divine punishment, as a social glue before philosophy is able to show that self-interest is best pursued within law-bound society as a whole. Religion is thus a "defensive reaction of nature against the dissolvent power of intelligence" [TS 101/127]. Second, ideas of ancestral spirits and immortal souls abound in religions because religion is a "defensive reaction of nature against the representation by intelligence", one that is debilitating and demotivating for the individual, "of the inevitability of death" [TS 109/137]. Third, religions involve beliefs in "favourable powers overriding or replacing natural causes" as "defensive reactions of nature against the representation by intelligence of a depressing margin of the unexpected between the initiative taken and the effect desired". There is often a gap between our goal and the means we use to pursue it, and religious belief intervenes to make us believe the effect will occur, for "in default of power we must have confidence" [TS 138/172].

Bergson's interpretation of religion is faithful to the etymological sense of the word as *binding again* or *reattachment*: "[r]eligion is that element which, in beings endowed with reason, is called upon to make good any deficiency of attachment to life" [TS 179/222], to life in society and the individual. What in 1900 was an object of laughter, namely a lack of attention or attachment to life, is now understood as the problem that religion solves. Fabulation, however, is merely static religion, and another source of attachment entirely, Bergson argues, is to be found in mysticism. Mysticism, which Bergson describes as "joy in joy, love of that which is all love" [TS 181/225], is but "the establishment of a contact, and consequently of a partial coincidence, with the creative effort which life itself manifests" [TS 188/233]. The "mystic genius" [TS 269/332] gains contact with this principle through the fundamental emotion that is love, and discovers an inexhaustible source of love and joy in doing so. In this sense, "the great mystic is to be conceived as an individual being, capable of transcending the limitations imposed on the species by its material nature, thus continuing and extending the divine action" [TS 188/233]. The great mystic gains contact with the *élan vital*, the principle of a *naturata naturans*, a nature in the making, rather than a nature ready-made, and in so doing discovers God. The mystic does not, for all that, "ask whether the principle with which it now is in contact is the transcendent cause of all things or if it is only its terrestrial delegation" [TS 180/224]. Bergson does not decide on this issue of whether the *élan vital* can be identified with God when he returns to it later, which leaves a fundamental ambiguity in his theology.[22]

In any case, it is through her love of God, and through the love that the mystic finds in God, that she "loves all humanity with a divine love" [TS 199/247]. But this love, in order to be complete, must consist in its realisation by "action, creation and love" [TS 192/238]. In this sense, Bergson can argue that mysticism is fully realised in the Christian mystics. The mystical aspects of ancient Greek thinking, for example, were still all too intellectual. In the East, Buddhism lacked warmth in failing to belief in the efficacy of human action, while Hinduism, with Ramakrishna or Vivekananda, focused on charity only with the influence of Christianity [TS 193/239]. In all of this reflection on love and charity, it should be noted, Bergson borrows much from Ravaisson's philosophy of religion, particularly as it is expressed in his *Philosophical Testament*.[23]

War and the will to power

After the first chapter on morality, the second chapter of *The Two Sources* is concerned with closed, static religion, while its third chapter addresses dynamic, open religion. All of this is followed, however, by a final chapter that bears the title "Final Remarks: Mechanism and Mysticism". Here Bergson asks whether "the distinction between the closed and the open, which is necessary to resolve or remove theoretical problems, is able to help us practically" [TS 234/288] in the present. That these are "remarks" seems to invite us to consider them as incidental to Bergson's philosophy, as merely the musings of a theorist on contemporary practical and political problems. Lacey took them in this way: although "philosophical material crops up here and there", they do little other than recommend "mysticism as a remedy for the discontents in modern industrial society".[24] In truth, these remarks are crucial in Bergson's philosophical trajectory, for in them, he returns to the key themes of his war writings, and makes explicit their philosophical grounds. The "Final Remarks" in Bergson's final monograph illuminate his war discourses, and the war discourses, as we will see, also serve to illuminate the dangers in the position that he lays out clearly in 1932.

Nadia Kisukidi has recently pointed out "two persistent difficulties" relating to Bergson's war writings: "How is it that the philosophical concepts of *Creative Evolution* are merged into this war rhetoric?" and "Why do passages of the war writings anticipate certain reflections" in *The Two Sources of Morality and Religion*?[25] What we first observed in Chapter 8 of this study allows us to answer the first question: the idea of creation that Bergson draws from an interpretation of the production of fine art, and subsequently applies to the processes of psychological and biological life in general, and then to the French nation at war with Germany, is the expression of a philosophy of the will. In the idea of the *élan vital* as a dynamic, creative force there lies a conception of the will as a self-grounding, self-asserting, self-augmenting voluntary power, and this becomes all the more evident in the way that Bergson mobilises his philosophy. The force that does not wear out, to refer to the title of Bergson's November article on the war, is the power of the will. Note that if creation were involuntary, Bergson would not have been able to invoke it for his propagandistic purposes: it would hardly be morale-boosting to characterise France, in the face of the German war machine, as a nation of "creatives" waiting for inspiration to arrive. Bergson had his own political and personal motivations for his interventions in the war, but the voluntarism in his philosophy of creation is what made possible its own mobilisation. The war writings can certainly be characterised, following Philippe Soulez, as a kind of "doubling [*dédoublement*]"[26] of the philosophical work that Bergson, in his testament, chose to separate from his more circumstantial writings, but in the heat of the moment they distil a fundamental position in his philosophy.

Chapter 1 of the present study briefly mentioned George Politzer's denunciation of Bergson in his 1928 *The End of the Philosophical Parade*. It is not necessary to agree with Politzer's view that the Great War was a clash internal to capitalist imperialism, or with his claim that Bergson's spiritualist philosophy, in the name of life and immediacy, was an ideological ruse obscuring the significance of Marxist dialectical materialism as a genuinely concrete philosophy of life, in order to see that he was right to assert a direct relation between Bergson's philosophy and its expression in his wartime writings. Politzer was

246 Ethics, religion and politics

right for reasons that are independent of his Marxist politics and his demand for a "concrete" philosophy: Bergson's philosophy of life as creation is a philosophy of the will as a self-propelling and self-constituting power, a power at one's command, a power that calls for its intensification from its own resources. Politzer was perhaps not wholly unaware of this, since he cites the following passage on Jean-Marie Guyau from Bergson's 1915 essay on "French Philosophy": "Less famous than Nietzsche, Guyau held, before the German philosopher, in more measured terms and in a more acceptable form, that the moral ideal is to be sought in the highest possible expansion of life" [M 1180]. It is hard to disagree with Politzer that this "reveals to us what Bergson thinks of himself" as much as of his predecessor Guyau.[27] But what Politzer does not state is that if the essence of life is will, and if the moral ideal is the expansion of life, then the aim of life is the expansion and intensification of the will. Will, if it wills well, wills its own expansion. The will wills dominion and power, but the principle of power is not external to the will. Will, therefore, is and should be a *will to will*. Will is a "wanting to will, a wanting to give oneself more will [*vouloir vouloir, vouloir se donner de la volonté*]" [EPL 205–6], as Bergson says in 1905. He may well have considered the form of Nietzsche's philosophy to be unmeasured and unacceptable in 1914, but his own ideas have more than a passing resemblance—we will see that he implicitly acknowledges this—to the Nietzschean doctrine of the will to power.

In order to respond to Kisukidi's second question—why, and in what way, do passages of the wartime writings anticipate certain reflections in *The Two Sources of Morality and Religion?*—we should note first of all how Bergson's position in 1932 has changed since 1914. He has clearly recognised that what he now terms the "open" and the "closed" are two tendencies inherent to all societies, and that no particular nation-state can be wholly determined by either one. Furthermore, when he evokes the "exaltation of a people at the outbreak of war", which could "perhaps" be explained as a "defensive reaction against fear" [TS 246/303], he is perhaps engaging in an implicit self-critique: the mobilisation of his philosophy in the service of the French war effort—*and this in the name of a concern for international justice and then of life*—was to a degree a function of a bellicose, perhaps fearful, but certainly partially closed mind.

In any case, the very real social and philosophical issue of technology in modern industrial society remains. In 1914, Bergson had speculated that "a philosopher of the future", when the guns have fallen silent and there is opportunity for reflection, might speak of the meaning of the war thus: modern science "had procured for man more tools than he had produced during the thousands of years in which he had previously existed on earth. Each new machine being for man a new organ—an artificial organ that comes to extend his natural organs—, his body has found itself suddenly and prodigiously enlarged, without his spirit being able to dilate itself quickly enough to extend itself to the whole of this new body. From this disproportion are born moral, social and international problems" [M 1114]. Bergson returns to the issue, as the philosopher of the future about whom he had speculated, in almost identical terms: the disproportion between the enhanced powers of the body and those of the soul produces "social, political and international problems which are just so many definitions of this gap, and which provoke so many chaotic and ineffectual efforts to fill it" [TS 267–8/330]. In fact, "humanity stands half-crushed by the progress it has made" and is perhaps on the verge, as Bergson adds presciently, 13 years before the detonation of the first atomic bomb, of developing military technologies that entail the total annihilation of the enemy population, and even the annihilation of mankind as a whole. Our enlarged physical and technological capacities have brought us to the point of imminent destruction, to the point where it is necessary to ask whether and how humankind wants to continue living. These enlarged capacities require "a supplement of spirit", a spiritual expansion enabling a return to a life more austere and simple, in which we are able to resist the commercial production of new, unnecessary "needs". Only with such an expansionary purification can we ensure, Bergson argues, that the basic alimentary needs of a rapidly increasing global population, rather than of just a few, can be met. Bergson promotes the necessity of eating less meat, and remarks—again, quite presciently—that we may soon discover it is rather bad for our general health. At the same time, he hopes that genuine equality between the sexes and an end to the subordination of women might bring about a decline in the pursuit of superfluous luxuries.

In modern societies beset by war, technological excess, numbing uniformity, pointless needs and overpopulation, mechanism "requires a mysticism" [TS 268/330]. This is not to say that the former is to be vanquished by the latter, since mysticism itself requires mechanism in order to gain the requisite freedom from immediate material needs. But is it realistic to hope for such a mystical transformation in societies governed by materialistic frenzy, societies driven by the production of pointless needs to distraction, depletion and destruction? Bergson offers the sketch of a philosophy of history—one that develops his previous account of biological life as differentiation—in order to justify his optimism. The mysticism that was so present in medieval society before the first stirrings of modernity, was, he argues, accompanied by asceticism, by a general indifference to the material conditions of life. This was as frenetic as modern materialism and expanded to the limits of its possibilities, but the frenzy was a function of pride rather than vanity, of self-mastery rather than mastery of the world [TS 277/320]. In order to move forward, and in order for democracy to be viable [TS 266/328], as Bergson notes, Western culture had to promote the machine, and to swop one form of frenzy for another. Now that this materialist frenzy has exhausted its own possibilities and outlasted its usefulness, progress can consist only in rediscovering on a higher level a principle of mysticism.

Modern life, then, requires a new synthesis of self-mastery and mastery of the world. Against this background, in the final pages of The Two Sources, Bergson responds to Ernest Seillière, his colleague at the French Academy of Moral and Political Sciences. Seillière is little read now, but "in a long series of writings, which for depth and forcefulness are beyond praise" [TS 268/1239], he attempts to illuminate the sense and sources of imperialism.[28] Seillière analyses the political reality of imperialism, understood as the tendency of social groups and modern nation-states to expand into foreign territory. Seillière does this, however, not economically in, say, a Marxist sense, but metaphysically, according to a philosophy of life: life is essentially imperialist in that its forms need to exploit and overcome their surroundings in order to survive and develop.[29] In the human being, this vital reality is expressed as a desire to dominate oneself, things and other people. As denominating such a vital, personal and social reality, the term "imperialism", for Seillière, does not possess a pejorative sense. Still, for him, imperialism becomes problematic when it loses its moorings in reason and experience and is led astray by improper forms of "mysticism", such as beliefs in the essential goodness of humankind, romantic beliefs in human genius, democratic beliefs in the essential rightness of the people, and doctrines of racial supremacy.

It was in this light that Seillière, before the war, had approached Bergson's work, which he took, like that of Nietzsche, to be one of the recent philosophies of "imperialism". In an article published initially in German in 1913, "Welche Moralphilosophie läßt Bergson erwarten?" ("What Moral Philosophy Can We Expect from Bergson?"), and then as the third chapter of his 1917 *L'avenir de la philosophie bergsonienne* (*The Future of Bergson's Philosophy*), Seillière wondered whether Bergson's philosophy of life could ground a moral doctrine contrasting with Nietzsche's allegedly irrationalist, individualist and violent imperialism.[30] Bergsonism is a "new mysticism," one that is "marvelously adapted [...] to the present state of human knowledge" and that is "the most useful tonic for the sort of action to which those of good will should rally". That said, this mysticism carries the risk of abuse by an "excessive will to power", and Bergson requires a moral doctrine to "oppose, as a brake, the temptations already assailing so visibly some of his readers". It is probable, Seillière proposes, that *sympathy* will occupy an important position in a Bergsonian moral doctrine, although Bergson himself has placed "the Will to power, much more insistently than sympathy, at the origin of active life".[31] Seillière, then, sees that Bergson's philosophy is a philosophy of the will, and even of the will to power, but he also sees the need for this philosophy to be tempered by a moral doctrine of "sympathy".

Bergson responds to Seillière by asserting that once genuine mysticism is distinguished from its improper forms in the imperialism of modern nation-states—which merely amount, one might say, to ideological mystification—it will become clear that mysticism is *not* tied to imperialism. Although he adds that he does not address the full senses of both terms in Seillière's work, Bergson's first point is that if "we keep to true mysticism, we shall judge it incompatible with imperialism" [TS 269/332]. Bergson's philosophy of mystical openness in 1932 is not imperialist, if by that we mean empire and dominion over other human beings and societies. Instead of empire in this ordinary sense, he now promotes openness, international law and the nascent League of Nations.[32] Bergson's position in 1932 is that the League of Nations to which he had professed France's allegiance in 1917 to Woodrow Wilson, and to which he had given many years of his professional life in the 1920s, is an expression of the "open", and non-imperialist, principle of morality.

Bergson distances himself from a "philosophy of imperialism", but he immediately qualifies his position: "at the most, we will have to admit, as we just put it, that mysticism cannot be expanded without encouraging a certain, very particular 'will to power'. It is a question of having dominion, not over men, but on things, precisely so that man should no longer have it so much on man" [TS 269/232]. Bergson admits, then, that his philosophy of mystical openness requires an expansionary and imperialist principle, a will to power, since the natural world, by means of modern technology, is to be dominated, its resources fully exploited, so that humanity as a whole can live without want and thus in peace. Julien Benda's remark in 1927 that "it is man" that Bergson "exalts for his genius in making himself master of the earth" was prescient.[33] Bergson's position is what could be called metaphysically expansionary and imperialist, but not imperialist in a narrowly political or social sense. There must be dominion, but this concerns the human being's relation to the tools it has made and to nature as a whole, but not the relation of person to person or group to group.[34] Still, it is the metaphysical imperialism of the will to power underlying Bergson's later philosophy of mystical sympathy and openness to humanity that is precisely what enabled the mobilisation of his philosophy in 1914 in order to advance the interests of a particular imperialist nation-state against another. This imperialism, ordinarily focused on exploiting nature, needed only to change direction, to change its object.

In one sense, the philosophy of *Creative Evolution*, as a philosophy of the will, culminates in *The Two Sources* as a philosophy of emotion and love. Bergson, however, never leaves this philosophy of the will behind.[35] The *élan vital* may find its ultimate motive source in the love of a divine principle, a principle that is itself pure love, and in a mystical contact with eternity, but, Bergson argues, the human relation to nature, precisely in order to facilitate this openness, must be one of empire, domination, command and control. To wonder whether Bergson can help to combat the modern techno-scientific "war against nature"[36] without remarking that he actively prescribes that war against nature is strange. To point this out is not to deny that in the contemporary context Bergson's vote, as Lacey wondered,[37] may well have gone to the Green party. Nor is it to deny that other aspects of his thinking could serve deeper ecological concerns. He recognises, as we have seen, that our intellectual grasp of nature, and thus the mathematisation of nature in modern science, reveals as much about our pursuit of power as the truth of the natural world, and that nature in this sense is derivative of a more primordial living principle. Moreover, mystical openness does not have to be limited to a love of the human species alone. Nevertheless, from the perspective of "deep ecology" in later-twentieth-century thinking, the humanist—recall that *Creative Evolution* wondered whether man "is the *raison d'être* of the development" of the *élan vital* "as a whole" [CE 279/ 265]—and voluntarist philosophy expressed in the final pages of the *Two Sources* offers only the shallowest of ecologies.

The war against nature that Bergson promotes in 1932 has the same source as the mobilisation of his philosophy in the war against Germany in 1914: a philosophy of the will as will to power. It is, of course, open to question whether this philosophy of the will can respond adequately to the problems of modern technology that Bergson first brought to light in 1914. He sensed then, with the fable of the sorcerer's apprentice, that modern technology was escaping human control, developing according to its own, autonomous logic. But in 1932 he states explicitly what it is that can get modern technology back in hand: an intensified, expanded, and purified will. Nearly a century after Bergson's *Two Sources*, we may be readier to entertain the idea that the goal of control over modern technology is illusory, and that the problems emerging from modern technology may actually derive from the same source as the desire for mastery that is supposed to solve them.

Summary

The *Two Sources of Morality and Religion* advances an anti-intellectualist ethics. Bergson argues that all of deontology, utilitarianism and intuitionism fail to provide a convincing response to the problem of moral motivation, to the problem of why I should act morally at all. That motivation has two extra-rational sources. "Closed" morality is conditioned by social habits binding particular social groups; habit in this sense, Bergson argues, is a war instinct that pits societies against each other. "Open" morality, in contrast, is the work of genius (Bergson takes seriously the idea that there is something superhuman and divine in genius) and expresses the sort of boundless love and generosity that Christianity discussed under the heading of *agape*. Any existing system of moral commitments is an expression of these two principles. Corresponding to open and closed morality, are open and closed religion. The former Bergson understands as a kind of instinctive, defensive reaction against the socially disruptive power of intelligence and the certainty of death, while the latter is pure joy as a mystical contact with the divine, a principle of love and generosity. In concluding *The Two Sources*, Bergson returns to the problems of the modern technological age that he had first reflected on in his war writings. He advocates a return to a simpler and more austere (as well as more vegetarian and feminist) form of life as a response to the problems of the age. However, his remarks about the will and the need to dominate nature in these pages allow us to see clearly what made possible the mobilisation of his philosophy for the French cause in 1914: an account of creation as a function of the will to power.

Notes

1 This is what Bergson related to Jacques Chevalier; see Chevalier, *Entretiens avec Bergson* (Paris: Plon, 1959), p. 176. For more on the genesis of *The Two Sources*, see Brigitte Sitbon-Peillon "*Les Deux Sources de la Morale et de la Religion* suite de *L'Evolution créatrice? Genèse d'un choix philosophique entre morale et esthétique*".

2 Bergson, *Cours II*, ed. H. Hude, pp. 109–11.

3 §135 of Hegel's *Philosophy of Right*, cited in John McCumber, *Understanding Hegel's Mature Critique of Kant* (Stanford, CA: Stanford University Press, 2014). See Chapter 5 as a whole: "Hegel's Critique of Kant's Moral Theory".

4 See, for example, Gary Banham, "Kantian Respect", *Kant Studies Online* (2014): www.garybanham.net/PAPERS_files/Kantian%20Respect.pdf.

5 For a longer treatment of Bergson's arguments against intellectualism in ethics than I am able to offer here, see Carl Power, "Bergson's Critique of Practical Reason", in *Bergson, Politics, and Religion*, ed. Alexandre Lefebvre and Melanie White (Durham, NC: Duke University Press, 2012), pp. 175–92.

6 See David Hume, *A Treatise of Human Nature*, 1.1.4.1.

7 Kant, *Anthropology from a Pragmatic Point of View*, ed. and trans. Robert B. Louden, in *The Cambridge Edition of the Works of Immanuel Kant: Anthropology, History and Education* (Cambridge: Cambridge University Press, 2011), §12, p. 261.

8 F. Keck and G. Waterlot notice this in their useful critical edition of *Les deux sources de la morale et de la religion* (Paris: Presses universitaires de France, 2008), p. 367, n.9.

9 Ravaisson, *Of Habit*, p. 57.

10 Emile Boutroux, *On the Contingency of the Laws of Nature*, pp. 194–6. For more in this connection, see Chapter 4 of my *Being Inclined: Félix Ravaisson's Philosophy of Habit*.

11 Alexandre Lefebvre, *Human Rights as a Way of Life: On Bergson's Political Philosophy* (Stanford, CA: Stanford University Press, 2013), p. 35 and the whole of Chapter 3. See also Alexandre Lefebvre and Melanie White, "Bergson and Durkheim: Society *sui generis*", *Journal of Classical Sociology* 10/4 (2010), 457–77.

12 Philippe Soulez objects in exactly this way: "Bergson commits a fault here: a philosopher has the right to play on the plurality of meanings of an ordinary language term, but he has no right to extend (expand) the meaning of that term, especially if, as in the case of 'biology', it is a technical term". See Soulez, "Bergson as Philosopher of War and Theorist of the Political", in *Bergson, Politics and Religion*, ed. Lefebvre and White, pp. 99–125, p. 105.

13 See Mullarkey, *Bergson and Philosophy*, p. 89.

14 Emile Durkheim, *Moral Education: A Study in the Theory and Application of the Sociology of Education*, trans. Everett Wilson and Herman Schnurer (New York: Free Press, 1961 [1922]), p. 77.

15 Lefebvre, *Human Rights as a Way of Life*, p. 13.

16 For a response to the question of how such a love that favours nobody in particular can be bestowed in concrete worldly circumstances on anyone at all, see Lefebvre, *Human Rights as a Way of Life*, Chapter 6.

17 See Eric Thiers, "Droit et culture de guerre 1914–1918. Le Comité d'études et documents sur la guerre", *Mil neuf cent. Revue d'histoire intellectuelle* 23/1 (2005), 23–48.

18 Emile Durkheim and Ernest Denis, *Qui a voulu la guerre? Les origines de la guerre d'après les documents diplomatiques* (Paris: Armand Colin, 1915) / *Who Wanted War? The Origin of the War According to Diplomatic Documents*, trans. A. M. Wilson-Garinei (Paris: Armand Colin, 1915) and Durkheim, *L'allemagne au-dessus de tout. La mentalité allemande et la guerre* (Paris: Armand Colin, 1915) / *Germany Above All: German Mentality and War*, trans. J. S. (Paris: Armand Colin, 1915).

19 On this point, see Robert Alun Jones, *Emile Durkheim: An Introduction to Four Major Works* (Beverly Hills, CA: Sage Publications, 1986), p. 21.

20 See Bergson, *Cours II*, ed. Hude, pp. 71–9.

21 For an extended discussion of this issue, see Lefebvre, *Human Rights as a Way of Life*.

22 This did not escape the notice of Bergson's Catholic contemporaries. On this point, see n.57 to Chapter III in Keck and Waterlot's edition of *Les deux sources*, and Bergson's letters to Father Tonquédec in M, pp. 766–7 and 963–4.

23 Ravaisson, "Philosophical Testament", in Ravaisson, *Selected Essays*, ed. M. Sinclair (London: Bloomsbury, 2016) and the Editor's Introduction to the volume.

24 Lacey, *Bergson*, p. 159.

25 Nadia Yala Kisukidi, "Bergson et la guerre de 1914–1918: Présentation du dossier", in *Annales bergsoniennes* VII: *Bergson, l'Allemagne, la guerre de 1914*, ed. Arnaud François, Nadia Yala Kisukidi, Camille Riquier, Caterina Zanfi and Frédéric Worms (Paris: Presses universitaires de France, 2014), pp. 101–13, p. 105.

26 See *Bergson politique*, 31–6, for Soulez's presentation of this problematic of "doubling".

27 *La fin d'une parade philosophique*, p. 225. On Bergson's relation to Guyau, see Keith Ansell-Pearson, "Morality and the Philosophy of Life in Guyau and Bergson", *Continental Philosophy Review* 47/1 (2014), 59–85.

28 See, in particular, Ernest Seillière, *La philosophie de l'impérialisme*, 4 vols. (Paris: Plon, 1903–8).

29 For this definition, see Ernest Seillière, *L'avenir de la philosophie bergsonienne* (Paris: Alcan, 1917), p. 37.

30 Ernest Seillière, "Welche Moralphilosophie läßt Bergson erwarten?", *Internationale Zeitschrift für Wissenschaft, Kunst und Technik* 8/2 (1913), 191–209, and *L'avenir de la philosophie bergsonienne*, pp. 34–50.

31 All citations in this paragraph: Seillière, *L'avenir de la philosophie bergsonienne*, pp. 34–5.

32 This position contrasts, it should be noted, with the apparent justification of French colonialism in Bergson's 1923 review of de Tarde's *Le Maroc, école d'énergie*: a developed "philosophy of colonialism" is still required, Bergson wrote there, but France needed to unleash its power of action, and Morocco needed to be awakened from its slumbers. See the conclusion of "Rapport sur 'Le Maroc, école d'énergie' d'Alfred de Tarde": M 1396.

33 Julien Benda, *The Treason of the Intellectuals* (Abingdon: Routledge, 2017), p. 141.

34 In 1937 Bergson returns to the necessity of "dominating" modern technology in his "Message au Congrès Descartes": M 1579. In this connection, see Worms and Zanfi's "Présentation" to *Revue de métaphysique et de morale* 84/4 (2014), 464.

35 See François, *Nietzsche, Schopenhauer, Bergson*, pp. 70–3.

36 See P. Y. A. Gunter, "Bergson and the War against Nature", in *The New Bergson*, ed. J. Mullarkey (Manchester: Manchester University Press, 1999), pp. 168–82.

37 Lacey, *Bergson*, p. 159.

Further reading

Alexandre Lefebvre, *Human Rights as a Way of Life: On Bergson's Political Philosophy* (Stanford, CA: Stanford University Press, 2013). A lucid account of Bergson's ethical and political thinking in the *Two Sources*.

Alexandre Lefebvre and Melanie White (eds.), *Bergson, Politics, and Religion* (Durham, NC: Duke University Press, 2012). An excellent collection remedying the relative lack of discussion of Bergson's 1932 text in English.

Keith Ansell-Pearson, *Bergson: Thinking Beyond the Human Condition* (London: Bloomsbury, 2018). Chapter 6, "Bergson and Ethics" is another good, recent account of Bergson's ethical thought.

Eleven
Legacy

Boom and bust

Bergson's thinking had a huge cultural influence in his own lifetime, as Chapter 1 of this study showed. It could be felt in the work of writers such as Marcel Proust and T. S. Eliot, in artistic movements such as cubism and futurism, in political thinkers and statesmen as diverse as Sorel and Charles de Gaulle.[1] It was present, in one way or another, almost everywhere in French and then European culture. This influence spread to North America, and can be seen in the work of writers such as Willa Cather and Wallace Stevens.[2] Nevertheless, in 1930s France Bergson's influence began to wane. French thinkers began to look across the Rhine to the new phenomenological and existential philosophies of Edmund Husserl and Martin Heidegger, and Hegel's philosophy of history made a delayed entrance into French thinking. Bergson, who seemed increasingly parochial and outdated to some, was being passed over by philosophers importing the national tradition that he had so vehemently and vociferously rejected in 1914.

Bergson's remarks about German philosophy in his war writings (see Chapter 1) were unjust, but so too was this later rejection of his thinking,[3] all the more so in that before and even after the war, the principal German philosophical schools developed in dialogue with Bergson's work, as Caterina Zanfi has shown in detail recently.[4] This applies to the phenomenological school in particular. Husserl wrote of the "genius Bergson",[5] and Heidegger (never wasting an opportunity to criticise Husserl) wrote this to his wife Elfrida in

1920: "I'm learning much in studying Bergson—what I said to you a few weeks ago about how little we know the French—is confirmed more and more—problems that often Husserl in present conversation [considers] as amazing novelties have been clearly defined and solved by Bergson 20 years ago".[6] Other prominent members of the phenomenological school such as Alfred Schutz, Max Scheler and Roman Ingarden all engaged significantly with Bergson.[7] Bergson, then, was rejected for phenomenologists in Germany without acknowledgement that his work played a role in the development of that school or that his work prepared French philosophers to turn to it. This rejection led to the peculiar situation in 1945 whereby Heidegger, clearly having learnt more about French philosophy in the meantime, could enthuse to Frédéric de Towarnicki, the first French philosopher to reach him at the end of the war, about the spiritualist tradition, about the work of Félix Ravaisson and Bergson's genial essay celebrating it, whereas when de Towarnicki arrived back in Paris, his report of Heidegger's enthusiasm met with Sartre's incredulity.[8] In its turn to German thinking, French philosophy had become alienated from its own roots.

Heidegger is hardly blameless in this development, since in his 1927 Being and Time he famously criticises, with no obvious indications of grace or generosity, Bergson's conception of time.[9] This is easily the most important critical response to Bergson's reflection on time not only because of Heidegger's own renown and influence on generations of French philosophers, but also because it is an immanent critique, a critique offered in an attempt to further develop Time and Free Will's attempt to grasp the nature of temporal experience. With the aim of understanding Bergson's legacy in twentieth- and twenty-first-century philosophy, we should assess briefly Heidegger's remarks on his French predecessor both in Being and Time and in his lecture courses of the 1920s.

From Time and Free Will to Being and Time

In Being and Time, Heidegger offers several remarks concerning Time and Free Will when sketching out the project of a critical delimitation of conceptions of time in the history of philosophy since Aristotle. This critical delimitation, which is part of, to cite the title of §6 of the text, "The Task of a Destructuring [*Destruktion*] of the History of Ontology", was supposed to appear in the projected second volume of *Being and Time* that Heidegger would never actually write in that form. With all the fervour and force of a philosopher claiming to have revealed a previously un-recognised, un-thought principle in the history of metaphysics as a whole, Heidegger aims to address a "traditional concept" of time "that has persisted since Aristotle and beyond Bergson". Bergson, according to Heidegger, remains within a traditional, Aristotelian paradigm in his account of time as duration. Heidegger's task, however, is to determine "in what way this concept of time and the common understanding of time in general originate from temporality [*Zeitlichkeit*]", which is his term for a lived time prior to time as recorded by clocks. "In this way", as he also notes, "the common concept of time receives again its rightful autonomy—contrary to Bergson's thesis that time understood in the common way is really space".[10]

There are two essential claims sketched out here: (1) Bergson's conception of time remains stuck within traditional boundaries, beyond which we can find a more fundamental conception of time as "temporality"; and (2) Bergson illegitimately claims that time in a derivative sense is really space. Let's examine the second claim first. Is it true that Bergson simply *identifies* time in its derivative sense with space? In one sense, it is, as we saw in Chapter 2: "time, understood in the sense of a medium in which one distinguishes and one counts is merely space" [TFW 91/68]. In another sense, however, Bergson *does not* identify time in its derivative mode with space. Recall that by the process of endosmosis we gain not only the *illegitimate* idea of a spatialised duration in the self, but also what Bergson treats as the surprising but *legitimate* experience of duration as somehow existing in things. Endosmosis goes in both directions, from space into duration, and from duration into space. Its result in the second sense is not immediately a mathematised time, but duration instantiated in the world; it is the time whereby movement in things is observed as movement, as a stretch, rather than constructed by some kind of association of ideas with whatever occupies the present instant. Perhaps *Time and Free Will* did not distinguish this homogeneous time, the time of common sense, from mathematised time quite as clearly as Camille Riquier has supposed,[11] but Bergson writes that "by a real process of endosmosis we get the mixed idea of a measurable time, which is space insofar as it is homogeneity, and duration insofar as it is succession, that is to say, at bottom, the contradictory idea of succession in simultaneity" [TFW 228/171]. Here there is an analogy, rather than an identity, of time in this sense with space. It is somehow half duration and half space, both at once, and perhaps neither. Bergson, the doctoral candidate, is clearly struggling to get to grips with his own insights, but his position in *Time and Free Will*, before he states his position more definitely and clearly in *Matter and Memory*, is not that derivative time is really space. Emmanuel Lévinas—who was always one of the most prominent of Bergson's advocates despite having gone to Freiburg to study with Husserl and Heidegger in 1928—seems to have understood this, even though he responds to an exaggeration with exaggeration: in an "absolutely inexplicable way Heidegger attributes to the French philosopher a thesis according to which time is space".[12] Heidegger's claim may be partial, but it is hardly "inexplicable".

Heidegger offers a more nuanced version of his critique on this point when he writes later in *Being and Time* that derivative time, the time in which the events of the world occur, "is not an externalization of a 'qualitative time' into space, as Bergson's interpretation of time—which is ontologically completely indeterminate and insufficient—would have it".[13] Now, it is undeniable that Bergson *begins* from the idea of pure duration, on the one hand, and pure space, on the other, and *then* comes to recognise that the twain shall meet, in a strange third form, by means of endosmosis. But it is not clear to what degree, if at all, the order of Bergson's philosophical discoveries limits his resulting philosophical position. Nor is it clear that anything Heidegger says about "world time"—time as forming the horizon of our experience of things—is incompatible with what Bergson says about the result of endosmosis in *Time and Free Will* and then more clearly in *Matter and Memory*. Heidegger, in some respects at least, can justifiably claim to go further than Bergson, and to gain more clarity than the French philosopher. Still, the claim that Bergson's reflection on time is indeterminate and insufficient, though perhaps true in a sense, says nothing about how much *Being and Time* borrows from him.

Let us turn back, then, to Heidegger's first claim: Bergson remains within the parameters of a traditional understanding of time, which passes over a more fundamental sense of lived time as temporality. Heidegger expands on the claim in the famous long footnote (to which Jacques Derrida devoted an essay in the 1960s without discussing in detail its remarks on Bergson[14]), which describes Hegel's ideas about time as operating within a traditional Aristotelian paradigm, before it turns to Bergson. Abstracting from Heidegger's claim here about Bergson's relation to Aristotle, about the French philosopher even having failed to see something essential in Aristotle's own work that leads beyond a traditional concept of time,[15] the point of real critical import is this: according to Bergson, "time as space (cf. *Essai* 69) is *quantitative succession*. Duration is described in a counter-orientation towards this concept of time as *qualitative succession*". Heidegger hastily adds that this is "not the place for a critical discussion of Bergson's conception of time",[16] but the claim is that Bergson has merely opposed qualitative succession to quantitative succession and thus remains with a conception of time as *succession*. Heidegger fullest elaboration of the claim is to be found in a lecture before *Being and Time*:

> a clear indication that Bergson failed to break through to a conception and categorical knowledge of primordial time is the fact that he understood even lived time—duration—as "*succession*", with the sole proviso that the *succession* of lived time is, he says, not a quantitative *succession* laid out in individual now-points. Instead, this *succession* is a qualitative one, in which the individual moments of time—past, present and future—permeate each other.[17]

Bergson's "sole proviso", however, is no small proviso, and, once again, in order to be faithful to his thinking, it is necessary to grasp it in its movement. Bergson certainly *begins* by separating duration from space as a principle of succession from a principle of simultaneity, but interesting things occur, as Chapter 2 showed, when he and we try to think about succession as *pure* succession, without any infiltration of space: the idea of *pure* succession, of non-spatial succession brings the very idea of time as a succession or series into question. Consequently, in defending Bergson against Heidegger's charge in *Being and Time*, Lévinas writes that according to *Time and Free Will* "an instant is not related to another, but is the other in some sense, without however being identified with it. The present big with the future is the present that *exists* the future".[18] Presence, on this account, is already a retention of the past and a protention of the future, such that Bergson could even, as Heidegger will in his account of temporality as "ecstatic", draw on the etymological sense of the verb *exist* (*existere, ex-istere*, to step out, to stand forth) in reflecting on duration and the being of the durational self. The later Merleau-Ponty will make the same point: "in 1889 it was a great novelty—one which had a future—to present as the basis of philosophy not an *I think* and its immanent thoughts but a being-oneself [*Etre-soi*] whose self-cohesion is also a tearing away from self".[19]

Bergson's notion of pure succession heads in the direction, as Lévinas and Merleau-Ponty were right to underline, of what Heidegger will think under the heading of "temporality". The real question, then, is whether Bergson goes far enough in this direction, and whether the notion of retention and anticipation in the present is sufficient. The question was posed by the Hegelian philosopher Jean Hyppolite in the late 1940s, a time of renewed attention to Bergson's work after his death in 1941 and the end of the war. The Société des amis de Bergson was instituted by his former students in 1947, and *Matter and Memory* appeared on the programme of the *agrégation* in 1947–8, together with two other French philosophical classics: Nicolas Malebranche's *Christian Meditations* and Maine de Biran's *Essay on the Foundations of Psychology*. As a result, Hyppolite devoted a whole lecture course to *Matter and Memory* in Strasbourg, and published four essays testing Bergson's work against phenomenological and existentialist theses, as well as against developments in the philosophy of history.[20] In one of these essays, Hyppolite notes that the "modern philosophies of temporalisation have criticised Bergson for making nothing more of duration than 'cohesion', for not having recognised the separations and the reunifications of the ecstasies of the past, present and future".[21] *Time and Free Will*, with its notion of a qualitative multiplicity, perhaps does not advance far beyond an indeterminate idea of the cohesion or fusion of the present with the past and future. Hyppolite responds to such a critique by noting that *Matter and Memory* already stands as an attempt "to raise the problem" of the separations and reunifications of past, present and future and to "resolve" it. This response, however, does not quite get to the heart of the matter. For although Bergson shows in 1896 how the past returns to constitute the present of perceptual experience, he remains with what, from the perspective of the modern philosophies of temporalisation, is the crippling notion of a pure past, a past-in-itself. Within a lecture course of 1928, Heidegger writes that time in the most original sense is not:

> what Bergson likes to illustrate with various images, the future unrolls, as it were, while the past is rolled up on another roll [...]. Presenting it in this way would be correct insofar as the immanent connection of future and having-been-ness [*Gewesenheit*] are suggested by the picture; but it would be misleading because the has-been is not something remaining by itself, nor is it an accumulating dead weight I have behind me and to which I could occasionally relate in one way or another. Rather, my having-been only "is", in each case, according to the mode of the temporalisation of the future, and only in the temporalisation.[22]

"Having-been-ness" is Heidegger's name for a past that is what it is only in terms of the present and future, a past that is precisely not a past-in-itself. This is the core of what Heidegger means by "temporalisation". To be sure, in *Matter and Memory* Bergson does not say that the past is a "dead weight" to which we could occasionally relate; as we saw in Chapter 5, the past has its own kind of dynamism in its constant return into the present. It remains the case, however, that Bergson posits a pure past, a past in itself that is the condition of the possibility of its return in the present.

On this issue, Merleau-Ponty makes the same point as Heidegger: when Bergson says that "duration 'snowballs upon itself'", and when he postulates memories in themselves accumulating in the unconscious, he makes time out of a "preserved present"[23]—out of a virtual, preserved present that will have to be brought into relation, after the fact of its separation, with the actual present and the future in order to constitute the unity of temporal experience. In one sense, then, Bergson's notion of a past-in-itself blocks the way to an understanding of the separations *and* reunifications of past, present and future. But is the problem here that *Matter and Memory* fails to notice, as Merleau-Ponty writes in 1945, that "our best reason for rejecting the physiological preservation of the past is equally a reason for rejecting its 'psychological preservation'"?[24] Has Bergson criticised, in other words, the conception of the brain as a storehouse of ideas without adequately criticising the idea of memory as a storehouse? This critique is perhaps unjust. Given that pure memory does not, as we saw, contain memory-images (it cannot do so, since memory-images are not pure), he is perhaps already close to rejecting the very idea of memory as conservation.[25] In this sense, perhaps the idea of pure memory is paradoxical and self-defeating in a way that points beyond a notion of conservation and that thus opens a path towards a notion of temporalisation.[26]

We might wonder how wedded *Matter and Memory* is to the idea of the pure past, particularly given that Bergson seems to have come to it relatively late in 1896, and also given his admissions that consciousness has no direct access to it. The fact is, in any case, that later he *does* challenge and reject the idea of a past in itself. In his reflection on history, and first of all art-history, as we saw in Chapter 8, Bergson argues that the present has a retroactive effect on the past. The meaning of canonical works, what canonical works are—and for Bergson, the meaning of a work and what it is are inseparable—is not given once and for all, but always remains to be determined. Bergson urges us to take seriously the thought, as we saw, that creative work is "plagiarism by anticipation". He advances this notion of retroactivity solely in relation to collective and social history, but, as we argued, it develops the notion that he borrowed from Boutroux in *Time and Free Will* of backwards causation in a free action, of my motives being determined by the decision that I make. Bergson, then, thinks about retroactivity in relation to both personal and social history. Hence, already in 1920, he could agree entirely with what Heidegger will write in *Being and Time* about the past: the individual's "own past—and this always means the past of its generation—is not something which follows along after it, but something which already goes ahead of it".[27] And thus perhaps he would not have found overly perplexing Heidegger's idea that "ecstatic temporality" "does not mean a 'succession' ['*Nacheinander*'] of the ecstases. The future is not later than having-been, and this is not earlier than the present".[28]

This is not the place to assess Heidegger's account of "ecstatic temporality" in depth, but Bergson's doctrine of retroactivity brings him into the closest proximity to the "modern philosophies of temporalisation".[29] At the same time, Bergson's thought is not wholly foreign to the idea of history that Heidegger's account of temporalisation involves. There was some debate in the 1940 and 1950s concerning a possible Bergsonian account of the historian's practice and a Bergsonian philosophy of history.[30] But although there are "only a few indicators", as Hyppolite was right to note, in Bergson's texts concerning history and "historical duration",[31] and although the emphasis on genius and novelty in his later works risks distorting some of his best insights in this connection, the idea of retroactivity means that it is false to claim, following Merleau-Ponty, that Bergson "did not think about history from within as he thought about life from within". This claim is based on a confusion of Bergson's diagnosis of retrospective illusions with his account of retroactivity: "Bergson seems to reject this depth history once and for all", when he maintains that each historical "period is all it can be, a complete event existing wholly in its actuality, and that pre-Romanticism for example is a post-Romantic illusion."[32] Although retrospective illusions arise as a result of retroactivity, they are not, as we have seen, the same thing. For Bergson, it is not illusory per se to consider, after the fact of Romanticism, Classicism as pre-Romantic. The illusion consists rather in thinking that the pre-Romantic aspect of Classicism was there all along, before Romanticism put it there retroactively. The key indicator, therefore, of a Bergsonian philosophy of history is this doctrine of retroactivity. The doctrine points towards and implies a "hermeneutic" conception of history (of the sort promoted in different ways by the young Nietzsche, and then Heidegger, and Hans-Georg Gadamer among others) and towards an "ecstatic" idea of temporality that would ground it. There is, of course, a risk of retrospective illusion in making this claim, but to be subject to that risk is the human, historical condition. In trying to avoid that risk at all costs, one would fail to avoid another pitfall: an absence of any generosity, of any principle of charity, in engaging with the history of philosophy.

In this light, Lévinas appears all the more justified in denouncing the "rather summary execution"[33] of Bergson in *Being and Time*. The denunciation is no laughing matter given Lévinas' wartime experiences and given that Heidegger in 1949 was still banned from teaching in West Germany as a result of his public commitment to National Socialism in the early 1930s. But Heidegger did not maintain for long his hurried and ungracious stance in relation to Bergson. In the first set of lectures he delivered after the publication of *Being and Time*, lectures that present some of what he projected under the heading of a "destructuring" of the history of ontology, he writes this about the history of the concept of time: "from the most recent period we may cite Bergson's investigations of the time phenomenon. They are by far the most independent". Although we cannot, Heidegger argues, content ourselves with them, "Bergson's investigations are valuable because they manifest a philosophical effort to surpass the traditional concept of time".[34] Lévinas put the point more emphatically in 1982: without Bergson, "Heidegger could not have dared to advance his conception of the finite temporality of *Dasein*, despite the radical difference that separates Bergson's conception of time from Heidegger's conception. The merit of having liberated philosophy from the prestigious model of scientific time falls to Bergson".[35]

Sartre's parricide

There are many issues—the relations of science and philosophy, the philosophy of technology, the will, conceptions of philosophical method, to name the most obvious—in addition to those of time and history, on which a productive debate could be staged between Bergson and Heidegger. On some issues, such as the nature of biological life and the mind–body problem, Bergson may well offer more, and risk more, than Heidegger. But, in the end, Heidegger had no real need to minimise the significance of *Time and Free Will*. Sartre, however, according to François Azouvi at least, "needed to kill Bergson".[36] Sartre admitted that he had been inspired to take up philosophy by reading Bergson,[37] but in his 1936 *The Imagination*, apparently written before he had he read Heidegger, Sartre aims to make a clean break with Bergson in turning Husserl's doctrine of the "intentionality" of consciousness against the author of *Time and Free Will*. Bergson may well have fought against associationism in the philosophy of mind, but

> he did not understand that associationism will always get the better of those who concede to it that the image is a thing, even if, in the face of this thing, they re-establish the mind. He did not see that the only means of being done with this invasive doctrine is to return to the image itself and to prove that is radically different from an object. He thus softened the notion of consciousness; he attempted to restore to it fluidity, spontaneity and life. But try as he might, he let these inert images remain within pure duration like cobblestones at the bottom of water. We must start all over again.[38]

We have to start over, independently of Bergson, because his philosophy of mind, Sartre claims, is all too realist. Bergson has treated "images" as real things able to exist independently of the mind and failed to apprehend their status as objects of consciousness. This, one might infer, is what would permit Bergson to write of "images in themselves" in the cases of both perception and memory. We have seen, however, that the idea of pure images or images-in-themselves is not Bergson's authentic thought. In writing *Matter and Memory*, in working through its problematic, as we showed in Chapters 4 and 5, he comes to see that *pure* perception, in truth, is as little a function of images as *pure* memory. Bergson's position is, in fact, Sartrean in one sense: images are precisely the meeting point of consciousness and objects in the world. In another sense, however, his claim that pure memory and pure perception are non-imagistic transcends the limitations of Sartre's own concern for images as the object of consciousness.[39] Sartre's critique hardly hits the centre of its target and perhaps even wholly misses it; and he is so focused on the notion of image that he ignores the importance of what transcends images in Bergson's philosophy.

Sartre's concern for an idea of nothingness in his 1943 *Being and Nothingness* also pitted him directly against Bergson.[40] Previously, on the basis of Husserl's notion that all consciousness is consciousness of *something*, Sartre had accepted Bergson's critique of nothingness: "Bergson's analyses remain valid here: an attempt to conceive death or the nothingness of existence directly is by nature doomed to fail".[41] In *Being and Nothingness*, however, he moves beyond Bergson's analysis. According to Bergson, as we saw in Chapter 8, the idea of nothingness derives from the negation of things, but given that negation, as he argues, is a covert affirmation, an implicit substitution of one thing with another, the idea of total nothingness is the idea of the substitution of everything by everything, which is absurd, like the idea of a square circle. Sartre, in contrast, with the celebrated example of Pierre's absence in the café, wants to show that there we do have a certain experience of nothingness that is the condition of negative judgment. Bergson took it for granted that nothingness could not be an *immediate given of experience*, and his argument that nothingness can be neither imagined nor conceived seemed also to take for granted that an experience of nothingness could not be given in another way, by and through, for example, intuition.[42] Sartre—influenced by the three German "Hs": Hegel, Husserl, Heidegger—brings to light the limitations of Bergson's approach, even though he does not address him directly on this score in *Being and Nothingness*.

Sartre replaces Bergson's philosophy of plenitude and positivity with an explicit confrontation with negativity, nothingness, anxiety, atheism and death. Sartre would doubtless have considered Bergson's thinking before *The Two Sources* to belong to a rather different, more genteel and more optimistic age—to, in short, the *belle époque*.[43] Instructive in this regard is that even though Bergson describes the *élan vital* as finite, he responds to André Lalande's 1899 *Dissolution in Opposition to Evolution*, "which shows us everything marching to its death", by claiming that "everything occurs *as if* this death", i.e. the death of the individual or species, "was willed or at least accepted, for the greater progress of life in general" [CE 273/247]. In this sense, in concluding the third chapter of *Creative Evolution*, he speaks of the *élan* in egregiously optimistic terms:

> all living beings hold together and all yield to the same tre-
> mendous push. The animal takes its stand on the plant, man
> bestrides animality, and the whole of humanity, in space and
> time, is an immense army that gallops next to each of us, in

front and behind each of us, in an overwhelming charge able to beat down every resistance, and clear the most formidable obstacles, perhaps even death. [CE 286/271]

After 1914, of course, the idea of "galloping armies beating down every resistance" can no longer suggest eternal life.

Bergson redivivus

Sartre was justified in moving beyond Bergson's position on nothingness, but he did not always reject his predecessor for good reasons. Merleau-Ponty was also critical of Bergson in the 1940s—for his still all too objective notion of embodiment, for his account of pure memory, for his supposed commitment to a notion of intuition as total co-incidence—but his later readings, beginning with his inaugural discourse at the Collège de France in 1953, tempered this critical approach, and expressed a fair-minded (even though, as we have just seen, it is not always immune to injustice) attempt to rediscover Bergson's philosophy.[44] Merleau-Ponty saw the error in his generation's desire to start all over again without Bergson:

> If we had been careful readers of Bergson, and if more thought had been given to him, we would have been drawn to a much more concrete philosophy [...]. It is quite certain that Bergson, had we read him carefully, would have taught us things that ten or fifteen years later we believed to be discoveries made by the philosophy of existence itself.[45]

The idea of a "concrete philosophy" was a philosophical watchword in 1930s France, but Merleau-Ponty came to recognise that elements of one could be found in Bergson. Indeed, when Bergson notes that "existence" in the case of human existence means that although "what we do depends on what we are", "we are, to a certain degree, what we do", and thus that "we continually create ourselves" [CE 8/7], he is several decades ahead of the French existentialists. Merleau-Ponty seems to have been led towards his view that Bergson can be read as offering a concrete, existential philosophy by Jankélévitch's *Henri Bergson*, first published in 1931 and then reworked and extended in 1959.[46] Despite Bergson's optimistic approach to the issue of death, Jankélévitch emphasised negative phenomena such as the finitude of the *élan vital*, its necessary dispersion as matter, as well as the irreversibility, nostalgia and regret in the concrete human experience of the vital "push". It was against this background that it was possible for Merleau-Ponty to claim that "the true sense of Bergson's philosophy consists less in eliminating nothingness than in incorporating it into the idea of being".[47]

This existential re-evaluation would hardly save Bergson from marginalisation by the waves of structuralist and then post-structuralist thinking in Paris. The rejection of humanist existentialism, a rejection motivated to a large degree by Heidegger's 1945 "Letter on Humanism",[48] implied a condemnation of Bergson at the same time. Bergson's critique of the powers of language, and his privileging of diachrony over synchronic structure, was anathema for the structuralist thinkers. The condemnation of Bergson was now even less forgiving than the one offered by the French existentialists themselves. As Giuseppe Bianco has shown recently, all of Louis Althusser, Jacques Lacan, Claude Lévi-Strauss and then Michel Foucault and Jacques Derrida, for slightly different reasons each time certainly, dismissed and rejected Bergson.[49] Against this background, Gilles Deleuze's return to Bergson in the 1950s and 1960s looks all the more idiosyncratic. In 1956 Deleuze published "Bergson's Concept of Difference", which he had presented as a paper two years earlier to the Société des amis de Bergson, as well as the entry ("Henri Bergson 1859–1941") on Bergson in Merleau-Ponty's coffee-table history-of-philosophy book *Les philosophes célèbres*. These essays led to Deleuze's longer *Bergsonism* a decade later.

"The notion of difference", Deleuze writes, "must throw a certain light on Bergson's philosophy, but inversely, Bergsonism must bring the greatest contribution to a philosophy of difference".[50] Deleuze seeks in Bergson a notion of difference that is prior and irreducible to a Hegelian conception of internal difference (according to which a thing is what it is only in relation to what it is not) as contradiction, negation and the "labour of the negative". In this, Deleuze responds to Hyppolite, his teacher and supervisor. In a 1954 review of Hyppolite's *Logic and Existence*,[51] Deleuze applauds his anti-anthropological and anti-humanist reading of Hegel. Against its prioritisation of Hegelian "speculative negation" in relation to "empirical negation", however, Deleuze argues that Bergson offers a notion of difference that proceeds any sense of negation. When Bergson distinguishes "two species of multiplicity, two possible senses of the word distinguish, two concepts, one qualitative and one quantitative, of the difference between the *same* and the *other*" [TFW 121/90], on Deleuze's reading this second concept of difference:

> will have to be distinguished from contradiction, alterity, neg-ation. This is where the Bergsonian theory and method of diffe-rence is opposed to that other method, to that other theory of difference that is called the dialectic, as much Plato's dialectic of alterity as Hegel's dialectic of contradiction, both implying the power and presence of the negative [...] To think internal difference as such, as pure internal difference, to reach the pure concept of difference, to raise difference to the absolute, such is the direction of Bergson's thought.[52]

Deleuze aims to retrieve from Bergson a non-anthropological and non-dialectical notion of difference—a notion of difference without negation, difference prior to any negation performed by a subject. In Chapter 2 we saw that Bergson seemed to reject the idea of a "pure difference", but Deleuze developed his anti-Hegelian and post-structuralist approach in his 1966 *Bergsonism*. A more orthodox French Bergsonian disputed whether Deleuze's interpretation, which "pru-dently remains close to much-discussed contemporary currents" of thought, could rightfully bear *Bergsonism* as a title.[53] Deleuze, of course, was aware of the singularity of his own interpretation: it was a matter of giving Bergson "a child that would be his own but mon-strous", a monster that quickly grew, in fact, into Deleuze's *Difference and Repetition* in 1968.[54] Once Deleuze was translated in the 1990s, English-language work (without a rich Bergsonian tradition of its own to build on given the rapid decline of the "Bergson boom" in the 1920s) on his *Bergsonism* sometimes struggled to distinguish the interpretation from the texts interpreted. Still, Deleuze's interpret-ation served to keep the flame of Bergson's philosophy alive, and it has been a key motivation for the renewed scholarly attention to it.

With and after Deleuze, Bergson's ideas about novelty and retro-activity have come to prominence in the much-discussed notion of the "event" in contemporary theory, a notion used to account for "occurrences that radically interrupt our sense of continuity".[55] According to Slavoj Žižek, the event is "something shocking, out of joint, that appears to happen all of a sudden and interrupts the usual flow of things", and it is a "manifestation of a circular struc-ture in which the evental effect retroactively determines its causes or reasons".[56] The influence of Bergson, and of Boutroux before him, is patent here, but it is less obvious that contemporary theory has worked though the sources of Bergsonian notions of "absolute nov-elty" and creation "from scratch", namely a voluntarist conception of genius. Contemporary notions of the "event" may well harbour some of the most problematic aspects of the modern metaphysics of the will, the modern metaphysics of voluntary subjectivity, and, as a consequence, may well preclude a true grasp of the real essence of history.

Bergson's influence lives on. It lives on, for example, in the process philosophy that, in drawing on Alfred North Whitehead's develop-ment of Bergson's ideas, is significant in many fields of philosophy and that is still inspiring critique of dominant paradigms in the phil-osophy of biology.[57] Outside of the confines of academic philosophy, Bergson's thinking finds perhaps its most popular prolongation in the work of Rupert Sheldrake, whose widely read and important *The Science Delusion* contains many restatements of nineteenth-century French positions. The contents page of Sheldrake's book looks like a list of Bergson's principal philosophical concerns: 1. Is Nature Mechanical?, 2. Is the Total Amount of Matter and Energy Always the Same?, 3. Are the Laws of Nature Fixed?, 4. Is Matter Unconscious?, 5. Is Nature Purposeless?, 6. Is All Biological Inheritance Material?, 7. Are Memories Stored as Material Traces? and so on.[58] I hope the present book has shown, however, that for the sake of philosophical reflection in the present, and in order to grasp adequately the philo-sophical possibilities of our own historical position, it is necessary to work through Bergson's own texts against the background of the history of modern philosophy, and to discern the promise, but also the occasional dangers, that lie within them.

Summary

Bergson's philosophy was hugely influential in his own lifetime, but by the 1930s French philosophers began to look to German phenomenology for a "concrete", "existential" philosophy. Bergson had influenced these German thinkers also, but in his 1927 *Being and Time*, a landmark of twentieth-century philosophy, Martin Heidegger criticised *Time and FreeWill*. In his lecture courses, however, Heidegger clearly recognised the importance of Bergson's breakthrough in the philosophy of time. French phenomenologists such as Jean-Paul Sartre and Maurice Merleau-Ponty often read Bergson unfairly, but the latter came to recognise this. Vladimir Jankélévitch interpreted Bergson's work with an existentialist accent, but this did not prevent the submergence of Bergson's ideas by waves of structuralist and post-structuralist thinking. Still, Bergson was never wholly forgotten, and Gilles Deleuze's post-structuralist and anti-Hegelian approach brought about a revival of interest in his thought within the English-speaking world.

Notes

1　See Ellen Kennedy, "Bergson's Philosophy and French Political Doctrines: Sorel, Maurras, Péguy and de Gaulle", *Government and Opposition* 15/1 (1980), 75–91.

2　See Tom Quirk, *Bergson and American Culture: The Worlds of Willa Cather and Wallace Stevens* (Chapel Hill, NC: University of North Carolina Press, 1990). I am grateful to Keith Ansell-Pearson for this reference.

3　Camille Riquier notes the injustice in "La durée pure comme ésquisse de la temporalité ekstatique: Heidegger lecteur de Bergson", in *Heidegger en Dialogue 1912–30*, ed. Servane Jollivet and Claude Romano (Paris: Vrin, 2009), pp. 33–67, p. 34.

4　See Caterina Zanfi, *Bergson et la philosophie allemande 1907–1932* (Paris: Armand Colin, 2014).

5　This appears in a letter from Husserl to the great historian of French philosophy, Henri Gouhier: Edmund Husserl, *Briefwechsel*, vol. VI: *Philosophenbriefe*, ed. K. Schuhmann (Dordrecht: Kluwer, 1994), p. 155.

6　Martin Heidegger, *Letters to His Wife 1915–70*, ed. Gertrud Heidegger, trans. R. Glasgow (London: Polity, 2008), p. 71.

7　On this, see Zanfi, *Bergson et la philosophie allemande*, pp. 183–93.

8　This is a paradox that Merleau-Ponty did not observe when noting that "there is more than one paradox in the fortunes of Bergsonism"; see Merleau-Ponty,

"Bergson in the Making", in *Signs*, trans. Richard C. McClearly (Evanston, IL: Northwestern University Press, 1964), pp. 182–92, p. 182. For the story of Heidegger enthusing about Ravaisson and Bergson's essay, see Frédéric de Towarnicki, *A la rencontre de Heidegger: Souvenirs d'un messager de la Forêt-Noire* (Paris: Gallimard, 1993), *Martin Heidegger: Souvenirs et chroniques* (2002) and the introduction to his edition of Ravaisson's *De l'habitude* (Paris: Payot, 1997).

9 Heidegger, *Sein und Zeit* (Tübingen: Niemeyer, 1984). My translations are based on Heidegger, *Being and Time*, trans. J. Stambaugh (Albany, NY: State University of New York Press, 1996), to which I do not refer each time since it contains the pagination of the German edition in the margins.

10 Heidegger, *Sein und Zeit*, p. 18.

11 See Riquier, "La durée pure comme ésquisse de la temporalité ekstatique: Heidegger lecteur de Bergson", p. 43, and *Archéologie de Bergson*, pp. 276–88.

12 Emmanuel Lévinas, *En découvrant l'existence avec Husserl et Heidegger* (Paris: Vrin, 1994 [1949]), p. 100.

13 Heidegger, *Sein und Zeit*, p. 333.

14 Jacques Derrida, "*Ousia* and *Gramme*: Note on a Note in *Being and Time*", in *Margins of Philosophy*, trans. A. Bass (Brighton: Harvester Press, 1982), pp. 29–68.

15 The section of Heidegger's 1925–6 lecture course offers a fuller, earlier version of the footnote, with more detail on the claim that Bergson has misinterpreted Aristotle: Heidegger, *Logik: Die Frage nach der Wahrheit* (Frankfurt am Main: Klostermann, 1995), pp. 263–70/*Logic: The Question Concerning Truth*, trans. Thomas Sheehan (Bloomington, IN: Indiana, 2010), pp. 218–24. In this connection, see also Heath Massey, *The Origin of Time: Heidegger and Bergson* (Albany, NY: State University of New York Press, 2016), pp. 155–61.

16 Heidegger, *Sein und Zeit*, p. 432.

17 Heidegger, *Logik: Die Frage nach der Wahrheit*, p. 207/*Logic: The Question Concerning Truth*, pp. 249–50. I follow Massey's translation of this passage; see *The Origin of Time*, p. 41.

18 Lévinas, *En découvrant l'existence avec Husserl et Heidegger*, p. 100.

19 Merleau-Ponty, "Bergson in the Making", p. 184.

20 On this point, see Giuseppe Bianco, "Le Bergson de Deleuze entre existence et structure", in *Gilles Deleuze. Politiques de la philosophie*, ed. Adnen Jdey (Geneva, Métis Presses, 2015), pp. 99–116, p. 108.

21 Jean Hyppolite, "Various Aspects of Memory in Bergson", trans. A. V. Coleman, in Leonard Lawlor, *The Challenge of Bergsonism* (London: Continuum 2003), pp. 112–28, p. 114. This is available in French in Hyppolite, *Figures de la pensée philosophique*, vol. II (Paris: Presses universitaires de France, 1969), pp. 468–88, together with "Vie et Existence d'après Bergson", pp. 488–98, and "Du Bergson à l'existentialisme", pp. 443–59. Hyppolite also published "Bergson et l'existentialisme", in *Les Etudes bergsoniennes* 2 (1949), 208–15.

22 Heidegger, *Metaphysische Anfangsgründe der Logik im Ausgang von Leibniz* (Frankfurt am Main: Klostermann, 1978), p. 266/*The Metaphysical Foundations of Logic*, trans. M. Heim (Bloomington, IN: Indiana University Press, 1984), p. 206.

23 Merleau-Ponty, *The Phenomenology of Perception* (London: Routledge, 2002), p. 482, n.3.

24 Merleau-Ponty, *The Phenomenology of Perception*, p. 479.

25 For the claim that he has criticised *all* ideas of conservation, see Riquier, *Archéologie de Bergson*, p. 330.

26 See also in this connection Keith Ansell-Pearson, *Bergson: Thinking Beyond the Human Condition*, p. 75, but my argument is that Hyppolite's approach is insufficient.

27 Heidegger, *Sein und Zeit*, p. 20.

28 Heidegger, *Sein und Zeit*, p. 350.

29 In his "Durée bergsonienne et temporalité", in *Bergson: La durée et la nature*, ed. J.-L. Vieillard-Baron (Paris: Presses universitaires de France, 2004), pp. 77–98, Jean-François Marquet does not address this. Nor do Riquier and Massey in their studies of Heidegger's relation to Bergson.

30 See Henri Davenson (this is a pseudonym of the historian Henri Marrou), "Bergson et l'histoire", in *Henri Bergson: Essais et témoignages recueillis*, ed. A. Béguin and P. Thévenaz (Neuchâtel: Editions de la Baconnière, 1943), pp. 205–13. See also Raymond Polin, "Y a-t-il chez Bergson une philosophie de l'histoire?" and Raymond Aron, "Notes sur Bergson et l'histoire", in *Les Etudes bergsoniennes* 4 (1956), pp. 7–40 and pp. 46–51, respectively. On all of this, see Bianco, "Le Bergson de Deleuze entre existence et structure", pp. 108–9.

31 Hyppolite, "Various Aspects of Memory in Bergson", p. 114.

32 Merleau-Ponty, "Bergson in the Making", p. 187.

33 Lévinas, *En découvrant l'existence avec Husserl et Heidegger*, p. 100.

34 Heidegger, *Die Grundprobleme der Phänomenologie* (Frankfurt am Main: Klostermann, 1975), p.328/*The Basic Problems of Phenomenology*, trans. A. Hofstadter (Bloomington, IN: Indiana University Press, 1988), p. 232.

35 Lévinas, *Ethique et infini* (Paris: Fayard, 1982), p. 34. For Lévinas' relation to Bergson, see Jean-Louis Vieillard-Baron, "Lévinas et Bergson", in *Bergson*, ed. C. Riquier (Paris: Editions du Cerf, 2012), pp. 191–221.

36 Azouvi, *La gloire de Bergson*, p. 193.

37 See "Interview with Michel Rybalka, Oreste Pucciani and Susan Gruenheck", in *The Philosophy of Jean-Paul Sartre*, ed. Paul Schilpp (La Salle, IL: Open Court, 1981), pp. 5–51, p. 6.

38 Jean-Paul Sartre, *The Imagination*, trans. K. Williford and D. Rudrauf (Abingdon: Routledge, 2012), p. 53.

39 For more on the inadequacy of Sartre's critique, see Riquier, *Archéologie de Bergson*, pp. 326–7.

40 See Sarah Richmond, "Sartre and Bergson: A Disagreement about Nothingness", *International Journal of Philosophical Studies* 15/1 (2007), 77–95, p. 83.

41 Sartre, *The Imaginary: A Phenomenological Psychology of the Imagination*, trans. J. Webber (Abingdon: Routledge, 2004), p. 187.

42 See Richmond's concluding remarks in "Sartre and Bergson: A Disagreement about Nothingness".

43 On this point, see Azouvi, *La gloire de Bergson*, p. 320.

44 See Merleau-Ponty, "In Praise of Philosophy", in *In Praise of Philosophy and Other Essays*, trans. J. O'Neill (Evanston, IL: Northwestern University Press, 1963).

45 Merleau-Ponty, "The Philosophy of Existence", in *Texts and Dialogues: On Philosophy, Politics, and Culture*, ed. Hugh J. Silverman and James Barry, Jr., trans. Michael B. Smith *et al.* (New York: Humanity Books, 1992), p. 132.

46 On this, see Alexandre Lefebvre's introduction to the English translation and Florence Caeymaex, "Négativité et finitude de l'élan vital. La lecture de Bergson par Jankélévitch", in *Annales bergsoniennes IV*, ed. Fagot-Largeault and Worms, pp. 629–40.

47 See Merleau-Ponty, *La Nature, Notes (Cours du Collège de France)* (Paris: Seuil, 1995), p. 97.

48 See Heidegger, "Letter on Humanism", trans. F. A. Capuzzi, in *Pathmarks*, ed. W. McNeill (Cambridge: Cambridge University Press, 1998).

49 Bianco, "Le Bergson de Deleuze entre existence et structure", pp. 99–101. See also Bianco's review of the English translation of Jankélévitch's *Henri Bergson*, H-France 16/113 (July 2016), 1–4.

50 Deleuze, "La Conception de la différence chez Bergson", *Les Etudes bergsoniennes 4* (1956), 77–112, p. 77/"Bergson's Conception of Difference", trans. Melissa McMahon, in *The New Bergson*, ed. John Mullarkey (Manchester: Manchester University Press, 1999), pp. 42–66, p. 42.

51 See Deleuze "Jean Hyppolite's *Logic and Existence*", in *Desert Islands and Other Texts 1953–74* (Cambridge, MA: MIT Press, 2004), pp. 15–19.

52 Deleuze, "Bergson's Conception of Difference", p. 49.

53 See M. Bartélemy-Madaule, "Lire Bergson", *Les Etudes bergsoniennes 8* (1968), pp. 86 and 120.

54 Deleuze wrote later that he saw the "history of philosophy as a sort of buggery or (it comes to the same thing) immaculate conception. I saw myself as taking an author from behind and giving him a child that would be his own offspring, yet monstrous. It was really important for it to be his own child, because the author had to actually say all I had him saying. But the child was bound to be monstrous too, because it resulted from all sorts of shifting, slipping, dislocations and hidden emissions that I really enjoyed. I think my book on Bergson a good example"; Deleuze, *Negotiations*, trans. Martin Joughin (New York: Columbia University Press, 1995), p. 6. For more on the phases of Deleuze's interpretation of Bergson, see Michael Hardt, *Gilles Deleuze: An Apprenticeship in Philosophy* (Minneapolis, MN: University of Minnesota Press, 1993).

55 Leon ter Schure, *Bergson and History* (Albany, NY: State University of New York Press, 2019), p. 251.
56 Slavoj Žižek, *Event: A Philosophical Journey through a Concept* (London: Penguin Books, 2014), p. 4.
57 See Daniel J. Nicholson and John Dupré, *Everything Flows: Towards a Processual Philosophy of Biology* (Oxford: Oxford University Press, 2018).
58 Rupert Sheldrake, *The Science Delusion* (London: Coronet, 2012).

Further reading

Giuseppe Bianco, *Après Bergson: Portrait de groupe avec philosophe* (Paris: Presses universitaires de France, 2015). A broad and brilliant study of Bergson's influence and legacy.

Michael Kelly (ed.), *Bergson and Phenomenology* (London: Palgrave Macmillan, 2010). A collection of essays examining the relation of Bergson to the phenomenological tradition from a variety of perspectives.

Heath Massey, *The Origin of Time: Heidegger and Bergson* (Albany, NY: State University of New York Press, 2016). A useful extended study of Heidegger's inheritance and critique of Bergson.

A. E. Pilkington, *Bergson and His Influence: A Reassessment* (Cambridge: Cambridge University Press, 1976). A study of Bergson's influence on Benda, Charles Péguy and Paul Valéry as well as Proust.

Rupert Sheldrake, *The Science Delusion* (London: Coronet, 2012). Sheldrake's hypothesis of "morphic resonance" is his own but it draws on Bergson's ideas in many respects.

Caterina Zanfi, *Bergson et la philosophie allemande 1907–1932* (Paris: Armand Colin, 2014). A fine study of Bergson's influence in Germany, of which German and Italian editions are also available, but not yet an English one.

Glossary

analysis the 1903 "Introduction to Metaphysics" opposes analysis
  to **intuition** as modes of knowledge. Analysis takes an external
  standpoint to its object and requires mathematical or linguistic
  symbols, whereas intuition does not. By 1907, Bergson interprets
  analysis as the work of the **intellect** as a faculty of mind.
animism this is a position opposed in the seventeenth century
  to Cartesian iatromechanism (according to which all bodily
  processes are mechanical). For the animist, all bodily processes,
  including even digestion and blood circulation, are a function
  of the mind, of the unconscious mind at least. Mind, for the
  animist, is the principle of biological **life**. Eighteenth-century
  vitalism attempted to forge a middle way between animism and
  iatromechanism.
attention to life from 1896 this is Bergson's name for the degrees
  of consciousness, and thus the degrees of durational fusion,
  involved in psychological life.
body *Matter and Memory* presents the "living-body" not as the site of
  representations of the external world, but as the means through
  which **perception** goes out to meet extended things. At the level
  of pure **perception**, what the living-body sees is a function of
  what it can do, of its practical orientation in the world. Given
  that this living-body operates mechanically and is in principle
  independent of memory and the self, it is quite different from
  what is thought under the heading of "one's own body" or the
  "lived body" in earlier and later French philosophy.

closed, the morality is "closed" when it serves the interests of a particular society pitted against others. This form of morality, contrasted with **open** morality, operates by habit and takes the form of a war-instinct. Similarly, closed religion acts as a social glue against the dissolving power of the intelligence and of the fear of death.

comic as what it is that makes us laugh, the comic is "mechanism plastered on the living". This, however, is not in *essence* what makes us laugh, for *Laughter* rejects the idea that "mechanism plastered on the living" is a genus under which all comic instances fall. "Mechanism plastered on the living" is rather a *source* of the comic, which is to be found *to a greater or lesser degree*, by means of association and analogies in less obvious cases, in all instances of the comic.

creation Bergson's concept of creation is pivotal in his philosophy as a whole. Following a Kantian conception of **genius** as the principle of fine-art production, creation, for Bergson, is not reducible to craft production as the realisation of an ideal model or blueprint. Nor is it *ex nihilo*, from nothing, which is impossible for Bergson, since he argues that **nothingness** does not "exist" in any sense. Creation is rather an immanent but original development of what is already given that allows what we might take to be sources and motives for the creative act to become apparent after the fact. In this sense, Bergson treats "creation" as synonymous with "maturation" and considers duration as such as "creative". That said, Bergson's affirmations about "radical novelty" and creation "from scratch", together with his affirmations that creation is a function of the **will**, might push him back towards a notion of *ex nihilo* creation. The difficulty consists in trying to grasp what creation is when recognising that it is from *no thing* but not from nothing.

duration this is time directly experienced as passage, as the stretch between any two moments that we might isolate within it. The condition of isolating such moments, and thus the condition of any measurement of time (by, for example, seconds, hours or days) is, Bergson argues, **space**. Duration is thus the unquantifiable experience of temporal passage that is prior to spatialised time.

élan vital (**vital impulse**) even though Bergson knew his own position was not a **vitalism**, but rather an **animism**, **spiritualism** or **panpsychism**, he could not resist borrowing the "image" of the *élan vital* from his contemporary, André Lalande, in order to characterise the temporal development of life as a whole.

extension in *Matter and Memory* extension is no longer synonymous with **space**, for it is a principle that stands between the traditional opposition of spatially extended things to those things (minds) which do not occupy space. On the basis of showing that a form of "lived", pre-objective spatiality precedes objective, mathematical space, Bergson argues that things are extended by degrees, and that these degrees are degrees of "extension". In *Creative Evolution*, Bergson understands extension in this sense as degrees of the rhythms or tensions of duration itself. The degree of extension in which things appear is a function of the relaxation of duration itself. In this sense, extension is ex-tension.

finalism this is the doctrine according to which particular processes involve the pursuit of ends or goals. *Time and Free Will* criticises finalism in the guise of libertarian accounts of human freedom, while *Creative Evolution* targets finalism in biology. That said, Bergson does not reject finalism altogether. In both texts, he implicitly advances a Kantian or post-Kantian notion of "finalism without an end" or "purposiveness without purpose" as constituting, respectively, the essence of human freedom and the nature of biological life.

free will on the basis of his account of duration Bergson defends a notion of free will while criticising traditional libertarian conceptions according to which free volition supposes alternative possibilities in action.

genius Bergson's account of **creation** relies on Kantian and post-Kantian, Romantic accounts of genius as the principle of fine-art production. See **creation.**

habit the second chapter of *Matter and Memory* seems to reject the pivotal vitalist or animist accounts of habit in earlier nineteenth-century French philosophy by interpreting an acquired motor habit in mechanical, neurological terms following the empirical psychology of his day. It is not clear whether this is Bergson's true position or one that he adopts only for the "convenience of the study" (as he writes concerning **mechanism** in general in concluding the book). This ambiguity is never really resolved in Bergson's work, although *Creative Evolution* seems to offer a more definite conception of motor habit as a tendency of life and thus as something other than a mechanical principle.

homogeneity it is possible to count, say, ten sheep only if the simultaneously existing, different sheep are treated at the same time as fundamentally identical, for otherwise there is nothing to count. Bergson understands the principle of this identity or homogeneity as mathematically calculable **space**, which is the same in all its parts, and indifferent to its contents.

image in *Matter and Memory*, a perceptual image is not a representation of something that exists beyond the image. Images are rather real things as I see them. The first chapter of the 1896 text alludes to "images in themselves", but the fourth chapter expresses Bergson's more developed position: the truth of things prior to my perceptual encounter with them is pre-imagistic. Similarly, Bergson initially gestures towards an idea of pure **memory**-images, but comes to realise in the course of *Matter and Memory* that pure memory exceeds any memory-image.

instinct according to *Creative Evolution*, instinct does not give rise to **intellect**, as the Darwinian evolutionary psychologist supposes, but nor does **intellect** give rise to instincts, as the Lamarckian supposes in viewing instincts as **habit**s acquired by effort and then inherited by descendants. Although Bergson considers both instinct and **intellect** to be forms of consciousness, and although in a given species they differ by the degree of consciousness they involve, instinct and intellect are nevertheless coeval principles that differ in nature. Instinct uses the **living body** rather than tools, and has a kind of blind lucidity that assures the living being of success.

intellect *Creative Evolution* offers a pragmatist and evolutionary account of the faculty of what Kant called the "understanding", the faculty of concepts. The understanding or intellect is apt for manipulating inert **matter** but the profound secret of **life** escapes it; every time it tries to explain **life**, it explains it away. The intellect is merely a particular product of biological evolution, as one of life's responses to the hurdles it has faced, and thus, Bergson argues, we should not be surprised that it is unable to account for life and biological evolution as a whole.

intensity the opening chapter of *Time and FreeWill* criticises the traditional notion of intensive magnitude, according to which psychological qualities, although they are not quantities, can be ordered according to a vague "more or less". Bergson attacked this hybrid notion as opening the gates to the reductive quantifying approach in the "psychophysics" of his time. It is not clear, however, whether he just rejects the notion of intensive magnitude or the notion of intensity *tout court*; if intensity is purely qualitative it is not easy to see how we can continue to speak of it.

intuition in "Introduction to Metaphysics" Bergson borrows from post-Kantian German philosophy the idea of intuition as a non-conceptual form of knowledge that attains the absolute, which in Bergson's case is duration. Bergson seems to use the term in different senses: in a broader sense, it denominates his philosophical method as a whole, including both conceptual thought and what transcends the latter; in a narrower sense, it denominates only what precedes and transcends conceptual thought. In the narrower sense, it is related to artistic intuition and genius.

laughter on Bergson's account, laughter has the purpose of chastising and correcting behaviour that is mechanical and inflexible. Mechanical inflexibility is socially deviant given that society essentially requires, as Bergson claims in 1900, flexibility. Since laughter gently attacks such slight social deviancy and is interested in its object, it is not quite an aesthetic response; since its object is inflexible behaviour rather than malicious wrongdoing, it is not quite an ethical response either. The Bergson of the *Two Sources* could claim that laughter is one of the disciplinary techniques of closed ethics and morality, but in the text of 1932 society is all rigidity rather than a principle of flexibility, so it is hard to relate the two approaches. See **comic**.

life *Time and FreeWill* had already suggested that the principle of psychological life and that of biological life are one and the same, namely time as duration, and *Creative Evolution* expands on this suggestion.

matter although *Time and Free Will* seemed to oppose space, and thus the matter within it, to mind, the final chapter of *Matter and Memory* tries to undo this opposition by showing that matter is purely movement which occurs according to rhythms or tensions of **duration**. This thought will be developed in the third chapter of *Creative Evolution*.

mechanism the first and second chapters of *Matter and Memory* suggest that the human body with its habits and the natural world as a whole operates according to mechanical laws, but the final paragraph of the text, in returning to the work of Boutroux, suggests that this commitment to a mechanistic philosophy was merely a working hypothesis followed "for the convenience of the study". Arguably, this ambiguity is never resolved in Bergson's work.

memory the second chapter of *Matter and Memory* opens by distinguishing mechanical **habit** from episodic memory as two species of memory while admitting, confusingly, that the former is not really a species of memory. Bergson also distinguishes memory as the contraction of the past in **duration** from episodic memory, and thus the book leaves us with the task of relating these apparently different distinctions of two forms of memory. *Matter and Memory* also argues that episodic memory presupposes a pure memory, a pure memory that is not composed of memory **image**s, but runs up against the problem of what exactly can be said of it.

metaphysics according to the 1903 "Introduction to Metaphysics", metaphysics is the form of knowledge that requires **intuition** and attains **duration** as an "absolute". It is thus contrasted with positive **science**, which requires **analysis**.

multiplicity *Time and Free Will* turns on the idea that there are two forms of multiplicity: quantitative and qualitative. The domain of quality is not devoid of difference and multiplicity, but it is not a domain of numerical or spatial multiplicity. There is a strange kind of identity in difference in **duration**, where interpenetration and fusion is the prior condition of discrete unities.

nothingness on Bergson's account, nothingness cannot be perceived or imagined, for to perceive or imagine is always to perceive or imagine something. Nor, he argues, can it be consistently conceived. *Creative Evolution* argues that the idea of nothingness is a kind of generalisation from particular negative judgments, and that the latter are merely covert affirmations bound up with a feeling of regret that one thing has been substituted by another. Nothingness is thus a pseudo-idea and merely an empty word.

novelty in his later work, Bergson explicitly thematises duration as the continual creation of unforeseeable novelty. Novelty is to be taken primarily in an epistemological sense: if something is new I could not have foreseen or guessed that it was going to happen before it did. That said, Bergson is sometimes tempted by a more absolute and metaphysical notion of novelty as constituting a radical temporal discontinuity between the present and the past.

number according to his intuitionist position in the philosophy of mathematics, Bergson argues that any genuine idea of number requires the counting of simultaneous units in a real or ideal space.

open, the this is one of the sources of morality and religion according to the Bergson of 1932. It is a boundless love without preference and a mystical experience of the divine as joy.

panpsychism this is not a term that Bergson favours, but his position in *Creative Evolution* is panpsychist insofar as he considers duration and thus the conscious principle that is life to constitute, by degrees, the existence of all that is.

perception *Matter and Memory* advances a direct realist theory of perception based on an extramission theory of vision, according to which we see things beyond us, where common sense tells us they are. This does not prevent Bergson from positing a world existing independently of our visual encounter with it, but the fourth chapter of the text claims that this world already has a share of mind and consciousness, since it has its own rhythm of duration.

possibility Bergson takes possibility in a traditional sense as conceivability. Bergson's is a combinatorial conception of possibility (ideas of what is possible are collated from experiences of actual things) as conceivability that offers a radical solution to the problem of "alien qualities" (i.e. of **novelty**) that combinatorial conceptions have faced: actions and events in their novelty are not possible before they occur. This critique of possibility as conceivability presupposes a more fundamental sense of modality in order to account for the relation of the past to the present in duration, but Bergson leaves us to fill in the gaps on this point.

purposiveness see **finalism**.

quality Time and Free Will separates the durational mind as the realm of quantity from **space** as the realm of quantity; nothing in the mind, it argues, is quantifiable. Matter and Memory tries to reduce this opposition of quality and quantity by showing that the difference is always merely one of degree.

quantity Time and Free Will separates the durational mind as the realm of **quality** from **space** as the realm of quantity. Any meaningful idea of number, and thus of quantity, requires **space** as a homogeneous milieu, as Bergson argues. See **homogeneity**.

science in 1889 Bergson sought to protect psychology from any incursion of the quantifying methods of supposedly "scientific" and "empirical" psychology, but subsequently he tries to reconcile philosophy and the natural scientific reliance on mechanistic notions of **matter** and on analytical method. This involves critically delimiting the sphere of applicability of scientific analysis, while allowing that it can attain in its own domain and in its own way an "absolute". Bergson's concern to reconcile science and philosophy motivated his 1922 response to Einstein's theory of relativity.

self Time and Free Will distinguishes between the superficial and the profound self. The former is that aspect of the self that is closest to **space** and the clear distinctions space enables. At the level of the superficial self, it is possible to speak, for example, of isolated, distinct motives that shaped a decision. At the level of the profound, durational self, in contrast, there is interpenetration and fusion through which everything is tainted by everything else. Time and Free Will suggests that the superficial and the profound selves are separated by degree, and this suggestion leads to Matter and Memory's notion of degrees of **attention to life**.

simultaneity Time and Free Will opposes **space** as a principle of simultaneity, which allows one to count, since counting a sum requires the units counted to be present at the same time, to time as a principle of **succession**.

substance Bergson reinterprets rather than rejects outright the traditional notion of substance, understood as the self-identical basis or essence of a thing that does not change over time. Bergson conceives "substance" in terms of **duration**: the substance of the self is its persistence as duration and nothing (*no thing*) besides. Substance is at once persistent change and the continuity, the enduring of a personal history.

succession Bergson's initial position involves separating duration from space as a principle of succession from a principle of **simultaneity**. However, the notion of "pure succession" brings the idea of duration as succession into question insofar as succession seems to require the distinct and simultaneous moments (moments on the "time line") that can be imagined or represented only in space.

space Bergson suggested in *Time and Free Will* that a qualitative, "lived" spatiality is the prior condition of mathematised, objective space, and he develops this thought explicitly in *Matter and Memory*. With this idea of a "lived" spatiality, Bergson attempts to think beyond traditional oppositions of the extended to the in-extended in modern philosophy. See **extension**.

spiritualism the leading philosophical school or tradition in the French universities throughout the nineteenth century was the "spiritualist" school. This school, in a variety of ways, held that the mind has an immediate knowledge of itself as an active principle, and (with Ravaisson's "new spiritualism") that mind can discover itself as the active principle in all things. "Spiritualism" in this context did not denominate an interest in the occult or in contact with the dead. That said, there was much interest in parapsychology and the occult in nineteenth-century France.

synthesis *Time and Free Will* characterises duration as a "qualitative synthesis". A quantitative synthesis is a combination of separate units or parts; a qualitative synthesis is not. Hence when Bergson later attacks a conception of **creation** as a synthesis of pre-existing elements he is not attacking the notion of a qualitative synthesis advanced in 1889; he is just using the term "synthesis" in a more traditional and straightforward sense. The qualitative synthesis that is **duration** is an immanent synthesis, since it does not bring together separate moments in time, and a "passive synthesis", since it is not a function of deliberate volition.

teleology see **finalism**.

time according to *Time and Free Will*, time is not a principle in its own right, but **duration** spatialised, duration seen through the prism of space. We spatialise duration when we measure time, for to measure the length of time something takes is merely to compare two completed simultaneous spatial movements (the marathon, for example, with the quarter of one revolution of the heavens it takes me to run it).

virtual this is a word used by Bergson in a variety of senses, but most often, particularly when he is reflecting on **possibility** and traditional problems of modality, as a synonym of "possible". That said, *Matter and Memory* attempts to account for the mode of existence of the past, in a positive sense, as virtual rather than actual.

vitalism properly speaking, vitalism is the doctrine that biological life is a principle irreducible to, on the one hand, the mechanical principles of matter and, on the other hand, the mind. Properly speaking, then, Bergson is not a vitalist, for he considers the principle of biological life to be continuous with consciousness and the **life** of the mind. It is not by accident that Bergson does not speak positively of vitalism in *Creative Evolution*, even when borrowing the image of the *élan vital* from one of his contemporaries. Bergson offers not a vitalist but rather an animist or spiritualist philosophy of life. See **animism** and **spiritualism**.

will when *Time and Free Will* conceives of duration as a kind of psychological power, force or energy, Bergson did not spell out the relation of this power in general to will-power in particular. After the interregnum that is *Matter and Memory*, which was concerned predominantly with the past rather than with free action oriented to the future, he begins to do so in *Creative Evolution* and the lecture courses of the period. If **duration** is intrinsically creative, **creation** (and thus **genius**) are at the same time intrinsically voluntary, and thus he arrives at a general metaphysics of duration as will.

Bibliography

Ansell-Pearson, K., "Morality and the Philosophy of Life in Guyau and Bergson", *Continental Philosophy Review* 47/1 (2014), 59–85.

———— *Bergson: Thinking Beyond the Human Condition* (London: Bloomsbury, 2018).

Ansell-Pearson, K., P.-A. Miquel and M. Vaughan "Responses to Evolution: Spencer's Evolutionism, Bergsonism and Contemporary Biology", in *The History of Continental Philosophy*, Vol. 3: *The New Century: Bergsonism, Phenomenology and Responses to Modern Science*, ed. K. Ansell-Pearson and A. D. Schrift (Abingdon: Routledge, 2013), pp. 347–79.

Antliff, M., *Inventing Bergson: Cultural Politics and the Parisian Avant-Garde* (Princeton, NJ: Princeton University Press, 1993).

Aristotle, *Categories, On Interpretation, Prior Analytics*, trans. H. P. Cooke and H. Tredinnick (Cambridge, MA: Loeb Classical Library, 1938).

———— *Metaphysics*, trans. H. Tredennick, 2 vols. (Cambridge, MA: Loeb Classical Library, 1933 & 1935).

———— *Poetics*, ed. D. W. Lucas (Oxford: Oxford University Press, 1968).

Armstrong, D. M., *A Combinatorial Conception of Possibility* (Cambridge: Cambridge University Press, 1989).

Aron, R., "Hommage à Bergson", January 14, 1941, in *Essais sur la condition juive contemporaine*, ed. P. Simon-Nahum (Paris: Editions de Fallois, 1989), pp. 16–20.

———— "Notes sur Bergson et l'histoire", *Les Etudes bergsoniennes* 4 (1956), 46–51.

Azouvi, F., *La gloire de Bergson. Essai sur le magistère philosophique* (Paris: Gallimard, 2007).

Bain, A., *The Emotions and the Will* (London: Longmans, 1865).

Balan, B., "L'Œil de la coquille Saint Jacques—Bergson et les faits scientifiques", *Raison présente* 119 (1996), 87–106.

Banham, G., "Kantian Respect", *Kant Studies Online* (2014): www.garybanham.net/PAPERS_files/Kantian%20Respect.pdf.

Bartélemy-Madaule, M., "Lire Bergson", *Les Etudes bergsoniennes* 8 (1968), 83–120.

Baugh, B., "Time, Duration and Eternity in Spinoza", *Comparative and Continental Philosophy*, 2/2 (2010), 211–33.

Bayard, P., *Le plagiat par anticipation* (Paris: Editions de Minuit, 2009).

Bayer, R., "L'Esthétique de Henri Bergson", *Revue philosophique de la France et de l'étranger* 131 (1941), 244–318.

Beaney, M., *Analytic Philosophy: A Very Short Introduction* (Oxford: Oxford University Press, 2017).

Becquemont, D., and L. Muchielli, *Le Cas Spencer: Religion, science, politique* (Paris: Presses universitaires de France, 1998).

Belot, G., "Une théorie nouvelle de la liberté", *Revue philosophique de la France et de l'étranger*, XXX (1890), 361–92.

Benda, J., *The Treason of the Intellectuals* (Abingdon: Routledge, 2017).

Benrubi, I., "Entretien avec Bergson", in *Henri Bergson: Essais et témoignages recueillis*, ed. Albert Béguin and Pierre Thévenaz (Neuchâtel: Editions de la Baconnière, 1943), pp. 365–71.

———— *Souvenirs sur Bergson* (Neuchâtel: Delachaux & Niestlé, 1942).

Bergson, H., "Banquet Speech", in *Nobel Lectures, Literature 1901–1967*, ed. H. Frenz (Amsterdam: Elsevier, 1969), pp. 246–7.

———— *Cours I: Leçons de psychologie et de métaphysique*, ed. H. Hude (Paris: Presses universitaires de France, 1990).

———— *Cours Vol. II: Leçons d'esthétique. Leçons de morale, psychologie et métaphysique*, ed. H. Hude (Paris: Presses universitaires de France, 1991).

———— *Correspondances* ed. A. Robinet (Paris: Presses universitaires de France, 2002).

———— *Creative Evolution*, ed. A. François, trans. D. Landes (forthcoming from Routledge).

———— 'De la simulation inconsciente dans l'état d'hypnotisme', *Revue philosophique de la France et de l'étranger*, 22 (1886), 525–531.

———— *Durée et simultanéité*, ed. E. During (Paris: Presses universitaires de France, 2009).

———— *Essai sur les données de la conscience*, ed. A. Bouaniche (Paris: Presses universitaires de France, 2007).

———— *L'Evolution créatrice*, ed. A. François (Paris: Presses universitaires de France, 2007).

———— *L'évolution du problème de la liberté. Cours au Collège de France 1904–05*, ed. A. François (Paris: Presses universitaires de France, 2017).

———— *Histoire de l'idé e de temps. Cours au Collège de France 1902–03*, ed. C. Riquier (Paris: Press universitaires de France, 2016).

———— *Histoire des théories de la mémoire. Cours au Collège de France 1903–04*, ed. A. François (Paris: Presses universitaires de France, 2018).

———— "Introduction à la métaphysique", *Revue de métaphysique et de morale* 1903/1 (1903), 1–36.

———— *La Pensée et le mouvant*, ed. A. Bouaniche et al. (Paris: Presses universitaires de France, 2009).

———— *Le Rire: Essai sur la signification du comique*, ed. Guillaume Sibertin-Blanc (Paris: Presses universitaires de France, 2012).

———— *Les deux sources de la morale et de la religion*, ed. F. Keck and G. Waterlot (Paris: Presses universitaires de France, 2008).

———— *Matière et Mémoire*, ed. Camille Riquier (Paris: Presses universitaires de France, 2012).

———— *Mélanges*, ed. A. Robinet (Paris: Presses universitaires de France, 1972).

———— "Mémoire et reconnaissance", *Revue philosophique de la France et de l'étranger* 16 (1896), 225–48 and 16 (1896), 380–99.

———— *Œuvres*, ed. A. Robinet (Paris: Presses universitaires de France, 1959).

———— "Perception et matière", *Revue de métaphysique et de morale* 4 (1896), 257–79.

———— *The Meaning of the War*, trans. H. Wildon-Carr (London: T. Fisher Unwin, 1915).

Berkeley, G., *A Treatise Concerning the Principles of Human Knowledge* (Oxford: Oxford University Press, 1998).

Bernecker, S. and K. Michaelian (eds.), *The Routledge Handbook of Philosophy of Memory* (Abingdon: Routledge, 2017).

Bernet, R., "Bergson on the Driven Force of Consciousness and Life", trans. T. Perri, in *Bergson and Phenomenology*, ed. M. Kelly (Basingstoke: Palgrave, 2010), pp. 42–77.

Berthelot, R., *Un romantisme utilitaire; étude sur le mouvement pragmatiste* (Paris: Alcan, 1911).

Bianco, G., *Après Bergson: Portrait de group avec philosophe* (Paris: Presses universitaires de France, 2015).

———— "Le Bergson de Deleuze entre existence et structure", in *Gilles Deleuze. Politiques de la philosophie*, ed. A. Jdey (Geneva, Métis Presses, 2015), pp. 99–116.

———— Review of Jankélévitch's *Henri Bergson*, H-France 16/113 (July 2016), 1–4.

Bishop, R., "The Causal Closure of Physics and Free Will", in *The Oxford Handbook of Free Will*, ed. R. Kane (Oxford: Oxford University Press, 2011), pp. 101–14.

Boutroux, E., *On the Contingency of the Laws of Nature*, trans. F. Rothwell (Chicago, IL: Open Court, 1920).

Bowler, P. J., *The Eclipse of Darwinism: Anti-Darwinian Evolutionary Theories in the Decades around 1900* (Baltimore, MD: Johns Hopkins University Press, 1983).

Bruyeron, R., *1914: L'entrée en guerre de quelques philosophes* (Paris: Hermann, 2014).

Callendar, C., *What Makes Time Special?* (Oxford: Oxford University Press, 2018).

Canales, J., "Einstein, Bergson, and the Experiment That Failed: Intellectual Cooperation at the League of Nations", *MLN* 120/5 (2005), 1168–91.

———— *The Physicist and the Philosopher: Einstein, Bergson, and the Debate That Changed Our Understanding of Time* (Princeton, NJ: Princeton University Press, 2015).

Canguilhem, G., *Œuvres complètes* vol. IV, ed. C. Limoges (Paris: Vrin, 2015).

Caro, E., "Les deux allemagnes: Madame de Staël et Henri Heine", *La revue des deux mondes* November (1871), 5–20.

Čapek, M., *Bergson and Modern Physics: A Reinterpretation and Re-evaluation*. Boston Studies in the Philosophy of Science, Vol. 7 (Dordrecht, D. Reidel, 1971).

Casey, E., "Habitual Body and Memory in Merleau-Ponty", *Man and World* 17 (1984), 279–97.

Caeymaex, F., "Les discours de guerre: Propagande et philosophie", in *Annales bergsoniennes VII: Bergson, l'Allemagne, la guerre de 1914*, ed. Arnaud François, Nadia Yala

Kisukidi, Camille Riquier, Caterina Zanfi and Frédéric Worms (Paris: Presses universitaires de France, 2014), pp. 143–66.

———— "Négativité et finitude de l'élan vital. La lecture de Bergson par Jankélévitch", in *Annales bergsoniennes* IV, ed. Anne Fagot-Largeault and Frédéric Worms (Paris: Presses universitaires de France, 2008), pp. 629–40.

Chapoutot, J., "La trahison d'un clerc? Bergson, la grande guerre et la France", *Francia* 35 (2008), 295–316.

Chevalier, J., *Entretiens avec Bergson* (Paris: Plon, 1959).

Comte, A., *Cours de philosophie positive*, 2 vols. (Paris: Hermann, 1975).

Couchoud, P.-L., "La métaphysique nouvelle, *Matière et Mémoire* de Bergson", *Revue de métaphysique et de morale* X (1902), 225–43.

Crocker, S., "Man Falls Down: Art, Life and Finitude in Bergson's Essay on Laughter", in *Bergson and Phenomenology*, ed. M. Kelly (Basingstoke: Palgrave, 2010), pp. 78–97.

Dainton, B., "Bergson on Temporal Experience. Durée Réelle", in *The Routledge Handbook of the Philosophy of Temporal Experience*, ed. I. Phillips (Abingdon: Routledge, 2017), pp. 93–106.

Davenson, H., "Bergson et l'histoire", in *Henri Bergson: Essais et témoignages recueillis*, ed. A. Béguin and P. Thévenaz (Neuchâtel: Editions de la Baconnière, 1943), pp. 205–13.

Delboeuf, J., *Essai de logique scientifique* (Liège: Desoer, 1865).

Deleuze, G., *Bergsonism* (New York: Zone, 1991).

———— "Bergson's Conception of Difference", trans. M. McMahon, in *The New Bergson*, ed. J. Mullarkey (Manchester: Manchester University Press, 1999), pp. 42–66.

———— *Desert Islands and Other Texts 1953–74* (Cambridge, MA: MIT Press, 2004).

———— *Difference and Repetition*, trans. P. Patton (London: Athlone, 1994).

———— "La Conception de la différence chez Bergson", *Les Etudes bergsoniennes* 4 (1956), 77–112.

———— *Le bergsonisme* (Paris: Presses universitaires de France, 1997).

———— "Lecture Course on Chapter Three of Bergson's *Creative Evolution*", trans. B. Loban, *SubStance* 36/3 (2007), 72–90.

———— *Negotiations*, trans. M. Joughin (New York: Columbia University Press, 1995).

Derrida, J., "Ousia and Gramme: Note on a Note in *Being and Time*", in *Margins of Philosophy*, trans. A. Bass (Brighton: Harvester Press, 1982), pp. 29–68.

Descartes, R., *Meditations on First Philosophy* (Cambridge: Cambridge University Press, 1996).

———— *The Philosophical Writings of Descartes*, ed. J. Cottingham, R. Stoothoff and D. Murdoch, vol. 1 (Cambridge: Cambridge University Press, 1985).

Dolbeault, J., "From Mind to Matter: How Bergson Anticipated Quantum Ideas", *Mind and Matter* 10/1 (2012), 25–45.

Durkheim, E., *Germany Above All: German Mentality and War*, trans. J. S. (Paris: Armand Colin, 1915).

———— *L'allemagne au-dessus de tout. La mentalité allemande et la guerre* (Paris: Armand Colin, 1915).

———— *Moral Education: A Study in the Theory and Application of the Sociology of Education*, trans. E. Wilson and H. Schnurer (New York: Free Press, 1961).

Durkheim, E. and Denis, E., *Qui a voulu la guerre? Les origines de la guerre d'après les documents diplomatiques* (Paris: Armand Colin, 1915).

———— *Who Wanted War? The Origin of the War According to Diplomatic Documents*, trans. A. M. Wilson-Garinei (Paris: Armand Colin, 1915).

Einstein, A., *Correspondances françaises*, ed. M. Biezunski (Paris, Editions du Seuil, 1989).

Egger, V., "La Naissance des Habitudes", *Annales de la faculté de lettres de Bordeaux* 1 (1880), 1–15.

———— *La parole intérieure* (Paris: Germer Baillière 1881).

Fedi, L., "Bergson et Boutroux. La Critique du modèle physicaliste et des lois de conservation en psychologie", *Revue de métaphsique et de morale* 2001/2 (2001), 97–118.

Ferejohn, M. T., "Aristotle on Focal Meaning and the Unity of Science", *Phronesis* 25/ 2 (1980), 117–28.

Fisher, J., "Frankfurt-Style Examples and Semi-Compatibilism: New Work", in *The Oxford Handbook of Free Will*, ed. R. Kane (Oxford: Oxford University Press, 2011), pp. 243–65.

François, A., *Bergson, Schopenhauer, Nietzsche: Volonté et réalité* (Paris: Presses universitaires de France, 2008).

———— "Bergson plagiaire de Schopenhauer? Analyse d'une polémique", *Etudes germaniques* 60/3 (2005), 469–91.

———— 'Les sources biologiques de l'*Evolution créatrice*", in *Annales bergsoniennes* IV, ed. Anne Fagot-Largeault and Frédéric Worms (Paris: Presses universitaires de France, 2008), pp. 95–109.

———— "Y a-t-il une théorie de la pulsion chez Bergson? Pulsion et actualisation", in *Pulsions*, ed. J.-C. Goddard (Paris: Vrin, 2006), pp. 183–211.

Friedman, G., "La prudence de M. Bergson, ou Philosophie et caractère", *Commune*, 30/3 (1936), 721–36.

Fujita, H., "Anarchy and Analogy: The Violence of Language in Bergson and Sorel", in *Bergson, Politics, and Religion*, ed. A. Lefebvre and M. White (Durham, NC: Duke University Press, 2012), pp. 126–43.

Gayon, J., "L'*Evolution créatrice* lue par les fondateurs de la théorie synthétique de l'évolution", in *Annales bergsoniennes* IV, ed. Anne Fagot-Largeault and Frédéric Worms (Paris: Presses universitaires de France, 2008), pp. 59–93.

Gervais, M. and D. S. Wilson, "The Evolution and Functions of Laugher and Humour: A Synthetic Approach", *The Quarterly Review of Biology* 80/4 (2005), 395–430.

Gorham, G., "Descartes on Time and Duration", *Early Modern Science and Medicine* 12 (2007), 28–54.

Grandjean, F., *Une revolution dans la philosophie. La doctrine de M. Bergson* (Geneva and Paris: Atar, 1916).

Guerlac, S., *Thinking in Time: An Introduction to Henri Bergson* (Ithaca, NY: Cornell University Press, 1996).

Gunn, J. A., *Bergson and His Philosophy* (London: Methuen, 1920).

Gunter, P. Y. A., "Bergson and the War against Nature", in *The New Bergson*, ed. J. Mullarkey (Manchester: Manchester University Press, 1999), pp. 168–82.

────── "Bergson's Creation of the Possible", *SubStance* 36 (2007), 33–41.

Guyer, P., *Kant* (Abingdon: Routledge, 2014).

Hardt, M., *Gilles Deleuze: An Apprenticeship in Philosophy* (Minneapolis, MN: University of Minnesota Press, 1993).

Heidegger, M., *Letters to His Wife 1915–70*, ed. G. Heidegger, trans. R. Glasgow (London: Polity, 2008).

────── *Being and Time*, trans. J. Stambaugh (Albany, NY: State University of New York Press, 1996).

────── *Die Grundprobleme der Phänomenologie* (Frankfurt am Main: Klostermann, 1975).

────── *Logic: The Question Concerning Truth*, trans. T. Sheehan (Bloomington, IN: Indiana University Press, 2010).

────── *Logik: Die Frage nach der Wahrheit* (Frankfurt am Main: Klostermann, 1995).

────── *Metaphysische Anfangsgründe der Logik im Ausgang von Leibniz* (Frankfurt am Main: Klostermann, 1978).

────── *Pathmarks*, ed. W. McNeill (Cambridge: Cambridge University Press, 1998).

────── *Sein und Zeit* (Tübingen: Niemeyer, 1984).

────── *The Basic Problems of Phenomenology*, trans. A. Hofstadter (Bloomington, IN: Indiana University Press, 1988).

────── *The Metaphysical Foundations of Logic*, trans. M. Heim (Bloomington, IN: Indiana University Press, 1984).

Heinamma, S. and T. Kaitaro, "Descartes' Notion of the Mind–Body Union and its Phenomenological Expositions", in *The Oxford Handbook of the History of Phenomenology*, ed. D. Zahavi (Oxford: Oxford University Press, 2018), pp. 25–44.

Herring, E., "'Great is Darwin and Bergson his poet': Julian Huxley's other evolutionary synthesis", *Annals of Science* 75/1 (2018), 40–54.

Heyd, D., "The Place of Laughter in Hobbes' Theory of the Emotions", *Journal of the History of Ideas* 43/2 (1982), 285–95.

Hobbes, *Human Nature and De Corpore Politico*, ed. J. C. A. Gaskin (Oxford: Oxford University Press, 2008)

────── *Leviathan*, ed. N. Malcolm (Oxford: Oxford University Press, 2012).

Hume, D., *Treatise of Human Nature* vol. 1: *The Text*, ed. D. F. Norton and M. J. Norton (Oxford: Clarendon Press, 2007).

Husserl, E., *Briefwechsel*, vol. VI: *Philosophenbriefe*, ed. K. Schuhmann (Dordrecht: Kluwer, 1994).

Husson, L., *L'Intellectualisme de Bergson. Genèse et développement de la notion bergsonienne d'intuition* (Paris: Presses universitaires de France, 1947).

Hyppolite, J., "Bergson et l'existentialisme", *Les Etudes bergsoniennes* 2 (1949), 208–15.

────── *Figures de la pensée philosophique* vol. II (Paris: Presses universitaires de France, 1969).

———— "Various Aspects of Memory in Bergson", trans. A. V. Coleman, in *The Challenge of Bergsonism*, ed. L. Lawlor (London: Continuum 2003), pp. 112–28.

Huneman, P. and D. M. Walsh (eds.), *Challenging the Modern Synthesis* (Oxford: Oxford University Press, 2017).

Jackson, H., "On Affections of Speech from Disease of the Brain", *Brain* 1/3 (1878), 304–330, republished in *Brain* 38/1–2 (1915), 107–129.

Jaffro, L., "Infinity, Intuition, and the Relativity of Knowledge: Bergson, Carrau, and the Hamiltonians", *British Journal for the History of Philosophy* 18/1 (2010), 91–112.

James, W., "On Some Omissions of Introspective Psychology", *Mind* 9/33 (1884), 1–26.

Janet, P., "Une nouvelle phase de la philosophie spiritualiste", *Revue des deux mondes* 108/2 (1873), 363–88.

Jankélévitch, V., *Henri Bergson* (Paris: Presses universitaires de France, 1959).

———— *Henri Bergson*, ed. N. F. Schott and A. Lefebvre (Durham, NC: Duke University Press, 2015).

Johnson, C., *Darwin's Dice: The Idea of Chance in the Thought of Charles Darwin* (Oxford: Oxford University Press, 2014).

Jones, D. V., "Mysticism and War: Reflections on Bergson and His Reception during World War I", in *Annales bergsoniennes VII: Bergson, l'Allemagne, la guerre de 1914*, ed. Arnaud François, Nadia Yala Kisukidi, Camille Riquier, Caterina Zanfi and Frédéric Worms (Paris: Presses universitaires de France, 2014), pp. 167–79.

Jones, R. A., *Emile Durkheim: An Introduction to Four Major Works* (Beverly Hills, CA: Sage Publications, 1986).

Joyce, R., "Cartesian Memory", *Journal of the History of Philosophy* 35/3 (1997), 375–93.

Kane, R. (ed.), *The Oxford Handbook of Free Will*, ed. R. Kane (Oxford: Oxford University Press, 2011).

Kant, I., *Anthropology from a Pragmatic Point of View*, ed. and trans. R. B. Louden. The Cambridge Edition of the Works of Immanuel Kant: Anthropology, History and Education (Cambridge: Cambridge University Press, 2011).

———— *Critique of Pure Reason*, ed. P. Guyer and A. Wood (Cambridge: Cambridge University Press, 1999).

———— *Kritik der Urteilskraft*, in *Gesammelte Schriften* vol. 5, ed. Preußische Akademie der Wissenschaften/Deutsche Akademie der Wissenschaften zu Berlin/Akademie der Wissenschaften zu Göttingen (Berlin: De Gruyter, 1963).

———— *Critique of Judgment*, trans. N. Walker (Oxford: Oxford University Press, 2007).

Kelly, M., (ed.), *Bergson and Phenomenology* (Basingstoke: Palgrave, 2010).

Kennedy, E., "Bergson's Philosophy and French Political Doctrines: Sorel, Maurras, Péguy and de Gaulle", *Government and Opposition* 15/1 (1980), 75–91.

Kisukidi, N., "Bergson et la guerre de 1914–1918: Présentation du dossier", in *Annales bergsoniennes VII: Bergson, l'Allemagne, la guerre de 1914*, ed. Arnaud François, Nadia Yala Kisukidi, Camille Riquier, Caterina Zanfi and Frédéric Worms (Paris: Presses universitaires de France, 2014), pp. 101–13.

Kołakowski, L., *Bergson* (Oxford: Oxford University Press, 1985).

Knuuttila, S., "Modal Logic", *The Cambridge History of Later Medieval Philosophy*, eds. N. Kretzmann, A. Kenny and J. Pinbourg (Cambridge: Cambridge University Press, 1982), pp. 342–57.

Lacey, A. R., *Bergson* (Abingdon: Routledge, 1999).

Lachelier, J., *Du fondement de l'induction* (Paris: Fayard, 1992).

——— "Psychologie et métaphysique", *Revue philosophique de la France et de l'étranger* 19 (1885), 481–516.

Lalande, A., *La dissolution opposée à l'évolution dans les sciences physiques et morales* (Paris: Félix Alcan, 1899).

——— *Vocabulaire technique et critique de la philosophie* (Paris: Presses universitaires de France, 1997 [1926]).

Laro, C., "Promesses et carences de l'esthétique bergsonienne", *Revue de métaphysique et de morale* 48/4 (1941), 301–13.

Lefebvre, A., *Human Rights as a Way of Life: On Bergson's Political Philosophy* (Stanford, CA: Stanford University Press, 2013).

Lefebvre, A. and M. White (eds.), *Bergson, Politics, and Religion* (Durham, NC: Duke University Press, 2012).

Lemoine, A., *L'habitude et l'instinct* (Paris: Germer Baillière, 1875).

Lévinas, E., *En découvrant l'existence avec Husserl et Heidegger* (Paris: Vrin, 1994 [1949]).

——— *Ethique et infini* (Paris: Fayard, 1982).

Lewens, T., *Darwin* (Abingdon: Routledge, 2006).

Lewis, D., *On the Plurality of Worlds* (Oxford: Blackwell, 1986).

Lorand, R., "Bergson's Concept of Art", *British Journal of Aesthetics* 39/4 (1999), 400–15.

Lovejoy, A., "Some Antecedents of the Philosophy of Bergson: The Conception of 'Real Duration'", *Mind* XXII/10 (1913), 465–83.

Maine de Biran, P., *Of Immediate Apperception*, ed. A. Aloisi, M. Piazza and M. Sinclair (London: Bloomsbury, forthcoming).

Marquet, J.-F., "Durée bergsonienne et temporalité", in *Bergson: La durée et la nature*, ed. J.-L. Vieillard-Baron (Paris: Presses universitaires de France, 2004), pp. 77–98.

Martineau, H., *The Positive Philosophy of Auguste Comte* (London: J. Chapman, 1853).

Massey, H., *The Origin of Time: Heidegger and Bergson* (Albany, NY: State University of New York Press, 2015).

Mathewson, L., "Bergson's Theory of the Comic in the Light of English Comedy", *University of Nebraska Studies in Language, Literature and Criticism* 5 (1920) 1–27.

McTaggart, J. M. E., "On the Unreality of Time", *Mind* NS 17 (1908), 457–74.

McCumber, J., *Understanding Hegel's Mature Critique of Kant* (Stanford, CA: Stanford University Press, 2014).

Merleau-Ponty, M., *In Praise of Philosophy and Other Essays*, trans. J. O'Neill (Evanston, IL: Northwestern University Press, 1963).

——— *La Nature (Cours du Collège de France)* (Paris: Seuil, 1995).

——— *The Incarnate Subject: Malebranche, Biran and Bergson on the Union of Mind and Body*, ed. A. G. Bjelland Jr. and P. Burke, trans. P. Milan (New York: Humanity Books, 2001).

———— *The Phenomenology of Perception* (Abingdon: Routledge, 1962).

———— *Signs*, trans. R. C. McClearly (Evanston, IL: Northwestern University Press, 1964).

———— *Texts and Dialogues*, ed. H. Silverman and J. Barry, Jr., trans. M. Smith, *et al.* (New York: Humanity Books, 1992).

———— *The Merleau-Ponty Aesthetics Reader*, ed. G. A. Johnson (Evanston, IL: Northwestern University Press, 1994).

Mill, J. S., *An Examination of Sir William Hamilton's Philosophy* (London: Longmans, 1865).

Miquel, P.-A., "Une harmonie en arrière", in *Annales bergsoniennes* IV, ed. Anne Fagot-Largeault and Frédéric Worms (Paris: Presses universitaires de France, 2008), pp. 133–45.

Moore, A. W., *The Evolution of Modern Metaphysics. Making Sense of Things* (Cambridge: Cambridge University Press, 2012).

Moore, F. C. T., *Bergson: Thinking Backwards* (Cambridge: Cambridge University Press, 1996).

Morreall, J., (ed.), *The Philosophy of Laughter and Humor* (Albany, NY: State University of New York Press, 1987).

Mossé-Bastide, R.-M., *Bergson Educateur* (Paris: Presses universitaires de France, 1955).

Mullarkey, J., *Bergson and Philosophy* (Manchester: Manchester University Press, 1999).

Mumford, S. and R. L. Anjum, *What Tends to Be: An Essay on the Dispositional Modality* (Abingdon: Routledge, 2018).

Nachtomy, O., "Modal Adventures between Leibniz and Kant: Existence and (Temporal, Logical, Real) Possibilities", in *The Actual and the Possible: Modality and Metaphysics in Modern Philosophy*, ed. M. Sinclair (Oxford: Oxford University Press, 2017), pp. 64–93.

Nahm, M., "The Theological Background to the Theory of the Artist as Creator", *Journal of the History of Ideas* 8/3 (1947), 362–72.

Nicholson, D. and J. Dupré, *Everything Flows: Towards a Processual Philosophy of Biology* (Oxford: Oxford University Press, 2018).

Nietzsche, F., *Kritische Studienausgabe*, ed. G. Colli and M. Montinari (Berlin: de Gruyter, 1988).

———— *The Gay Science*, trans. W. Kaufmann (New York: Vintage, 1974).

Nizan, P., *Les chiens de garde* (Marseille: Agone, 2012).

Parodi, D., "Le Rire. Essai sur la signification du comique par H. Bergson", *Revue de métaphysique et de morale* 9/2 (1901), 224–36.

Pilkington, A. E., *Bergson and His Influence: A Reassessment* (Cambridge: Cambridge University Press, 1976).

Plato, *Theaetetus, Sophist*, trans. H. N. Fowler (Cambridge, MA: Loeb Classical Library, 1921).

Polin, R., "Y a-t-il chez Bergson une philosophie de l'histoire?", *Les Etudes bergsoniennes* 4 (1956), 7–40.

Politzer, G., *Contre Bergson et quelques autres. Ecrits philosophiques 1924–1939*, ed. R. Bruyeron (Paris: Flammarion, 2013).

Power, C., "Bergson's Critique of Practical Reason", in A. Lefebvre and M. White (eds.), *Bergson, Politics, and Religion* (Durham, NC: Duke University Press, 2012), pp. 175–92.

Pross, A., *What is Life? How Chemistry Becomes Biology* (Oxford: Oxford University Press, 2012).

Proust, M., *A la recherche du temps perdu* (Paris: Gallimard, Bibliothèque de la Pléiade, 1988).

Quirk, T., *Bergson and American Culture: The Worlds of Willa Cather and Wallace Stevens* (Chapel Hill, NC: University of North Carolina Press, 1990).

Ravaisson, F., *De l'habitude*, ed. F. de Towarnicki (Paris: Payot, 1997).

———— *Of Habit*, ed. C. Carlisle and M. Sinclair (London: Continuum, 2008).

———— *Rapport sur la philosophie en France au XIXème siècle* (Paris: Hachette, 1889 [1867]).

———— *Selected Essays*, ed. M. Sinclair (London: Bloomsbury, 2016).

———— *Testament Philosophique* (Paris: Boivin et Cie, 1933).

Richmond, S., "Sartre and Bergson: A Disagreement about Nothingness", *International Journal of Philosophical Studies*, 15/1 (2007), 77–95.

Riquier, C., *Archéologie de Bergson: Temps et métaphysique* (Paris: Presses universitaires de France, 2009).

———— "La durée pure comme ésquisse de la temporalité ekstatique: Heidegger lecteur de Bergson", in *Heidegger en Dialogue 1912–30*, ed. S. Jollivet and C. Romano (Paris: Vrin, 2009), pp. 33–67.

Robinet, A., "Le passage à la conception biologique de la perception de l'image et du souvenir chez Bergson", *Les Etudes philosophiques* 15/3 (1966), 375–88.

Robson, M., "Is Ultimate Moral Responsibility Metaphysically Impossible? A Bergsonian Critique of Galen Strawson's Argument", *Philosophy* 92/4 (2017), 519–38.

Roosevelt, T., "The Search for Truth in a Reverend Spirit", *Outlook* 99 (1911), 819–26.

Russell, B., *The Collected Works of Bertrand Russell: Logical and Philosophical Papers* vol. 6: 1909–1913 (Abingdon: Routledge, 1992).

———— "The Philosophy of Bergson", *The Monist* 22 (1912), 321–47.

———— "The Professor's Guide to Laughter", *The Cambridge Review* 33 (1912) 193–4.

Ruyer, R., "Bergson et le Sphex ammophile", *Revue de métaphysique et de morale* 64/2 (1959), 165–79.

Sartre, J.-P., "Interview with Michel Rybalka, Oreste Pucciani and Susan Gruenheck", in P. Schilpp (ed.) *The Philosophy of Jean-Paul Sartre* (La Salle, IL: Open Court, 1981), pp. 5–51.

———— *The Imaginary: A Phenomenological Psychology of the Imagination*, trans. J. Webber (Abingdon: Routledge, 2004).

———— *The Imagination*, trans. K. Williford and D. Rudrauf (Abingdon: Routledge, 2012).

Scharfstein, B.-A., *Roots of Bergson's Philosophy* (New York: Columbia University Press, 1942).

Schrift, A. D., *Twentieth-Century French Philosophy* (Oxford: Blackwell, 2006).

Schure, L. ter, *Bergson and History* (Albany, NY: State University of New York Press, 2019).

Séailles, G., *Essai sur le genie dans l'art* (Paris: Germer Baillière, 1883).

Seillière, E., *L'avenir de la philosophie bergsonienne* (Paris: Alcan, 1917).

———— *La philosophie de l'impérialisme*, 4 vols. (Paris: Plon, 1903–8).

———— "Welche Moralphilosophie läßt Bergson erwarten?", *Internationale Zeitschrift für Wissenschaft, Kunst und Technik* 8/2 (1913), 191–209.

Sheldrake, R., *The Science Delusion* (London: Coronet, 2012).

Sinclair, M., *Being Inclined: Félix Ravaisson's Philosophy of Habit* (Oxford: Oxford University Press, 2019)

———— "Habit and Time in Nineteenth-Century French Philosophy: Albert Lemoine between Bergson and Ravaisson", *British Journal for the History of Philosophy* 26/1 (2018), 131–53.

———— *Heidegger, Aristotle and the Work of Art* (Basingstoke: Palgrave, 2006).

———— "Is Habit the Fossilised Residue of a Spiritual Activity?: Ravaisson, Bergson, Merleau-Ponty", *Journal of the British Society for Phenomenology* 42/1 (2011), 33–52.

Sitbon-Peillon, B., "*Les Deux Sources de la Morale et de la Religion* suite de *L'Evolution créatrice?* Genèse d'un choix philosophique entre morale et esthétique", in *Annales bergsoniennes* IV, ed. Anne Fagot-Largeault and Frédéric Worms (Paris: Presses universitaires de France, 2008), pp. 325–38.

Sorel, G., *Reflections on Violence*, trans. T. E. Hulme and J. Roth (New York: Dover, 1950).

———— *Réflexions sur la violence* (Paris: Marcel Rivière, 1908)

Soulez, P., *Bergson politique* (Paris: Presses universitaires de France, 1989).

———— "Bergson as Philosopher of War and Theorist of the Political", in *Bergson, Politics and Religion*, ed. A. Lefebvre and M. White (Durham, NC: Duke University Press, 2012), pp. 99–125.

Soulez, P. and F. Worms, *Bergson* (Paris: Presses universitaires de France, 2002).

Spencer, H., *First Principles* (London: Watts & Co., 1937 [1862]).

Stallknecht, N., *Studies in the Philosophy of Creation with Especial Reference to Bergson and Whitehead* (Princeton, NJ: Princeton University Press, 1934)

Stebbing, L. S., *Pragmatism and French Voluntarism* (Cambridge: Cambridge University Press, 1914).

Sully, J., *Les illusions des sens et de l'esprit* (Paris: Baillière, 1883).

Tarde, A. de, *Le Maroc, école d'énergie* (Rabat: Imprimerie du Bulletin Officiel du Protectorat, 1915): http://gallica.bnf.fr/ark:/12148/bpt6k62652277.

Thibaudet, A., *Trente ans de vie française III: Le bergsonisme* (Paris: Gallimard, 1923)

Thiers, E., "Droit et culture de guerre 1914–1918. Le Comité d'études et documents sur la guerre", *Mil neuf cent. Revue d'histoire intellectuelle* 23/1 (2005), 23–48.

Towarnicki, F. de, *A la rencontre de Heidegger: Souvenirs d'un messager de la Forêt-Noire* (Paris: Gallimard, 1993).

———— *Martin Heidegger: Souvenirs et chroniques* (Paris: Rivages, 2002).

Tycerium-Lightner, D., "Hume on Conceivability and Inconceivability", *Hume Studies* 23/1 (1997), 113–32.

Vaughan, M., "Introduction: Henri Bergson's *Creative Evolution*", *SubStance* 36/3 (2007), 7–24.

Vieillard-Baron, J.-L., *Bergson* (Paris: Presses universitaires de France, 1993).

——— "Lévinas et Bergson", in *Bergson*, ed. C. Riquier (Paris: Editions du Cerf, 2012), pp. 191–221.

Vollet, M., "Créativité comme Tendencialité", in *Bergson*, ed. C. Riquier (Paris: Editions du Cerf, 2012), pp. 359–73.

Ward, J., "Psychology", in *Encyclopaedia Britannica*, 9th edition, Vol. 20 (Edinburgh: Black, 1886), pp. 37–85.

Watson, W., *The Lost Second Book of Aristotle's Poetics* (Chicago, IL: Chicago University Press, 2012).

White, M., "Bergson and Durkheim: Society *sui generis*", *Journal of Classical Sociology* 10/4 (2010), 457–77.

Wildon-Carr, H. (ed.), *The Philosophy of Bergson* (Cambridge: Bowes and Bowes, 1914).

Worms, F., and C. Zanfi (eds.), "Presentation: L'Europe philosophique des congrès à la guerre", *Revue de métaphysique et de morale* 2014/4 (2014), 459–66.

Wolsky, M. and Wolsky, A., "Bergson's Vitalism and Modern Biology", in F. Burwick and P. Douglass (eds.), *The Crisis in Modernism: Bergson and the Vitalist Controversy* (Cambridge: Cambridge University Press, 1992), pp. 153–69.

Worms, F., *La philosophie en France au XXe siècle* (Paris: Gallimard, 2009).

Wundt, W., "*Plagiator Bergson, membre de l'Institut. Zur Antwort auf die Herabsetzung der deutschen Wissenschaft durch Edmond Perrier, président de l'Académie des Sciences par Hermann Bönke*", *Literarisches Zentralblatt für Deutschland* 66 (1915), 1131–8.

Zanfi, C., *Bergson et la philosophie allemande 1907–1932* (Paris: Armand Colin, 2014).

Žižek, S., *Event: A Philosophical Journey Through a Concept* (London: Penguin Books, 2014).

Index

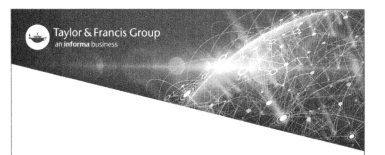

Made in the USA
Monee, IL
07 April 2023